*Volume I*

# WE PEOPLE HERE:
# NAHUATL ACCOUNTS OF
# THE CONQUEST OF MEXICO

Geoffrey Symcox
*General Editor*
UCLA

M. J. B. Allen
Philip Levine
Norman J. W. Thrower
Edward Tuttle
UCLA

Luciano Formisano
UNIVERSITY OF BOLOGNA

Juan Gil
Consuelo Varela
UNIVERSITY OF SEVILLE

*Publication of this volume was made possible
by the generous support of the*

NATIONAL ENDOWMENT FOR THE HUMANITIES
*Washington, D.C.*

*and the*

SOCIEDAD ESTATAL QUINTO CENTENARIO
*Madrid*

*Published under the auspices of the*

UCLA CENTER FOR MEDIEVAL AND RENAISSANCE STUDIES

*Volume 1*

# WE PEOPLE HERE:
# NAHUATL ACCOUNTS OF
# THE CONQUEST OF MEXICO

James Lockhart

*Editor and Translator*

*Wipf & Stock*
PUBLISHERS
*Eugene, Oregon*

Wipf and Stock Publishers
199 West 8th Avenue, Suite 3
Eugene, Oregon 97401

We People Here
Nahuatl Accounts of The Conquest of Mexico
By Lockhart, James
Copyright©1993 UCLA Center for Medieval and Renaissance Studies
ISBN: 1-59244-681-7
Publication date 5/6/2004
Previously published by University of California Press, 1993

Lockhart
would've
been 60

# SERIES PREFACE

The Repertorium Columbianum is a collection of contemporary sources relating to Columbus's four voyages, and the interpenetration of the hitherto separate worlds that resulted from them. This multivolume series will provide in readily accessible form the basic documents that are the starting point for research into this pivotal moment in world history; they form the indispensable tools for all scholarly inquiry into the encounter. The series provides accurate editions of the essential texts in their original languages, for the use of specialists, while at the same time making them available to students and scholars in related fields through parallel translations into modern English.

The Repertorium Columbianum was originally conceived by the late Professor Fredi Chiappelli, former director of the Center for Medieval and Renaissance Studies at the University of California, Los Angeles. The series is respectfully dedicated to his memory. He intended it to be an up-to-date, greatly expanded version of the Raccolta Colombiana published on the occasion of the Columbian quatercentenary in 1892. He laid down the basic lines of editorial policy that are being followed in these volumes, in an approach that blends philological and historical methodologies. Because of the dual approach, the editing of most volumes is an interdisciplinary undertaking among specialists in the field represented by the source materials in that volume. Each text is preceded by a historical and philological introduction; the text itself follows, with comprehensive lists of textual variants at the foot of the page and the translation *en face;* it is supplemented by a detailed commentary and a glossary of problematic terms; finally each volume is rounded off by complete indexes of sources and subjects. A final, cumulative index volume will enable users of the series to make connections and trace thematic linkages among the wide variety of documentary materials that the series contains. The Repertorium's scope is generally limited to sources from the period between Columbus's first voyage and the Spanish conquest of Mexico in 1519–1521, although certain volumes, by their nature, may extend the chronological range of the series beyond these dates.

Since 1892 historical perspectives on the Columbian encounter have shifted, and the techniques of philological analysis have made enormous strides. The Repertorium's presentation of the sources reflects these changes. Centennial commemorations such as

the Columbian quincentenary serve to remind us of the way in which scholarly methods and concerns have altered over the intervening years; they are occasions for taking stock of the past century's achievements, for seeing how interpretations have changed, for scrutinizing new material that has come to light, and for charting the course for future research. These are the purposes that inform the editorial policy of the Repertorium Columbianum. It seeks to sum up what has been achieved in the field of Columbian studies over the past century, to throw new light on the encounter and its immediate aftermath, to collect in a standardized format the essential materials for research, and to suggest lines of inquiry for the years ahead.

The original Columbian ventures were international in conception and execution, and in this same spirit the Repertorium Columbianum is an international undertaking. The contributing scholars and the members of the editorial board are drawn from both sides of the Atlantic, and the costs are being borne with the help of generous funding from the United States National Endowment for the Humanities, the Italian Comitato Nazionale per le Celebrazioni del V Centenario della Scoperta dell'America, and the Spanish Sociedad Estatal para la Ejecución de Programas del Quinto Centenario. The administrative and editorial work for the series is being performed by the UCLA Center for Medieval and Renaissance Studies, under whose auspices these volumes will appear. As general editor it is my pleasant duty to acknowledge a profound debt of gratitude to the three government sponsors, without whose generous and enlightened support this project would have been impossible.

Geoffrey Symcox
General Editor

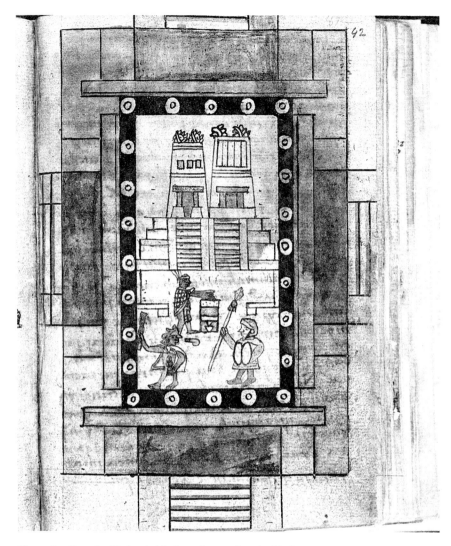

Illustration from the Codex Aubin (text 3), reproduced with the permission of the Trustees of the British Museum.

*ce cioatl nican titlaca*

a woman, one of us people here . . .


*Totomoniliztli, inic micque nicā tlaca*

a disease of pustules, from which the people here died . . .


*in iuh mochichioa nican tlaca: no iuh mochichioaia*

they dressed as the people here dress

FLORENTINE CODEX, BOOK TWELVE


*i nican titlaca i nican tichaneque yn nueva España*

we people here, who dwell here in New Spain

HUEJOTZINGO LETTER, 1560

# CONTENTS

# ACKNOWLEDGMENTS

Far and away my greatest debt is to the work of Arthur J. O. Anderson and Charles E. Dibble, whose translations of the Nahuatl of Book Twelve of the Florentine Codex were indispensable to my own version. I have also profited substantially from the work of Ernst Mengin and Angel María Garibay with the Annals of Tlatelolco and from the edition of the Historia Tolteca-Chichimeca done by Paul Kirchhoff, Lina Odena Güemes, and Luis Reyes García. I was greatly helped in getting started with the Spanish version of Book Twelve by having access to the unpublished transcription and English translation prepared by Howard F. Cline, which S. L. Cline kindly made available to me.

Let me also take this occasion to acknowledge the contribution of Kimberly Gauderman, who prepared drafts of the transcriptions of both Nahuatl and Spanish of Book Twelve, as well as of some of the other texts, and did a great deal of difficult bibliographical spadework. In addition, I wish to express my gratitude to José Luis Martínez and Andrea Martínez for making it possible for me to acquire a copy of the entire color facsimile edition of Book Twelve from the Archivo General de la Nación in Mexico City. Without it I could never have prepared this volume. The library of California State University, Fullerton, was gracious in lending its rare copy of the facsimile of the Annals of Tlatelolco for an extended period.

The illustrations of the Florentine Codex are reproduced with permission of the Biblioteca Medicea Laurenziana, Florence. I am especially grateful to the School of American Research, to the University of Utah Press, and to Norma B. Mikkelsen, its executive editor, for the generous loan of photographs used in a previous publication of Book Twelve. The frontispiece, from the Codex Aubin, is reproduced by courtesy of the trustees of the British Museum.

I am grateful to Saloman Bejarano, Richard and Ruth Lavine, the Sidney Stern Memorial Trust, the National Endowment for the Humanities, and the Sociedad Estatal para la Ejecución de Programas del Quinto Centenario for generous financial support.

# INTRODUCTION

# INTRODUCTION

The voluminous early histories and reports the Spaniards wrote about their first experiences with the Indians of the Americas have long been familiar to the world. Observers across the centuries have frequently expressed the sentiment that we should balance the Spanish corpus with some accounts from the Indian side. In sixteenth-century central Mexico, some relevant texts were in fact written, set down in Roman letters in the indigenous Nahuatl, and during the twentieth century scholars have published those extant, translating them into various languages. Now the time has come to bring them together, taking advantage of the achievements of the existing editions, without which such an enterprise would have been impossible, or at least impractical. I present transcriptions of the originals as well as translations, so that readers who know Nahuatl can themselves grapple with the many remaining conundrums. For despite a century of scholarly activity, some of it by minds of true distinction, the field of older Nahuatl philology can still be described as nascent.

Among the Nahuatl conquest accounts, one outweighs the rest: Book Twelve of the encyclopedic history of Nahua culture organized by the Franciscan friar Bernardino de Sahagún and generally known as the Florentine Codex.[1] Sahagún's Nahua aides composed the original text in their own language under their mentor's supervision—how close and of exactly what nature will perhaps always remain controversial—and Sahagún later produced a parallel Spanish text, translating or paraphrasing and sometimes offering explanations or expressing his own opinions.

Because my purpose here is to let the Nahuas speak, it is perhaps ironic that the primary innovation of this volume is to include Sahagún's Spanish along with his aides' Nahuatl, both translated into English.[2] (To my knowledge, the Nahuatl and the

---

1. The true title, or the most generally used version thereof, is *General History of the Things of New Spain*, and the Florentine Codex is merely the best and fullest copy of it. Because usage in English is not yet entirely solidified, let me make it clear that I use "Nahuatl" to refer to the language and "Nahua" (pl. "Nahuas") to refer to the people; both are also used adjectivally.

2. Howard F. Cline prepared a complete transcription and English translation of the Spanish of Book Twelve, which remained unpublished but to which I have had access (see acknowledgments).

Spanish are not to be found facing, or even contained in the same volume, in any published form other than the color facsimile edition.) [3] Yet the intention even here is above all to throw light on the Nahuas' version and vision of things, partly through the contrast between the Nahuatl and the Spanish, partly by virtue of the fact that Sahagún often elicited further information not directly contained in the Nahuatl text, and partly because his translation has infinite value for our attempts to decipher the Nahuatl today. Sahagún often veers so far from the literal shape of the Nahuatl that (his propensity to paraphrase aside) he would seem to be in error, and translators in this century have sometimes rather hastily assumed that he was. The more we learn about older Nahuatl idiom, however, the more we find Sahagún right after all (not that some actual error does not exist), and he can no doubt continue to guide us as we attempt to improve the accuracy of our versions. [4] Another important reason for including the Spanish text is that it was copied by a Nahua, who in doing so has left us precious direct testimony about his comprehension, construction, and even pronunciation of Spanish, and hence about the place of himself and his fellow aides in the broader picture of cultural interaction.

The other Nahuatl texts dealing with the conquest are all fragments included in larger writings created for more general purposes. They were all done under less Spanish supervision than the Florentine Codex, in several cases under none at all, and some of them come from other locations in central Mexico; thus they serve as a kind of control. None of them was translated into Spanish at the time, and the lack is sorely felt in the type of translation that can be achieved today, although with perseverance and comparison between texts (toward which this volume is a step) fuller comprehension should come in time.

My translations, cast in a colloquial contemporary English as far as that is feasible, participate in the general current tendency in Nahuatl philology to emphasize pragmatics, the intended sense and effect, over a literal rendering. Recent work in grammar and idiom analysis, together with the study of a vast body of mundane Nahuatl texts previously left out of consideration, has made it possible to detect formulas and comprehend meanings whose presence we had hardly suspected. [5] The newer style of translation meshes well with, if indeed it is not a part of, the movement in history and an-

3. Sahagún 1979: vol. 3.

4. Let me give one example from my own experience. In chap. 6, fol. 10, we find the Nahuatl "aoc ie quilhuiaia in çaço tlein quichioaia," which appears to be "they said nothing to him, whatever he did." Such a rendering does not fit the context at all, however. Comparing Sahagún, I found that he said at this juncture "ni hazia de buena gana ninguna cosa" ("nor did he take joy in anything he did"). This reading gave me courage to continue searching for some special idiom, which eventually appeared in an entry in Molina 1970: fol. 3v of the Nahuatl-to-Spanish section, as "aye niquilhuitica" ("to be stupefied or pensive, paying no attention to what is said to one"). This parallel justified the translation "whatever he did, he was abstracted."

5. See Andrews 1975; Anderson, Berdan, and Lockhart 1976; Karttunen and Lockhart 1976; Launey 1979; Cline and León-Portilla 1984; Ruiz de Alarcón 1984; Lockhart, Berdan, and Anderson 1986; Karttunen and Lockhart 1987; and Lockhart 1991.

thropology to study the mental world, the attitudes and concepts, of those who produce texts instead of the facts and artifacts the texts appear to describe. Such a philosophy of translation is all the more appropriate with the present body of texts because  their strictly factual reliability seems low or at least clouded. The conquest accounts were all written appreciably later than the events of which they speak, in most cases by more than a generation, and I would maintain that even the apparently earliest, the Annals of Tlatelolco, should be dated no earlier than the 1540s, some twenty years after the conquest. The art of alphabetic writing was not to be transferred across cultures in a day.

Not all is gain in the newer style of translating, nor is everything changed. Many phrases and sentences will receive virtually the same translation no matter how one proceeds. In giving the intention of the original, one can lose part of its flavor (though a literal version also loses part). As a formal greeting, the Nahuas frequently uttered a phrase on the order of *oticmiiyohuilti, oticmociahuilti,* which could be rendered somewhat literally as "It (the effort of getting here) has tired you, has wearied you."[6] I translate this expression as "you are doubly welcome," for not only was that the effect, but the phrases are actually glossed as "welcome" in some dictionary entries. Sahagún, normally avoiding literal renditions, treats this phrase sometimes one way, sometimes the other. Indeed, many translators of formal Nahuatl texts have so strongly felt the need of two translations, one a literal reproduction of the elements, and the other a rendering of the sense, that they have included both in the same edition.[7] To attempt such a thing here, with an already overloaded format, is impractical, but a reader seeking more of an element-by-element rendition might do well to consult previous translations, above all Anderson and Dibble's work with Book Twelve, which was the first guide and point of departure of my own efforts. The new wave of interpretation concerns primarily syntax, idiom, formula, and semantic range; it does not much affect the primary reference of individual words. Thus the change is at the level of interpreting narrative, conversation, and general concepts. Little if any progress has been made with costumes, artifacts, or flora and fauna; nor does the new insight help identify exact locations and the like. Here I rely heavily on my predecessors, and again above all on Anderson and Dibble.[8]

Even if one's aim is to reveal the specific intention of a metaphor or formula, little can be done if that intention has not been fathomed. Here many Nahuatl expressions have been, by my own lights, translated too literally, sometimes consciously, *faute de*

6. Some examples are in the Nahuatl text of Book Twelve on fols. 4v, 8, 25, and 62.

7. For example, Garibay K. 1943; Tezozomoc 1949; Karttunen and Lockhart 1987.

8. Interested readers will find much useful specific information in the apparatus of Anderson and Dibble's edition of Book Twelve (Sahagún 1950–1982: part 13), including a speculative map of Tenochtitlan/ Tlatelolco, locating many of the sites named in the text, and notes of identification giving scientific names of species, further references, and so on. I have used the second revised edition of Book Twelve, published in 1975, and my page references are to that version. See also the introductory matter and notes in Sahagún 1978.

*mieux,* and other times no doubt without my realizing it. As knowledge of idiom mounts over time, the next generation of translations may be less literal yet.

## PERCEPTUAL-EXPRESSIVE
## MODES, GROUP CONSCIOUSNESS,
## AND GENERAL VIEW IN THE TEXTS

Before entering into more detailed discussion of the texts and my principles of editing them, I wish to range quite widely—if provisionally, given the state of our knowledge—over the general attitudes and concepts they reveal.

One of the more central aspects of recent Spanish American ethnohistorical research is to highlight the extent of the similarities between the cultural systems of the Europeans and those of the Nahuas of central Mexico (probably the Mesoamericans generally).[9] The Nahuas had reasonably close analogues of the concepts structuring nearly all facets of European society and culture. After first contact, each side was able to operate for centuries on an ultimately false but in practice workable presumption that the other side's analogous concepts were essentially identical with its own, thus avoiding close examination of the unfamiliar and maintaining its own principles. The truce obtaining under this partial misconception permitted for a long period the preservation of indigenous structures of all kinds while intercultural ferment went on gradually, hardly attaining the level of consciousness. I have called this phenomenon the process of Double Mistaken Identity.[10]

Within the perspective of a broad comparability between the two cultures in contact, Nahuatl-language texts show us a world of well-defined indigenous concepts, far from identical with their closest Spanish parallels, embodied in special vocabulary; as a corpus these fixed ideas organized sociopolitical, economic, and household life (and art as well), often making extensive use of the principles of cellular subdivision, rotation, and numerical ordering. Most of this lore and its vocabulary survived for more than a hundred years after the conquest, and large and basic parts were still operative at the time of Mexican independence. The Nahuas continued to be primarily self-centered, judging things within the framework they had developed for themselves, concerned above all with life inside the local ethnic states that had always been their primary arena. Yet they did not shy away from contact with things Spanish, readily adopting any new artifacts, practices, or principles that struck them as comprehensible and useful for their own purposes. Clearly they had maintained their balance past the cataclysms of first contact in a way that many less sedentary peoples, who had less cultural ground in common with the newcomers, did not.

More than 250 years of pragmatism, flexibility, self-absorption, and corporate survival on the part of the postconquest Nahuas presumably say something about their

9. Consider especially Gibson 1952, 1964; Taylor 1972, 1979; Lockhart 1991, 1992; and Farriss 1984.
10. Lockhart 1985.

reaction in the moment of contact itself. The common notion of their first reaction to Europeans, however, is very different indeed, of a people shocked out of its senses, amazed, bewildered, overwhelmed, benumbed by the intruders, paralyzed, fate-ridden, prepared for imminent doom and disappearance.[11] I am sure that that image is erroneous but, as it happens, it is not possible to investigate the first twenty-five years or so after contact—the first generation—in the same way as later decades, for a very simple and basic reason. The inevitable source for anyone who would study postconquest Nahua conceptual vocabulary and self-view is the corpus of alphabetic writing in a large variety of genres produced in Nahuatl by Nahuas; and not before 1545 or 1550, for understandable reasons, did the production of Nahuatl texts become a standard feature of the scene.

What we find, picking up about 1550, is a picture dominated in so many aspects by patently untouched preconquest patterns that it does not take much imagination to reconstruct a great deal of the situation during the missing years. It would be a most unlikely scenario for a people to have spent twenty-five undocumented years in wide-mouthed amazement inspired by some incredible intruders, and then, the moment we can see them in the documents, to have relapsed into going about their business, seeking the advantage of their local entities, interpreting everything about the newcomers as some familiar aspect of their own culture, showing concern with the Spaniards only insofar as they impinged on local life.

The body of material assembled here purports to speak directly of actions, speech acts, and emotions of the Nahuas during the first year or two after the arrival of the Spaniards in central Mexico. It is thus obviously to the purpose in reconstructing first reactions, and as such has been copiously used by several generations of scholars; at the same time it is highly suspect, for the versions we know, having been written down many years after the events, show numerous signs of legend formation, as well as of other distortions—distortions, that is, if we are interested in Nahua reactions of 1520 or 1525, as opposed to the attitudes of certain Nahuas in certain places writing between 1545 and 1565 for the most part, and looking back to the events of the earlier period. The small corpus of literature of this type is dominated by the Mexica of Tenochtitlan/ Tlatelolco, the leading power of the "Triple Alliance" of the Valley of Mexico. The single most well-developed and well-known account, as we have seen, is Book Twelve of Sahagún's Florentine Codex, composed by Tlatelolca under Sahagún's sponsorship, and I will concentrate on that work in this discussion.

The Nahuatl material on the conquest presents historiographic questions that cannot be ignored and had best be taken into consideration from the very beginning. We have seen that all known accounts were put on paper toward the middle of the sixteenth century or later; some of them were done under Spanish supervision, as is notably the case with Book Twelve. Nor are contact/conquest narratives distributed evenly

---

11. For early and late examples of this view, see Prescott 1931 and Todorov 1984. The entire tradition is well represented in León-Portilla 1992.

according to point of origin. From the thriving local states (altepetl; on this term see my remarks below, between notes 40 and 41) spread all across central Mexico we have virtually nothing; while from the center of the Triple Alliance, the double state of Tenochtitlan/Tlatelolco, comes the great bulk of all we have, and in that corpus Tlatelolco—the junior cousin and partner of Tenochtitlan and its immediate neighbor on an island base in Lake Tetzcoco—happens to predominate, providing both Book Twelve and the next most systematic account, a portion of what I have called in this volume the "Annals of Tlatelolco." One might think this state of affairs the result of simple chance, that is, chance in association with the natural concentration of certain activities in the imperial capital both before and after the Spaniards arrived. Furthermore, the prodigious philologist Sahagún was long stationed precisely in Tlatelolco. Under these conditions it could well be thought that the geographic distribution of the texts is not particularly problematic, that they are likely to be as representative as any and have the additional advantage of a kind of centrality.

In fact, the spatial distribution turns out to be of considerable interest; in itself it can tell us a good deal about who reacted most intensely to the intrusion. Although we are not flooded with indigenous histories from across the face of central Mexico, written in the postconquest period, neither are they lacking. All take the form of annals of an altepetl, with a goodly amount of material on surrounding states, going far back into the preconquest period and bringing the story up past the conquest to the time of writing. Prominent among them are the so-called "Historia Tolteca-Chichimeca," being annals of Quauhtinchan (Cuauhtinchan) east of Puebla; the annals of Quauhtitlan (Cuauhtitlan) just north of Mexico City; and the vast work of the Chalco historian Chimalpahin. [12] All have a postcontact section of greater or lesser extension, and what is remarkable about all of them, compared to the Tenochtitlan texts, is that they march right by the appearance of the Spaniards and the conquest with minimal comment. The Spanish advent receives mention primarily insofar as that particular altepetl is directly affected when the Spaniards physically move through in the course of their campaign, bring about changes in the local rulership, realign the jurisdiction, or assign tribute. Chimalpahin and the authors of the Historia Tolteca-Chichimeca show far more concern about Mexica inroads into local sovereignty in preconquest times than about the Spaniards, who merely replaced the Mexica. The conclusion I draw is that Tenochtitlan/Tlatelolco as the great loser cared much more intensely about the conquest than other Nahua groups, wrote more about it, and doubtless harbored certain attitudes that were not representative of the broader culture group.

It is likely that the Tlaxcalans, who were in some sense the great winners and who made their corporate living in postconquest times by harping on the glories of their role as the main auxiliaries of the Spaniards in the conquest, were also relatively preoccupied with the contact years. Yet no relevant writing has survived other than a promotional literature (and even it is mainly in Spanish) aimed at getting favors from the

---

12. Nothing from Chimalpahin is included here, despite the fact that his work contains some material on the conquest, because he belongs primarily to the seventeenth century.

Spanish government, plus the late Spanish-language chronicle of the Tlaxcalan mestizo Diego Muñoz Camargo. [13] A set of annals in Nahuatl by the Tlaxcalan Tadeo de Niza could have told us a great deal, but it has disappeared.

We are left, then, with a corpus in some ways clearly atypical. Only the Mexica and their closest associates put up prolonged resistance to the Spaniards, and only they made any written record of the experience that was at all detailed. Yet questions of conscious allegiance versus conscious resistance, or the relative intensity of local reaction based on political-ethnic self-interest, are quite superficial. The Mexica must have shared most of their basic view of the Spaniards and of themselves with other Nahuas, and once an attempt has been made to discover the main lines of that view as seen in their conquest narratives, perhaps we can detect some connection with what can be deduced from more general analysis.

A most striking aspect of Book Twelve of the Florentine Codex is the degree to which it is visual and episodic; much of the story, sequential though it is, is a series of snapshots of individual scenes. Consider the catapult episode of chapter 38. The Spaniards had pushed the Mexica back into a fortified portion of the Tlatelolcan section of the island, in the north, and, contrary to their usual practice in the Indies, were tending to adopt full-scale siege tactics:

And then those Spaniards installed a catapult [literally, "wooden (stone) sling"] on top of an altar platform with which to hurl stones at the people. And when they had it ready and were about to shoot it off, they gathered all around it, vigorously pointing their fingers, pointing at the people [i.e., the Mexica], pointing to where all the people were assembled at Amaxac, showing them to each other. The Spaniards spread out their arms, [showing] how they would shoot and hurl it at them, as if they were using a sling on them. Then they wound it up, then the arm of the catapult rose up. But the stone did not land on the people, but fell behind the marketplace at Xomolco.

Because of that the Spaniards there argued among themselves. They looked as if they were jabbing their fingers in one another's faces, chattering a great deal. And the catapult kept returning back and forth, going one way and then the other; bit by bit it righted itself. Then it could be seen clearly that there was a stone sling at its point, attached with very thick rope. Then because of that they named it a "wooden sling."

Here we have the Nahuas observing the Spaniards closely but entirely from the outside, making no judgments per se but drawing realistic conclusions about their actions and purposes on the premise that their opponents are much like themselves. This is precisely the same posture detected in the early linguistic reaction of Nahuatl to the intrusive phenomena (in fact, the passage includes a classic example of one of the main adaptive strategies, the qualified identification: *quauhtematlatl* 'wooden sling'). [14]

13. See Assadourian and Martínez Baracs 1991 and Muñoz Camargo 1984.
14. See Lockhart 1992: chap. 7.

Let us look at one more example. Chapter 30 speaks of the experience of the Mexica with guns and crossbows as the siege of Tenochtitlan got under way.

> A gun went in the prow of each of their boats, and where the [Mexica] boats were close together and assembled, they fired on them; many people died from it. [When hit, each boat] quickly lifted its prow, wavered, and sank. Likewise when they took good aim at someone with the iron bolts, he did not escape; immediately he died, he expired.
>
> But when the Mexica had been able to see and judge how the guns hit, or the iron bolts, they no longer went straight, but moved back and forth, going from one side to the other, zigzagging. Also, when they saw that the big gun was about to go off, everyone hit the ground, spread out on the ground, crouched down, and the warriors quickly went in among the houses. The road cleared off; the highway was as if swept clean.

The second example is in all basic respects identical to the first, but it shows in addition the ability to turn the conclusions gained from close observation into an appropriate reaction or adaptation. Here we see the Mexica almost instantaneously adopting the same defensive tactics toward artillery and small-arms fire that have prevailed in Europe.

At times the detail of the observation is overwhelming. Let us pick out some passages on European dogs and horses (chapters 7, 15).

> Their dogs were huge creatures, with their ears folded over and their jowls dragging. They had burning eyes, eyes like coals, yellow and fiery. They had thin, gaunt flanks with the rib lines showing; they were very tall. They did not keep quiet, they went about panting, with their tongues hanging down. They had spots like a jaguar's, they were varicolored.

> The second contingent and file [entering Tenochtitlan] were horses carrying people, each with his cotton cuirass, his leather shield, his iron lance, and his iron sword hanging down from the horse's neck. They came with bells on, jingling or rattling. The horses, the deer, neighed, there was much neighing, and they would sweat a great deal; water seemed to fall from them. And their flecks of foam splatted on the ground, like soapsuds splatting. As they went they made a beating, throbbing, and hoof-pounding like throwing stones. Their hooves made holes, they dug holes in the ground wherever they placed them. Separate holes formed wherever they went placing their hindlegs and forelegs.

At this point it becomes necessary to look into the background of the visual-episodic (or sensory-episodic) mode of perception of things Spanish in the Florentine Codex. As suggestive as it is, one must ask if the circumstances of the work's composition have not had a strong effect on the result. Book Twelve is part of a great encyclopedic enterprise in which Sahagún hoped to capture, through original Nahuatl texts produced on humanistic, philological principles, the breadth of preconquest Nahua civilization.

Above all, Sahagún was interested in vocabulary; he often spoke as if his work was meant primarily as raw material for a Nahuatl dictionary, and indeed he was preparing such a dictionary.[15] Reading the Sahagún corpus overall in comparison with other older Nahuatl documents, one becomes aware of a particular type of wordiness. Now most Nahuatl verbal expression of a formal or elevated nature was wordy, compared to recent European modes, conforming to an elaborate rhetorical protocol that included among other things a feast of double phrases. But Sahagún is both different and more extreme. Pairs by no means always dominate; rather, whole series pile up, often with absolutely minimal variation between one element and the next, as though one were creating a grammatical paradigm or listing all of the possible acceptable variants. Again and again the reader gets the feeling that at some point of the work's composition Sahagún must have looked at the texts and exhorted his writer-aides to produce more words; in fact, he virtually admitted as much.[16] I think that he sometimes drove them to their wits' end, and beyond. Somehow or other, a recognizable "Sahagún style" arose, to be found in a great many compartments of the corpus (not all), and not quite like anything else in older Nahuatl writing. The study of style, usage, and genre in older Nahuatl is in its infancy, and we must be diffident. I cannot absolutely assert that the Sahagún microvariational, agglutinative style is not partly grounded in some oral storyteller's art of heightening attention and building up suspense. I do feel certain that Sahagún's prodding has had the effect of increasing the detail, hence the visuality and sensuality, of the contents of Book Twelve.

On the indigenous side too, there are some considerations that might deter us from too quick an equation of the visuality of Book Twelve with a general Nahua perceptual mode. Preconquest Nahua record-keeping was a complex system operating simultaneously on two tracks, the visual and the oral. An impressive visual artifact was one of the components, consisting of colored pictures and glyphs preserved on paper, but it was not entirely self-interpreting, nor was it complete; it needed the complement of a memorized oral presentation, which often went far beyond simple explanation of the visual component. Some kinds of things were more easily reduced to pictorial communication than others. Tribute lists and censuses, with graphic representation of tangible items, precise dating and specification of amounts, and well-developed glyphs for personal and place-names came close to conveying the entire message. The pictorial part of historical narratives, in annals form, contained only the barest skeleton of the account, primarily restricted to the type of information just mentioned in the case of surveys. The elaborate set speeches so important in every branch of Nahua life were apparently not represented pictorially at all.

15. One such statement is in the preface to Book Twelve; for Sahagún's lexical interests see Campbell and Clayton 1988.

16. In the prologue to Book Seven, Sahagún apologizes for the displeasure the reader may experience from the many synonymous words given for a single thing and the different ways presented of making the same statement. It was done on purpose in order to have a full record, he says, and not only in Book Seven but throughout the work (Sahagún 1950–1982: 1.68).

If we try to imagine a historical record, or one might almost say journalistic record, of the events of the conquest, made by the Nahuas before they came under Spanish domination or in the first years thereafter, when they had not yet taken to alphabetic writing, the visual component presumably would have pictured certain key events or scenes, in addition to giving a number of names and dates. The burden of the narrative would have been conveyed through a memorized oral text. We cannot be absolutely positive that such a record ever existed, but it is at least very likely.

Book Twelve contains some elements that have every appearance of being authentic oral tradition carried down from the very moment of the events. The Nahua aides working on the account in the 1550s and 1560s no doubt had seen horses and Euro-pean dogs, which they could have described out of their own experience, but only someone who was present could have originated the picture of the Spaniards arguing and gesticulating around the catapult, or of its pendulumlike return to a vertical posi-tion. Further, if a pictorial skeleton for the conquest narrative did exist (though no such thing seems to be extant now),[17] it might very likely have survived the intervening years of catastrophe and monumental change better than the oral component. The Tlatelolcan authors of Book Twelve may have worked on the basis of a highly frag-mentary oral narrative, leading them to transfer the pictorial component into prose in the version we know, with an automatic emphasis on visuality.

Because no preconquest convention for the pictorial representation of specifically Spanish phenomena could have existed, it is hard to guess what parts of the description of such things go back to pictures, what parts to visual observation orally preserved. The visual emphasis I have spoken of, however, applies not only to the Spanish side of the narrative, but to everything recorded (one indication among many of how the Spaniards are treated within the normal framework). Pictographic conventions on the indigenous side were well established, and it is easier to recognize their precipitation in prose. A large department of preconquest pictorial communication was the depiction of costume, with each of the multitudinous insignia of a god, priest, ruler, or warrior shown in color and conventionally reproduced for easy recognition. Several passages of Book Twelve seem to go back to visual models of this type. When Moteucçoma's emissaries first go to meet Cortés on board ship, the episode is dominated by a long description of the four gods' or priests' outfits they presented to him. The narrative of the Spanish massacre of participants in the festivities of Toxcatl is nearly overshadowed by a minute description of the dough image of the god Huitzilopochtli specially cre-ated for the occasion, together with all of its accoutrements. Time and again the exact outfit worn by Mexica heroes is detailed, including the style of the cloaks worn by the leaders at the final surrender.[18]

It is ironic that none of these things is actually elaborately portrayed in the pictorial material accompanying Book Twelve in its present form. Although the pictures in the

---

17. The so-called Lienzo de Tlaxcala (see Gibson 1952) is an equivalent for the Tlaxcalan region.

18. These descriptions could have been pulled from sources not related to the conquest.

volume are many and useful, there is every indication that they are essentially a back-formation from the alphabetic text rather than the primary pictorial elements on which much of the text was probably based. A version intermediate between any pictorial-oral account and the Florentine account—the so-called Madrid Manuscript—lacks pictures entirely, and the set accompanying Book Twelve in the Florentine Codex is incomplete. The main function of the pictures in the existing manuscript is to make up for the difference in length between the Nahuatl and the Spanish versions, and the amount of space so left seems to have been the deciding factor in determining their topic and location. The illustrations are so posterior, coming last when the volume was being brought to a hasty completion, that few of them got colored, and in several cases spaces where pictures should have been were left entirely blank. [19]

Perhaps we can get some perspective on the Florentine Codex's account by looking beyond it. Briefer, less well-developed versions can be equally indicative, and indeed because of their stripped down and accidental nature perhaps even more so. The so-called Codex Aubin is a set of pictorial-alphabetic annals written in Tenochtitlan start-ing perhaps in the 1560s, with contemporary entries covering the remainder of the century, but the author also collected material for earlier times, both pre- and postcon-quest. [20]

Some seven or eight pages are devoted to the conquest, virtually all of it concerning things happening in Tenochtitlan itself. A full-page drawing (the frontispiece of this volume) depicts the massacre at Toxcatl, but it is more an architectural blueprint than a detailed vision of what happened; other pictures are small, stylized, and serve primarily to mark topics and make subdivisions. In the text itself there is very little of the visuality so marked in the prose of Book Twelve of the Florentine Codex. Of the elaborate de-scriptions of costumes and processions there is no hint. Perhaps one or two action de-tails are a bit reminiscent of the other work: the drummers' hands being hacked off; the nose cut off the dough image of Huitzilopochtli; or Quauhtemoc laying a friendly hand on the back of the neck of Tzihuacpopoca, whom he suspected of plotting against his life, before striking and killing him.

Yet the impression left by the Codex Aubin is remarkably similar to that given by the Florentine Codex. Visuality is replaced by orality; that is, instead of the detail of costume, color, and action, we have the detail of conversation. In this version, Mo-teucçoma asks permission for the festivity of Toxcatl to be held:

"The day of the festivity of our god has come; today is the tenth day [of the month]. Well then, shouldn't we still celebrate it? We won't do anything. We will just dance; when they are about to take up the dough [image], they will make a clamor, that's all."
Then the captain said, "Very well, let them do it; I have understood."

19. This is not to say that the illustrations would not reward intensive study, which I regret not being able to dedicate to them at present, but perhaps their inclusion in this edition will make it easier for others to analyze them. Brief identifications of each illustration are included as the appendix to this volume.
20. See Dibble 1963: introduction.

Actually, Spaniards participate only briefly in these conversations, which are primarily exercises in traditional Nahua discourse, little different whether they refer to the new arrivals or not.

The similarity of effect between the two versions is heightened by the fact that both are equally episodic. Because the Codex Aubin's version is so short, this facet stands out all the more. By no means are the seven pages given over to a summary of the events of two years. Rather, the Toxcatl massacre takes more than a third of the space. It is followed by a consultation between Moteucçoma and some high leaders about whether the Spaniards' horses should be fed, then by Moteucçoma's death. The death itself is passed over in favor of telling the story of the difficulty in getting Moteucçoma's body buried because of his unpopularity. This material is followed by a recital of the sequence of the months, with an event or two, including the succession of kings and the final fall, indicated rather than told. The Florentine Codex also gives a full account of the procession of the months, though separate from the main narrative. In the Nahua tradition of historical writing, it is the calendar that marches along step by step with no abbreviation or deviation, while actions that occur are individual episodes inserted somewhere in that framework. The Florentine Codex's account is rather superficially arranged in the European fashion in which the flow of the narrative, not the passage of time per se, gives the structure, but it remains a set of discrete staged episodes even if the temporal structuring has been somewhat mutilated. Book Twelve, alone of the texts included here, has topically organized chapter divisions, but in a great many cases it is clear that the heading and the division were created at a later stage than the text proper. [21]

The above may tend to give us the impression that the Nahua annals genre has very considerably colored the view of the Spaniards shown in the extant sources. Nevertheless, that the annals genre is what it is cannot be regarded as an accident; rather, it corresponds closely to general modes of Nahua culture. The Nahua view of almost anything was in some sense episodic. In political life, household organization, land management, song, visual representation, really in everything they did, the Nahuas built symmetrical, numerically ordered structures in which larger units consisted of markedly separate independent parts. [22] The conquest annals show us that they were not shaken out of their usual modes by the Spaniards, did not ultimately view them differently than anything else, but perceived them as an encapsulated element within their general lore. The accounts also show that the Mexica and Tlatelolca were more impressed with what happened—the siege, the fighting, their loss of preeminence—than with the Spaniards as such. People of the other altepetl of central Mexico were apparently much less impressed even with the transcendence of the events. None of the versions could be said to be *about* the Spaniards, or even primarily concerned with them. This too is important evidence toward an understanding of their reaction to the new arrivals.

21. For example, one half of a battle cry is at the end of chap. 33, the other half at the beginning of chap. 34.

22. See Lockhart 1992: throughout, but especially chap. 10.

One way of addressing the topic of the early Nahua vision of themselves and the Spaniards is to examine the descriptive categories used in this connection in the texts. First we must note (despite the title I have given to this collection) how little any general term for indigenous people is seen—no surprise, for the same can be said of the mass of Nahuatl sources written over the following two and a half centuries. As in other kinds of Nahuatl texts, the Spanish word *indio* 'Indian' fails to appear as a loan,[23] though *españoles* 'Spaniards' is prominent; nor do we find any close equivalent of the term "Indian," for under precontact conditions the indigenous people of the Americas were without the prerequisites for developing a concept "inhabitants of the Western Hemisphere as opposed to other humans." The most general category to be found is *nican tlaca* 'here people', which indicated generally the local, native inhabitants of central Mexico and specifically those inhabitants in distinction to the Spaniards. The "here" may have extended to all indigenous Western Hemisphere peoples of whom the Nahuas were aware, such as the Maya of the south or the less sedentary peoples of the north; the texts give us no sure way to test its scope, for in the corpus it only occurs three times in Book Twelve and twice in the letter from the council of Huejotzingo that I have included in this volume. In every case it is a last resort, when using altepetl names would have been awkward or impossible.[24]

"Mexica," very frequently seen in Book Twelve, refers only to the inhabitants of the island capital of the empire, the paired altepetl of the Tenochca and the Tlatelolca (in fact, it often means the dominant Tenochca specifically; the Tlatelolca mainly use their altepetl name and only rarely call themselves Mexica). The rest of the population of central Mexico is also referred to by separate altepetl names. No unity of the various altepetl is expressed or implied. In Book Twelve, "we" always means the Mexica or even just the Tlatelolca, who in the two documents they authored cast aspersions on Mexica courage and wisdom and in other ways show resentment of their more prominent cousins. Although words for the Nahuatl speakers as a group existed, they fail to appear in these texts; a certain awareness of the language and culture group is shown indirectly by occasional references in Book Twelve to the Otomi, the second language group of central Mexico, over and above their altepetl affiliation, and to non-Nahuatl speech as babbling. All central Mexicans other than the island inhabitants are "they," and the Tlatelolca often refer to even the Tenochca in that fashion (the Tenochca, in the few texts we have, hardly refer to the Tlatelolca at all).[25]

23. Sahagún, by contrast, uses it constantly in his Spanish version of Book Twelve.

24. In Book Twelve the expression will be found on fols. 13v, 53, and 74. Very interesting is the passage (fol. 67) in which the non-Spanish enemies are called *hueca tlaca* 'distant people' (as though the Spaniards were not), because it is supremely illustrative of the Nahua reluctance to change their categories of thought. Another partial equivalent was *macehualtin;* see the discussion of translation practices below. For the whole question of postconquest indigenous self-terminology, see Lockhart 1992: chap. 4.

25. See the selection from the Codex Aubin; some of the portions of the song collection, the Cantares Mexicanos, that refer to the conquest (in Bierhorst 1985) are much the same. Such items could even be considered Nahuatl texts concerning the conquest and so be included here, but they are distinctly not narratives, and in any case they are so obscure at present that working out a reasonable rendering and explanation of them would unduly delay the present publication.

Nor is there much emphasis on classification by subregion. Once the eastern Nahuas are lumped together as *tlatepotzca* 'people from the other side of the mountains', a term not apparently laden with either good or bad connotations, and once the name Tlalhuica, an ethnic group dominating several altepetl in the basin to the south of Mexico City, appears in a context showing that to the Mexica they were crude backlanders.[26] For the people located around the southern lakes of the Valley of Mexico, who lived primarily from intensive chinampa[27] agriculture on the marshes and lake borders, we sometimes see the term *chinampaneca* 'the chinampa people', but this usage is closely defined by altepetl, as the individual altepetl are usually mentioned concurrently.

Book Twelve frequently calls the auxiliaries and the Spaniards, taken together, *toyaohuan* 'our enemies', sometimes with no ethnic distinction at all. When distinctions are made, those mentioned are the Spaniards and the individual altepetl groups. Indigenous people, then (and this is emphatically true of the whole corpus of Nahuatl annals and conquest accounts), are overwhelmingly categorized by altepetl grouping, each one separate. Any one altepetl has its friends and its enemies among the rest; from the point of view of each altepetl, all others are outsiders. The Spaniards, it appears, enter into this scheme as one more player. "We" and "they" divides along altepetl lines, not between New Worlders and Old Worlders.

When the invaders are not being called simply "our enemies," which as we have seen does not distinguish them from central Mexican enemies of the Mexica, Book Twelve mainly terms them Spaniards, *españoles*, with the loanword used in the Nahuatl text. I have no way of knowing whether the word itself entered the language at this time, either in the Tenochtitlan vicinity or elsewhere. The Florentine Codex's writers show a good deal of sensitivity to first-generation versus second-generation usage, employing the former in direct quotes and the latter in narrative; but, alas, the correspondence is not absolutely perfect. In general, despite the frequency of *españoles* in the text, it is not seen in the many quotes, but once in fact it does appear. The populace is said to have cried out in the last moment of the siege that Quauhtemoctzin was going to surrender to "the Spaniards."[28]

In the other texts the new arrivals are called Christians *(x̄pianome)*, Castilians *(caxtilteca)*, and "Castile people" *(Caxtillan tlaca)*, most often by the narrator, as well as Spaniards. ("Christian" continued in popular usage as a way of referring to Spaniards long after everyone had become Christian, often in an early form that nearly disguised its origin: *quixtiano*. In all likelihood it is a reflection of the fact that the Spaniards often so referred to themselves in the first years, rather than any specific comment on religion.) The Annals of Tlatelolco also occasionally use the term *totecuiyohuan* 'our lords (or masters or rulers)'.

---

26. Folio 23v has "tlateputzcatl" and fol. 74 "tlalhuicatotonti."

27. A chinampa is an intensively cultivated bed formed by heaping up earth and vegetable matter until it rises above the level of the shallow water that surrounds it.

28. Folio 81. One would have expected rather *caxtilteca* during this time period, but it fails to appear in the whole text. As explained below in the particular discussion of Book Twelve, Sahagún was likely responsible for the uniform use of *españoles*.

In none of these sources is mention of the Spaniards accompanied by much overt commentary, whether positive or negative. Surely no moral judgments are issued. Some actions by the Spaniards that moderns often tend to judge, including the massacre of Toxcatl and the execution of some Nahua rulers after the victory, are indeed told in detail, with a sense of shock and deep imprint; but the tagwords usually employed in modern descriptions, "cruel" and the like, are entirely absent. In the Florentine Codex, the capture, sacrifice, dismemberment, and display of several Spaniards is told in exactly the same fashion and the same spirit, as a notable event. Moralizing or any kind of active evaluation can hardly be said to be a part of these writings. Almost the only statements in this vein are put in the mouths of enemies of the Mexica and their allies, who were egging the Spaniards on to action against them. Thus the Tlaxcalans are said to have told the Spaniards that the Cholulans were evil people. And the people of Teocalhueyacan are said to have told Cortés that the Mexica were inhuman and oppressive.

Again we encounter questions of genre. The annals genre called for everything to be told as simple fact, event, occurrence, though of course it was always slanted. Direct evaluation and expression of emotion were largely limited to words uttered by the characters. In Book Twelve, a Mexica warrior taunts the Spaniards, calling them barbarians and backlanders. [29] Early in the game, the wizards and Moteucçoma say "We are not their match." [30] (We will later see that the first portion of Book Twelve must be taken a bit differently from the rest.) One could say that much is made of the Spaniards' equipment and animals and their efficacy. But it is the same with many plans and individual actions of the Mexica, especially the Tlatelolca. Once again we are dealing up to a point with the annals genre, which whenever it goes beyond simple declaration aims above all to heighten, to make each battle the fiercest, each hero the bravest, each coward the most cowardly.

To me, the overall, unspoken Mexica perspective on the Spaniards that arises from a reading of this corpus is that they were formidable adversaries who wanted much the same thing as the Mexica themselves. This is the rationale for opposing them. In the final section of Book Twelve, when the Mexica decide further resistance is impossible, they have a conference among themselves on how they should pay tribute to the Spaniards, assuming that the Spaniards would exact payments from them not unlike those they had exacted from other central Mexicans. The last speech in the book is a Mexica dignitary's explanation to the Spaniards of the tribute-payment system in the time of Moteucçoma. The actions of the other central Mexicans, as portrayed both here and in Spanish records, speak of a similar attitude, though with a different result. They also think that the Spaniards are like the Mexica, a group seeking dominance and tribute, content to leave local states otherwise to themselves; therefore from the first moment they are willing to play power politics with them against the Mexica. Actually, the central Mexican assessment was essentially correct; the Spanish encomienda system was a

29. Folio 74.
30. Folio 13.

form of indirect rule and tribute extraction, and Spanish intentions matched indigenous expectations on a great many fronts. It was the unforeseen effect of European
technology, diseases, and continued immigration that eventually transformed the situation.

At one point in Book Twelve (chap. 12) it does seem that the Mexica are making
negative comments on the Spaniards' attitude about gold (which, as the Nahuas did
not realize and a good many moderns still do not, was their only viable export product
at that time and therefore their only source of financial reward, European goods, logis-
tical support, and much else).

> Thereupon Moteucçoma named and sent the noblemen and a great many other agents of
> his, with Tzihuacpopocatzin as their leader, to go meet [Cortés] between Popocatepetl
> and Iztactepetl, at Quauhtechcac. They gave [the Spaniards] golden banners, banners of
> precious feathers, and golden necklaces.
>
> And when they had given the things to them, they seemed to smile, to rejoice and be
> very happy. Like monkeys they grabbed the gold. It was as though their hearts were put to
> rest, brightened, freshened. For gold was what they greatly thirsted for; they were glutton-
> ous for it, starved for it, piggishly wanting it.

Another passage (chap. 18) describes what happened when the Spaniards first went
to Moteucçoma's personal home. The message is similar, but noticeably more re-
strained and objective, with emphasis on how the Spaniards valued gold alone and not
the other things precious to the Nahuas.

> And when they got there and went into the storage place, they seemed to disperse in all
> directions, quickly going in everywhere, as though covetous and greedy. Thereupon [Mo-
> teucçoma's] own personal property was brought out, belonging to him alone, his own
> portion, all precious things: necklaces with pendants, arm bands with quetzal feathers,
> golden arm bands, bracelets, golden bands with shells for the ankles, and the turquoise dia-
> dem, insignia of the ruler, and the turquoise nose rods, and other things without number
> belonging to him. They took all of it; they appropriated it, assigned and apportioned it to
> themselves. And when they had taken off each and every piece of the gold, when it had
> been detached, then they assembled all of the precious feathers in the courtyard, in the
> middle of the courtyard [to be disposed of].

Here I must address a question that I have been holding in reserve. Most of what I
have been saying is, I believe, applicable to the entire corpus of Nahua contact narratives. In this corpus, however, a large portion of Book Twelve (including the passages
just quoted) is quite anomalous. The part from the Toxcatl massacre forward, including all of the fighting in and around Tenochtitlan, in many ways stands together with
the Annals of Tlatelolco and the Codex Aubin, both of which virtually begin their

conquest story with the events of Toxcatl, in contrast to the first part of Book Twelve. This part, dealing with the arrival of the Spaniards at the coast and their gradual progress toward Tenochtitlan, with the reactions of Moteucçoma and the Mexica population, up to and including the meeting of Cortés and Moteucçoma, has only a few parallel sentences in the other texts. My belief is that the part from Toxcatl forward in all three sources rests closely on oral tradition (and probably pictorial documents as well) actively preserved from nearly the time of the events, whereas the part dealing with what preceded is reconstructed from the merest fragments of authentic oral tradition (that is, in origin going back to the time of the events and faithfully preserved over the intervening years) and incorporates recent legend formation as well as, apparently, a great deal of simple embroidery. The overloaded style of which I have spoken is much more characteristic of the first part than of the second. [31] Yet it is precisely this suspect first part that has given rise to the general impression of the Mexica reaction to the Spaniards that has reigned ever since the work of William Prescott.

Here and here alone are omens vital to the story. [32] In my view they are the typical attempt of a vanquished group to explain, after the fact, what has happened, saying that the gods were against us, we should have seen what was coming, instead of evidence of fatalism and undue superstition on the part of the indigenous people who were actually living the experience. Note that there are eight of the omens, the canonical number of any set of things in the Nahua world. The inventor of an omen set would surely not be content until there were eight of them. No other Nahuatl source mentions any such phenomena. One source in Spanish does, the history of the Tlaxcalan mestizo historian Diego Muñoz Camargo, written about 1580. The spatial distribution might seem impressive substantiation, but Muñoz Camargo gives much evidence of having known the work of Sahagún and having been influenced by it. Above all, the omens he lists are virtually the same as those in Book Twelve, and all are related to Tenochtitlan, with nothing special to Tlaxcala, an unimaginable attribute of a source resting on authentic Tlaxcalan tradition. [33] The truth seems to be that the Tlaxcalans and others had nothing to explain and far less to regret, so they did not look back for omens. That the Mexica did I do not doubt, but I imagine it as a cumulative tradition arising over the twenty or thirty years after the culmination of the conquest.

Another feature of the early part of Book Twelve is the quaking, indecisive, quiescent, effete Moteucçoma. This I view as another of the classic reactions of a people after defeat, to blame their leader as a scapegoat. The whole process occurred time and

31. It is also seen in the parts referring to events taking place outside of Mexico/Tenochtitlan after the Spanish evacuation.

32. Burning temples being seen with dismay (fol. 68v) is a different thing, and so is the last-ditch attempt to determine fate with the Quetzaltecolotl (fols. 77v–79); the blood-fire apparition (fols. 79v–80) is perhaps similar.

33. Muñoz Camargo 1984: 209–212. Juan López y Magaña, doing doctoral research on Muñoz Camargo, was the first to see the probable origin of the omens in his history. After the list, which follows Sahagún down to minute details, in order and in many other respects, Muñoz Camargo adds as an afterthought two rather pitiful meteorological omens seen in Tlaxcala.

again in the Spanish Indies. A standard procedure of Spanish campaigners was to get into the presence of the local ruler peacefully, seize him, and use his powers to reap rewards and get a foothold in the country. This tactic usually worked only for a brief time, after which a strong rebellion would take place, by now as much against the ruler, who had lost all credibility and popularity in the process, as against the Spaniards. We must not look to the Moteucçoma portrayed in the Florentine Codex as a true expression of the first Mexica reaction to the Spaniards. The fawning and fearful character projected upon him has been heightened in the eyes of later observers by the elaborate speeches he gave, especially the one to Cortés on their first encounter. This speech may have been enhanced in the version we have or invented from the whole cloth, but the bowing down, the looking up to the new arrival as a towering figure who can protect his humble welcomer, the offer of the realm to him as his due, are hardly more than the ordinary rhetoric of polite greeting among Nahua lords and rulers.

It is also only in this first more mythical part that we hear much of great fright, grief, and dazed preoccupation on the part of the general Mexica populace, the streets deserted, the people inside their houses sorrowfully greeting each other as if for the last time. And it is here and only here that we hear about the doings of sorcerers and prognosticators.

One might object that some of the material in the first part of Book Twelve partakes of that convincing visuality which I have associated with oral tradition based ultimately on eyewitness experience. Leaving aside the description of gods' costumes, which could have come from codices of various kinds, and the dramatized account of a putative epiphany of the god Tezcatlipoca, there are certain dramatic details of considerable verisimilitude. In the account, the Mexica emissaries who had been sent to the Spaniards while they were still on the coast sprinkled the blood of human sacrifices on their food, to which they are said to have reacted with nausea. They blinked, they spat, they shook their heads. It is entirely convincing, yet it is also the general reaction of humankind to an unexpected sickening experience; there is no reason the skilled dramatists of Book Twelve could not have invented it (or reinvented it). As a rough parallel of the incident also appears in the Annals of Tlatelolco, we have some reason to believe that something of this nature may in fact have occurred. The latter version, however, lacks the sensual details. There blood is offered to Cortés, and he takes out his sword and kills the person offering it.

In a word, I suggest that the first part of Book Twelve, which has virtually dictated the European view of how the Nahuas first received the Spaniards, is a late reconstruction, seriously at odds with the pragmatism seen everywhere else in the narrative corpus, in those portions which by every indication were much closer to tradition actually handed down from the time of the events. Although I cannot accept 1528 as the time of writing of the Annals of Tlatelolco, there can be no doubt that it is much earlier than the version of Book Twelve that has reached us, and it lacks the perspectives and the incidents of the first portion of the latter. I do not doubt that Moteucçoma became unpopular; both the Tlatelolcan manuscript and the Codex Aubin confirm it, and it fits

well into the general pattern of postcontact events all over the Indies. But instead of putting this unpopularity down to some particular quality of Moteucçoma as a representative of the indigenous people, I think of it as a generic quality, inherent in the contact situation, which gave a good foothold to the reshaping of his image by a later generation. In their portrayal of Moteucçoma I imagine the writers of Book Twelve not to have been arbitrary, but to have reflected the attitude of a whole cohort of Mexica smarting under their loss of preeminence and looking for someone to blame. Later generations, in need of symbols, gave both Cortés and Moteucçoma a meaning they hardly had at the time.

Yet I do not mean to deprive the two of meaning. They were each most meaningful, at the time, to the other camp. Following their "seize the cacique" policy, the Spaniards from the first moment were intent on finding out as much as possible about the Mexica ruler in order to get him in their power, as they in fact managed to do. And from the accounts it emerges, hardly ever explicitly, that the Nahuas took Cortés to be the ruler, the *tlatoani,* of the Spaniards. The bows that Cortés made to the emperor and the pope either were not translated or made no impression. As I have indicated, it is as good as impossible to decide with certainty what Spanish words, all with some flavor of proper names, entered Nahuatl at this time, but one of the prime candidates for that honor is the word *capitán* 'captain', which in the sources virtually always refers to Cortés, as though there were no other captain, although in fact from the Spanish point of view there were several.

A few other individuals appear to have entered the Mexica consciousness during the siege. Pedro de Alvarado, Cortés' chief lieutenant, is referred to in the corpus (not in Book Twelve, actually) as *Tonatiuh* 'the Sun', supposedly because of his skin and hair coloring, though nothing is explicitly said in the Nahuatl accounts. And one Rodrigo de Castañeda appears to have become known to them by name, apparently because he entered into the spirit of their bouts of single combat, wearing devices and hurling insults at his enemies. For the rest, the Spaniards remain in the eyes of the Mexica (and of the Nahuas generally, as we know from sources of a later time) an unanalyzed corporate entity, as though they were a single altepetl grouping instead of containing among themselves the equivalent of many altepetl, a fact of which the Spaniards themselves were highly conscious even if the Nahuas were not, for it was a prime factor in their internal politics.

A final point I have reserved for the end: the question of whether the Mexica and the Nahuas in general at first viewed the Spaniards as gods, and if so what was meant thereby. Even from the time before I began to learn Nahuatl, I was highly skeptical on this point. All of the Nahuatl texts saying that the Spaniards were called gods were written in a later generation, as we have seen. With accounts in Spanish, which are the best known, it might be imagined that the Spaniards were creating a myth for their own purposes, and it is clear that their comprehension of Nahua culture was limited. Nevertheless, all three of the Nahuatl texts I have been discussing, written down under quite different auspices, do contain the same usage (that is, as something characteristic of the first year or two after first contact). Although we may never know the details of

meaning, connotation, and use, one can hardly doubt that the word did in fact circulate in the first generation in reference to Spaniards, and there is no doubt at all that by the 1540s or so the Nahuas of that generation were convinced that the generation of 1519–1521 had used the term.

We are still far from a full understanding of the semantic range of the Nahuatl word *teotl*. It surely was the primary term for a pantheon of divinities who run parallel in some ways to Old World gods of the Indo-Europeans, East Asians, and others, and after the conquest it also came to serve as a generic description of the God of the Christians. As in some other traditions, however, the human and the divine interpenetrated extensively among the Nahuas. Their altepetl gods were often also ancestors and former leaders of the group. Priests impersonated gods, taking their names as titles, and ritual god impersonators, dressed in all of the god's accoutrements, were feted and then sacrificed. Furthermore, it was said [34] that in ancient Tula men addressed one another as *teotl*.

As to the well-aired notion of Cortés being imagined to have been the god Quetzalcoatl returning, the suspect first portion of Book Twelve contains the only such references in the Nahuatl corpus (two of them to my knowledge). [35] The word *teotl*, by contrast, is spread widely through the texts; it occurs in conversational passages, not on every page but enough to render it part of their standard vocabulary, both in the singular (always I believe in reference to Cortés) and in the plural, in reference to all of the Spaniards or a group of them. An exhaustive list of the occurrences and an analysis of their context is a task for future research. Another question still to be investigated is whether there is any evidence that Nahuas other than the Mexica ever called or considered the Spaniards gods. It is reasonable to presume that the categorization, whatever its meaning, was general across the culture area, but we have seen that in certain ways the Mexica as the only truly resisting power were different from the rest.

Ultimately, although this aspect of the Nahua or Mexica reaction has often been taken as an indication of the perception of the Spaniards as something radically distinct, I view it rather as another attempt to include the intruders within the existing framework and bypass (thus implicitly denying or obscuring) the notion of radical distinctness.

In general, the posterior Nahua accounts of the events of the first contact period manifest a core of congruity with other existing evidence (much of it linguistic) on the first Nahua reaction to Spanish phenomena. In both sets of material, visuality reigns (along with other sensual perception). The Nahuas observe the Spaniards and the things they bring with them, taking each phenomenon as a separate item to be integrated into their general lore and modes, which otherwise remain unchanged. They

34. Sahagún 1950–1982: Book Ten, chap. 29.
35. In chaps. 2 and 3. Moteuccoma's speech to Cortés in chap. 16 can surely be read in that light, as it usually is, but it is indirect and nonspecific, and much of it can be read as normal greeting formula. See Gillespie 1989 for a large-scale demonstration of the gradual evolution of the "returning Quetzalcoatl" notion over the two generations after the conquest.

are interested in the newcomers but hardly overwhelmed. The kinds of assessments and adjustments they make belong to the general human equipment for evolution and change, hardly even reaching, during this first generation, the level of what we could call specifically culture contact.[36] Their responses are more like the ways in which a culture evolves within itself.

The so-called "other" hardly figures in this picture. The Nahuas simply do not recognize any new "other." Their most basic, frequently used means of categorizing human groups is "we" and "they." In most contexts, "we" are the individual altepetl group and "they" are all other humans, imagined as other altepetl groups. The Spaniards coming on the scene are viewed as one more such group. Their altepetl is Caxtillan and they are Caxtilteca (or other names meaning the same), just as there is an altepetl Tepoztlan, land of the Tepozteca. In other words, the Spaniards did not have the effect of creating a polarization between the indigenous inhabitants and the intruders. The Nahuas continued to see the world as they had before, divided between the altepetl group and all outsiders, be they indigenous or Spaniards.

## CONVENTIONS AND PROCEDURES

The present volume is far from representing a definitive edition of the texts it contains. Under present conditions, an attempt to indicate all doubts, spell out the trains of thought behind all new translations, and offer all of the possible alternative renderings of various words and passages would lead to an apparatus at least as large as the texts themselves and inappropriate in view of the probable readership of the Repertorium Columbianum of which this book is part.[37] Therefore, notes are relatively few and brief, confined largely to extreme cases of puzzlement, clear-cut alternative translations, minor points of information, and elucidation of slips and unusual spellings in the manuscript.[38] Sometimes a high degree of uncertainty or speculativeness is indicated

---

36. See Lockhart 1992: especially chaps. 7 and 10.

37. At present, few if any older Nahuatl texts of any length have received such an edition, a situation I view as appropriate given the state of the art and the present quick rate of progress.

38. A full-scale concordance and analysis of the vocabulary and phraseology of the corpus, including Book Twelve, would be a most useful enterprise. I will mention a few aspects of usage, previously unknown to me and which I have been unable to find in dictionaries, that gradually became clearer to me in close work with the texts. The verb *tlaça* is usually and properly defined as "to cast, hurl (especially but not necessarily downward)." Its use in Book Twelve shows that it goes farther semantically in related directions, including "let loose, drop, lose, get loose." With *cen-* 'entirely' it repeatedly means "let loose with everything, all of the forces available." The word is used in connection with the Spaniards losing or dropping things at the Tolteca canal and again when good-looking Mexica women were trying to get loose from the Spaniards at the end of the war. The reflexive form of *mana* 'to offer, place (in a spread-out position)', already well known to have the meaning of meteorological phenomena taking shape, in Book Twelve is repeatedly used in the sense of a squadron forming up, taking position, or the like. The verb *olini* 'to move' (usually with a directional prefix) has specific meanings, not all yet clear to me, relating to movements of parties, columns, or formations. Sometimes it seems to be "to break camp"; other times it seems more like "to mobilize." The distributive reflexive of *cenquetza*, literally, "to rise entirely," proves to mean "to bunch up, to be gathered in a bunch."

simply by putting a phrase of the text or translation in angled brackets, omitting a note; such items should be viewed as being accompanied by a question mark.

In the preceding section the general nature of the translations has already been explained. Let me concentrate here on the rendering of some special terms running through the corpus. A key word in several of the texts is *mexicatl* (plural *mexica*), designating members of the ethnic group inhabiting Tenochtitlan and Tlatelolco. Sahagún, like his Spanish contemporaries, translated the term as *mexicano,* which is the same word used to mean "Mexican, citizen of Mexico," today. It did not, of course, at that time yet have the broader meaning.[39] To translate *mexicatl* as "Mexican," though it has excellent recent precedent,[40] is therefore to invite misinterpretation. I prefer to use the form "Mexica"—taken from the stem of the Nahuatl word and in standard use among anthropologists in reference to the ethnic group in the narrower sense—for it is clearly distinct from the word for the citizens of the modern nation. I use the same translation even for Sahagún's *mexicano* (except when he is speaking of the language).

Conversely, although a similar situation exists with the primary designation in both Nahuatl and Spanish for the seat of the group and the corporate entity—Mexico—I have let it stand, feeling that the reader will immediately grasp that the modern nation is not meant. To use "Mexico City" for the time before a Spanish municipality was founded would be to commit a serious anachronism.

A fixture of older Nahuatl, naming a pivotal structure in the Nahua world, was the word *altepetl,* literally, "water(s) and mountain(s)," a territorial metaphor for any sovereign state but especially for the local ethnic states of central Mexico, which might be compared with ancient Greek city-states with respect to their range in size. "City-state," however, will hardly do as a translation, because of its emphasis on an urban entity, an element lacking in the rationale of the altepetl. Indeed, such was the specificity and complexity of altepetl structure that it is hard to find any sociopolitical term in English that is a reasonable equivalent on all counts (such as nation, kingdom, land, province, town, or people; village and chiefdom may be dismissed out of hand). The one possible rendering that seems to me to have few wrong connotations is "realm," and given my ambition to make the translations readable, I was tempted to use it. But though innocuous enough, it is not informative. Historical and anthropological scholarship on late preconquest and early postconquest times is profiting vastly from a better understanding of the altepetl, long virtually unrecognized in a picture emphasizing on the one hand imperial alignments and on the other the microstructure called the calpulli (a constituent part of the altepetl). Each new shade of meaning and different context of the use of the word "altepetl" adds significantly to our comprehension, so I have retained it in the English translation despite its currently exotic status. I trust that

---

39. The Spaniards did immediately begin to broaden the scope of the term, above all by using it for the Nahuatl language, starting the process that gradually led to its present significance. See Lockhart 1992: chap. 4.

40. Anderson and Dibble do so in Sahagún 1950–1982.

in time it will become a normal part of the English vocabulary for dealing with central Mexico (and indeed it is well on its way), just as in Spanish American history no one would try to translate the now-familiar "encomienda" (referring in fact to the grant of an altepetl or similar entity to a Spaniard, to whom its tribute and draft labor would be channeled).

A term much used in the Nahuatl of Book Twelve is *tiacauh,* usually appearing in the plural form *tiacahuan.* The great sixteenth-century lexicographer Molina glosses it as "brave man, courageous and valiant soldier" (see Molina 1970: Nahuatl to Spanish, fol. 112v). It refers primarily to the body of experienced fighters above the neophytes and below the leaders or captains (though collectively it can include the latter as well). In Book Twelve, it refers in the vast majority of cases, if not all, to the Mexica, not to the other side; thus it acquires something of the sense of "our men." I have uniformly translated it simply as "warriors."

An important and interesting term is *macehualli,* normally glossed as "commoner," though there is good reason to believe that the original sense, not entirely lost by the sixteenth century, was "human being."[41] In the texts reproduced here the word occurs quite frequently in the plural *(macehualtin)* as a collective. I have not found a satisfactory uniform translation. On occasion the term seems to designate a group distinct from nobles or war leaders, and then I may translate "common people." Much of the time, however, it seems to denote the entire local population as a body, and in that case I translate simply "the people." The word is in fact more used in the texts than *nican tlaca* to indicate indigenous people. It does not do so, however, generically, but is always tied explicitly or implicitly to a certain altepetl. Later, at the very end of the sixteenth century and first years of the seventeenth, it was to transcend this limitation and become (though still not much used) the main referential equivalent of "Indian" in Nahuatl when one was needed.[42]

In Sahagún's Spanish one frequently finds the word *principal* for an indigenous person of importance. In sixteenth-century Mexican Spanish in general, *principal* often equates with Nahuatl *pilli* 'nobleman'. But it was used more broadly for people in prominent positions, sometimes for lords high above simple noblemen, and other times for ward heads and the like who may have lacked noble status altogether. Sahagún's usage conforms with this broader pattern, and I have translated the word as "leader."

Proper names from the Nahuatl texts appear in the translations in a standard form representing the orthographic system of the great seventeenth-century grammarian Horacio Carochi, minus the diacritics he added (I use the same system when I have any other occasion to use a Nahuatl word). Proper names from the Spanish text of Book Twelve are standardized in the translation in the same way if they are of Nahuatl origin, or if Spanish are put in the normal modern form, including accents.

41. See Lockhart 1992: chap. 4.
42. See ibid.

In the case of Sahagún's Spanish version of Book Twelve, I have retained untranslated the loans from Nahuatl, leaving them italicized for easier identification, because they help pinpoint Nahua cultural influence on Sahagún specifically and on early Mexican Spanish more generally. [43] Sahagún's *pueblo* I have translated as "settlement" rather than town, village, or the word itself as English, for I am convinced that in the sixteenth century it lacked most of the connotations it has today.

In transcribing the texts I have tried to leave as much as possible unchanged, including diacritics and abbreviations. The most common of these phenomena is the overbar, a line over a vowel to indicate a following nasal (*n* or *m*). [44] In many hands, there was no external distinction between the tilde over *n* and the overbar, and one could argue that there is usually none in Book Twelve. Nevertheless, I have represented the overbar as a macron, distinct from the intended tilde. [45] Ecclesiastical Spanish writing made much use of a series of abbreviations of *qu* plus vowel: *q* with an overbar (*q̄*) meant *que;* with a more or less vertical stroke over it (*q̇*), *qui;* and with a line over it somewhat like a *w* (*q̈*), *qua;* for convenience, the last sign is shown here as *q̃*. An alternate way of representing *que* was a combination that looked for all the world like *qz* and may be so represented. In some usage, reflecting secular Spanish handwriting, *q̄* was the most used by far and might also on occasion stand for the others.

These abbreviations are used in the original texts along with the spelled-out variants with no detectable nuancing of meaning; rather, they tend to come at the ends of lines and sections when saving space is a consideration, or for simple variety. Yet although they are nearly meaningless within any one text, I have felt it worthwhile to represent them, for they are a means of tracking cultural influence. In the Florentine Codex the *qua* sign is rare; in the Historia Tolteca-Chichimeca, common. The writer of the Codex Aubin, located in Tenochtitlan though he was, had clearly not been exposed to Sahagún's system. All of the writers of the Nahuatl texts included here, by their relatively heavy use of this set of abbreviations, show their relative closeness to ecclesiastical instruction, for when the Nahuas were left more to themselves they quickly dropped all of the signs not in vogue with secular writers of Spanish.

I have attempted to reproduce capital letters, which can be done with some certainty where there are two sets of characters (for example, Book Twelve has a distinct uppercase and lowercase *q* regardless of the size of the particular letter). Generally speaking, however, the size of letters varies along a continuum. Although there is a

43. Actually, not quite all of the loans from indigenous languages come from Nahuatl. *Cu* for a temple in indigenous style was taken from Yucatecan Maya and was a standard word in Mexican Spanish for a few decades.

44. Sixteenth-century writers in general tended to write *n*, not *m*, even before labial consonants (*b* and *p*), and though writers in the ecclesiastical tradition, in which Sahagún instructed his aides, came closer to modern practice, even among them *n* was used more than today.

45. Especially the copyist of the Spanish of Book Twelve could be said to have minimized any distinction. Indeed, most of his tildes look like overbars on the following vowel, and it is conceivable that he did not grasp the pronunciation and significance of the tilde.

certain tendency in these texts to capitalize proper names and beginnings of sections, it is a tendency only, and arbitrary decisions are involved, which no two transcribers would probably make identically. [46]

In the transcription of older Nahuatl, the justifiable practice has arisen of ignoring punctuation marks other than such clearly recognizable items as the diagonal, partly because it is often impossible to distinguish rare commas or periods from haphazard strokes, and partly because the intention in any case is often not discernible. [47] With the texts included here, the situation is rather different. Signs recognizable, at least externally, as periods, commas, semicolons, colons, and even question marks occur with regularity. They are not used by any means as they would be today, nor even apparently as they would have been used in the Spanish ecclesiastical writing of that time (that being their origin, for secular Spanish calligraphy was virtually innocent of punctuation). Nor are they, as sometimes happens in Nahuatl writing, consistently employed to demarcate the important Nahuatl constituent element that we can call the phonological phrase. [48] In the Florentine Codex, there seem to be few if any functional differences among the comma, semicolon, colon, and period, though the latter is most often used to end a section. Sometimes the signs are clearly misplaced, by most standards. [49] It would be wrong to call them meaningless, however—they generally separate major constituents—and they represent one of the limited number of clues we

46. Generally speaking, there is no problem in identifying the letters themselves, which are the same as in today's English or Spanish alphabet. One exception is the question of *i* and *j*. Secular Spanish writing had two distinct characters, but ecclesiastical writing, following the tradition of Latin, still tended not to make a clear distinction. In the Florentine Codex, as in many similar writings, one will see a normal *i* alternating with a character that differs from it only in ending in a downward stroke rather than a horizontal stroke connecting it with the next character. Some have taken this longer character for a *j*, but I maintain that it is simply an alternate way of writing *i,* or *i/j* if you will. The longer character tends to be used word-internally and especially word-finally; the Roman numeral "3" is often seen written as two normal *i*'s plus a final one with the downward stroke. In the Nahuatl of the Florentine Codex, I have been able to discover no context in which one variant is much more likely than the other, and I have not hesitated to transcribe them all uniformly as *i.*

The Spanish I have treated differently. Nahuatl after all had only one sound corresponding to the two variants. In Spanish, there were two very different phonemes, the syllabic vowel *i* and the fricative *j*. When the long *i* comes where a *j* is expected in the Spanish version, I have so transcribed it. I even fancy that there was an incipient differentiation in the writer's practice. Long *i*'s intending *j* are much more frequently separated from surrounding letters, especially on the left side, than those intending *i*.

Another problem in the Florentine Codex, virtually confined to the Nahuatl text, is that of distinguishing *o* from *v*. Fully closed and rounded *o*'s are unmistakable, as are elaborately formed *v*'s. When *o*'s are left unclosed and *v*'s written hastily, however, they approach each other to the point that identifying the letter as one or the other is an arbitrary act. The problem is all the more acute because *v* was often used by Sahagún's aides to represent syllabic *o* as well as *u;* furthermore, there is no distinction in Nahuatl pronunciation between [o] and [u]. The situation is compounded by the fact that in Sahagún's system both letters were employed to represent [w]. It is quite possible that the copyist of the Nahuatl of Book Twelve did not always make the distinction in his own mind.

47. Such in fact has been my normal procedure in the past.

48. See Lockhart 1992: chap. 8.

49. Consider the use of the period in the following example from the Spanish of Book Twelve, fol. 74v: "ansi se retruxeron. Otra vez al tianquez . . ." ("so they retired. Again to the marketplace . . .").

have to the culture of the writers and copyists, so I have attempted to reproduce them fully.

Problems do arise. Just as I am not convinced that the Florentine Codex's writers recognized any difference of function among various signs, it appears to me that they often made no attempt to differentiate clearly between the form of comma and period, semicolon and colon, leading to arbitrary decisions on the part of the transcriber. Most puzzling at first is the matter of the question mark. Book Twelve has many examples of a sign that, if not exactly the same as a printed question mark, is a close approximation and does in fact often coincide with the end of a spoken question. In some cases, however, the question is indirect and would not call for a question mark by most norms. In others, there is no question at all, but a forceful or emotional statement, so that the reader eventually comes to understand that this sign also served for an exclamation mark, and when appropriate I have so transcribed it. In other cases, neither a question mark nor an exclamation mark would be at all suitable; here I have transcribed a question mark. I believe that the copyist involved had conceived some notion that the question mark was associated with direct address, much like modern quotation marks. I feel confident that he was in considerable doubt about when to use the sign. [50]

All of the principles of transcription I have been discussing have been applied to the Spanish text of Book Twelve as well as to the various texts in Nahuatl. Nor have I added modern punctuation and accents to the Spanish, as is quite frequently done even in critical editions. Such a practice is often fully justified, but here it is important to have the exact form of the orthography available as an avenue of approach to the mind of the Nahua copyist (some of the implications of the orthography will be explained below).

With respect to spacing I have, in the name of easier intelligibility, departed from the policy of leaving the originals unchanged. The spaces between words in the transcriptions all rest on my own decisions, following present-day grammatical norms for both languages. In most sixteenth-century manuscripts, whether Spanish or Nahuatl, what we would consider words are most often run together indefinitely, until the writer runs out of ink or takes it into his mind to halt. An interval is as likely to occur in the middle of a word as between words. Not only is it difficult to ascertain where intervals are; even when a perceptible interval indisputably exists, it cannot be interpreted as a "space," the demarcator of words to which we are so accustomed. Respacing is thus standard in modern transcriptions of this kind of material. The reason I am expatiating on the matter in some detail is that in the body of texts included here, one is almost tempted to retain the original spacing; in the Florentine Codex especially, it often approximates modern practice. Yet exceptions and dubious instances are many, not to

---

50. These remarks apply above all to the copyist of the Spanish, but there are one or two similar instances from the copyist of the Nahuatl. The hands of the two are quite distinct; each did his own column all the way through Book Twelve, except that on fols. 26 through 27v the copyist of the Spanish appears to have written the Nahuatl as well.

speak of the fact that no distinction is made between a space and continuation at a line break, so I have not made the attempt.

The manuscripts vary in the extent to which they indicate division at the level of the paragraph, but generally speaking they contain fewer subdivisions than would be expected in present practice. The Annals of Tlatelolco are essentially not subdivided at all. In Book Twelve, chapters have no internal divisions in either the Nahuatl or the Spanish except after a blank column or picture when the two fail to equal each other in length, and though in those cases the new section will start with an extra-large capital letter, it does not appear that anything is being asserted about the content. Some of the other manuscripts have some paragraph signs (which have been retained in the transcription), but there too subdivision is inconsistent. I have thus divided the material arbitrarily into paragraphs, which are for the reader's convenience only and are not to be imagined to reflect anything about the organization of the originals.

### PARTICULARS ABOUT THE TEXTS

The following is not part of the general introduction, which at this point may be viewed as complete, but includes the type of material that might well have been put at the beginning of each text as a special introduction to it and that may be read separately according to the reader's need.

1. *Book Twelve of the Florentine Codex.*   This is not the place to recapitulate the complex, much discussed, though not yet fully understood process through which Sahagún's encyclopedia and history of Nahua culture came into existence.[51] Briefly, in various places and on various occasions Sahagún collected statements from indigenous people, especially those of relatively advanced age and high status, having what was said written down in Nahuatl by the aides he had trained; he had his aides work over and reshape the material several times, in addition to his own reorganization of the larger blocks. The process having started about 1547, not until 1569 had most of the Nahuatl taken on a form close to that which we see in the Florentine Codex, and not until about 1577 was a Spanish version complete. The Florentine Codex itself was probably put on paper about 1578–1579. Book Twelve is thought to have been first drafted about 1555.[52]

The paramount question that must concern us about the Nahuatl text of Book Twelve (as with the whole of the Florentine Codex and other texts produced under

---

51. For a detailed history of the evolution of the work, with many further references, see Dibble 1982; also d'Olwer and Cline 1973 and other articles in the same volume; as well as the material in Klor de Alva, Nicholson, and Quiñones Keber 1988; Edmonson 1974; and Martínez 1982.

52. See Dibble 1982: 10; in a note to the reader of the emended version of 1585, Sahagún says that the original was written "ha ya mas de treinta años" ("more than thirty years ago"; Sahagún 1989: 147, 417). He could of course have meant any number of years up to forty, or perhaps up to thirty-five, but most commentators have construed it, as I tend to, as meaning only a little more than thirty.

Sahagún's direction) is the extent to which it can be considered an authentic product and expression of indigenous people, Nahuas and Nahuatl speakers. It is beyond doubt that Sahagún gave the impetus, trained the writers,[53] and in the broadest lines determined the topics and overall organization. Without Sahagún there would have been no Florentine Codex or Book Twelve. But granted that, much room remains for an indigenous role, for indigenous ideas, frameworks, and imperatives.

Let us first look at the matter from the perspective given by Sahagún himself in his prologues to various parts of the Florentine Codex. Sahagún's views are complex, even, apparently, ambivalent and highly inconsistent. At times he makes the outright claim to have written the whole work, and he considered himself its author.[54] Elsewhere he speaks of compiling rather than writing[55] and emphasizes how indigenous people of various communities were asked to provide pictures and statements that then became the core of the text. For the Florentine Codex as a whole he says he repeated this process three times, first at Tepepolco (in the Tetzcoco region), second in Tlatelolco, and third in Tenochtitlan (by then Mexico City).[56] In yet other contexts he draws attention to the role of his literate aides, at times seeming to make them the true authors.[57]

The respective parts played by the informants and the aides will perhaps prove impossible ever to determine with any clarity, but I believe Sahagún had great respect for the integrity of the texts written down by the aides and representing some mixture of their own views, language, and concepts with those of the informants. I think that in speaking of "writing" the texts, Sahagún was in part addressing an audience of uninformed outsiders who had no notion of philological complexities and would not have comprehended the full truth. He really meant, I imagine, that he was in charge of the process that led to the writing of the texts.

In recent years Sahagún has frequently been called an ethnographer, centuries ahead of his time.[58] I have little argument with such a proposition, which contains much truth, but viewed as a general model by which to understand Sahagún's enterprise, the analogy with anthropological ethnography as practiced in the past couple of generations or so carries with it some false implications.[59] Unlike most ethnographers of the twentieth century, he was interested not so much in facts about the people he was

53. Even at the level of simple orthography, Sahagún's pupils stand out from all others writing Nahuatl in several of their conventions, above all the use of *o* or *ho* for [w] and of *i* for the glide [y] as well as syllabic [i].

54. Statements of having written everything are in the prologue to Book Two (Sahagún 1950–1982: 1.53, and at the beginning of the 1585 version of Book Twelve (Sahagún 1989: 147, 417); an aside in Spanish of Book Twelve, chap. 39, is headed "author."

55. Sahagún mentions compiling in the prologue to Book Ten (Sahagún 1950–1982: 1.73).

56. The fullest statement of this kind is in the prologue to Book Two (Sahagún 1950–1982: 1.54–55).

57. See the prologue to Book Two and Sahagún's remarks in chap. 27 of Book Ten (Sahagún 1950–1982: 1.55, 83–84).

58. Klor de Alva, Nicholson, and Quiñones Keber 1988 illustrates this view in the title and in much of the contents.

59. Although it is technically unobjectionable, I feel uncomfortable speaking of Sahagún's "informants," and I object to the use of the term "field work" in describing any of Sahagún's activities.

studying as in texts, texts that would illustrate those people's vocabulary, concepts, and stock of commonplace metaphor and idiom. In this emphasis he had a great deal in common not with the ethnographic tradition but with the current of interest in texts and "tropes" that is so strong today in anthropology (and some other disciplines). Sahagún was not, however, a "postmodern." He was a humanistic philologist. His was the world of polyglot bibles, of editions and compendia of Greek, Latin, or Hebrew works wherein establishing and respecting an authentic text was the inescapable means by which anything further could be accomplished, and wherein the preservation of full original texts, separate from the editor's glosses, was the core of the work.

Some of Sahagún's contemporaries thought he was producing a *calepino,* a dictionary of usage like that done by Ambrosio Calepino for Latin. In one of his prologues he responds that he is fully aware of the value such a work would have, but that he was unable to do it for lack of authoritative texts by poets, orators, and other writers, such as those on whom Calepino based his entries. But, he says, "I have laid the foundation, so that whoever should wish to can easily do it, because through my effort twelve books have been written in language proper and natural to the Mexican tongue, where, aside from its being very enjoyable and profitable reading, there will be found all of the expressions and words that this language employs, as authoritative and reliable as what was written by Vergil, Cicero, and other Latin authors."[60] In other words, not finding the requisite written Nahuatl texts available to practice Renaissance philology, Sahagún set about getting them created, organizing and guiding, it is true, but avoiding direct intervention in the same spirit as with a Latin text. He was later to give a good illustration of his attitude in a 1585 reworking of Book Twelve, partly in line with Franciscan polemics relating to the vision of the conquest, and partly in order to develop the text as an example of polished Nahuatl composition. He felt it his duty, however, to keep the original Nahuatl text, with all of its perceived roughnesses or insufficiencies, in addition to the more polished version, so that readers could see what the Nahuas had originally produced. (Unfortunately, both Nahuatl versions of the 1585 redaction have disappeared; only a copy of the Spanish remains.)[61]

Intentions and principles are one thing, of course, and within the framework of Sahagún's theoretical respect for texts any amount of intervention could have taken place. Let us look at the matter from the other side, searching for evidence of the relation between the indigenous people involved and the actual Nahuatl text, which seems to have arisen and taken on something approaching its definitive shape in Tlatelolco about 1555. Perhaps Sahagún proceeded as he has told us he did in a later sojourn in Tlatelolco (1561–1565), when he requested from the indigenous municipal council eight or ten prominent local citizens as consultants, the writing being done by the assistants he had trained in the academy there. The one who did the most, Sahagún says, was a Martín Jacobita, "citizen of Tlatelolco in the district of Santa Ana."[62] In his

---

60. Prologue to Book One (Sahagún 1950–1982: 1.50).
61. Sahagún 1989: 147–148, 417–418.
62. Dibble 1982: 13; prologue to Book Two (Sahagún 1950–1982: 1.54).

grand accolade to his aides he again included Martín Jacobita among the "grammarians," and another citizen of Tlatelolco, Diego de Grado, among the copyists. [63]

There is good reason to believe, then, that the group of indigenous participants in the composition of Book Twelve was overwhelmingly weighted toward Tlatelolco. If we look for a Tlatelolcan orientation in the text, we will not be disappointed. Itzquauhtzin, the Tlatelolcan ruler, is placed as much as possible on the same level as Moteucçoma (though he is popular where Moteucçoma is hated), and the Tenochca are seen as cowards who desert their part of the island and leave the real fighting to the Tlatelolca, aside from their later trying to blame the Tlatelolca for taking the gold the Spaniards left at the Tolteca canal (in all of these matters the independently written Annals of Tlatelolco are very similar). Not only does action on the island overshadow things happening elsewhere, but within that focus, the final Tlatelolcan phase is told in greater detail than events in Tenochtitlan, and Tlatelolcan heroes and deeds of arms get pride of place. Sahagún, left to himself, would surely not have given the story this twist. His focus would doubtless have been much broader. His interest is shown in his prologue, where he starts out speaking of "the conquest of New Spain." One of the two Spanish titles given to Book Twelve restricts the subject matter to Mexico City (already something of an exaggeration), but the other returns to the broader ambition before narrowing it: "Book Twelve, of the Conquest of New Spain, that is, Mexico City." [64]

Going beyond the specifically Tlatelolcan flavor of Book Twelve—one example of the micropatriotic perspective from which all indigenous central Mexicans viewed the conquest—we have seen in a previous section that the general categorization of groups in the Nahuatl of Book Twelve, as well as the general way of perceiving and presenting things, are profoundly indigenous, allied to what we find in other Nahuatl texts and different from what we find in Spanish writings, including the Spanish version of Book Twelve (in which the frequent use of *indio* 'Indian' alone alters the perspective vastly). The Nahuatl chapter titles are perhaps an intrusive element to be attributed to Sahagún alone. In one of his prologues Sahagún takes sole responsibility for dividing the Nahuatl corpus into twelve books, and those into chapters, during a stay at the Franciscan monastery in Mexico City about 1566–1568, in other words, at a very late stage in the evolution of the Nahuatl texts that were to become part of the Florentine Codex. Very likely Sahagún himself devised the chapter titles, in Spanish, and the Nahuatl chapter titles may well be a translation of them, reversing the usual process. If the chapter divisions and titles are foreign to the text, however, they do not seem to have affected it in any other way. Beginnings and endings were not rewritten to reflect the chapter structure. The Nahuatl text retains its own episodic organization; sometimes a continuous episode falls into more than one chapter, [65] sometimes one chapter contains more than one episode. [66]

---

63. Prologue to Book Two (Sahagún 1950–1982: 1.55).
64. Unnumbered folio (fol. 406 of the volume foliation); fol. 1.
65. See note 21 above for the most egregious case.
66. Chapter 38 contains three separate well-defined sections.

Coming to the level of the language itself, we can see that certain portions show the overladen quality discussed above, to which Sahagún's methods seem to have contributed, but I for one have failed to find anything Spanish about the syntax, usage, or general vocabulary. There are, it is true, a few Spanish loanwords, some of them of frequent occurrence. Whether we think of them as originating with the first draft of the text in the mid 1550s or at some later time up to 1569 or the 1570s, there is no need to imagine that they were inserted at Sahagún's behest, for words like them, and almost all of the very items appearing in Book Twelve, are abundantly attested in the Nahuatl of the time.[67] So few are they, indeed, that one could better imagine Sahagún expunging loanwords his aides spontaneously produced. Given the subject matter and the location in time of the events narrated, however, few were needed. Several of the loans in the text have something of the flavor of proper names. The only two ordinary generic words among them are *caballo* (written *cavallo,* where the *v* must have been pronounced [w] and the *ll* as geminate rather than palatalized) 'horse' and *diablo* 'devil'. I would not count *capítulo* 'chapter', which is seen only in chapter titles, or *bergantín* 'brigantine', which appears only in the title of chapter 31; in the text proper the brigantines are always called just *acalli* 'boats'. *Diablo* (used about four times) always has the meaning "preconquest indigenous deity," and the indigenous gods are never called anything else, at least not in the third-person narrative. Sahagún's influence is probably in evidence here, not that he would have had to direct the aides to use the word in specific passages, for through his instruction his circle would already have been imbued with that manner of speech; and, in fact, it had been spread by Spanish ecclesiastics more generally among their Nahua associates.

Among the loans that are proper names or close to it, *Castilla* or *Castillan* 'Castile, Spain' is used twice, put in the mouths of Spaniards, but it was in fact prominent among the first loans into Nahuatl generally.[68] By far the most common loan in Book Twelve, to be found somewhere in nearly every chapter and often several times on a page, is *español* 'Spaniard'. The word is virtually always in the plural, referring to the whole group present (never to Spaniards generically), but once it does occur in the singular, describing a specific person.[69] I suspect that Sahagún's influence is somehow related to the use of *españoles* in Book Twelve. Not that *español* was not a common loanword in the 1550s and after, for it is widely attested; but not one of the alternative terms seen in most other texts—*caxtilteca, Caxtillan tlaca, cristianos*—appears in all of the long text. This absence is all the more remarkable because the other terms seem to have been in vogue earlier than *españoles.* It is also worthy of note that the normal Spanish plural, without the addition of a Nahuatl plural suffix, is the only form used, whereas with *caballo* we find a welter of variants.[70] It appears to me that Sahagún for some reason greatly preferred *españoles* to any alternative and in one way or another conveyed as

67. To be found in the loanword lists in Karttunen and Lockhart 1976.

68. See Lockhart 1992: chap. 7, section "Stage 1."

69. Folio 74v.

70. Folio 22v has "cavallos" and "cavallosme"; fol. 23, "cavallotin"; fol. 42v, "cavallome"; fol. 57, "cavallostin." This list covers all of the possibilities. The singular "cavallo" also occurs once (fol. 74v).

much to his aides, whether merely through his own choice of words in general conversation or through a specific directive.

Scattered through the text is the loanword *capitán* 'captain', always in reference to Cortés, for whom in effect it serves as an alternate appellation. Once one of the Mexica leaders is made to employ it in direct address to Cortés, so the aides imagined that it belonged to the vocabulary of the Nahuas of the conquest years.[71] It would be hard to say how the Nahuas took the term, whether with its normal meaning in Spanish, as the equivalent of one of their lordly titles, or as an actual name. From its use, and the manner of its use, here and in other texts, I have the impression that the word entered Nahuatl very early, perhaps during the conquest itself as Sahagún's aide assumed, and that Sahagún had nothing to do with its appearance in Book Twelve.[72]

Nor is he to be thought responsible for the appearance of the title *marqués* a few times, also in reference to Cortés. Rather, Sahagún's influence seems to have worked to reduce the frequency of the word in Book Twelve. By 1550 if not before, Cortés was normally referred to in central Mexico, by both Spaniards and Nahuas, simply as "the Marqués." Such might have been the normal way of referring to him in the Nahuatl of Book Twelve had it not been for Sahagún, and the few occurrences seem to be in the nature of relapses, or possibly relics of an earlier draft in which the word was more prominent. Perhaps Sahagún considered the term anachronistic in the context, because Cortés did not yet have the title at the time in question; or perhaps his position on the matter had to do with his tendency, also that of his order, to emphasize Cortés the person as a Moseslike symbol of the benefit of the Spanish conquest; in his 1585 reworking, that tendency came even more to the fore.[73] As seen in his Spanish, *don Hernando Cortés* or *el capitán don Hernando Cortés* was the style Sahagún preferred.[74] He even consistently transforms the Nahuatl's *marques* into one of his own favorite forms in the Spanish.[75] Oddly, once the Spanish has the word when the Nahuatl lacks it, "adonde estaua el marques" ("where the Marqués was").[76] This exception was likely a slip, falling back into the vernacular, or possibly it is one of the liberties taken by the

71. Folio 85v. I have in the past taken it from the fact that the aides often use a different kind of vocabulary in quotes from actors of the time than in their own third-person narrative that they were aware of a distinction between the manner of speech of the two epochs. I still tend to think so. It is conceivable, however, that the archaic vocabulary got there through copying word-for-word the testimony of by then elderly eyewitnesses. In this case, the eyewitnesses could by then themselves have picked up manners of speech not current earlier. We know for sure that the Spaniards did so. Cortés and his fellows never use the word *soldados* for the body of Spanish conquerors; Bernal Díaz, who was one of them, because he wrote many years later, does use it, and frequently.

72. Except as part of the set sequence "capitan don hernando cortes," which occurs once (fol. 37) and does seem to come from Sahagún; see below. Also see below for the predominance of *capitán* in the relatively early Annals of Tlatelolco.

73. See Sahagún 1989: especially the editor's introduction.

74. This style too is anachronistic, for Cortés did not bear the *don* by birthright and acquired it only along with the title of Marqués when he was in Spain in 1529, returning with it to New Spain in 1530.

75. Folios 25v, 26, 54, 55, 85.

76. Folio 80v.

Nahua copyist. *Don Hernando Cortés,* variously capitalized and of course without accent, is the most common way of mentioning Cortés in the Nahuatl text itself.[77] This form, I feel sure, is the direct result of Sahagún's intervention and does not correspond to the Nahuas' spontaneous manner of speech. Indeed, I rather suspect that it was at Sahagún's insistence that Cortés is mentioned in the Nahuatl, in any form, as frequently as he is. Even in the manuscript as we know it, the Nahuatl retains a much stronger tendency to speak of the Spaniards as an anonymous block than the Spanish version, which frequently mentions Cortés even when the Nahuatl does not.[78]

Only three other Spanish names appear in the Nahuatl of Book Twelve. (Doña) Marina, the name of the indigenous interpreter for the Spaniards, is rendered frequently in Nahuatl texts as Malintzin. Other sources confirm the authenticity of this form, which apparently goes back to the time of the conquest itself. The name arises from the Spanish Marina by substituting *l* for *r* (which Nahuatl lacked), omitting the final *a* for reasons that are not clear, and adding the honorific ending *-tzin.* Rodrigo de Castañeda appears without a first name but with a Nahuatl epithet as Castañeda Xicotencatl,[79] and again this form apparently goes back to the days of the siege. Pedro de Alvarado is mentioned with his first name,[80] which was probably not known to the Nahuas of 1519–1521, though by the 1550s they were likely aware of it.

In addition to outright Spanish loans, Book Twelve contains a frequently used set of words newly coined or extended to describe Spanish introductions; they include *maçatl* 'deer', for horse; *tlequiquiztli* 'fire trumpet', for firearm; *quauhtemalacatl* 'wooden circular stone', hence 'wooden wheel', for cart; *tepoztli* 'copper, usable nonprecious metal', for iron and steel; and some compounds using the latter, such as *tepozmacquahuitl* 'iron hand-stick' (i.e., war club), for sword. These are spontaneous and general Nahuatl speech phenomena of the first postcontact generation, attested also in Molina's dictionary and in other early texts, including some of the ones in this volume. Far less even than the Spanish loanwords are they in any way connected with Sahagún. They are to be attributed primarily to the informants and the early oral tradition rather than to the aides and the redaction of about 1555. As mentioned earlier, the writer or writers of the Nahuatl appear to show quite a strong awareness of the generational distinction in usage.[81]

In general, then, the Nahuatl of Book Twelve gives evidences of being an authentic expression of indigenous people, above all of Tlatelolca, containing lore and attitudes both from the time of the events and from the time of composition (1555 and thereaf-

---

77. *Don* as a title can be considered another loanword, much like the others in being namelike, in this case to the extent of becoming part of the name.

78. As on fols. 16 (where in the Nahuatl the Spaniards ask, while in the Spanish Cortés asks), 25v (where in the Nahuatl the Spaniards take Moteucçoma by the hand and show their great interest in him, while in the Spanish Cortés takes him by the hand and the others are not mentioned), or fol. 28 (where in the Nahuatl Marina simply calls to the Mexica, while in the Spanish Cortés orders her to do so).

79. Folio 65.

80. Folio 54.

81. See Lockhart 1992: chap. 7.

ter). Signs of active intervention by Sahagún are minimal. Nevertheless, if one resorts to comparison with the substantial section of the Annals of Tlatelolco describing the conquest, some differences can be seen that might be attributable to Spanish influence on Book Twelve. The latter, markedly episodic and fragmentary though it is, approaches much closer to a thorough running narrative than the Annals, and this difference may be the result of elicitation and prodding by Sahagún. Although, compared to a European history, Book Twelve seems to abound in speeches and conversation, it pales in that respect compared to the Annals. Here too Sahagún, without actually telling anyone what to say, merely by what he wanted and expected may have had the effect of bringing the account closer to the European style and farther from the indigenous style, which emphasized dramatization. [82] And if Book Twelve seems a strongly partisan and parochial Tlatelolcan document, the Annals are far, far more so. Possibly Sahagún's broader interests and the presence of aides from elsewhere worked to dilute the micropatriotism to an extent.

Sahagún's part in the Nahuatl texts of the Florentine Codex has been often and deeply considered; it is also instructive to look at the obverse side of the coin, the part the Nahua aides may have had in shaping the Spanish texts. Even a quick glance will tell the reader conversant with Spanish that the orthography is often deviant and the grammar itself sometimes very odd. How did these mistakes, if they are that, arise? We might wonder if the text was dictated by Sahagún to a Nahua secretary. He does speak once of dictation. [83] It is well known that for many years his hand shook to the extent that he seems to have been reluctant to write much more than his signature. About the time that the Spanish version was produced, he made the outright statement that he could write nothing. [84] Thus dictation was very possibly involved at some point, but the Florentine Codex was not the first, nor probably even the second copy made of the Spanish text. Some of the deviances are of the kind that must have come about through visual rather than aural misapprehension. Consider the following examples: [85]

| | | |
|---|---|---|
| *ausan* (fol. 5v) | for | *auian* 'they had' (involves long *s* for long *i*) |
| *desportade* (fol. 10v) | | *despertalde* 'awaken him' |
| *entrarse* (fol. 35) | | *entrasse* 'should enter' |
| *se desperauā* (fol. 38) | | *se despeñauā* 'they jumped off' |

82. Admittedly, there was a European style of history, rooted in antiquity, that did much the same, but the Spanish chronicles of the conquest emphasized straightforward third-person narrative prose marching forward day by day, event by event. Even when European histories resort to first-person dramatization, one usually sees set speeches by protagonists, rather than the back-and-forth conversational dialogue of Nahuatl accounts.

83. Prologue to Book Two (Sahagún 1950–1982: 1.54).

84. Ibid., pp. 55–56.

85. Examples of this type must be distinguished from normal sixteenth-century usage that varies from today's, including many spelling conventions, such as *u* for intervocalic *v* or *b*, and special forms such as *via* as the imperfect of *ver* 'to see', the metathesis of *l* and *d* in imperatives with a pronominal object (*dezilde* for *dezidle* 'tell him'), or *asconder* as a variant spelling of *esconder* 'to hide'.

| | |
|---|---|
| *hizieron* (fol. 74v) | *hirieron* 'they struck' |
| *cendidumbre* (fol. 78) | *certidumbre* 'certainty' |

These instances and others like them imply the writer's ignorance of the form involved, either replacing it with something more familiar or taking a stab at the letters regardless of meaning. It is true that we all do similar things when copying even very familiar matter mechanically. On the whole, the copyist seems to have had a good understanding of the intention of the Spanish.

If, then, the Nahua copyist was working from a written text, how can we explain the Nahuatlisms that appear? Some may already have been there, of course; we do not know the quality of earlier copies. But apparently the copyist did as both Spanish and Nahua secretaries were wont to do, innerly pronouncing the material to himself and then writing it according to his own canon. In this way he has left some record of his Spanish pronunciation and even syntax, one measure of his level of acculturation and that of his fellows.

The copyist's Spanish pronunciation probably involved little if any use of sounds and distinctions not already in the Nahuatl phonological system. Most of the "misspellings" in the text are letter substitutions reflecting Nahuatl habits carried into Spanish. Nahuatl made no distinction between voiced and unvoiced stops; its basic series was the unvoiced *p*, *c* [k], and *t*. These sounds would normally be substituted for the voiced *b*, *g*, and *d*, and writers of Nahuatl in the sixteenth and seventeenth centuries frequently made the corresponding letter substitutions when they reproduced Spanish loanwords.

The expected substitutions in fact appear in the present text: "supita" for *subita (súbita)* 'sudden, unexpected' (fol. 68); "delcadas" for *delgadas* 'slim, light' (fol. 35v); "moternas" for *modernas* 'modern' (fol. 15). (Throughout this introduction and the commentary, I place literal reproductions of the actual or expected spellings of a particular writer or copyist in quotation marks, distinguishing them from purely abstract standard forms, in italics.) And as in many Nahuatl texts, here too we find examples of hypercorrection, the use of the symbol for a new Spanish sound even when a familiar one is intended. As the Nahuas at first discerned no difference between the voiced and the unvoiced stops, they would sometimes write *b* for *p*, and the like. In the Spanish of Book Twelve we find "bueblo" for *pueblo* 'settlement' (fol. 44v), and "desde" (normally "from, since") for *deste* 'of this' (fol. 21v et al.). The copyist also probably pronounced *r* as *l*, the closest Nahuatl equivalent, because he wrote the hypercorrect form "abrir" for *abril* 'April' (fol. 52).

Somewhat similar is the situation with *o* and *u*. Nahuatl had only *o*, long and short. Thus in the copyist's text one frequently sees *o* for *u*, as in "arcaboceros" for *arcabuceros* 'harquebusiers' (fol. 15v) or "yocatan" for *yucatan* 'Yucatan' (fol. 28), but almost equally often *u* for *o:* as in "su pena" for *so pena* 'under penalty' (fol. 13), or "estamus" for *estamos* 'we are' (fol. 77v). Nahuas also often had trouble telling Spanish unstressed *e*

from *i*. This confusion too shows up in the text, as in "se rendieron" for *se rindieron* 'they surrendered' (fol. 58), or "los siguian" for *los seguian* 'they followed them' (fol. 71). One result of the vowel merging was that the copyist seems to have had no conception at all of how Spanish verbs of the third conjugation change the stem vowel in the preterit and allied tenses; thus we find "morieron" for *murieron* 'they died' (fol. 71), and "veniese" for *viniese,* 'should come' (fol. 14v), along with standard forms in which the vowel changes according to the rule.

Some of the copyist's modifications go beyond spelling to affect grammar and idiom. A good many slips are to be found with the use of prepositions, a natural phenomenon in view of the fact that Nahuatl had none. Sometimes one sees *a* 'to' used where it does not belong: "podrian a hazer," 'they could do' (fol. 12), or the rather subtle example "otros officiales a quien concernia a esta prouision," 'other officials whom this provision concerned', with *a* before the subject (fol. 27). Conversely, as location was often built into Nahuatl expressions, *en* 'in' is sometimes missing where needed: "enterraronlos diuersas partes," 'they buried them [in] various places' (fol. 34v), or "Este lugar estaua una aguila." 'an eagle was [in] this place' (fol. 57). In "començaron de caminar," 'they began to walk' (fol. 76v), *de* should be *a*.

The copyist's vagaries go farther perhaps than will the reader's patience in following them. Nahuatl made no external distinction between direct and indirect objects. Sixteenth-century Spanish did, then obscured the distinction in some gender and number combinations, so it is understandable that the copyist did not grasp that although *les,* normally indirect 'to them', might occasionally be direct, *los* 'them' could under no circumstances be indirect, as the copyist constantly makes it. Nahuatl indication of number varied considerably from Spanish, and we are not surprised to see the copyist making many errors of singular for plural and vice versa, aided perhaps by the weakness or absence of final *n* in Nahuatl pronunciation. [86]

At times the copyist changed the syntax, resorting to a Nahuatl phrase type. Thus in "Sancto antonio yglesia" (fol. 54v) he puts the name of the church first, as one would in Nahuatl and might in English, whereas Spanish would require the saint's name to come afterward, preceded by *de*. In "todos se mostrarō de paz estos pueblos de la chināpan" (fol. 20v) 'all these settlements of the chinampa country showed their peaceful intent', we find "all" preceding the verb and "these settlements" after it, just as is often done in Nahuatl, but hardly in Spanish. [87] It is not a remarkable fact, but never-

86. In other words, the final *n* that indicates plurality in so many Spanish verb forms would hardly have been pronounced by a Nahuatl speaker. Apparently there was also some problem with *s;* perhaps final *s* was notably weak in the Spanish spoken around the copyist, as it is in some varieties of Spanish today. At any rate, the confusion goes beyond the plural, for the copyist often wrote "ante" for *antes* 'before' and "entonce" for *entonces* 'then'.

87. Nahuatl syntax (along with misspelling and error in number) probably accounts for the oddness of one of our copyist's greatest leaps into Spanish composition, "estaua su coraçon parecia que se leuauan en agua de chilli" (fol. 10v). I have not identified the Nahuatl model, however. The phrase is not, by the way, an attempt to go back to the corresponding passage in the Nahuatl text, which I have the sense the copyist of the Spanish was not following.

theless one worth noting, that the copyist's Spanish was very much like that produced by Nahuas when they began writing Spanish texts extensively in the late eighteenth century. [88]

As the Nahua copyist was consciously or unconsciously taking rather great liberties with Sahagún's Spanish, and Sahagún either never noticed or decided against revision attempts, we must ask if the role of the aides in the preparation of the Spanish version went yet farther. Does the Spanish really represent Sahagún? Is it possible that the aides actually did the translations? In many places, minor deviances aside, the Spanish is wooden, pedestrian, making no attempt even to avoid multiple repetition of the same word in a short section. The general impression is not at all that given by Sahagún's prologues. But a translation is not a prologue, and Sahagún was well aware of it; he specifically apologized for the "low" style of the translation of Book Seven, but defended it as appropriate. Although I would not know how to go about proving it, I doubt that Sahagún's aides did much direct translation of the Nahuatl. In Book Twelve (though the same could apparently be said of all parts of the vast work), the Spanish not only sometimes contains technical explanation and amplification, [89] which the aides might have been equipped to provide, but offers some editorial comments not in the Nahuatl. These asides—like the most formal of them, which is set off with the label "Author" [90]—manifest the general point of view of a Spaniard when not, as in this case, specifically that of a Franciscan. The categorization is Spanish, vastly changing the microperspective of the Nahuatl by lumping groups together under "Indian," and using the peculiarly Spanish notion of *principal* 'leader'. We have already discussed Sahagún's use of the Spanish as a vehicle to draw a certain kind of attention to Cortés in connection with a broader Franciscan campaign. With some exceptions, the Spanish tends to be more abbreviated than the Nahuatl, a general tendency of translations from Nahuatl by Spaniards of the time; Sahagún's patience was clearly finite when it came to detail in narrative, dialogue, or description. Considering everything, I have little reason to doubt that the Spanish text faithfully represents Sahagún's intentions and views, and even for the most part his phrasing. [91]

*2. Extract from the Annals of Tlatelolco.* The important document usually called simply the "Annals of Tlatelolco," because of its far greater right to that title than any compet-

---

88. See Lockhart 1991: item 7.

89. Significant explanatory detail will be found in chaps. 4, 21, 28, and 37. There are several cases of apparent error, such as the bear for a wolf in chap. 31, or having Indians displayed on the skull rack when the Nahuatl says they were not (chap. 35). The Spanish often seems to display considerable disorientation about which indigenous personal names go with which titles, or indeed which elements are personal names, and which are titles (chaps. 24, 37, 40).

90. Chapter 39.

91. As an aside, given the false, stereotypical modern view of the Spanish conqueror/immigrants as "soldiers," let it be noted that Sahagún repeatedly calls the Mexica warriors *soldados*, but rarely indeed does he use that term in reference to Spaniards. (For more on the inadequacies of the concept of "soldier" in this context see Lockhart 1968: especially 137–141; Lockhart 1972: especially 17–22; and Lockhart and Schwartz 1983: especially 78–80.)

ing text, deals for the most part with the preconquest history of the entity. It ends, however, in a substantial account of the conquest, included here, that makes it (after Book Twelve of the Florentine Codex) easily the second most extensive item in the Nahuatl literature on that subject. Of its Tlatelolcan provenience there can be no doubt; I have already had occasion to allude to the intensity of its Tlatelolcan preoccupations. But about the circumstances of its origin, and most especially about its dating, certainty has been hard to attain. The manuscript material now extant consists of two separate versions, one clearly very old, the other set down much later—to my eye, in the late seventeenth or the eighteenth century.[92] Aside from varying orthographic systems and relatively minor phrasing differences, the two are to a great extent identical, though the later version does contain some sections and comments not in the earlier. It is also less damaged and has complete reproductions of some passages missing or obscured in the earlier (though it is impossible to establish beyond all doubt that they were ever actually in it). The second version openly purports to be a copy of an older document.

Eduard Seler and after him Ernst Mengin were inclined to think that the newer version did not rest directly on the one extant;[93] some of the additions are located in sections well preserved in the older version, where it is clear that nothing is missing. The presence of these amplifications might be taken to imply the existence of another, perhaps fuller version of the older text, which must have been contemporary with it, or possibly even older. Such an interpretation becomes yet more likely when we take into consideration that the later text is accompanied by a number of pictorial representations. The putative unknown manuscript would then have had a pictorial component, whereas in the one extant the pictorial element is entirely lacking.

If this hypothesis is correct, we must imagine a complex scenario. The first version made would have been the unknown manuscript, for the spontaneous written expression of the Nahuas in the earlier postconquest period, when it came to historical material, usually involved a combination of the pictorial and the alphabetic. Immediately thereafter, almost concurrently, the older version we now know would have been prepared, whether a copy or a further development it would be hard to guess. The older extant manuscript does show distinct signs of being a copy, the most obvious being many things crossed out that are mentioned earlier or later, as though one had returned to the task and begun in the wrong place. The two manuscripts would then have been kept together, in indigenous hands in Tlatelolco, for the writer of the later text was a

92. Eduard Seler judged it to be of the mid seventeenth century, but it is hard to reach precise conclusions on these matters without a great deal of closely related material, some of which would have to be firmly dated; in any case, I doubt that Seler knew much about Mexican calligraphy of the seventeenth and eighteenth centuries. Mengin 1939 contains a transcription and a German translation of the material, giving only the older version where they are virtually identical and including parts of the newer where they are not. Mengin 1945 contains a facsimile of both texts. Spanish translations of the conquest section (but no transcriptions) are to be found in Toscano 1948 and Sahagún 1975. The older text is MS 22, the newer one MS 22[bis].

93. Mengin 1945: introduction.

Tlatelolcan Nahua, interested in the history of his own entity for his own purposes. After the later writer had used the illustrated version as the basis for his own, it would have become separated from the rest and then lost.

As attractive and even in part plausible as this hypothesis is, the more I have studied the texts, the more I have returned to my first thought, that the later manuscript is a direct copy of the earlier, with some digressions based on other late texts, oral tradition, or the writer's imagination. The vast majority of the relatively minor variations between the texts prove to stem from the later writer's inability to read the older text (in which it is easy to have sympathy with him). Some of the added material is clearly discordant with the early manuscript; passages not in the earlier version often have to do with Quauhtemoc, whose popularity grew with every passing generation. Nor are the pictorial representations as impressive as they appear at first sight. Some of them could pass for copies of authentic sixteenth-century items and are not at all in the extravagant, quasi-traditionless manner of what purported to be indigenous in the late period. Even they, however, tend to be generic. Some are merely ornaments in the style of a later time. Mengin took the newer version's interpolations seriously enough to include them in the main text of his transcription and translation, though enclosing them in brackets and giving the precise origin in notes. Later translators of the conquest section followed him, not always indicating the distinction as carefully as he did. My skepticism about the newer text being as strong as it is, I have relegated these passages to the notes, but because such a high degree of uncertainty attaches to the whole origins question, I have not felt it proper to omit them entirely.

In any case, none of this discussion yet tells us much about the single point of greatest interest: when the earlier version was composed, or rather when it was set down on paper. It would be wrong to put credence in the newer text's assertion that it was a copy of an old text of 1528.[94] Nothing of the kind is found in the extant older manuscript. The dates found in historicizing documents of the later period are notoriously incorrect, and their writers have a general tendency to push them back far beyond credibility, often in the attempt to establish antiquity and authenticate some claim or other.[95] The notion that by 1528 Spanish ecclesiastics could have learned the language well enough to have developed such a refined orthography, much less to have trained expert indigenous calligraphers capable of writing great amounts of complex prose, is so improbable as to verge on the ridiculous. Such distance in years between the putatively oldest example and the mass of dated documents is also highly suspicious.

We must resort, then, to direct evidence in the older manuscript alone, which as already seen contains no reference to a date of composition, nor any current date mentioned in passing. The first thing one notices in this respect is the presence of Spanish loanwords not thought to be characteristic of the first years after the conquest. We find

94. MS 22[bis]: 15 says "ye huecauh mochiuh nican Tlatilulco ypan xihuitl de 1528 años" ("it was done a long time ago here in Tlatelolco, in the year of 1528").

95. See Lockhart 1991: item 3, and Lockhart 1992: chap. 9, especially the sections on annals and titles.

not only some of the same loans as in Book Twelve, for which the mid 1550s is the decisive date, but also loans avoided and types of formations not seen there, so that one has no hesitation in saying that other things being equal, even the older manuscript of the Annals of Tlatelolco would seem from linguistic evidence to be a product of a later time than Book Twelve and surely not to go back to the first couple of decades after the conquest. Where Book Twelve has the indigenous neologism *tepozmacquahuitl* 'iron war club' for "sword," the Annals of Tlatelolco have the loanword *espada*.[96] Moreover, the word is once combined with a native ligature and relational word in the form "espadatica," 'with a sword', a type of construction with no parallel in Book Twelve or the other texts reproduced in this volume. Such a form cannot be pegged to any particular time period distinct from other loans, but it represents a more advanced stage of language contact and incorporation of loans than what we see elsewhere. The same can be said of the construction "quipelloqualtiqz,"[97] which in addition to containing the loan *perro* 'dog', not seen in Book Twelve despite its frequent mention of Spanish dogs, incorporates the word into a complex verbal form meaning "to have someone eaten by dogs." Nor is there anything in the other texts remotely like "yey hora,"[98] 'for three hours', wherein not only is the Spanish temporal noun *hora* borrowed, it is used in a very advanced durative sense.[99]

The loan phenomena and the fact that the date is given only in the later manuscript would tend to make one estimate the actual time of composition for the earlier text at probably not before the 1550s or 1560s, surely not before the late 1540s. Other factors, however, call for some sort of explanation. The earlier manuscript is written on indigenous paper, the only one of the entire set of texts included here of which that can be said. The native papers faded out of use with great speed; they are virtually not seen in the great corpus of alphabetic Nahuatl documentation that came into existence from about 1545, except for some aberrant texts of the late seventeenth and eighteenth centuries purporting to be original land titles of indigenous corporations and actually very close to simple fakes.[100] They do not, however, at all resemble the Tlatelolcan manuscript, and I for one do not question its authenticity, or its dating to some time in the sixteenth century.

One other major set of Nahuatl documents is written on indigenous paper: the censuses of the Cuernavaca region, which many scholars regard as the oldest known examples of alphabetic Nahuatl texts. On consideration (for I am very familiar with the Cuernavacan texts) I am of the opinion that the hand of the Tlatelolcan manuscript is

---

96. MS 22: 27, 37.

97. MS 22: 38.

98. MS 22: 28.

99. Before I knew the manuscript at all well, I was impressed with the presence of the loan *marques*, which would indicate a time at least into the 1530s and probably later; but it turns out to be contained only in the later manuscript. I have not included the section, having to do mainly with the story of Quauhtemoc, which contains the word, because I view it as most likely belonging to a much later time.

100. See Lockhart 1991: item 3; and Lockhart 1992: chap. 9, section on titles.

very similar, and that both are different from anything else I have seen in the way of sixteenth-century Nahuatl manuscripts. [101] The Cuernavacan texts mainly use an orthographic system very much like that which gained general currency after 1545 or 1550, or at least like variants of it, but they do have certain peculiarities. The greatest is that whereas the vast majority of later texts distinguish clearly between *tz* and *ç* or *z*, no such distinction is found in the Cuernavacan corpus; *tz* is completely lacking. Apparently at that time those who were developing the system either did not yet hear the distinction or had not devised a way to represent it. Looking at the Tlatelolcan manuscript, we will find a great number of examples of standard *tz* being written as *z*; [102] nevertheless, perhaps an even greater number are written as *tz*, in the ordinary way of the later period. The conclusion I draw from these facts is that the Tlatelolcan manuscript indeed has some signs of unusual earliness compared to the corpus of Nahuatl documents in general, but it seems to be somewhat later than the Cuernavacan texts.

One can also compare the two sets with regard to language-contact phenomena. Here the difference leaps to the eye, for loans of any kind other than personal names are very rare in the Cuernavacan texts. They are not, however, entirely absent; moreover, some of the few to be found are of a rather surprising nature, including words not later definitively borrowed at all, such as small numerals. [103] Perhaps, then, some of the extreme phenomena of the Tlatelolcan manuscript indicate not so much a very late time period as the experimentation of a time before all of the conventions were set. Loans are not truly numerous in the conquest section of the Tlatelolcan manuscript. The word *capitan* alone accounts for almost half of all occurrences, and it always refers to Cortés; as he is given no other appellation, it serves as a proper name. To me, this usage also smacks of relative earliness.

The Cuernavacan corpus and the Tlatelolcan manuscript are alike in that, despite being in indigenous genres and eminently suited for pictorial representation, they show no pictures or glyphs at all. The Cuernavacan censuses often seem to be the description of a pictorial document, or rather the realization of a mixed pictorial-oral account. Possibly in both cases there was originally a manuscript with pictures only, and outside prodding of one kind or another eventuated in a form to which Spaniards could more easily relate. To keep things in proportion, it is necessary to remind ourselves at this point that the Annals of Tlatelolco are far less visual than Book Twelve of the Florentine Codex, and that they show far fewer signs of active Spanish participa-

101. The comparison must of course be carried out much more methodically on the entirety of both sets. I rely above all on a strong impression. For now let me point in particular to the great size of many capital letters and to the frequently elongated form of the *y*. The orthography, by the way, has none of the earmarks of that of Sahagún, with whom some have wanted to connect the manuscript. The Cuernavacan censuses are in Mexico City's Museo de Antropología, Archivo Histórico, Colección Antigua, vols. 549–551. A selection is published in Carrasco 1972, transcribed and translated into Spanish. Most of vol. 550 is in Hinz et al. 1983, transcribed and translated into German. A transcription and English translation of vol. 549 will shortly be published by S. L. Cline.

102. There is also a bit of *tz* for *z*, another indication of the newness of the distinction to the writer.

103. See Karttunen and Lockhart 1976: 40–41.

tion. At any rate, the Cuernavacan censuses and the Annals of Tlatelolco both seem to belong to a time before the integration of indigenous pictorial and European alphabetic styles of writing that occurred, in general, by the mid sixteenth century. Herein we have still another reason to doubt the existence of another, profusely illustrated alphabetic version of which the existing older Tlatelolcan manuscript would have been a copy.

If, as appears to be so, the Tlatelolcan set is a bit later than the Cuernavacan set, it becomes important to date the latter. That itself is not an easy matter. The entire corpus contains no precise date (in itself a rarity and one more point of affinity with the Tlatelolcan manuscript). Suffice it to say that those who have worked most with the material favor a time hovering around 1540, perhaps a few years earlier in some cases and quite definitely a little later in others (for the censuses were not done simultaneously, and some were maintained current over a period of time).[104] We might say, then, that about 1545 would be a reasonable estimate of when the Annals of Tlatelolco were set down. By 1550 their orthography and calligraphy, and the paper on which they were written, would have been anomalous, especially in the vicinity of Mexico City, home of the new. All in all, I expect that the present form of the older version is a product of some time during the 1540s; I hope that fuller examination of all relevant texts and perhaps the location of some new ones will bring greater certainty and precision.

Meanwhile, we appear to have a text done not in the wake of the events but some twenty years after them, and hence quite comparable in its perspective to the other texts reproduced here. It does give every indication of being the earliest known Nahuatl conquest account and deserves corresponding attention. It shares a great deal with Book Twelve, including the Tlatelolcan provenience and emphasis, certain indigenous neologisms for Spanish introductions, many narrative details, and much else. We must consider the extent to which it represents an earlier stage of a tradition leading to something like Book Twelve.

The fact that the manuscript ended up in indigenous hands seems to differentiate it from the Florentine Codex, but the distinction is not absolute. This writer too was trained by Spanish ecclesiastics, though probably of the generation of fray Pedro de Gante rather than the generation of Sahagún and Molina. Turning a pictorial-oral expression into a purely alphabetic one, if that is what happened, reminds one of the process by which Sahagún himself was later to develop his work; perhaps in this case the papers simply remained with the aides and informants instead of going into Spanish custody.

In view of the number and extent of the mysteries in the text, the reader will find a somewhat heavier concentration of notes here than elsewhere, but let it not be imagined that they are in any sense exhaustive. With one exception, which bears on the sense, no notice is taken in the transcription of the many words and letters crossed out

104. See the sources mentioned in n. 101.

in the original manuscript, because most are clearly mechanical errors repeating or anticipating something else in the text.

*3. Extract from the Codex Aubin.* The manuscript usually known by this name is a set of annals of Tenochtitlan, put on paper by an anonymous citizen who seems from internal evidence to have lived in the San Juan Moyotlan quarter in the second half of the sixteenth century. He apparently started writing about 1562, at which point the entries become current, prefaced with the word "today," and sometimes they concern himself and his family. It must have been about this time that he collected material from various sources on the migrations of the Mexica, the foundation of Tenochtitlan and its subsequent history, the conquest, and events of the postconquest years up to the point at which he began to rely on his own observations. [105]

Included here is the section dealing with the conquest. In a previous section I commented at some length on the form and content, seen in comparison to Book Twelve. One might add that the author/compiler does not give much sign of great historiographic expertise or even in a sense interest. Like a good many other practitioners of the annals genre, he apparently felt that certain topics and years should be covered and hence put in whatever he could find, not carefully rethinking and integrating it, as the great annalist Chimalpahin did. The material is thus quite disjointed; a speech of Moteucçoma's stops in midstream. The advantage of the writer's procedure is that in all likelihood he has given us quite untouched and authentic elements of Tenochca oral and written tradition.

Note that whereas the Tlatelolca in their writings were obsessed with the Mexica, forever trying to pull them down or at least put themselves on the same plane, the Tenochca here show no concern with the lesser Tlatelolca. Not a word is said in the Codex Aubin's conquest account about Tlatelolco, the Tlatelolca, or their leader, Itzquauhtzin.

*4. Fragments from the Annals of Quauhtitlan.* This set of annals, by internal evidence, was written in 1570 at Quauhtitlan (modern Cuauhtitlan or Cuautitlan, just north of Mexico City) [106] and deals primarily with the political history of that altepetl, from the early migrations of the ethnic group through the founding and vicissitudes of the polity to the arrival of the Spaniards, with some genealogical information on postconquest times. Inward-looking like most exemplars of the genre, it nevertheless speaks fre-

---

105. See the introduction to Dibble 1963. The publication contains a facsimile, a full transcription of the Nahuatl text, and a Spanish translation. I used the facsimile as the source of my own transcription; later, on ordering photographs of some pages of the original in the British Museum, I became aware that the Dibble facsimile is a redrawing that at times actually redistributes the written words somewhat differently on the page. Although I detected no actual errors in the sections of which I obtained photographs, it is quite possible that some exist. The publication of a true photographic facsimile and an updated translation of the entire manuscript, with a full critical apparatus, would be a very worthwhile undertaking.

106. See Velázquez 1975: 9.

quently of the Mexica. The reason may be the propinquity of the two groups and the influence Tenochtitlan/Tlatelolco exercised on Quauhtitlan, well nigh incorporating it, or it may be that the author or authors had been exposed to the broader world and had a more cosmopolitan view. There is no doubt that he or they had been among Spaniards and even had access to Spanish documents. The work's editor, noticing that two of Sahagún's best-trained aides, Alonso Bejerano and Pedro de San Buenaventura, were from Quauhtitlan, and that in 1570 the Sahaguntine enterprise was at its height, concludes that these two were likely the authors. [107]

However that may be (one must note that the manuscript does not use Sahagún's orthographic system), the work reverts to a typical Nahua genre and typical indigenous interests, showing no effect of Sahagún's concern with language and lore as such. I include here all of the portions that relate to the Spanish conquest in the whole work— namely, a total of two paragraphs—primarily in order to show how the historians of even an entity so closely connected with the Mexica as Quauhtitlan gave the conquest very short shrift. In the first of the two passages, the coming of the Spaniards is mentioned only in passing, and only as it relates to Quauhtitlan; the primary purpose of the mention is simply to help date internal events. The second paragraph is actual conquest history, repeating the story of the first encounter with some details in agreement with Book Twelve, and possibly even relying on it to some extent. An additional item not in Book Twelve, the highlight of the passage indeed, is a detailed listing of the gifts the Spaniards sent Moteucçoma, based perhaps on some pictorial record, for it hardly seems that two pairs of shoes, and so on, would enter into general oral tradition. The account goes no farther. [108]

5. *Extract from the Historia Tolteca-Chichimeca.* Thought to have been written about 1547–1560, the set of annals now called the Historia Tolteca-Chichimeca is from Quauhtinchan (modern Cuauhtinchan) in the eastern part of the Nahua-speaking region, southeast of Puebla. [109] In several ways it is, without being on the same scale, the primary counterpart and corrective to the Florentine Codex. The altepetl of Quauhtinchan was not only far removed from Tenochtitlan/Tlatelolco, it was (unlike Quauhtitlan) outside the entire political and economic web encompassing the Valley

107. Ibid. 9–11. Velázquez was by far the best modern translator of Nahuatl working before the past couple of decades. He did not, however, publish a transcription of the Annals of Quauhtitlan in addition to his Spanish translation, offering only a facsimile. An edition by John Bierhorst is forthcoming from the University of Arizona Press and will contain, in addition to an up-to-date English translation, a full and very reliable transcription of the Nahuatl text.

108. That is, the work ends at that point. One could speculate that the intention was to go ahead with the history of the conquest on a scale as grand as Book Twelve or grander, or even that such a history was written and is not preserved. That sort of account would not be very congruent with the work we know, however, and at any rate we do not have it.

109. Kirchhoff, Güemes, and Reyes García 1976 includes an excellent color facsimile, a complete transcription of the Nahuatl (standardizing and hence changing the way certain sounds are written), and a good Spanish translation.

of Mexico and centered on the Mexica. And whereas the writers of the Nahuatl of the Florentine Codex were elaborately supervised, working within the framework of a Spanish enterprise, the person or persons who wrote the Nahuatl text of the Historia Tolteca-Chichimeca and executed its many drawings and glyphs were working on their own, for their own factional and corporate purposes, thereby showing us how they spontaneously expressed themselves and what their most urgent concerns were.[110] No Spaniard, ecclesiastical or not, is mentioned in connection with the manuscript, and it remained for generations in indigenous custody.[111] It is not that Spanish ecclesiastical training was absent; the hand and orthography of the Nahuatl text are in that tradition and are as fine as anything in the Florentine Codex, or finer; the pictorial element evinces a quite similar combination of preconquest and European conventions.

Much as with the Annals of Tlatelolco and Quauhtitlan, the bulk of the work concerns the preconquest sociopolitical tradition of the local corporate group, in this case with strong implications of jockeying for advantage in interethnic disputes over borders and jurisdiction. A brief final section brings the story through and past the conquest, nearly up to the time of composition (the extract here includes everything from the appearance of the Spaniards to the end of the manuscript). The interest in jurisdiction, borders between indigenous groups, and tribute arrangements remains much the same as in the large preconquest portion. The style of presentation also resembles that of many sections of the preconquest account, but it is spare and noncommittal, not in the detailed and dramatized manner of the high points of the earlier history; also, the pictorial component is dropped. Even in this section, the ramifications of the preconquest invasion by the Tenochca and Tlatelolca loom almost as large as the Spaniards and their doings. The text gives no indication that the Quauhtinchan people were bowled over by the Spanish advent, though they tell in a matter-of-fact way of a number of adjustments; rather, the postconquest entries show them still looking above all for the good of their particular entity in terms that have hardly changed.

6. *Letter from the council of Huejotzingo, 1560.*[112] This is the only text in the volume that does not belong to the Nahuatl annals genre; even Book Twelve is ultimately an-

110. The entire Nahuatl text, compiled from various sources that were doubtless transformed in the process, appears to have been set down by a single writer. It is not so easy to say how many people may have been involved with the pictorial component, or whether the writer was one of them. The ongoing dissertation project of Dana Leibsohn, doctoral student in art history at UCLA, may answer some of the questions. Leibsohn is also preparing a complete transcription and English translation.

111. On an early page of the manuscript is a Nahuatl comment on it in a hand of the late seventeenth or the eighteenth century, clearly written by a Nahua in whose possession it still was at that time.

112. A color facsimile of the Nahuatl text is in *Cartas de Indias* (1877), though not properly identified. The archival location of the manuscript is unknown to me. A transcription of the Nahuatl and an English translation are in Anderson, Berdan, and Lockhart 1976. I have mainly reproduced that version, in the case of the transcription reproducing the overbars instead of writing out *n* or *m* as there, and with the translation introducing a few minor changes.

nals material in a very good disguise. The notion of the letter as a form, a message written on paper and sent to a distant recipient, is European, but the Nahuas quickly took it up by adopting some of the beginning and ending formulas and otherwise equating it with a genre of which they were great masters, the speech—sometimes more conversational, sometimes more oratorical. In this case we have oratory. The purpose is to appeal against a tax that has just been levied; the means is to review in cascading words and pairs of phrases the exemplary behavior of the altepetl of Huejotzingo from the moment the Spaniards arrived until the present. Each step of the process gets its own long paragraph, beginning with a weighty vocative and making a single point in a hundred ways.

What the noble members of the Huejotzingo council say cannot, of course, be accepted as the simple truth, any more than the contents of Book Twelve or any of the other texts in this collection can be. And given the transparent self-interest, we may even wish to question the sincerity of some of the affirmations made. But it is useful to absorb even the public perspective on the conquest and its aftermath as reported from a major altepetl in the eastern part of the Nahua world. Here we see once again the Nahua micropatriotism, the drive of each entity for maximum advantage and autonomy, often with other indigenous groups, not the Spaniards, cast as rivals and obstacles. Although the letter resorts to an umbrella term for indigenous people, "we people here in New Spain," it does so primarily in order to compare itself favorably with all others. The most bitterly resented rival of Huejotzingo is neighboring Tlaxcala, which, as a somewhat larger and more prominent ally of the Spaniards in the war against the Mexica, got the lion's share of the credit. In the historical core of the presentation, each paragraph has its coda, castigating the Tlaxcalans for their failings, to put them in their place and to make Huejotzingo's virtues shine more brightly by contrast.[113]

113. See also the comments on this letter in Lockhart and Otte 1976.

TEXTS AND TRANSLATIONS

## 1.

# BOOK TWELVE OF
# THE FLORENTINE CODEX

| *Spanish* | *English Translation of Spanish* |
|---|---|
| EL DOZENO LIBRO | THE TWELFTH BOOK |
| Tracta de como los españoles conquistaron a la ciudad de Mexico. | Treats of how the Spaniards conquered Mexico City. |

I

## Al lector.

Aunque muchos an escrito en romance la conquista desta nueua españa, segun la relacion de los q̄ la conquistaron: quise la yo escreuir en lengua mexicana, no tanto por sacar algunas verdades de la relacion de los mismos indios, que se hallaron en la conquista: quanto por poner el lenguaje de las cosas de la guerra, y de las armas que en ella vsan los naturales: para que de alli se puedan sacar vocablos y maneras de dezir proprias, para hablar en lengua mexicana cerca desta materia, allegase tambien a esto que los que fuero [1] conquistados, supieron y dieron relacion de muchas cosas, que passaron entre ellos durante la guerra: las quales ignorarō los que los conquistarō, por las quales razones, me parece que no a sido trabajo superfluo, el auer escrito esta estoria. [2] la qual se escuiuio en tiempo que eran viuos, los que se hallaron en la misma conquista: y ellos dieron esta relacion personas principales, y de buen juizio y que se tiene por cierto, que dixeron toda verdad.

## To the Reader.

Although many have written in Spanish about the conquest of New Spain according to the accounts of those who conquered it, I wanted to write about it in the Mexican language, not so much in order to extract some truths from the very Indians who took part in the conquest as in order to set down the language of the things of war and of the weapons that the natives use in it, so that from there one can take appropriate words and expressions for speaking in the Mexican language on this topic. It can also be added that those who were [1] conquered found out and gave account of many things that happened among them during the war, things that those who conquered them did not know. For these reasons it seems to me that it was not a superfluous effort to have written this history, [2] which was written at a time when those who took part in the conquest itself were alive, and those who gave this account were important people of good judgment who are considered certain to have told the entire truth.

2

| Nahuatl | English Translation of Nahuatl |
|---|---|

[fol. 1] Inic matlactetl omume amoxtli, itechpa tlatoa in quenin muchiuh iauiotl in nican ipan altepetl Mexico.

Twelfth book, which speaks of how war was waged here in the altepetl of Mexico.

I

Inic ce capitulo vncā mitoa in nez, in mottac in machiotl yoā in tetzavitl, in aiamo valhui españoles, in nican tlalli ipan, in aiamo no iximachoa in nicā chaneque. [3]

First chapter, where it is said that before the Spaniards came here to this land, and before the people who live here were known, [3] there appeared and were seen signs and omens.

In aiamo vallaci españoles, oc matlac-xivitl, centlamātli tetzavitl achto nez, il-huicatitech, iuhqui in tlemiiaoatl, iuhqui in tlecueçalutl, iuhquin tlavizcalli, pipi-xauhticaca inic necia; iuhq̄n ilhuicatl quiçoticac: tzimpatlaoac, quapitzaoac: vel inepantla in ilhuicatl; vel yiollo [fol. 1v] in aciticac ilhuicatl, vel ilhuicaiollotitech aciticac, in iuh ittoia vmpa tlapcopa: in oalmoquetzaia, oiuh onquiz ioalnepantla in necia tlatviliaia, ipan tlatvia, q̄n iehoatl quioalpoloaia in tonatiuh, in iquac oal-quiçaia: vel ce xivitl in oalmoquetzaia

Ten years before the arrival of the Span-iards an omen first appeared in the sky, like a flame or tongue of fire, like the light of dawn. It appeared to be throwing off [sparks] and seemed to pierce the sky. It was wide at the bottom and narrow at the top. It looked as though it reached the very middle of the sky, its very heart and center. It showed itself off to the east. When it came out at midnight it appeared like the dawn. When dawn came, then the sun on coming out effaced it. For a full year it showed itself (it was in [the year] Twelve

3

[fol. 1] Libro doze de la conquista de la nueua españa, que es la ciudad de Mexico.

Book Twelve, of the conquest of New Spain, that is, of the City of Mexico.

4

I

Capitulo primero de las señales y pronosticos que aparecieron antes que los Españoles veniesen a esta tierra ni vuiese noticia dellos.

First Chapter, of the signs and omens that appeared before the Spaniards came to this land or had been heard of.

Diez años ante que viniesē los españoles desta⁴ tierra: parecio en el cielo, vna cosa marauillosa, y espantosa: y es que parecio vna llama de fuego, muy grande y muy resplandecieto: parecia que estaua tendida en el mismo cielo, era ancha de la parte de abaxo, y de la parte de arriba aguda, como quando el fuego arde parecia que la punta della llegaua hasta el medio del cielo, leuātauase [fol. 1v] por la parte del oriente, luego despues de la media noche, y salia con tanto resplandor que parecia el dia: llegaua hasta la mañana entonce se perdia de

Ten years before the Spaniards came to this⁴ land there appeared in the sky something marvelous and frightful. It was that a tongue of flame appeared, very large and resplendent; it seemed to be suspended in the very sky. It was wide below and pointed above; when the fire burned it seemed that the tip of it reached the middle of the sky. It would rise in the east, right after midnight, and it came out with such splendor that it seemed to be daytime; it continued until morning, then it was lost from view. When the sun rose, the flame

(ipan matlactli omume calli in peuh). Auh in iquac necia tlacaoacaia, netenvitecoia, neiçaviloia, tlatemma [5]

House that it began). And when it appeared there would be an outcry, and people would hit their hands against their mouths as they yelled. People were taken aback, they lamented. [5]

Inic vntetl tetzavitl muchiuh, nican mexico: çan monomavi in tlatlac, cuetlan, aiac ma quitlecavi, çan monomatlecavi in ical diablo vitzilobuchtli: mitoaia, iteioc [8] itocaiocan Tlacateccan: in nez ie tlatla in tlaquetzalli, in itoc, oalquiça in tlemiiaoatl, in tlenenepilli, in tlecueçalutl, cenca çan iciuhca compalo in [fol. 2] ixquich calquauitl: niman ie ic tlacaoaca, quitoa. Mexicae ma vallatotoca, tlaceviloz, amaapilol: auh in iquac caatequiaia, in quiceviznequia, çan ie ilhuice mopitza, aocmo vel ceuh, vel tlatlac.

The second omen that happened here in Mexico was that of its own accord the house of the devil Huitzilopochtli, what they call his mountain, [8] named Tlacateccan, burned and flared up; no one set fire to it, it just took fire itself. When the fire was seen, the wooden pillars were already burning. Tongues and tassels of flame were coming from inside; very quickly they consumed all the building's beams. Then there was an outcry. They said, "O Mexica, let everyone come running, it must be put out, [bring] your water jars!" But when they threw water on it, trying to extinguish it, it blew up all the more. It could not be put out; it burned entirely.

Inic etetl tetzavitl: vitecoc ipan tlatlatzin teucalli, çan xacalli catca, itocaiocan tzūmulco: iteupan in xiuhtecutli, amo tilaoaia, çan aoachquiavia in iuh tetzammachoc: iuh mitoa in çan [9] tonalhuitecoc, amo no caquiztic in tlatlatziniliztli.

The third omen was that a temple was struck by lightning, hit by a thunderbolt. It was just a building of straw at the temple complex of Xiuhteuctli, called Tzonmolco. The reason it was taken for an omen was that it was not raining hard, just drizzling. It was said that it was struck when the sun was shining, [9] nor was thunder heard.

5

Inic nauhtetl tetzavitl; oc vnca in tonatiuh in xivitl vetz ieteietia, vmpa oalpeuh in tonatiuh icalaquiampa; auh vmpa

The fourth omen was that while the sun was still out a comet fell, in three parts. It began off to the west and headed in the di-

vista, quando salia el sol, estaua la llama en el lugar que esta el sol a mediodia esto duro por espacio de vn año cada noche: començo en las doze casas y quando parecia a la medianoche toda la gente gritaua y se espantaua todos sospechauan que era señal de algū grā mal.

was in the place where the sun is at midday. This lasted for a year, every night, beginning in Twelve House. When it appeared at midnight, all the people would shout and take fright; everyone suspected that it was a sign of some great evil.

La segunda senal,[6] que acontecio, fue que el chapitel[7] de vn cu de vitzilobuchtli que se llamaua Tlacatecca, se encendio milagrosamente, y se quemo: parecia que las llamas del fuego salian de dētro de los maderos de las colunas, y muy de presto se hizo ceniza, quando ardia començaron los satrapas a dar vozes diziendo. O Mexicanos venid presto a apagar el fuego con cantaros de [fol. 2] agua: y venida el agua, echauanla sobre el fuego, y no se apagaua: sino antes mas se encendia: y asi se hizo todo brasa.

The second sign[6] that occurred was that the ornamented pillar[7] of a *cu* [temple] of Huitzilopochtli, called Tlacateccan, miraculously took fire and burned. The tongues of flame seemed to come from inside the wooden columns, and when it burned it quickly turned to ashes. The satraps [priests] began to shout, saying, "O Mexica, come quickly to put out the fire with jars of water!" And when the water came, they threw it on the fire, but it did not go out; rather, it flamed up more, and thus it was all left in embers.

6

La tercera señal o pronostico fue, cayo un rrayo sobre el cu, de xiuhtecutli dios del fuego: el qual estaua techado con paja llamauase tzūmulco: espantarōse desto porque no lluuia, sino agua menuda que no suele caer rayos quādo ansi llueue, ni vuo tronido: sino que no saben como se encendio.

The third sign or omen was that a bolt of lightning struck the *cu* of Xiuhteuctli, god of fire, which was roofed with thatch; it was called Tzonmolco. They were shocked by it because there was no rain except a drizzle, and lightning does not usually strike when it rains in this fashion. Nor was there thunder, so that they do not know how it took fire.

7

La quarta señal o pronostico, fue que de dia haziendo sol cayo, vna cometa, parecian tres estrellas, juntas que corrian a la

The fourth sign or omen was that during the day, when the sun was out, a comet fell. Three stars appeared together,

itztia in iquiçaianpa, iuhqui in tlesuchtli
pipixauhtiuh, veca mocuitlapiltitiuh, veca
acitiuh in icuitlapil: auh in oittoc cēca
tlacaoacac, iuhquin oiovalli ōmoman.

[fol. 2v] Inic macuiltetl tetzavitl: poçon
in atl, amo iehecatl quipoçonalti, iuhquin
momomoloca, iuhquin xixittemomoloca,
cenca veca in ia, inic macoquetz: auh in
calli tzitzintla cacic, auh capapachiuh, xixi-
tin in calli: iehoatl in vei atl totlan mani
nican mexico.

Inic chiquacentlamantli tetzavitl:
miecpa cioatl cacoia chocatiuh, tzatzitiuh,
ioaltica cenca tzatzi; quitotinemi. No
nopilhoantzitzin, ie ic çan ie tonvi: in
quenmanian quitoa. No nopilhoantzitzin,
campa namechnoviquiliz.

Inic chicuntlamantli tetzavitl: ceppa tla-
tlamaia, manoço tlamatlaviaia in atlaca;
centetl cacique tototl nextic, iuhquin to-
cuilcoiotl: nimā quittitito in Moteucçoma,
tlillan, calmecac: ommotzcalo [11] in
tonatiuh, oc tlaca, iuhq̄n [fol. 3] tezcatl
icpac mani, malacachtic, tevilacachtic, iuhquin xapotticac: vmpa onnecia in ilhuicatl,
in cicitlaltin, in mamalhoaztli. Auh in
motecuçoma, cenca quimotetzavi in iquac
quimittac cicitlaltin, yoā mamalhoaztli.
Auh inic vppa ontlachix in icpac tototl,
ene quittac, iuhqui on in ma acame,
moquequetztivitze, tepeuhtivitze, moiao-
chichiuhtivitze, quinmama mamaça. Auh
niman quinnotz in tlaciuhque, in tlamati-
nime: quimilhui: Amo anquimati in tlein
onoconittac, iuhquin acame moquequetz-

rection of the east, looking as if it were
sprinkling glowing coals. It had a long tail,
which reached a great distance. When it
was seen, there was a great outcry, like the
sound of rattles.

The fifth omen was that the water [of
the lake] boiled up; it was not the wind
that caused it. It bubbled and made exploding sounds, rising high in the air. It
reached the foundations of the houses; it
flooded them, and they collapsed. This is
the great lake that extends around us here
in Mexico.

The sixth omen was that many times a
woman would be heard going along
weeping and shouting. She cried out
loudly at night, saying, "O my children,
we are about to go forever." Sometimes
she said, "O my children, where am I to
take you?"

The seventh omen was that once the
water folk were hunting or snaring and
caught an ash-colored bird, like a crane.
Then they went to the Tlillan calmecac to
show it to Moteucçoma; the sun was in-
clining, [11] it was still full day. On top of its
head was something like a mirror, round,
circular, seeming to be perforated, where
the sky, the stars, and the Fire Drill [con-
stellation] could be seen. And Moteucçoma took it for a very bad omen when he
saw the stars and the Fire Drill. The second
time he looked at the bird's head he saw
something like a multitude of people coming along, coming bunched, outfitted for
war, carried on the backs of deer. Then he
called the soothsayers, the sages, and said to
them, "Do you not know what I've seen,

par, muy encendidas: y lleuauan muy largas colas partieron de hazia el occidente: y corrian hazia el oriente, yvan echãdo centellas de si, desque la gente las vio, comē̃-çarõ a dar gran grita sono grandissimo ruydo, en toda la comarca.

[fol. 2v] La quinta señal o pronostico fue, que se leuanto la mar de Mexico: con grandes olas parecia que heruia sin hazer ayre ninguno la qual nūca se suele leuantar, sin gran vieto llegaron las olas muy lexos y entraron entre las casas sacudian en los cimientos de las casas, algunas casas cayeron, fue grande el espanto de todos por ver, que sin ayre se auia de tal manera ē̃brauecido el agua.

La sesta señal o pronostico es que se oya, en el ayre de noche, vna voz de muger: que dezia. O hijos mios, ya nos perdemos: algunas vezes dezia. O hijos mios donde os lleuare.

La septima señal o pronostico es que los cazadores de las aues del agua, cazaron vna aue parda, del tanmaño [10] de vna grulla: y luego la fueron a mostrar a Motecuçoma que estaua en vna sala que llamauan Tlillancalmecac, era despues de mediodia, tenia [fol. 3] esta aue, en medio de la cabeça, vn espejo redondo, donde se parecia el cielo: y las estrellas y especialmente los mastelejos, [12] que andã cerca de las cabrillas: como vio esto Motecuçoma espantose. Y la segūda vez, que miro en el espejo que tenia el aue de ay a vn poco vio muchedumbre de gente iunta q̃ venian todos, armados encima de cauallos. Y luego Motecuçoma mando llamar a los agureros, y adiuinos, y preguntolos no sabeys ques esto que e visto? que viene mucha gente junta?

running along parallel, lit up very brightly and bearing large tails. They started to the west and ran toward the east; they went along casting off sparks. As soon as the people saw them, they began a great outcry; a huge noise sounded through the whole district.

The fifth sign or omen was that the sea [lake] of Mexico rose up with great waves. It seemed to boil, although there was no wind and it ordinarily never rises without strong winds. The waves reached a great distance and came in among the houses, shaking their foundations, and some houses fell. Great was the fright of all to see that without wind the water should have become so wild.

The sixth sign or omen is that in the night air the voice of a woman was heard, saying, "O my children, we are about to be lost." Sometimes she said, "O my children, where am I to take you?"

The seventh sign or omen is that the hunters of waterfowl caught a dark bird the size [10] of a crane, and then they went to show it to Moteucçoma, who was in a hall that they called Tlillan calmecac. This was after midday. This bird had in the middle of its head a round mirror in which appeared the sky and the stars, especially Castor and Pollux, [12] which move close to the Pleiades. When Moteucçoma saw this, he took fright. The second time he looked in the mirror on the bird, a little later, he saw a multitude of people all coming along together, armed and on horseback. Then Moteucçoma ordered the soothsayers and prognosticators to be called, and he asked them, "Do you not know what this is that I have seen? For many people are coming

tivitze: auh ie quinanquilizquia, in conittaque, opoliuh, aoctle quitoque.

9

Inic chicuetetl tetzavitl: miecpa motenextiliaia, tlaca, tlacanetzolti, ontetzon-
tecomeque, çan çe in intlac, vmpa quimō-
vicaia in tlillan calmecac, vmpa quimittaia
in motecuçoma, in oquimittac nimā
polivia./.

2

[fol. 3v] Inic vme capitulo, vncan mitoa
in quenin acico, in achto acalli oalla: in iuh
quitoa ca çan centetl in acalli.

Auh in oittoque, in aquique ovallaque
ilhuicaatenco, in acaltica ie onotinemi.
Niman inoma ia in cuetlaxtecatl pinotl, vei
calpixqui, ānvicac oc cequintin calpixque:
Mictlan, quauhtla calpixqui, Iaotzin. Inic
ei, Teuciniocan calpixqui: itoca Teuciniacatl. [13] Inic navi iehoatl in cuitlalpitoc, çan
tetlan nenqui tlaiacanqui. Inic macuilli
Tentlil, çanno tlaiacanqui;

çan oc iehoantin in, in quimittato, çan
iuhquin ma quintlanamaquiltito, inic
quinnaoalittato, inic quinnemilito: quin-
macato tlaçotilmatli, tlaçotlanqui, çan vel
itech itilma in Motecuçoma, in aoc ac oc
çe quiquemi, çan vel ineixcavil, vel itonal:

acaltica in iaque [fol. 4] inic quimittato,
inic iuh quichiuhque in: quito in pinotzin.
Ma tiquiztlacaviti in tlacatl Motecuçomatzin, ca iaocmo annenca ma çan tehoantin
tivia, ma tonmiquiti, inic vel melaoac

something like a multitude of people coming along?" But when they were going to
answer him, what they saw disappeared,
and they said nothing more.

The eighth omen was that many times
people appeared, thistle-people with two
heads but one body; they took them to the
Tlillan calmecac and showed them to Moteucçoma. When he had seen them, they
disappeared.

Second chapter, where it is said how the
first boat that came arrived; they say that
there was only one boat.

When those who came to the seashore
were seen, they were going along by boat.
Then Pinotl of Cuetlaxtlan, a high steward, went in person, taking other stewards
with him: [second], Yaotzin, the steward
of Mictlanquauhtla; third, the steward of
Teocinyocan, named Teocinyocatl; [13]
fourth, Cuitlalpitoc, who was only a de-
pendent, a subordinate leader; and fifth,
Tentlil, also a subordinate leader.

These were the only ones who first
went to see [the Spaniards]. They went as
if to sell them things, so that they could spy
on them and contemplate them. They
gave them precious cloaks, precious goods,
the very cloaks pertaining to Moteucçoma
which no one else could don, which were
assigned to him alone.

It was by boat that they went to see
them. As they were doing it, Pinotzin said,
"Let us not lie to the lord Moteucçoma,
for you would live no longer. Let's just go,
lest we die, so that he can hear the real

Y antes que respondiessen los adiuinos, desparecio el aue: y no respondieron nada.

La octaua señal o pronostico es que aparecieron muchas vezes mostruos, en cuerpos mostruosos. lleuauālos a Motecuçoma, y en viendolos el en su aposento que se llamaua Tlillancalmecac luego desaparecian.

2

[fol. 3v] Capitulo segundo, de los primeros nauios, que aportaron a esta tierra: que segun dizen fue Juā de grisalua.

La primera vez, que parecieron nauios en la costa desta nueua españa, los capitanes de Motecuçoma que se llamauan calpisques, que estauā cerca de la costa: luego fueron a uer, que era aquello que venia, que nunca auian visto nauios, vno de los quales fue el calpisqui de cuestecatl, que se llamaua pinotl: lleuo consigo otros calpisques, vno que se llamaua Iaotzin, que residia en el pueblo de Mictlanquauhtla: y otro que se llamaua Teociniocatl, que residia en el pueblo de Teociniocan, y otro que se llamaua Cuitlalpitoc. Este no era calpisqui, sino criado de vno destos calpisques, y principalejo: y otro principalejo que se llamaua Tentlil.

Estos cinco fueron a uer que cosa era aquello, y lleuauā algunas cosas, para venderlos so color de ver que cosa era aquella, [14] y lleuaronlos algunas mantas ricas, que solo Motecuçoma las vsaua ningū otro, [fol. 4] tenia licencia de vsarlas.

together." But before the prognosticators could answer, the bird disappeared, and they gave no reply.

The eighth sign or omen is that many times monsters appeared, in monstrous bodies. They took them to Moteucçoma, and after he had seen them in his lodging, called Tlillan calmecac, they immediately disappeared.

Second chapter, of the first ships that happened on these shores; according to what they say, it was Juan de Grijalva.

The first time that ships appeared on the coast of New Spain here, Moteucçoma's captains, called *calpisques,* who were near the coast went right away to see what it was that was coming, for they had never seen ships. One of them was the *calpisqui* of Cuextecatl [of Cuextlan], whose name was Pinotl; he took with him other *calpisques,* one of whom was named Yaotzin, residing in the settlement of Mictlanquauhtla, and another named Teocinyocatl, residing in the settlement of Teocinyocan, and another named Cuitlalpitoc. The latter was not a *calpisqui,* but the subordinate of one of these *calpisques,* and a lower-level leader, along with another low-level leader named Tentlil.

These five went to see what it was, and they took along some things to sell as a pretext for seeing what manner of thing it was. [14] They took some rich cloaks that only Moteucçoma wore, nor did any one else have permission to use them.

quimocaquitiz (in motecuçomatzin ipiltoca, auh Tlacatecutli in itlatocatoca:

niman ie ic vi in atl itic omma-
calaquique, ommatoctique, quintlanel-
huique atlaca. Auh in o intech ompa-
chivito españoles: niman imixpan
ontlalquaque acaliacac, in momatque, ca
iehoatl in Quetzalcoatl Topiltzin, in
oacico,
quinoalnotzā in españoles: quimilhuique. Acamique campa oanvallaque, can
amochan?
Çan niman quitoque: ca vmpa in mexico tioallaque.
Quinoalnanquilique: intla nelli anme-
xica tle itoca in tlatoani mexico?

Quimonilhuique: Totecuiovane ca
Motecuçoma itoca.
Nimā ie ic quinmaca in izquitlamantli
quitquique tlaçotilmatli: iuhqui in, iehoatl
in, in nicā moteneoa. Tonatiuhio xiuhtlalpilli; tecomaio, xaoalquauhio, coaxaiacaio,
[fol. 4v] coacozcaio, [17] Tolecio, [18] anoço
amalacaio, Tezcapocio:

in izquitlamātli in in quimōmacaque,
quinoalcuepcaiotilique, quinoalmacaque
cozcatl, xoxoctic, coztic: iuhquin ma
mapoçonalnenequi: auh in oconcuique, in
oquittaque, cenca tlamaviçoque,

yoan quinoalnaoatique: quinoalilhuique: xivian oc ie tivi in castilla, amo
tivecaoazā tacitivi in mexico:

nimā ie ic vi, niman ie no ic vitze, oalmocuepque. Auh in o tlalhoacca quiçaco:
niman oallamelauhque in Mexico, cecemi-
lhuitl, ceceioal in oalnenenque, inic
quinonotzaco in motecuçoma, in melaoac

truth." (Moteucçoma was his personal
name, and Tlacateuctli was his title as
ruler.)
Then they embarked, launched off, and
went out on the water; the water folk paddled for them. When they approached the
Spaniards, they made the eartheating gesture at the prow of the boat⟨s⟩. They
thought that it was Quetzalcoatl Topiltzin
who had arrived.
The Spaniards called to them, saying to
them, "Who are you? Where have you
come from? Where is your homeland?"
Immediately they said, "It is from Mexico that we have come."
They answered them back, "If you are
really Mexica, what is the name of the
ruler of Mexico?"
They told them, "O our lords, Moteucçoma is his name."
Then they gave them all the different
kinds of precious cloaks they carried, to
wit, like those mentioned here: the sun-
covered style, the blue-knotted style, the
style covered with jars, the one with
painted eagles, the style with serpent faces,
the style with wind jewels, [17] the style with
⟨turkey blood⟩, [18] or with whirlpools, the
style with smoking mirrors.
For all these things that they gave them,
[the Spaniards] gave them things in return;
they gave them green and yellow strings of
beads, which one might imagine to be
amber. And when they had taken them
and looked at them, greatly did they
marvel.
And [the Spaniards] took leave of them,
saying to them, "Go off, while we go to
Spain; we will not be long in getting to
Mexico."
Thereupon they went, and [the local
people] also came away, coming back. And
when they came out on dry land, they
came straight to Mexico, moving along in
this direction day and night to come in-

Entrarō en vnas canoas, y fueron a los
nauios: dixeron entre si, estamos aqui en
guarda desta costa, conviene que sepamos
de cierto, que es esto para que lleuemos la
nueua cierta a Motecuçoma:

entraron luego en las canoas, y començaron a remar hazia los nauios, y como llegaron junto a los nauios, y vieron a los españoles besaron todos las pruas de las
canoas, en señal de adoracion: pensaron
que era el dios. Quetzalcoatl: que boluia, al
qual estauan, y estan esperando, segun
parece en la historia deste dios: [15]

luego los españoles los hablaron. Dixeron. Quien soys vosotros donde [16] venis?
de donde soys?
Respōdieronlos, los que yuan en las
canoas, emos venido de Mexico.
Dixeronles los españoles: si es verdad
que soys mexicanos, dezidnos, como se
llama el señor de Mexico?
Ellos les respondieron, señores nuestros
llamase Motecuçoma el senor de mexico:
y luego les presentarō todo lo que lleuauan, de aquellas mantas ricas, que lleuauan
vnas se llamauan xiuhtlalpilli, otras tecomaio, otras xaoalquauhio, otras [fol. 4v]
Ecacozcaio, otras tolecio o amalacoio,
otras, tezcapucyo: todas estas maneras de
mantas, las presentaron al que yua por
principal en aquellos nauios que segun
dizen, era grisalua.
Y los españoles dieron a los indios cuētas
de vidro, vnas verdes, y otras amarillas; y
los indios como las vieron marauillaronse
mucho, y huuieronlas en mucho,
y despidieronse de los indios diziendo.
Ya nos boluemos a castilla, y presto
bolueremos: y yremos a mexico.

Los indios se boluieron a tierra, y luego
se partieron para mexico donde llegaron en
vn dia, y en vna noche a dar la nueua a

They embarked in some canoes and
went to the ships, saying among themselves, "We are here to watch over this
coast; we need to know for certain what
this is so that we can take a true report to
Moteucçoma."
Then they got in the canoes and began
to row toward the ships. And when they
arrived next to the ships and saw the Spaniards, they all kissed the prows of the
canoes as a sign of worship. They thought
it was the god Quetzalcoatl who was returning, whom they had been and are expecting, as appears in the history of this
god. [15]
Then the Spaniards spoke to them, saying, "Who are you? Where [16] are you
coming from? Where is your home?"
Those who were in the canoes answered, "We have come from Mexico."
The Spaniards said to them, "If it is true
that you are Mexica, tell us, what is the
name of the ruler of Mexico?"
They answered them, "Our lords, the
ruler of Mexico is named Moteucçoma."
Then they presented to them everything they had brought. Some of those rich
cloaks they had brought were called *xiuhtlalpilli,* others *tecomayo,* others *xahual-
quauhyo,* others *ecacozcayo,* others *tolecyo* or
*amalacayo,* others *tezcapocyo.* They gave all
these kinds of cloaks to the person who
went in charge in those ships, who according to what they say was Grijalva.
And the Spaniards gave the Indians glass
beads, some of them green and others yellow, and when the Indians saw them they
marveled greatly, esteeming them highly.
They took leave of the Indians, saying,
"Now we are returning to Castile, but
soon we will come back and go to Mexico."
The Indians went back to land, and then
they departed for Mexico, where they arrived in a day and a night to give the news

in iveliaca [19] quilhuico, quicaquitico: intlatqui oalmochiuhtia in oquicuito.

Auh niman ie ic quinonotza. Totecuioe,
notelpotzine, ma xitechmotlatlatili ca iz
catqui otiquittaque, iz catqui oticchiuhque, ca in vmpa mitzonmotlapielilia in
moculhoan, in teuatl ixco. Ca otiquimit-
tato in totecuioan, in teteu in atl itic: in ixquich motilmatzin otiquinmacato: auh iz
catqui techmacaque intlatquitzi. [fol. 5]
Quitoque; intla nelli vmpa oanoallaque
mexico, iz catqui anquimacazque in
tlatoani Motecuçoma, ic techiximatiz:
much iuh quilhuique, in iuh quimilhuique
atl itic.

Auh in Motecuçoma quimilhui, oan-
quihiovique, oanquiciauhque: ximocevicã,
ca onontlachix in topco, petlacalco; aiac tle
quitoz, aiac tle contenquixtiz, aiac tle con-
chitoniz, aiac tle concamacaoaz, aiac qui-
teneoaz, çan amitic.

form Moteucçoma, to tell him and report
to him the truth [. . .]. [19] They took the
goods they had received.

Then they spoke to him: "O our lord, o
master, destroy us [if you will, but] here is
what we have seen and done at the place
where your subordinates stand guard for
you beside the ocean. For we went to see
our lords the gods out on the water; we
gave them all your cloaks, and here are the
fine things belonging to them that they
gave us. They said, 'If you have really
come from Mexico, here is what you are
to give to the ruler Moteucçoma, whereby
he will recognize us.' " They told him everything [the Spaniards] had told them out
on the water.

And Moteucçoma said to them, "You
are doubly welcome; take your rest. What
I have seen is a secret. No one is to say
anything, to let it escape from his lips, to
let a word slip out, to open his mouth, to
mention it, but it is to stay inside you."

3

Inic ei capitulo: vncan mitoa in tlein ic
tlanaoati Motecuçoma in iquac oquicac
intlatol, in iehoantin in quittaque acalli in
achto valla.

In motecuçoma, niman ie ic q̃nnaoatia
in Cuetlaxtecatl, yoan in izquintin: quimilhui. Xitlanaoaticã, ma tlapielo, in noviã
atenco; inic mitoa. Nauhtlan Toztlan, [21]
mictlanquauhtla: in campa ie quiçaquivi:
nimã ic iaque in calpixque, tlanaoatique
inic tlapieloia.

Auh in motecuçoma: quincentlali in
itecuioan, Cioacoatl, Tlilpotonqui, Tlacochcalcatl, Quappiaztzin, [fol. 5v]

Third chapter, where it is said what
Moteucçoma ordered when he heard the
statement of those who saw the first boat
that came.

Thereupon Moteucçoma gave instructions to the man from Cuetlaxtlan and the
rest, telling them, "Give orders that watch
be kept everywhere along the coast, at [the
places] called Nauhtlan, Toztlan, [21] and
Mictlanquauhtla, wherever they will come
to land." Then the stewards left and gave
orders for watch to be kept.

And Moteucçoma assembled his lords,
the Cihuacoatl Tlilpotonqui, the Tlacochcalcatl Quappiaztzin, the Ticocyahuacatl

Motecuçoma, de lo que auian visto: y truxeronle las cuētas, que les auian dado los españoles,

y dixeronle desta manera. Señor nuestro dignos somos de muerte, oye lo que emos visto: y lo que emos hecho. Tu nos posiste en guarda a la orilla de la mar emos visto, vnos dioses dentro en la mar, y fuymos a recebirlos, y dimosles vuestras mantas ricas: y veys aqui lo que nos dieron, estas cuentas: y dixeronnos, si es verdad que soys mexicanos, veys aq̃ [fol. 5] estas cuentas, daldas a Motecuçoma para que nos conozca: y dixeronle todo lo que auia pasado, q̃n [20] estuuieron con ellos en la mar en los nauios.

Respondioles Motecuçoma y dixoles Venis cansados y fatigados yos a descansar yo e recibido esto en secreto, yo os mando que a nadie digays nada de lo que ha pasado

to Moteucçoma of what they had seen, and they brought him the beads that the Spaniards had given them.

They spoke to him as follows: "Our lord, we deserve death. Hear what we have seen and what we have done. You set us to watch the seashore; we have seen some gods in the sea, and we went to receive them and gave them your rich cloaks. You see here what they gave us, these beads, and they told us, 'If you are really Mexica, here are these beads; give them to Moteucçoma so that he will know us.'" And they told him everything that had happened when [20] they were with them in the ships on the sea.

Moteucçoma replied, saying to them, "You come tired and worn out; go and rest. I have received this in secret; I order you not to say anything to anyone about what has happened."

3

Capitulo tercero de lo que Motecuçoma proueyo despues q̃ oyo la Relacion de los que vieron los primeros nauios.

Third chapter, of what Moteucçoma decreed after he heard the account of those who saw the first ships.

Como vuo oydo Motecuçoma las nueuas de los que vinieron de la mar mando luego llamar al mas principal dellos que se llamaua Cuetlaxtecatl y los demas que auian venido con la mensajeria y mandolos que pusiesen guardas y atalayas en todas las estancias de la ribera de la mar. La vna se llama Nauhtlan toztlan otra mictlanquactla [22] para que mirasen q̃n boluiesen aquellos nauios para q̃ [fol. 5v] luego diesen relacion con esto se partieron los

When Moteucçoma had heard the news of those who came from the sea, he immediately had summoned the highest ranking of them, named Cuetlaxtecatl, and the rest who had come with the message, and ordered them to place guards and lookouts in all the small settlements of the seacoast— one is called Nauhtlan Toztlan, another Mictlanquauhtla [22]—in order to be looking out for when those ships should return, so that then they would report on it. With

Ticociaoacatl, Quetzalaztatzin, Vitznaoa-
tlailotlac, hecatenpatiltzin: quincaquiti in
tlatolli, yoan quimittiti, quimixpanti in
quioalcuique cozcatl:

quimilhui. Ca oticmaviçoque in matlal-
teuxivitl, vel mopiaz, in tlatlatique vel qui-
piazque: intla centetl quichitonizque toca-
cal, topipilhoan, titeheoan.


Auh niman ie mocuepa in xivitl, ie
imonamicioc in matlactli omei tochtli: auh
ie tlamiznequi, ie itzonquizian in xivitl
omei tochtli, in quiçaco, in ie no ceppa ittoque. Auh niman quinonotztivetzico in
Motecuçoma;

in oquicac, niman iciuhca tlaioa, in iuh
quima, in iuh moma, ca iehoatl in topiltzin
Quetzalcoatl in oquiçaco: ca iuh catca iniollo in çan oallaz, in çan quiçaquiuh, qui-
oalmatiz in ipetl, in icpal: ipampa ca
vmitztia, in iquac ia. Auh in quimioa macuiltin, in quinamiquitivi, in quitla-
mamacativi: in teiacantia Teuoa, in
itecutoca, in ipiltoca Ioalli ichan. Inic vme
Tepuztecatl. Inic ei, tiçaoa. Inic navi
vevetecatl. Inic macuilli Veicamecatl heca.

Quetzalaztatzin, and the Huitznahuatlailotlac Ecatenpatiltzin. He reported the
account to them, and showed them, put
before them, the beads they had brought.

He said to them, "We have beheld the
fine blue turquoise; it is to be guarded
well, the custodians are to take good care
of it; if they let one piece get away from
them, [their] homes, children, and women
with child will be ours."

Then the year changed to the one following, Thirteen Rabbit, and when it was
nearly over, at the end of the year Thirteen
Rabbit, [the Spaniards] made an appearance and were seen once again. Then the
stewards quickly came to tell Moteucçoma.

When he heard it, he quickly sent out a
party. He thought and believed that it was
Topiltzin Quetzalcoatl who had landed.
For they were of the opinion that he
would return, that he would appear, that
he would come back to his seat of authority, because he had gone in that direction
[eastward] when he left. And [Moteuc-
çoma] sent five [people] to go to meet him
and give him things. The leader had the
official title of Teohua [custodian of the
god] and the personal name of Yohualli
ichan. The second was Tepoztecatl, the
third Tiçahua, the fourth Huehuetecatl,
and the fifth Hueicamecatl eca.

<hr />

4

[fol. 6] Inic naui capitulo: vncan mitoa
in tlein ic tlaonaoati[26] Motecuçoma, in
oquima in quenin çan oalmocuepque Españoles, inic vppa oallaque, iehoatl in don
hernando Cortes.

Fourth chapter, where it is said what orders[26] Moteucçoma gave when he found
out that the Spaniards had returned. The
second time they came it was [with] don
Hernando Cortés.

calpisques o capitanes y mandaron luego poner atalayas en las dichas estancias.

Y Motecuçoma junto luego sus principales, vno que se llamaua Cioacoatl. Otro Tlilpotonqui otro Tlacochcalcatl otro Quappiatzin otro Ticociaoacatl otro Quetzalaztatzin otro Vitznaoatlaylotlac otro Hecatempatiltzin. A todos estos comunico las nueuas que ausan²³ llegado y mostrolos las cuentas de vidro que auian traydo los mensajeros, y dixolos

pareceme que son piedras preciosas quardense²⁴ mucho en la recamara no se pierda ninguna y si alguna perdiere pagarla an los que tienen cargo de guardar la recamara.

Desta ay a vn año en el año de treze conejos vieron en la mar nauios los que estauan en las atalayas y luego vinieron dar mandado a Motecuçoma con gran priesa

como oyo la nueua Motecuçoma despacho luego gente para el recibimiento de Quetzalcoatl porque penso que era el el que venia porque cada dia le estauā esperando y como tenia relacion q̄ Quetzalcoatl auia ydo por la mar hazia el oriēte y los nauios veniā de hazia el oriente por esto pēsarō q̄ era el, enbio cinco p̄ncipales a que le recibiesen y le presentasē vna grā presente que le ēbio de lo²⁵ que fuerō el mas principal dellos que se llamaua yoalli ichā 2º tepuztecatl el 3º tiçaoa. y el 4º Veuetecatl. y el 5º Veicamecatl heca.

this the *calpisques* or captains departed and immediately ordered that lookouts be put in the said settlements.

Then Moteucçoma assembled his leaders, one of whom was called Cihuacoatl, another Tlilpotonqui, another Tlacochcalcatl, another Quappiatzin, another Ticocyahuacatl, another Quetzalaztatzin, another Huitznahuatlailotlac, and another Ecatempatiltzin. To all these he communicated the news that had²³ arrived, and he showed them the glass beads that the messengers had brought, telling them,

"These appear to me to be precious stones; let them be guarded²⁴ well in the chamber. Let none be lost, and if any is lost, those who are in charge of guarding the chamber will pay for it."

A year from that time, in the year of Thirteen Rabbits, those who were at the viewpoints saw ships in the sea and right away came in a great hurry to give notice to Moteucçoma.

When Moteucçoma heard the news, he immediately sent people for the reception of Quetzalcoatl, because he thought it was him who was coming, because they were expecting him daily. And because they had accounts that Quetzalcoatl had gone by sea toward the east, and the ships came from the direction of the east, they thought it was him. Moteucçoma sent five leaders to receive him and give him a great present that he sent him. The highest ranking of those²⁵ who went was named Yohualli ichan, the second Tepoztecatl, the third Tiçahua, the fourth Huehuetecatl, and the fifth Hueicamecatl eca.

4

[fol. 6] Capitulo .4. de lo que proueyo Motecuçoma quando supo la segunda vez que los Españoles auian buelto: este fue don hernando cortes.

Fourth chapter, of what Moteucçoma decreed when he found out that the Spaniards had returned a second time; this was don Hernando Cortés.

Quimilhui tla xioalhuian moceloquichtle, tla xioalhuian quil ie quene oquiçaco
in totecuio tla xicnamiquiti, vel xitlacaqui-
can, vel xinacaçocan, tlein quitoz, vel nacaztli in anquioalcuizque: iz catqui ic itech
amacizque in totecuio.

He said to them, "Come, o men of
unique valor, do come. It is said that our
lord has appeared at last. Do go to meet
him; listen well, make good use of your
ears, bring back in your ears a good record
of what he says. Here is what you will take
to our lord."

iehoatl in itlatqui Quetzalcoatl: coa-
xaiacatl, xiuhtica tlachioalli, Quetzalapanecaiotl, chalchiuhcozcapetlatl nepantla
mantiuh teucuitlacomalli, yoan centetl
chimalli, teucuitlatica nenepaniuhqui,
anoço teucuitlatica epnepaniuhqui, quetzaltençouhqui, yoā quetzalpanio; yoan
tezcacuitlapilli quetzallo: auh inin tezcacuitlapilli, iuhquin xiuhchimallo tlaxiuh-
tzacutli, xiuhtica tlatzacutli, tlaxiuhçalolli,
yoan chalchiuhcuecuextli, teucuitlacoiol-
lotoc: niman ie iehoatl xioatlatl, çan motquitica xivitl, iuhquin coatzontecome[fol.
6v]tica,²⁷ coatzontecome, yoan itzcactli.

[First] were the appurtenances of Quetzalcoatl: a serpent mask, made of turquoise; a quetzal-feather head fan; a plaited
neckband of green-stone beads, with a
golden disk in the middle of it; and a shield
with gold [strips] crossing each other, or
with gold and seashells crossing, with quetzal feathers spread about the edge and
with a quetzal-feather banner; and a mirror
with quetzal feathers to be tied on his back;
and this mirror for the back seemed to
have a turquoise shield, with turquoise
glued on it, and there were green-stone
neck bands with golden shells on them;
then there was the turquoise spear
thrower, entirely of turquoise, with a kind
of serpent head;²⁷ and there were obsidian
sandals.

A los sobredichos hablo Motecuçoma y los dixo. Mirad que me an dicho que a llegado nuestro señor Quetzalcoatl yd y recebilde y oyd lo que os dixere con mucha diligencia mirad que no se os oluide nada de lo que os dixere veys aqui estas joyas que le presenteys de mi parte que son todos los atauios sacerdotales que a el le conuienen

primeramente vna mascara labrada de mosayco de turquesas tenia esta mascara labrada de las mismas piedras vna culebra doblada y retorcida cuya dublez era el pico de la nariz y lo retorcido yua hasta la frente era como lomo de la nariz luego se diuidia la cola de la cabeça y la cabeça con parte del cuerpo yua por sobre el vn ojo de manera que hazia ceja y la cola com parte del cuerpo yua por sobre el otro ojo y hazia otra ceja. Estaua esta mascara enxerida en vna corona alta y grāde llena de plumas ricas largas y muy hermosas de manera que poniendose la corona sobre la cabeça se ponia la mascara en la cara lleuaua por joel vna medalla de oro redonda y ancha estaua asida con nueue sartales [fol. 6v] de piedras preciosas que echadas al cuello cubrian los hombros y todo el pecho: lleuauā tanbien vna rodela grande bordada de piedras preciosas con vnas vandas de oro que llegauan de arriba abaxo por toda ella: y otras vandas de perlas atrauesadas sobre las de oro de arriba abaxo por toda ella y los espacios que haziā estas vandas los quales eran como mallas de red yvan puestos vnos sapitos de oro tenia esta rodela vnos rapacejos en lo baxo yva asido en la rodela vna vandera que salia deste la manixa de la rodela hecha de plumas ricas lleuaua tanbien vna medalla grande hecha de obra de mosaico que la lleuaua atada y ceñida sobre los lomos lleuauā tanbien vnos sartales de piedras preciosas cō vnos cascaueles de oro entrepuestos a las piedras para atar a la garganta de los pies lleuauā tanbien vn cetro como cetro de obispo todo labrado de obra

Moteucçoma spoke to the above-mentioned, telling them, "Listen, I have been told that our lord Quetzalcoatl has arrived; go to receive him, and listen with great care to what he should say to you. See to it that you forget nothing he tells you. You see here these jewels that you are to present to him on my behalf, which are all the priestly accoutrements proper to him."

First, a mask of turquoise mosaic work; this mask had, worked in the same stone, a snake folded upon itself and twisted, the bend of which was the tip of the nose, and the twisted part went as far as the forehead and was like the bridge of the nose; then the tail and the head went in different directions, and the head with one part of the body went over one eye in such a way that it formed an eyebrow, and the tail with part of the body went over the other eye, making another eyebrow. This mask was set in a large high crown, full of very beautiful, long, rich plumes, so that when one put the crown on one's head one also put the mask on one's face. It bore as an ornament a round, wide medallion of gold, attached to nine strings of precious stones that, when placed at the neck, covered the shoulders and the whole chest. They also took a large, round shield, embroidered with precious stones, with some golden bands that reached across its whole extent, from top to bottom, and other bands of pearls crossing over those of gold, from top to bottom over the whole extent; and in the spaces between these bands, which were like the mesh of a net, some little golden toads were placed. This shield had edgings below, and attached to the shield was a banner that projected from the handle, made of rich plumes. It also bore a large medallion made of mosaic work that they wore tied and girded at the small of the back. They also took some strings of precious stones, with some small golden bells interspersed among the stones, to be

Cortés = Quetzalcoatl

Inic vntlamantli quimacato, iehoatl in itlatqui catca Tezcatlipuca: hivitzoncalli, coztic teucuitlatica cicitlallo, yoan iteo-cuitlacoiolnacoch; yoan chipolcozcatl; elpan cozcatl, cilin ic tlatlatlamachilli, ic tenchaiaoac; yoan xicolli, çan tlacuilolli, in itenixio, hivitica tenpoçonqui: yoan cen-tetl tilmatli, xiuhtlalpilli, motocaiotiaia; tzitzilli, quioalnacazvitzana inic mocui-tlalpia: no ipan mantiuh tezcacuitlapilli: yoā oc no centlamātli, teucuitlacoiolli, itlanitzco molpiaia, yoā centlamantli, iztac cactli.

The second set of things they went to give him were the appurtenances of Tez-catlipoca: a feather headpiece, covered with golden stars, and his golden bell ear-plugs; and a seashell necklace; the chest or-nament, decorated with many small sea-shells, with its fringe made of them; and a sleeveless jacket, painted all over, with eyes on its border and teased feathers at the fringe; and a cloak with blue-green knots, called a *tzitzilli,* tied on the back by taking its corners, also with a mirror for the back over it; and another item, golden bells tied to the calves of the legs; and another item, white sandals.

Inic etlamantli, iehoatl in inechichioal catca, Tlalocā tecutli: quetzalaztatzontli, çā moca quetzalli, motquitica quetzalli, iuh-quin xoxoquivi, xoxoquiuhtimani: auh in ipan teucuitlatica epnepaniuhqui; yoan ichalchiuhcoanacoch; ixicol, tlachalchiuh-icuilolli: in icozqui chalchiuhcozcapetlatl no teucuitlacomallo, no tezcacuitlapile, in iuhqui omito, no tzitzile; tenchilnaoacaio in til[fol. 7]matli inic molpia: yoan icxicoi-olli teucuitlatl: yoan icoatopil, xiuhtica tla-chiuhtli.

Third was the outfit of the lord of Tlalo-can: the heron-feather headdress full of quetzal feathers, entirely of quetzal feath-ers, like a blue-green sheet, and over it [a strip of] shells crossed with [a strip of] gold; and his green-stone serpent earplugs; his sleeveless jacket sprinkled with green-stone; his necklace was a plaited green-stone neckband, also with a gold disk, also with a mirror for the back, as was said before, also with a *tzitzilli;* the cape to tie on, with red rings at the border; and

de mosayco de tosquesas [28] y la buelta de arriba era vna cabeça de vna culebra rebuelta o enroscada. Tanbiē lleuauā vnas cotaras como los grādes señores se las suelen poner.

2ọ lleuaron tanbien los ornamentos o atauios con que se atauiaua Tezcatlipuca que era vna cabellera hecha de pluma rica que colgaua por la parte de tras hasta cerca de la cintura estaua sembrada toda de estrellas de oro, lleuauan tanbien vnas orejeras de oro que lleuauā colgadas vnos [fol. 7] cascauellitos de oro y sartales de caracolitos marinos blancos y hermosos destos sartales colgaua vn cuero que era como peto y lleuauale cenido de manera que cubria todo el pecho hasta la cintura, lleuaua este peto muchos caracolitos sembrados y colgados por todo el: lleuauā tanbien vn cosete de tela blanca pintado la orilla de abaxo deste cosete yva bordada com plumas blancas tres listas por todo el rededor: lleuauā vna manta rica la tela della era vn açul claro y toda labrada encima de muchos labores de vn açul muy fino llamauase esta manta tzitzilli esta manta se ponia por la cintura atada por las esquinas al cuerpo sobre esta manta, yva vna medalla de mosayco, atada al cuerpo sobre los lomos. Tābien lleuauā vnos sartales de cascaueles de oro para atar a las gargantas de los pies: y tambien vnas cotaras blancas, como los señores las solian traer.

lleuaron tanbien los atauios, y ornamentos, del dios que llamauan tlalocan tecutli, que era vna mascara con su plumaje, como la que se dixo arriba, con vna vādera, como la que arriba se dixo. Tambien vnas orejeras de chalchiuitl, anchas que tenia dētro vnas culebritas de chalchiuites: y tanbien vn cosete pintado de labores verdes, y vnos sartales, o collar de piedras preciosas, con vna medalla de piedras preciosas: y tanbien lleuauan vna medalla, con que se cenia los lomos, como la que arriba se dixo, con vna

tied above the ankles. They also took a scepter, like a bishop's scepter, all covered with turquoise [28] mosaic work, and the hook above was a head of a snake twisted or coiled. They also took some sandals like those the great lords are accustomed to wear.

Second, they also took the ornaments or accoutrements with which Tezcatlipoca was outfitted, which was a headpiece made of rich plumes hanging down behind nearly to the waist, all sprinkled with golden stars. They also took some golden earplugs, from which hung some little golden bells and strings of small, beautiful white seashells. From these strings hung a hide that was like a breastplate; they wore it attached in such a way that it covered the chest down to the waist. This breastplate bore many small seashells hung sprinkled all over it. They also took a corselet of painted white cloth; the lower edge of this corselet had embroidered on it three strips of white feathers going all around. They took a rich cloak, the cloth of which was a light blue; it was embroidered above with many designs of a very fine blue. This cloak was called a *tzitzilli*. This cloak was placed at the waist, tied by its corners to the body. Over this cloak went a mosaic medallion, tied to the body at the small of the back. They also took some strings of small golden bells to be tied above the ankles, and also some white sandals such as the lords used to wear.

They also took the accoutrements and ornaments of the god whom they called Tlalocan teuctli, which was a mask with its plumage, like the one mentioned above, with a banner, like the one abovementioned. Also some wide earplugs of *chalchihuitl*, which had inside some little snakes of *chalchihuitl* stone. Also a painted corselet with green embroidery, and some strings of precious stones, or necklace, with a medallion of precious stones. And they also took a medallion girded on at the

Inic nauhtlamantli çan ie no iehoatl in itlatqui catca Quetzalcoatl, ie ne cen-tlamantli: Ocelocopilli, coxoliio; veitepul in chalchivitl yicpac ca ic quatzacutica; yoan xiuhnacochtli, malacachtic, itech pil-catica teucuitlaepcololli; yoan chalchiuh-cozcapetlatl, çanno teucuitlacomalli in ine-pantla mantia; yoan tilmatli tentlapallo inic molpia; çanno teucuitlacoiolli in icxi itech monequia: yoan chimalli teucuitlatica iti-xapo, quetzaltençouhqui, no quetzalpanio: yoã hecaxonecuilli, quacoltic, iztac chal-chivitl inic citlallotoc, yoan ipoçolcac.

O ca izquitlamãtli in, in moteneoa teu-tlatquitl, in intlatqui mochiuhtia titlanti, yoan oc cenca miec tlamantli in quit-quique in intenamiquia Teucuitlaquatec-ciztli toztlapilollo, teucuitlacopilli .&.

Niman ie ic tlatanatemalo, tlacacaxchi-chioalo. Auh in omoteneuhque macuiltin; niman ie ic quinnaoatia in Motecu[fol. 7v]coma: [32] quimilhui. Tla xivian, ma cana anvecauhti, xicmotlatlauhtilican [33] in tote-cuio in teutl: xiquilhuican, ca otechalioa in motechiuhcauh Motecuçoma: iz catqui mitzalmomaquilia, ca omaxitico in ichã-tzinco mexico:

golden bells for the feet; and his serpent staff made of turquoise.

Fourth were likewise appurtenances of Quetzalcoatl, but of a different kind: a miter of jaguar skin, covered with pheasant feathers; a very large green-stone at the top of it, glued on the tip; and round turquoise earplugs, from which hung curved golden seashells; and a plaited green-stone neck-band, likewise with a golden disk in the middle of it; and a cloak to tie on, with a border dyed red; likewise, golden bells used on his feet; and a shield with gold in-serted in it, with quetzal feathers spread along its edge, also with a quetzal-feather banner; and the curved staff of the wind [god], bent at the top, sprinkled with white green-stone stars; and his foam sandals.

These then were the things, called gods' appurtenances, that the messengers carried with them, and they took many other things by way of greeting: a shell-shaped gold headpiece with yellow parrot feathers hanging from it, a golden miter, etc.

Then baskets were filled and carrying frames were adjusted. And then Moteuc-çoma [32] gave orders to the aforementioned five [emissaries], saying to them, "Now go, don't tarry anywhere, and address yourselves to [33] our lord the god. Tell him, 'Your agent Moteucçoma has sent us; here is what he is giving you. You have arrived in Mexico, your home.'"

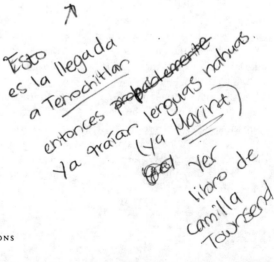

manta rica con que se cenia, como se dixo arriba, y cascaueles de oro pa poner a los pies, y su baculo como el de arriba.

[fol. 7v] Otros ornamentos, tanbien que llamauan era del mismo. Quetzalcoatl, vna mitra de cuero de tigre, y colcagaua [29] de la mitra, sobre las espaldas, vna capilla grande, hecha de plumas de cueruo, lleuaua la mitra vn chalchiuitl grāde: y redondo, en la punta. Y tambien vnas orejeras redondas, de mosayco de turquesas con vn garauato de oro, que salia de la orejera, lleuauan tanbien, vn collar de oro, del qual colgaua vna medalla de oro, que llaman hecacozcatl, y vna manta rica, con que se cenia, y vnos cascaueles de oro para los pies, y vna rodela q̄ tenia en el medio vna plancha de oro redonda: la qual rodela estaua bordada com plumas ricas en lo baxo de la rodella [30] salia vna vanda de plumas ricas en la forta [31] que se dixo arriba lleuaua vn baculo labrado de mosayco de turquesas y en la buelta de arriba puestas vnas piedras ricas o perlas enminentes en lo alto de arriba. Tanbien, lleuauan vnas cotaras, como los señores las solian traer:

Todas estas cosas lleuauā los mensajeros y las presentaron segun dizen a don Hernando cortes, otras muchas cosas le presentaron que no se escriuen como fue vna mitra de oro hecha a manera de caracol marisco cō vnos rapacejos de plumas ricas que colgauan hazia las espaldas y otra mitra llana: Tanbiē de oro, y otras joias de oro que no se escriuen.

Todas estas cosas metieron en sus petacas, y tomada la licencia de Motecuçoma dixoles yd cō priesa y no os detengays y adorad en mi nombre al dios que viene, y dezilde aca nos a embiado v̄ro sieruo Motecuçoma, estas cosas que aqui traemos os embia pues aveys venido a v̄ra casa que es mexico.

small of the back, like the one mentioned above, with a rich cloak girded on as was said above, and small golden bells to be put at the feet, and his staff like the one above.

Other ornaments that they took belonged to Quetzalcoatl as well: a miter of jaguar skin, and from the miter hung [29] onto the shoulders a large hood made of crow feathers; the miter bore a large round *chalchihuitl* at its tip. Also some round earplugs of turquoise mosaic, with a golden hook coming from the earplug. They also took a golden necklace, from which hung a gold medallion that they call an *ecacozcatl,* and a rich cloak to gird around one, and some small golden bells for the feet, and a round shield that had a round plate of gold in the middle. This shield was edged with rich plumes; from the lower part of the shield [30] projected a band of rich plumes in the fashion [31] mentioned above. They took a staff encrusted with turquoise mosaic, and in the curve above were set some rich stones or fine pearls, in the highest part of the top. They also took some sandals such as the lords used to wear.

The messengers took all these things and presented them, according to what they say, to don Hernando Cortés. They presented to him many other things not written here, such as a golden miter made in the fashion of a seashell, with some edgings of rich plumes that hung down toward the shoulders, and another plain miter, also of gold, and other gold jewels not written down.

They put all these things in their containers, and as they took leave of Moteucçoma he told them, "Go quickly, do not dally, and in my name worship the god who is coming. Tell him, 'Your servant Moteucçoma has sent us here. He sends you these things that we carry here, for you have come to your home, which is Mexico.'"

Auh in oacito atenco, quimōpanavique, acaltica quimonvicaque in xicalanco: ie no ceppa vncan oneoaq̄ acaltica quinvicaque in atlaca, moch onmacalaqui, onmacalten, conacaltenque in tlatquitl. Auh in ontla-acaltemaloc, niman ie ic vi, ommatoctique, itech onacito in imacal, itech compachoque in imacal.

nimā quinoalilhuique. Ac ameoan? campa anoallaque?

niman iuh quinnanquilique. Ca vmpa tioallaque in Mexico:
oc ceppa quinoalilhuique. Acaçomo, aço çan vmpa anmotlamia, aço çan anquipiqui, aço çā toca anmocacaiaoa.

Auh in o vel yiollo macic, in o iniollo pachiuh. Niman ic quioaliacatzopinique in acalli, tepuztopiltica, ic quinoaltilinique: niman no quioalquetzque ecaoaztli.

5

[fol. 8] Inic macuilli capitulo: vncan mitoa in tlein muchiuh, in iquac ititlanoan motecuçoma in vmpa callacque in iacalco don hernando Cortes.

Niman ie ic tleco, quinanapalotivi in tlatquitl: in otlecoto acalco ceceniaca ontlalquatimani yixpan in capitan: Niman ie ic contlatlauhtia: quilhuique:

Ma quimocaquilti in teutl: ca quioalmotlatlauhtilia in itechiuhcauh Motecuçoma in cōmotlapielilia mexico; ca conitoa. Oquimihiovilti, oquimociavilti in teutl:

niman ie ic quichichioa in capitan vel iehoatl conaquique in xiuhcoaxaiacatl, itech ietiuh in quetzalapanecaiotl, yoan itech ieietiuh, itech aactiuh, itech pipil-

And when they reached the coast, they were taken across [a river or inlet] by boat at Xicalanco. There again they left by boat, taken by the water folk. Everything went into the boats; the goods were placed in boats. And when the boats were full, they left. They cast off and reached [the Spaniards'] boat[s], bringing their own boat close.

Then [the Spaniards] said to them, "Who are you? Where have you come from?"

Then [the emissaries] answered them, "Why, we have come from Mexico."

Again [the Spaniards] replied to them, "Perhaps not. Perhaps you are just claiming to be from there, perhaps you are making it up, perhaps you are deceiving us."

But when they were convinced and satisfied, they hooked the prow of the boat with an iron staff and hauled them in; then they also put down a ladder.

Fifth chapter, where it is said what happened when Moteucçoma's messengers went into don Hernando Cortés's boat.

Then they climbed up, carrying in their arms the goods. When they had gotten up into the boat, each of them made the earth-eating gesture before the Captain. Then they addressed him, saying,

"May the god attend: his agent Moteucçoma who is in charge in Mexico for him addresses him and says, 'The god is doubly welcome.' "

Then they dressed up the Captain. They put on him the turquoise serpent mask attached to the quetzal-feather head fan, to which were fixed, from which hung the

Tomarō luego el camino los mensajeros, y llegarō a la orilla de la mar, y alli entraron en canoas, y llegarō a v̄ lugar que se llama Xicalanco, dalli tornarō, otra uez a entrar ē otras canoas, cō todo su hato, y llegarō a los nauios;

luego los pregū̄tarō de los nauios. Quienes soys vosotros de dōde aveys venido:

dixerō los de la canoa, Venimos de mexico

y dixeron los de la nao. Por uētura no soys de mexico? Sino q̄ dezis cō falsedad q̄ soys de mexico y no os enganays.

Y sobre esto tomaron, y dierō y desq̄ se satisficierō lo vnos a los otros juntaron la canoa cōn el nauio y echarōlos vna escalera con q̄ subierō al nauio donde estaua don hernā̄do Cortes.

5
[fol. 8] Capitulo quinto de lo que paso quando los mensajeros de Motecuçoma entraron en el nauio del capitan don hernando cortes.

Començaron a subir al nauio, por la escalera: y lleuauan el presente que Motecuçoma. los mando lleuar como estuuieron delante de don Hernando cortes: besaron todos la tierra en su presencia, y hablaronse desta manera;

sepa el dios a quien venimos a adorar en persona de su sieruo Motecuçoma, el qual le rige, y gouierna, la su ciudad de mexico. Y dize a llegado con trabaxo el dios:

y luego sacarō los ornamentos que lleuauan: y se los pusieron al capitan don hernā̄do cortes atauiandole con ellos pusieronle primeramente la corona, y mas-

The messengers then took to the road, arriving at the seashore, where they entered canoes and reached a place called Xicalanco; from there they again entered in different canoes, with all their gear, and reached the ships.

Then they were asked from the ships, "Who are you, and where have you come from?"

Those in the canoe said, "We come from Mexico."

Those of the ship said, "Perhaps you are not from Mexico, but you are falsely saying that you are from Mexico and deceiving us."

They talked back and forth over this, and when each side had satisfied the other, they hauled the canoe to the ship and put down a ladder for them, with which they climbed up into the ship where don Hernando Cortés was.

Fifth chapter, of what happened when the messengers of Moteucçoma entered Captain don Hernando Cortés's ship.

They began to climb up into the ship by the ladder, carrying the presents that Moteucçoma had ordered them to take. When they were before don Hernando Cortés, they all kissed the ground in his presence and spoke to him in the following manner:

"May the god, whom we come to worship in person, know from his servant Moteucçoma, who rules and governs his city of Mexico for him, that he says that the god has had a difficult journey."

Then they took out the ornaments that they carried and put them on Captain don Hernando Cortés, outfitting him with them. First they put on him the crown and

catiuh chalchiuhcoanacochtli: yoan conaquique xicolli, conxicoltique, yoan con-
cozcatique in chalchiuhcozcapetlatl
nepantla mantiuh in teucuitlacomalli, ic
conxillancuitlalpique in tezcacuitlapilli, no
ic contzinapanque in tilmatli in itoca tzitzilli, yoan [fol. 8v] icxic contlalilique in
chalchiuhtecuecuextli teucuitlacoiollo:
yoan conmacaque imac cōmanilique chimalli teucuitlatica nenepaniuhqui, yoan
epnepaniuhcaio, quetzaltençouhtiuh que-
tzalpaniotiuh: yoan ixpā contemilique itzcactli.

Auh in oc etlamantli nechichioalli, teu-
tlatquitl, çan ixpan contecpāque, con-
vipanque:

auh in ie iuhqui, quimilhui in capitā.
Cuix ie ixquich in, in amotenamiquia, in
amotetechacia?

quinnanquilique ca ie ixquich inic tioal-
latiaque totecue.

Niman tlanaoati in capitan inic il-
piloque, tepoztli imicxic quintlalilique,
yoan inquechtlan: in ie iuhqui niman ic
quitlazque in tomaoac tlequiquiztli: auh in
titlanti in iquac in vel iolmicque, yoan
çoçotlaoaque, vehuetzque, nenecuiliuh-
tivetzque, aocmo quimatque: auh in españoles quimeeuhq̄ quimecoatitlalique,
quimoniitique vino: nimā ie ic quintla[fol.
9]maca, quintlaqualtique, ic imihio quicuique, ic oalihiocuique:

auh in ie iuhqui in, niman quimilhui in
capitan. Tla xiccaquican, onicma, oniccac,
quilmach in iehoantin mexica cenca chicaoaque, cenca tiacaoan, cenca maiavini,
intla ce mexicatl vel quintocaz, vel quin-
topeoaz, vel quinpanaviz, vel quinteputztiz
in manel matlactin, in manel noço centec-
pantin in iiaovan. Auh in axcan noiollo pa-
chiviznequi, namechittaznequi, namech-
ieiecoznequi, in quenin anchicaoaque, in
quenin antlapalivi; nimā ic quinoalmacac
coachimalli, yoan tepuzmacquavitl, yoā
tepuztopilli:

green-stone serpent earplugs. And they put
the sleeveless jacket on him, and around
his neck they put the plaited green-stone
neckband with the golden disk in the middle. On his lower back they tied the back
mirror, and also they tied behind him the
cloak called a *tzitzilli*. And on his legs they
placed the green-stone bands with the
golden bells. And they gave him, placing it
on his arm, the shield with gold and shells
crossing, on whose edge were spread quetzal feathers, with a quetzal banner. And
they laid the obsidian sandals before him.

And the other three outfits, the gods'
appurtenances, they only arranged in rows
before him.

*Cortes*

When this had been done, the Captain
said to them, "Is this everything you have
by way of greeting and rapprochement?"

They answered, "That is all with which
we have come, o our lord."

Then the Captain ordered that they be
tied up; they put irons on their feet and
necks. When this had been done they shot
off the cannon. And at this point the messengers truly fainted and swooned; one
after another they swayed and fell, losing
consciousness. And the Spaniards lifted
them into a sitting position and gave them
wine to drink. Then they gave them food,
fed them, with which they regained
strength and got their breath back.

When this had been done the Captain
said to them, "Do listen, I have found out
and heard that by what they say these
Mexica are very strong, great warriors, able
to throw others down. Where there is one
of them he can chase, push aside, overcome, and turn back his enemies, even
though there should be ten or twenty.
Now I wish to be satisfied, I want to see
you, I want to try out how strong and
manly you are." Then he gave them
leather shields, iron swords, and iron
lances. [He said,]

cara que arriba se dixo: y todo lo demas
echarōle al cuello los collares de piedras
que lleuauā con los joeles de oro pusieronle en el braço yzquierdo, la rodela de q̄ se
dixo arriba:

y todas las otras cosas se las pusierō delante ordenadas como suelen poner sus
presentes

el capitan les dixo. Ay otra cosa mas que
esto?

dixerole señor nuestro, no emos traydo
mas cosas destas que aq̄ estan.


El capitan mandolos luego atar: y mando
soltar tiros de artilleria, y los mensajeros
que estauā atados de pies, y manos como
oyerō los truenos de las lombardas, cayeron
en el suelo, como muertos: y los españoles
leuātaronlos [fol. 8v] del suelo, y dieronles
a bever vino con que los esforçaron: y tornaron en si.

Despues desto el capitan don hernādo
cortes les dixo por su interprete oyd lo que
os digo: anme dicho que los mexicanos son
valientes hombres que son grandes pelea-
dores: y grādes luchadores son muy diestros en las armas dizenme que vn solo
mexicano es bastante para vencer a diez: y
a veynte de sus enemigos. [fol. 9] Quiero
prouaros, si es esto verdad si soys tan
fuertes como me an dicho: luego les mādo
dar espadas y rodelas para que peleasen con
otros tantos españoles para ver quien ven-
ceria a los otros.

mask mentioned above, and [then] all the
rest. They placed around his neck the
necklaces of stones with golden baubles.
On his left arm they placed the shield
mentioned above.

All the other things they put before him,
laid out as they customarily do with their
presents.

The captain said to them, "Is there anything more than this?"

They told him, "Our lord, we have not
brought more than the things that are
here."


Then the captain ordered them bound,
and he ordered the artillery pieces fired.
When the messengers, whose hands and
feet were tied, heard the thunder of the
cannon, they fell to the floor as if dead.
The Spaniards raised them from the floor
and gave them wine to drink, with which
they invigorated them, and they revived.

After this Captain don Hernando Cortés
told them through his interpreter, "Hear
what I tell you: I have been told that the
Mexica are valiant men, great battlers and
fighters, very dexterous with weapons.
They tell me that a single Mexica is
enough to overcome ten or twenty of his
enemies. I want to try you out and see if
this is true, if you are as strong as I have
been told." Then he ordered that they be
given swords and shields to fight with an
equal number of Spaniards to see who
would overcome the others.

auh inin vel oc iovatzinco, tlavizcalpan in muchioaz, in titomaiztlacozque, titone-neuhcavizque, tinevivicantlamatizque, ac ie tlani vetziz:

quinanquilique in Capitan: quilhuique. Tla quimocaquitin tlacatl, achcamo ic technaoati in itechiuhcauh in Motecu-çoma; ca çan tiquixcavico in tictociauh-quechi[fol. 9v]lico, in tictotlapalhuico, ca amo tonaoatil in quimonequiltia tlacatl: auh intla iuh ticchioazque, cuix amo cenca ic qualaniz in Motecuçoma, amo ic tech-tlatlatiz.

Niman quito in capitan ca amo ca ça mochioaz niquittaznequi, nicmaviçoz-nequi ca in omachiztito in castillan quil cenca anchicaoaque, antiiacaoan, ma oc veca ioac in xitlaquacan, oc no ioan in ni-tlaquaz, ma vel ximochichioacā.

"Well now, very early in the morning, as dawn is about to come, we will struggle against each other, we will challenge each other, we will find out by comparison who will fall down first."

They answered the Captain, saying, "May the lord pay heed, this is not at all what his agent Moteucçoma ordered us. All we came to do was to greet and salute you. We were not charged with what the lord wishes. If we should do that, won't Moteucçoma be very angry with us be-cause of it, won't he destroy us for it?"

Then the Captain said, "No indeed; it is simply to be done. I want to see and be-hold it, for word has gone to Spain that you are very strong, great warriors. Eat while it is still before dawn, and I will eat then too. Outfit yourselves well."

14

Y los mexicanos dixeron luego al capitā
don hernādo cortes, oyanos v̄ra merced n̄r̄a
escusa porque no podemos hazer lo que
nos mandays: y es porque Motecuçoma
n̄r̄o señor no nos embio a otra cosa sino a
saludaros y a daros este presente, no
podemo hazer otra cosa, ni podemos hazer
lo que nos mandays: y si lo hizieremos
enojarse a mucho n̄r̄o señor Motecuçoma,
y mandarnos a matar:

y el capitan res[fol. 9v]pondioles, ase de
hazer en todo caso lo que os digo tengo de
ver que hōbre soys: que alla en nuestra
tierra emos oydo que soys valientes hombres aparejaos con esas armas y disponeos
para que mañana luego de mañana nos
veamos en el campo.

Then the Mexica said to Captain don
Hernando Cortés, "May your grace hear
our excuse why we cannot do what you
order us, which is that Moteucçoma our
lord sent us here for nothing else than to
greet you and give you this present. We
cannot do anything else, nor can we do
what you order us. If we should do it, our
lord Moteucçoma would become greatly
angered and would have us killed."

The captain replied to them, "What I
tell you is to be done in any case. I must
see how manly you are, for in our land we
have heard that you are valiant men. Equip
yourself with these weapons and prepare
yourselves so that tomorrow, the first thing
in the morning, we will meet on the
field."

15

↑ cortés

Inic chiquacencapitulo: vncā mitoa, in quenin ititlanoan Motecuçoma, oalmocuepque in nican mexico quilhuico in motecuçoma in quittaque.

Sixth chapter, where it is said how Moteucçoma's messengers came back here to Mexico to tell Moteucçoma what they had seen.

Niman ie ic quincauh, quinoaltemovique in imacalco: auh in ovaltemoque acalco, niman ie ic tequitlaneloa, ontetemi in tlaneloa, cequintin matlaneloa. centlaquauh oalmotlaloa, quimolhuitivitze, tiacaoane ixquich amotlapal, xitequitlanelocan, ma itla nican taxti ma itla nican topan muchiuh:

[fol. 10] iciuhca acitivetzico in atl iitic in itocaiocan xicalanco, çan tequitl vncan oalihiocuitiquizq̄, ic ie no ceppa centlaquauh oaltotoca: niman acico in tecpan tlaiacac, niman ie no ic oalmeoaltia, oalmotlaloa, acitivetzico in cuetlaxtlan, çanno oalquiztiquizqueque, vncan ihiocuique.

Auh in cuetlaxtecatl quimilhui ma oc cemilhuitzintli ximocevicā ma oc amihio xiccuican.

Auh quilhuique, ca amo ca çan ticiuhtivi tictononochilizque in tlacatl tlatoani Motecuçoma, tictolhuilizque in tlein otiquittaque, in cenca temamauhti, in aic iuhqui omottac, cuix ie cuel ie teachto, toconcaquiz:
niman iciuhca oalpeuhque, acitivetzico in mexico, çan ioaltica in acico, çan oalioalcalacque.

Auh in iquac in aoquicochiz, aoquitlaqual quimatia, aoc ie quilhuiaia in çaço tlein quichioaia, ça iuhquin nentlamatia, iuhquin achica elcicivi, mociauhquetza, mociauhpoa, aoctle velic, aoctle tepac, aoctle teavialti ipan [fol. 10v] quimatia;

Then [Cortés] let them go. [The Spaniards] lowered them into their boat, and when they had descended into the boat, they paddled hard; each one paddled as hard as he could, and some used their hands to paddle. They fled with all possible speed, saying to one another as they came, "O warriors, exert all your strength, paddle hard! Let's not do something [wrong] here, lest something happen to us!"

By water they quickly reached the place called Xicalanco, where they did nothing but catch their breath, then again came running along as fast as possible. Then they reached Tecpantlayacac, whereupon they again left and came fleeing. They quickly got to Cuetlaxtlan, where they caught their breath and also quickly came away.

And the ⟨ruler or steward⟩ of Cuetlaxtlan said to them, "First take your rest for a day or so, until you recover your strength."

But they said to him, "No, rather we are going hurrying to talk to the lord ruler Moteucçoma, to tell him what we saw, these very terrifying things the like of which have never been seen. Should you be the very first to hear them?"

Then they quickly got on their way and soon reached Mexico. It was night when they got there; they came in by night.

During this time Moteucçoma neither slept nor touched food. Whatever he did, he was abstracted; it seemed as though he was ill at ease, frequently sighing. He tired and felt weak. He no longer found anything tasteful, enjoyable, or amusing.

## 6

Capitulo .6. de como los mensajeros de Motecuçoma boluieron a mexico con la relacion de lo que auian visto.

Chapter Six, of how Moteucçoma's messengers returned to Mexico with an account of what they had seen.

16

Hecho lo que esta dicho, luego se despidieron del capitan, y se baxarō a sus canoas, y començaron luego a yrse hazia tierra remando con gran priesa y diziendo los vnos a los otros: ea valientes hōbres esforçaos a remar antes que nos acontezca algo:

When the above-said had been done, they took leave of the captain, descended into their canoes, and immediately began to go paddling landward with great haste, telling one another, "Up and at it, brave men, paddle hard, before something happens to us!"

llegarō muy presto al pueblo de Xicalanco remādo alli comieron, y descansaron bien poco: y luego entrarō [fol. 10] otra uez en las canoas y con grā priesa remando llegaron al pueblo que se llama Tecpantlaiacac y de alli començaron a caminar por tierra corriendo con gran priesa y llegarō al pueblo que se lla³⁴ Cuetlaxtla alli comieron y descansaron poco:

Paddling along, they very quickly reached the settlement of Xicalanco; there they ate and rested a very short while. Then they reembarked in the canoes, and paddling with great haste reached the settlement called Tecpantlayacac. From there they commenced to travel by land, running with great haste. Reaching a settlement called ³⁴ Cuetlaxtlan, they ate there and rested little.

y los del pueblo les rogauā que descāsasen. Siquiera vn dia

The people of the settlement asked them to rest even for a day.

ellos les respondierō que no podian porque yuā cō grā priesa a hazer saber a Motecuçoma lo que auian visto cosas muy nueuas y nunca vistas ni oydas las quales a ninguno otro podian dezir

But they answered them that they could not because they were going with great haste to inform Moteucçoma what they had seen, very new things never seen or heard, which they could tell to no one else.

y caminando con gran priesa de noche y de dia, llegaron a mexico de noche.

Traveling with great haste night and day, they reached Mexico at night.

En el tiempo que estos mensajeros fueron y boluieron. Motecuçoma no podia comer ni dormir ni hazia de buena gana ninguna cosa, sino estaua muy triste: y suspiraua espesas vezes, estaua cō grā congoxa, ninguna cosa de pasatiempo le daua placer, ninguna cosa le daua contento,

In the time while these messengers went and returned, Moteucçoma was unable to eat or sleep or take joy in anything he did, but was very melancholy, sighing frequently; he suffered great anxiety, and no pastime gave him pleasure, nothing made him happy.

y dezia que sera de nosotros? quien a de çufrir estos trabaxos? ninguno otro sino yo! pues que soy señor y rey! que tengo cargo

He said, "What is to come of us? Who is to suffer these travails? None other than I, for I am lord and king who is in charge of

ipampa in quitoaia, tlein ie topan muchioaz, ac nel icac, ha ieppa nehoatl, [35] vel
patzmiqui in noiollo, iuhquin ma chil-
atequilo, vel toneoa chichinaca campanel
totecue.

Niman quimōnaoatique in quipia in
itzontlan tlapia quimonilhuique intla
mocochitia xicmolhuilican ca ovallaque
in tiquinmotitlani atl itic.

Auh in oconilhuito: niman quioalito.
Amo nican niccaquiz, vmpa niccaquiz in
coacalco, ma vmpa vian, yoan oallanaoati:
quioalito: ma onteticavilo in mamalti.

Auh niman vmpa iaque in coacalco in
titlanti: no iehoatl in motecucomatzin,
nimā ie ic imixpan micoa quimeltetequi in
mamalti, in imezio ic quimonatzelhuiaia in
titlanti (ipampa in iuh quichiuhque in, ca
cenca ovican in ovia ca oquimittato,
imixco imicpac otlachiato, vel oquin-
notzque in teteu.

Therefore he said, "What is to come of
us? Who in the world must endure it? Will
it not be me [as ruler]? [35] My heart is tor-
mented, as though chile water were
poured on it; it greatly burns and smarts.
Where in the world [are we to turn], o our
lord?"

Then [the messengers] notified those
who guarded [Moteucçoma], who kept
watch at the head of his bed, saying to
them, "Even if he is asleep, tell him,
'Those whom you sent out on the sea have
come back.' "

But when they went to tell him, he replied, "I will not hear it here. I will hear it
at the Coacalco; let them go there." And
he gave orders, saying, "Let some captives
be covered with chalk [for sacrifice]."

Then the messengers went to the Coacalco, and so did Moteucçoma. Thereupon the captives died in their presence;
they cut open their chests and sprinkled
their blood on the messengers. (The reason
they did it was that they had gone to very
dangerous places and had seen, gazed on
the countenances of, and spoken to the
gods.)

7

[fol. 11] Ic chicome capitulo: vncan
mitoa in tlatolli inic quinonotzato in
Motecuçoma, in titlanti in quittato acalli.

Seventh chapter, where is told the account that the messengers who went to see
the boat gave to Moteucçoma.

Auh in ie iuhqui, niman ie ic quinonotza in Motecuçoma iuh quilhuique in
iuhqui oquimaviçoto, yoan quittitique in
iuhqui intlaqual.

When this was done, they talked to Moteucçoma, telling him what they had beheld, and they showed him what [the
Spaniards'] food was like.

de todos! [fol. 10v] estaua su coraçon parecia que se leuauan[36] en agua de chilli, y ansi tenia grã tormento: y dezia O señor a donde yre? Como escapare?

llegando los mensajeros a donde estaua la guarda de Motecuçoma dixeronlos: aunque duerma n̄ro señor Motecuçoma desportade[37] y dezilde que somos venido de la ribera de la mar donde nos enbio:

luego los de la guarda le dixerō aquello: y el respondio no quiero oyr aqui las nueuas que traen alla quiero yr a la sala alla me hablarã vayanse alla: y luego mando que vntasen cō greda todo el cuerpo a ciertos captiuos para sacrificarlos:

los mensajeros fueronse a la sala: y tambien Motecuçoma se fue alla, y alli delante los mensajeros mataron los captiuos, y rociaron a los mensajeros con la sangre de los captiuos: hizieron esta cerimonia?[38] porque auian visto grãdes cosas: y auian visto a los dioses, y hablado con ellos.

everyone!" His heart seemed as though it had been washed[36] in chile water, and so he was greatly tortured. He said, "O lord, where am I to go? How am I to escape?"

When the messengers got to where Moteucçoma's guards were, they told them, "Even though our lord Moteucçoma should be sleeping, wake him[37] and tell him that we have come from the seashore where he sent us."

Then the guards told him, and he answered, "Here I don't want to hear the news they bring; I want to go to the hall; there they are to speak to me. Let them go there." Then he ordered that the whole bodies of certain captives be anointed with chalk for them to be sacrificed.

The messengers went to the hall, and Moteucçoma went too. There they killed the captives in the presence of the messengers and sprinkled the blood of the captives on them. They performed this ceremony[38] because they had seen great things; they had seen the gods and talked with them.

17

7

[fol. 11] Capitulo .7. de la relacion que dieron a Motecuçomatzin los mensajeros que boluieron de los nauios.

Chapter Seven, of the account that the messengers returning from the ships gave to Moteucçoma.

Hecho lo que arriba es dicho dierō la relacion a Motecuçoma de todo lo que avian visto y oydo y dieron la relacion de la comida que comian: y de las armas que

When the above-said had been done, they gave account to Moteucçoma of everything they had seen and heard, and told of the food that they ate and the weapons

Auh in oquicac in iuh tlanonotzque in titlanti cenca momauhti, miçavi, yoan cenca quimaviço in intlaqual: oc cenca iehoatl in quiiolmicti in oquicac in quenin vetzi in innaoatil[39] in tlequiquiztli, iuhqn tlatlatzini ic caquizti in iquac vetzi, vel teçotlauh, motzatzaqua in tonacaz. Auh in iquac vetzi iuhquin telolotli oalquiça yitic, tlepipixauhtiuh, chichitocatiuh: auh in ipocio cenca hiiac, xoquiiac, vel tetzonvitec: auh in quimotla tepetl iuhqn xitini, xixitica: auh in quavitl quimotlatetextia, iuhquin atetlachialti, iuhquin aca conilpitza; çan muchi tepuztli[40] in iniautlatqui, tepuztli in cōmaquia, tepuztli in conaquia intzontecon, tepuztli in inma[fol. 11v] quauh, tepuztli in intlavitol, tepuztli in inchimal, tepuztli in intopil:

auh in quinmama in inmaçaoa, iuhquin tlapantli ic quaquauhtique yoan novian quimilivi in innacaio, çanio neci in inxaiac, cenca iztac, ixtetenextique, tzoncoztique, tel cequi tliltic in intzon, viiac in intentzon no coztic, tētzōcoztique, cocototztique ocolochtic: auh in intlaqual iuhquin tlacatlaqualli,[41] veitepul, iztac, amo etic iuhquin tlaçolli, iuhquin ovaquavitl, iuhquin ovaquauhtextli inic aviac, achi tzopelic, achi nenecutic monecticaqua,[42] motzopelicaqua:

auh in imitzcuioan veveipopul, nacazcuecuelpachtique, tenvivilaxpopul, ixtletletique, ixtletlesuchtique, ixcocoztique, ixtlecocoztique, xillanvicoltique, xillāoacaltique, xillancapitztique vel quaquauhtique, amo tlaca mani, neneciuhtinemi, nenenepilotinemi, ocelocuicuiltique, mocuicuiloque:

Auh in o iuh quicac in Motecuçoma, cenca momauhti iuhquin iolmic, moioltequipacho, moiollacoma./.

And when he heard what the messengers reported, he was greatly afraid and taken aback, and he was amazed at their food. It especially made him faint when he heard how the guns went off at [the Spaniards'] command,[39] sounding like thunder, causing people actually to swoon, blocking the ears. And when it went off, something like a ball came out from inside, and fire went showering and spitting out. And the smoke that came from it had a very foul stench, striking one in the face. And if they shot at a hill, it seemed to crumble and come apart. And it turned a tree to dust; it seemed to make it vanish, as though someone had conjured it away. Their war gear was all iron.[40] They clothed their bodies in iron, they put iron on their heads, their swords were iron, their bows were iron, and their shields and lances were iron.

And their deer that carried them were as tall as the roof. And they wrapped their bodies all over; only their faces could be seen, very white. Their faces were the color of limestone and their hair yellowreddish, though some had black hair. They had long beards, also yellow-reddish. [The hair of some] was tightly curled. And their food was like fasting food,[41] very large, white, not heavy, like chaff, like dried maize stalks, as tasty as maize stalk flour, a bit sweet or honeyed, honeyed and sweet to eat.[42]

And their dogs were huge creatures, with their ears folded over and their jowls dragging. They had burning eyes, eyes like coals, yellow and fiery. They had thin, gaunt flanks with the rib lines showing; they were very tall. They did not keep quiet, they went about panting, with their tongues hanging down. They had spots like a jaguar's, they were varicolored.

When Moteucçoma heard it, he was greatly afraid; he seemed to faint away, he grew concerned and disturbed.

vsauan, y de todo lo que les acontecio con los españoles.

Oyda Motecuçoma la relacion que le dieron sus embaxadores, espantose mucho: y comēço a temer marauillose de la comida de los españoles, y de oyr el negocio del artilleria especialmēte de los truenos que quiebran las orejas, y del hedor de la polvora, que parece cosa infernal, y del huego que echā por la boca, y del golpe de la pelota, que desmenuza vn arbol de golpe: y de la relacion que le dieron de las armas muy fuertes que vsauā asi offensiuas como defensiuas, como son cosoletes, cotas, celadas, etᵃ Espadas, ballestas arcabuces, lanças etᵃ

Tambien de la relacion de los cauallos, y de la grādeza dellos: y como subian en ellos los españoles, armados [fol. 11v] que no se les parecian mas de la cara: y de como tenian las caras blancas, y los ojos garços, y los cabellos rosos, y las barbas largas: y de como veniā algunos negros entre ellos, que teniā los cabellos crespos, y prietos: tanbiē le dieron relacion de lo que comian los españoles, y de los perros que trayan, y de la manera que erā, y de la ferocidad que mostrauan, y de la color que tenian.

Oyda esta relacion Motecuçoma, espantose: y començo a temer, y a desmayarse, y a sentir gran angustia.

they used, and of everything that happened to them with the Spaniards.

When Moteucçoma had heard the account that his ambassadors gave him, he was greatly shocked and began to be afraid. He marveled at the Spaniards' food and at hearing the business of the artillery, especially the thunderous sounds that burst the eardrums and the stench of the powder, which appears to be something infernal, and the fire that they hurl from the mouth, and the impact of the ball, which reduces a tree to shreds at one blow, and the account of the very strong weapons they used, offensive as well as defensive, such as cuirasses, coats of mail, visored helmets, etc., and swords, crossbows, harquebuses, lances, etc.

Also the account of the horses and of their great size, and how the Spaniards mounted them in armor, so that nothing but their faces could be seen, and how they had white faces, blue eyes, red hair, and long beards, and how some blacks came among them who had crisply curled dark hair. They also told him of what the Spaniards ate, and of the dogs they brought along and how they were, and of the ferocity they showed, and what color they were.

When Moteucçoma heard this account, he was shocked. He began to be afraid, to lose heart, to feel great anxiety.

18

19

[fol. 12] Inic chicuei capitulo: vncan mitoa in quenin iehoatl motecuçoma, quimioa in nanaoalti in tlatlacateculo, in tetlachivianime, inic itla impan quichioazque in Españoles.

Niman iquac tlaioa in Motecuçoma in quimioa mocheoantin in atlaca, in tlaciuhque, in nanaoalti: [43] yoan quimioa in achcacauhti, chicaoaque, in tiacaoā in ipan tlatozque in ixquich intech monequiz in qualoni in totoli in totoltetl, in iztac tlaxcalli; yoā in tlein quitlanizque, yoan inic ça oc vel pachiviz in iniollo, vel quimittazque, quimioa in mamalti, ic monemachti, cuix quizque in imezço: auh iuh quichiuhque in titlanti.

Auh in iquac oquittaque: cenca motlaeltique chichicha, ixtetenmotzoloa, ihicopi, motzontecōvivixoa: auh in tlaqualli eztica catzelhuique, queezvique, cenca invic eoac, quintlaelti: iehica ca cenca xoquiiac in eztli.

Auh inic iuh quichiuh motecuçoma, ca quinteuma, teteu impan quinma quinteutocac: ic notzaloque, ic tocaiotiloque, teteu ilhuicac [fol. 12v] vitze: auh in tliltique teucacatzacti mitoque,

quin iehoatl quiquaque iztac tlaxcalli, tlatzincuitl, totoltetl, totoli: auh in ie ixquich xochiqualli, quauhtzaputl, teçontzaputl, atztzaputl, [44] totolcuitlatzaputl, camutli, quauhcamutli, poxcauhcamutli xochicamutli, tlapalcamutli, xicama, maçaxocotl, atoiaxocotl, xalxocotl, in quauhxilotl, aoacatl, oaxi, texocotl, in capoli, in nochtli, in amacapuli, iztac nochtli, coznochtli, tlatocnochtli, tzaponochtli, anochtli: auh in maçatlaqualli, pipillo, tlachicaztli:

Auh quil inic quimioa Motecuçoma in nanaoalti, in tlaciuhque, inic quimittazque

Eighth chapter, where it is said how Moteucçoma sent witches, wizards, and sorcerers to do something to the Spaniards.

Then at that time Moteucçoma sent out emissaries. Those whom he sent were all bad people, soothsayers and witches. [43] He also sent elders, strong warriors, to see to all [the Spaniards] needed as to food: turkey hens, eggs, white tortillas, and whatever they might request, and to look after them well so that they would be satisfied in every way. He sent captives in case [the Spaniards] should drink their blood. And the emissaries did as indicated.

But when [the Spaniards] saw it, they were made sick to their stomachs, spitting, rubbing their eyelids, blinking, shaking their heads. And [the emissaries] sprinkled blood in the food, they bloodied it, which made their stomachs turn and disgusted them, because of the great stench of the blood.

Moteucçoma did this because he took them for gods, considered them gods, worshiped them as gods. They were called and given the name of gods who have come from heaven, and the blacks were called soiled gods.

After that they ate white tortillas, grains of maize, turkey eggs, turkeys, and all the fruits: custard apple, mammee, yellow sapote, [44] black sapote, sweet potato, manioc, white sweet potato, yellow sweet potato, colored sweet potato, jicama, plum, jobo, guava, *cuajilote,* avocado, acacia [bean], *tejocote,* American cherry, tuna cactus fruit, mulberry, white cactus fruit, yellow cactus fruit, whitish-red cactus fruit, pitahaya, water pitahaya. And the food for the deer was *pipillo* and *tlachicaztli.*

They say that Moteucçoma sent the witches, the rainmakers, to see what [the

[fol. 12] Capitulo .8. de como motecuçoma enbio sus encantadores y maleficus para que empeciesen a los españoles.

Despues de lo arriba dicho luego Motecuçoma junto algunos adivinos, y agureros: y algunos principalejos, y los embio al puerto donde estauan los españoles para que procurasen que no les faltase comida, y todo lo que demandasē, y para que mirasen diligentemente para que le diesen la relacion de todo lo que pasava y enbio con ellos algunos captiuos para que sacrificasen delante del dios que venia si viesen que cōuenia, y si demandasen sangre ṗa beber.

Fueron aquellos embaxadores, y llegaron a donde estavan los españoles, y offrecieronles tortillas, rocidas con sangre humano: como vieron los españoles aquella comida tuuieron grande asco della. Començaron a escupir y abominarla, porque hedia el pan con la sangre.

Esto se hizo por mandado de Motecuçoma, y el lo mando hazer porque tenia que aquellos erā dioses que venian del cielo: y los negros [fol. 12v] pensaron que eran dioses negros.

Todos ellos comieron el pan blanco que lleuauan sin sangre, y los veuos y aves, y la fruta que los presentaron: y recibieron, tanbien comida para los cavallos.

Chapter Eight, of how Moteucçoma sent his enchanters and casters of evil spells to do harm to the Spaniards.

After the above-said, Moteucçoma convoked some diviners and soothsayers, along with some lower leaders, and sent them to the port where the Spaniards were so that they would arrange that they should not lack food or anything they should demand, and should diligently see to it that they report to him everything that was going on. He sent with them some captives to be sacrificed before the god who was coming, if they should deem it fitting and if he should demand blood to drink.

Those envoys went and reached the place where the Spaniards were. They offered them tortillas sprinkled with human blood; when the Spaniards saw that food, it made them very nauseous. They began to spit and detest it, because the bread reeked of blood.

This was done by order of Moteucçoma, and he ordered it done because he considered that those were gods who came from heaven, and they thought that the blacks were black gods.

They all ate the white bread, without blood, that they brought, and the eggs and fowl, and the fruit that they presented to them, and they also received food for the horses.

in quenamique in aço vel quintlaca-
teculovizque, quintlachivizque, in aço vel
quimipitzazque quinxoxazque in aço oc
itla ic quinmotlazque, in aço itla tlaca-
teculotlatolli, ic quintlanonochilizque, inic
aço cocolizcuizque, mimiquizque, in
anoce ic ilotizque. Auh in iehoantin in
quichiuhque in intequiuh, in innaoatil in
intechpa españo[fol. 13]les, çan nimā
avelitque, atle vel quichiuhque: niman ic
oalmocueptivetzque quinonotzaco in Motecuçoma inic iuhque, inic chicaoaque,
amo titenamicoan, iuhquin atitleme:

niman ic tetlaquauhnaoati in Motecuçoma, vel quincocolti, vel quintenizti,
quinmiquiznaoati in calpixque: auh in ixquich in tecutli, in achcauhtli in quit-
tazque, in quimocuitlavizque in ixquich
intech monequiz. Auh in ovallalhoacaquizque iequene ic vitze: in ie oaloli-
nizque, in ie oalolini, in ie oalotlatoca,
cenca necuitlaviloque, mavizmachoque,
çan temac in oallatiaque, in oalotlatocaque,
cenca inca nechioaloc.

Spaniards] were like and perhaps be able to
enchant them, cast spells on them, to use
conjury or the evil eye on them or hurl
something else at them, perhaps addressing
some words of wizardry to them so that
they would take sick, die, or turn back.
But when they performed the assignment
they had been given concerning the Spaniards, they could do nothing; they had no
power at all. Then they quickly returned
to tell Moteucçoma what they were like,
how strong they were, [saying,] "We are
not their match; we are as nothing."

Then Moteucçoma gave strict orders;
he scolded and charged the stewards and all
the lords and elders, under pain of death,
that they see to and take care of everything
[the Spaniards] might need. And when
[the Spaniards] came onto dry land and
finally started moving in this direction and
coming along the road toward here, they
were well cared for and made much of.
They were always in the hands of someone
as they came progressing; they were very
well attended to.

9

Inic chicunavi capitulo: vncā mitoa in
quenin chocac Motecuçomatzin, yoan in
chocaque mexica, in iquac oquimatque, ca
cenca chicaoaque in Españoles.

Auh in motecuçoma cenca tlatenma,
motenma, momauhti, miçavi, quitlaten-
machili in altepetl; yoan in ie ixquich
tla[fol. 13v]catl, cenca momauhtique, ne-
mauhtiloc neiçaviloc, tlatēmachoc, netēn-
machoc, nenonotzalo, nececentlalilo,

Ninth chapter, where it is said how Moteucçoma wept, and the Mexica wept,
when they found out that the Spaniards
were very strong.

And Moteucçoma lamented his troubles
at length; he was afraid and shocked. He
told the troubles of the altepetl. And everyone was very afraid. Fear reigned, and
shock, laments, and expressions of distress.
People talked, assembled, gathered, wept

Embio Motecuçoma a aquellos adiuinos, agureros, y nigromanticos para que
mirasen si podrian a[45] hazer contra ellos
algun encantamiento o hechizeria para con
que enfermasen o muriesen o se boluiesen:
y estos hizierō todas sus diligencias como
Motecuçoma les auia mandado contra los
españoles pero ninguna cosa les aprouecho
ni tuvo effecto: y ansi se boluieron a dar las
nueuas a Motecuçoma de lo que auia
pasado dixerōle que aquella gente que
auian visto era muy fuerte y que ellos no
erā nadie para contra ellos.

[fol. 13] Luego Motecuçoma embio
otros mesajeros y embaxadores principales
y calpisques, para que fuesen a donde estauan los españoles: y mādolos su[46] pena de
muerte que con grā diligēcia procurasen
todo lo que les fuesen[47] necesario a los españoles āsi para en la mar como para en la
tierra fuerō estos mesajeros con gran
priesa: y hizieron todo lo que motecuçoma
les mando por todo el camino procurauā
de proveer a los españoles de todo lo necesario y seruianlos, con grā diligencia.

Moteucçoma sent those diviners, soothsayers, and necromancers to see if they
could make[45] some enchantment or be-
witchment against them so that they
would sicken or die or go back. They used
all their procedures against the Spaniards,
as Moteucçoma had ordered them, but
nothing did them any good or had any effect, so they returned to tell Moteucçoma
the news of what had happened. They told
him that those people whom they had seen
were very strong, and that they were nothing against them.

Then Moteucçoma sent other messengers, envoys, leaders, and *calpisques,* to go
where the Spaniards were, ordering them
on[46] pain of death that with great diligence
they should arrange whatever the Spaniards should need,[47] whether on land or on
the sea. These messengers went with great
haste and did everything that Moteucçoma
ordered them. All along the way they arranged to supply the Spaniards with all
they needed and served them with great
diligence.

21

9

Capitulo .9. del llanto que hizo
Motecuçoma; y todos los mexicanos,
desque supieron, que los Españoles: eran
tan esforçados.

Oydas las cosas arriba dichas por
Motecuçoma, concibio en si vn sen-
timiento, que venian grandes males, sobre
el,[48] y sobre su reyno: [fol. 13v] y començo a temer grandemente no solamente el
pero todos aquellos q̄ supieron estas nueuas

Chapter Nine, of the lament that Moteucçoma and all the Mexica made when
they learned that the Spaniards were so
strong.

When Moteucçoma had heard the
things mentioned above, he conceived a
sentiment that great evils were coming
upon him[48] and his realm. He began to
experience great fear, and not he alone but
all those who heard the news just men-

neohololol, nechoquililo, nechocho-
quililo, techoquililo, ça tlaquechpilivi,-
ça tlaquechvi, nechoquiztlapalolo, te-
choquiztlapalolo, teellaquaoalo, neel-
laquaoalo, tepepetlalo, pepetlalo in pipiltzitzinti; in tetaoan quitoa: Veh nopil-
hoātzitzine, quen vel ameoantin in o
amopan muchiuh, in tlein ie muchioaz:
auh in tenanoan quitoa. No nopilhoantzitzin, queço uel amehoanti in anquima-
viçozque in tlein ie topan muchioaz:

   yvan ilhuiloc, ixpantiloc, machtiloc,
nonotzaloc, caquitiloc, yiollo itlan tlaliloc
in Motecuçoma: ce cioatl nican titlaca in
quinoalhuicac, in oalnaoatlatotia: itoca
Malintzi teticpac ichan, in vmpa atenco,
achto canaco.


   Auh niman iquac peuh in aocmo on-
necxitlalilo, in ça mocuitlacueptinemi in
titlanti, in ipan ontlatoa in izquitlamantli,
in izquican icac in intech monequiz.


   Auh çan nimā no iquac in qui[fol.
14]temotivitze Motecuçoma: quenami
cuix telpuchtli, cuix yiolloco oquichtli,
cuix ie veve, cuix ie tlachicalhuia, cuix ie
veve tlamati, cuix ie veve tlacatl, cuix ie
quaiztac? Auh quinnanquiliaia in teteu in
Españoles: ca yiolloco oquichtli, amo tomaoac, çan pitzactōtli, çan pipitzactontli,
çan cuillotic, cuillotcatontli.


   Auh in iuh quicaquia in, Motecuçoma,
in cenca temolo, in cenca matataco cenca
ixco tlachiaznequi in teteu iuhquin patz-
miquia yiollo, iolpatzmiquia, cholozquia,
choloznequia, mocholtiznequia, mochol-
tizquia, motlatizquia, motlatiznequia,

for themselves and for others. Heads hung,
there were tearful greetings, words of encouragement, and stroking of hair. Little
children's heads were stroked. Fathers
would say, "Alas, my children, how is it
with you, that what is about to happen has
happened to you?" And mothers said, "O
my children, how is it with you who are to
behold what is about to happen to us?"


   And it was told, presented, made
known, announced, and reported to Moteucçoma, and brought to his attention,
that a woman, one of us people here, came
accompanying them as interpreter. Her
name was Marina and her homeland was
Tepeticpac, on the coast, where they first
took her.
   And then at this time the messengers
who saw in each place to everything [the
Spaniards] needed began hardly to pause
[on arrival in Mexico], but to run right
back [from whence they came].
   At this same time [the Spaniards] came
asking about Moteucçoma: "What is he
like? Is he a youth, a mature man, already
old, advanced in age, or an old man but
able? Is he aged, is he white-haired?" And
they replied to the gods, the Spaniards,
"He is a mature man, not corpulent, but
slim and slender, on the thin side."


   When Moteucçoma heard this, that
many and persistent inquiries were being
made about him, that the gods wanted to
see his face, he was greatly anguished. He
repeatedly wished to flee, to hide, to take
refuge from the gods. He thought of,

ya dichas, Todos llorauan, y se angustia-
uan, y andauan tristes, y cabizbaxos hazian
corrillos, y hablauan con espanto de las
nueuas que auian venido: las madres llo-
rando tomaũã en braços a sus hijos, y tra-
endoles la mano sobre la cabeça, dezian: o
hijo mio en mal tiempo as nacido! que
grandes cosas as de ver! en grandes trabaxos
te as de hallar!

Fue dicho a Motecuçoma como los españoles trayan vna india mexicana que se
llamaua Marina vezina del pueblo de teticpac que es a la orilla de la mar del norte, y
que trayan esta por interprete que dezia en
la lengua mexicana todo lo q̃ el capitan don
hernando cortes la mandaua:

luego Motecuçoma començo a embiar
mensajeros y principales a donde estauã los
españoles para que mirasen lo que se hazia:
y procurasen lo que era menester al serui-
cio de los españoles cada dia yuã vnos y
boluian otros no parauã mensajeros que
yuã, y venian:

y los españoles no cesauã de preguntar
por motecuçoma, queriendo saber que
persona era, Si era viejo. O si era moço, o
si era de media edad, o si tenia canas,[49] [fol.
14] Respondian los indios mexicanos a los
españoles hombre es de media edad no es
viejo, ni es gordo: es delgado y enxuto.

Quando oya motecuçoma la relacion de
los mensajeros como los españoles pregun-
tauã mucho por el y que deseauã mucho
de verle angustiauase en gran manera:
penso de huyr o de esconderse para q̃ no le
viesen los españoles ni le hallasen pesaua de

tioned. All wept and were anxious, going
about melancholy and with head down.
They formed small groups and spoke with
shock of the news that had come. The
mothers, weeping, took their children in
their arms, and patting their heads said, "O
my child, you have been born in a bad
time! What great things you are to see!
You are to be in great travails!"

Moteuccoma was told how the Spaniards were bringing along with them a
Mexica [Nahuatl-speaking] Indian woman
called Marina, a citizen of the settlement of
Teticpac, on the shore of the North Sea
[Caribbean], who served as interpreter and
said in the Mexican language everything
that Captain don Hernando Cortés told
her to.

*Malinche*

Then Moteuccoma began to send messengers and leading figures to where the
Spaniards were to see what was going on
and provide what was necessary for the
service of the Spaniards. Every day some
were leaving and others returning; messengers were constantly coming and going.

And the Spaniards were continually asking after Moteuccoma, wanting to know
what kind of a person he was, whether he
was old or young or of middle age, or
gray-haired. The Mexica Indians replied[49]
to the Spaniards, "He is a man of middle
age, not old, nor is he fat; he is slender and
lean."

When Moteuccoma heard the messengers' account of how the Spaniards were
asking so much about him and that they
greatly desired to see him, he was seized
with great anxiety. He thought of fleeing
or going into hiding so that the Spaniards

22

quinnetlatilizquia, quinneinailiznequia in
teteu. Auh quimoiollotica, quimoiol-
lotiaia, quimopictica, quimopictiaia, qui-
iocuxca, quiiocoaia; ic moiolnonotzca, ic
moiolnonotzaia yitic: quimolhuica, yitic
quimolhuiaia cana oztoc calaquiz, auh cēca
intech moiollaliaia intech vel catca yiollo,
intech tlaquauh tlamatia; cequintin quimo-
mo[fol. 14v]machiztiaia, in quitoaia. Ca
vmmati in mictlan, yoan tonatiuh ichan,
yoan tlalocā yoan cincalco [50] inic vmpatiz
in campa ie vel motlanequiliz.

Auh ie vel vmpa motlanequiliaia, mo-
tlanequili in cincalco: vel iuh machoc, vel
iuh tepan motecac. Auh inin amo velit,
amo vel motlati, amo vel minax, aoc ievat,
aoctletic, aoc ievatix, aoc ie onneltic, aoctle vel muchiuh in intlatol tlaciuhque, inic
quiiolcuepca, inic quiiollapanca, inic qui-
iolmalacachoca, inic quitlacuepilica, in
quimomachitocaca in ommati, in vmpa
omoteneuh; çan quinmochielti, çan mo-
iollotechiuh, moiollochichili, quioalcen-
tlami, quioalcentlanqua in iiollo, quimo-
cenmacac in çaço tlein quittaz,
quimaviçoz.

imagined, invented, weighed, and turned
over in his mind that he would go into a
cave somewhere. He made it known to
some people with whom he consoled himself, with whom he was comfortable, with
whom he frequently conversed, and they
said, "The way is known to Mictlan,
Tonatiuh ichan, Tlalocan, and Cincalco [50]
for remedy, whichever suits you."

The one he preferred was Cincalco. It
became well known, word spread among
the public. But he was not able to do it,
not able to hide and take refuge. He took
no steps; it came to nothing. What the
rainmakers had said when they influenced
and instigated him, confusing him and
turning things around on him, when they
claimed they knew the way to the above-
mentioned places, was not carried out,
could not occur. [Moteucçoma] just
awaited [the Spaniards]; he strengthened
his resolve, mastered his emotions, and resigned himself entirely to whatever he was
to see and behold.

esconderse en alguna cueua o de salirse deste mundo, y yrse al infierno o al parayso terrenal, o qualquiera otra parte secreta: y esto trataua con sus amigos aquellos de quien se confiaua y ellos le dezian. Ay quien sepa el camino para yr al infierno: y tanbien al parayso terrenal, y a la casa del sol, y a la cueua que se llama Cincalco que esta cabe atlacuioaian detras de chapultepec donde ay fama que ay grādes secretos en vnos destos lugares se podra [fol. 14v] v̄ra magestad remediar escoxa vuestra magestad el lugar que quisiere que alla le lleuaremos: y alli se consolara sin recebir ningun daño.

Motecuçoma se inclino a yrse a la cueua de cincalco: y asi se publico por toda la tierra pero no vuo effecto este negocio ninguna cosa de lo que dixeron los nigromanticos se pudo verificar. y ansi Motecuçoma procuro desforçarse y de esperar a todo lo que veniese, y de ponerse a todo peligro.

would not see or find him. He thought of hiding in some cave, or leaving this world and going to the inferno or to terrestrial paradise or some other secret place, and he spoke of this with his friends in whom he trusted. They told him, "There are people who know the way to go to the inferno, and also to the terrestrial paradise and the house of the sun, and to the cave that they call Cincalco, which is close to Atlacuihuayan [Tacubaya], behind Chapultepec, where it is said that there are great secrets. Your majesty could find remedy in one of these spots. Let your majesty choose the one you want and we will take you there, and there you can console yourself without receiving any harm."

Moteucçoma was inclined to go to the cave of Cincalco, and so it was published throughout the whole land, but this business did not come to pass. Nothing of what the necromancers said could be verified. And so Moteucçoma tried to take courage, awaiting whatever should come and exposing himself to all the dangers.

23

Inic matlactli Capitulo: vncan mitoa in quenin Españoles çan ivian, oallalhoac-caquizque, oallotlatocatiaque yoā in quenin Motecuçoma quicauh in vei tecpan, vmpa ia in ipilchan.

Niman quioallalcavi in ive[fol. 15]ve-chan in vei tecpan, vncan oallamattia, vncan oallama, quioalma, quioaltocac in ipilchan in iehoatl Motecuçoma.

Auh in iequene vitze, in ie vitze, in ie ovalmolinique: ce tlacatl, cempoaltecatl, itoca tlacochcalcatl, no achto canaco; in iquac quittato tlalli, in altepetl, no oal-naoatlatotia, q̄noaloquechilitia, quinoalo-tlaxilitia, quinoallaixtlatitia, quinoaliacan, quinoaliacantia.

Auh in oacico Tecoac: intlalpan tlaxcal-teca vncan onoque imotonoan. Auh in otomi iautica quinnamicque, chimaltica quinnamicque: auh in otomi in Tecoaca vel quimixtlatique, vel ixpoliuhque, quinxixilque, texixilioac, quintlequiquiz-vique, quintepuzmivique, quintlavitol-huique, amo çan quexquichtin, vel ixa-chintin in ixpoliuhque.

Auh in ontlalpoliuh Tecoac; in tlaxcal-teca in oconcacque in ocōmatque, in onil-huiloto, cenca mauhcaçonecque, mocue-tlaxoque, cenca intlan ia in maviztli, mavizcuique: nimā mocentlalique mono-notzque, motecuiononotz[fol. 15v]que, motlatocanonotzque, quimoottitique in tlatolli:

Tenth chapter, where it is said how the Spaniards landed uncontested and came on their way in this direction, and how Moteucçoma left the great palace and went to his personal home.

Then Moteucçoma abandoned his pa-trimonial home, the great palace, and came back to his personal home.

When at last [the Spaniards] came, when they were coming along and moving this way, a certain person from Cempoallan, whose name was Tlacochcalcatl, whom they had taken when they first came to see the land and the various altepetl, also came interpreting for them, planning their route, conducting them, showing them the way, leading and guiding them.

And when they reached Tecoac, which is in the land of the Tlaxcalans, where their Otomis lived, the Otomis met them with hostilities and war. But they annihilated the Otomis of Tecoac, who were de-stroyed completely. They lanced and stabbed them, they shot them with guns, iron bolts, crossbows. Not just a few but a huge number of them were destroyed.

After the great defeat at Tecoac, when the Tlaxcalans heard it and found out about it and it was reported to them, they became limp with fear, they were made faint; fear took hold of them. Then they assembled, and all of them, including the lords and rulers, took counsel among themselves, considering the reports.

Capitulo .10. de como los españoles començaron a entrar la tierra adētro: y de como Motecuçoma dexo la casa rreal y se fue a su casa propria.

Moteucçoma teniendo ya por [fol. 15] aueriguado ansi por las cosas que auia oydo de los españoles como por los pronosticos que auian pasado y profecias antiguas y moternas que tenian que los españoles auiā de reynar en esta tierra: saliose de las casas reales, y fuese a las casas que el tenian ante que fuese rey o emperador.

Desque los españoles partieron de la ribera de la mar para entrar la tierra dentro, tomaron a vn indio principal que llamauā Tlacochcalcatl, para que los mostrase el camino: al qual indio auian tomado de alli de aquella prouincia los primeros nauios que vinieron a descubrir esta tierra el qual indio el capitan don hernando cortes truxo consigo, y sabia ya de la lengua española algo. Este juntamente con marina, erā interpretes de don hernādo cortes, a este tomaron por guia de su camino, para venir a mexico.

En llegando a la prouincia de tecoac que es tierra de tlaxcalla, alli estauan poblados los otomies y gente de guerra que guardaua la frontera o terminos de los tlaxcaltecas: estos salieron de guerra contra los españoles. Los españoles [fol. 15v] començaron a pelear con ellos y los de caballo alancearon mucha: y los arcaboceros, y ballesteros mataron tanbien muchos, de manera ḡ desbaratarō a todo aḡllo exercito que venia y huyerō los que ḡdaron: los españoles tomaron el pueblo y robaron lo ḡ hallarō y asi destruieron aḡllos pueblos.

Como los de tlaxcalla oyeron lo que auia acontecido a sus soldados y otomies espātaronse començaron a temer luego se juntarō a consejo y conferieron todos sobre el negocio para ver si saldrian de guerra contra los españoles o si se darian de paz

Chapter Ten, of how the Spaniards began to go into the interior of the country, and how Moteucçoma left the royal palace and went to his own house.

Moteucçoma, considering because of the things he had heard about the Spaniards, as well as the prophecies that had been made in ancient and modern times, that the Spaniards were to rule in this land, left the royal palace and went to the house that he had before he was king or emperor.

From the time that the Spaniards left the seacoast to go into the interior of the country, they took a leading Indian named Tlacochcalcatl to show them the way; the first ships that came to discover this land had taken him from that province; Captain don Hernando Cortés brought this Indian along with him, and he already knew something of the Spanish language. He was an interpreter for don Hernando Cortés along with Marina, and he was the one they took to guide the way coming to Mexico.

When they reached the province of Tecoac, which is Tlaxcalan territory, they found settled there the Otomis and warriors who guarded the border or jurisdictional limits of the Tlaxcalans, and they came out to do battle against the Spaniards. The Spaniards began to fight with them; the horsemen lanced many of them, and the harquebusiers and crossbowmen also killed many, so that they routed the whole army that was coming, and those who remained fled. The Spaniards took the settlement and stole what they found, and so they destroyed those settlements.

When the Tlaxcalans heard what had happened to their soldiers and Otomis, they were shocked and began to be afraid. Then they assembled in council and all conferred about the matter, to see if they should do battle against the Spaniards or if they should submit peacefully.

quitoque. Quen toiezque, cuix tiquin-
namiquizque: ca vei oquichtli vei tiacauh
in otomitl, atle ipan oquittac, atle ipan
oconittac, çan ixquich cavitontli in çan ix-
peioctli in oconpopolo maceoalli. Auh in
axcan ma çan itlan toncalaquicã, ma çan
tictocniuhtican, ma çan titocniuhtlacan,
motolinia in maceoalli.

Auh nima ie ic vi in quīnamiquizque in
tlaxcalteca tlatoque: quitquique in tlaqualli,
in totoli, in totoltetl in iztac tlaxcalli, in
chipaoac tlaxcalli: quimilhuique. Oan-
quimimihiovíltique totecuioane:
quinoalnanquilique. Can amochan?
Campa oanoallaque?

Conitoque. Titlaxcalteca, oanqui-
mociavíltique, oanmaxitico, otlaltech an-
maxitico in amochantzinco quauhtlaxcalla [51]
(auh in ie vecauh moteneoaia Texcalla,
in maceoalti mitoaia, Texcalteca.)

They said, "How is it to be with us?
Should we face them? For the Otomis are
great and valiant warriors, yet they thought
nothing of them, they regarded them as
nothing; in a very short time, in the blink
of an eyelid, they destroyed the people.
Now let us just submit to them, let us
make friends with them, let us be friends,
for something must be done about the
common people."
Thereupon the Tlaxcalan rulers went to
meet them, taking along food: turkey
hens, eggs, white tortillas, fine tortillas.
They said to them, "Welcome, our lords."

[The Spaniards] answered them back,
"Where is your homeland? Where have
you come from?"
They said, "We are Tlaxcalans. Welcome, you have arrived, you have reached
the land of Tlaxcala, [51] which is your
home."
(But in olden times it was called Texcallan and the people Texcalans.)

11

Inic matlactli oce capitulo: vncã mitoa
in quenin Españoles acico in vncã tlaxcalla:
in mitoa Texcalla.
[fol. 16] Quimõiacanato, quinoalhuicaque, quinoaliacantiaque, inic quim-
oncaoato, inic quincalaquito in intec-
panchan, cenca quinmavizmatque,
quinmacaque in intech monequi inca mo-
chiuhq̃ yoan niman quinmacaque imich-
puchoan:
niman quintlatlanique canin Mexico,
quenamican? oc veca?

Quīnanquilique, ca aocmo veca, aço ça
eilhuitl axioaloz, cenca qualcã, yoã cenca
chicaoaque, cenca tiacaoã, tepeoanime,
novian tepeuhtinemi.

Eleventh chapter, where it is said how
the Spaniards reached Tlaxcala, [also]
called Texcallan.
[The Tlaxcalans] guided, accompanied,
and led them until they brought them to
their palace⟨s⟩ and placed them there.
They showed them great honors, they
gave them what they needed and attended
to them, and then they gave them their
daughters.
Then [the Spaniards] asked them,
"Where is Mexico? What kind of a place is
it? Is it still far?"
They answered them, "It's not far now.
Perhaps one can get there in three days. It
is a very favored place, and [the Mexica]
are very strong, great warriors, conquerors,
who go about conquering everywhere."

dixerō: sabemos que los otomies son muy valientes y pelean reziamente y todos son destruidos ninguna resistencia vuo en ellos en vn cerrar y abrir de ojo los destruieron que podemos hazer nosotros sera bien que los recibamos de paz y los tomemos por amigos esto es mejor que no perder toda nuestra gente: y ansi acordaron los señores de tlaxcalla de recebirlos de paz y tomarlos por amigos.

Salieron luego los señores y principales con grā multitud de tamemes cargados de comida de todas maneras: llegando a ellos asaludaron de paz a don hernando cortes

y el los pregunto, diziendo: de donde soys vosotros? y de donde venis?

Ellos dixerō somos de la ciudad de taxcala: y venimos a recebiros porque nos holgamos de v̄ra venida, aveys llegado a n̄ra tierra, seays muy bienvenidos es v̄ra casa y v̄ra tierra dōde estays que se llama Quauhtexcalla. [52]

La ciudad q̄ agora se llama tlaxcalla, ante que viniesen los españoles se llamaua texcalla.

Capitulo .ii. de como los españoles llegaron a tlaxcalla que entoce se llamaua texcalla.

[fol. 16] Los señores y principales de tlaxcalla metieron en sociedad a los españoles, rescibiendoles de paz, lleuarōles luego derechos a las casas reales alli los aposentaron: y los hizieron muy buen tratamiento administandoles todas las cosas necesarias con grā diligencia: y tambien les [53] dieron a sus hijas donzellas muchas y ellos las recibieron y vsarō dellas como de sus mugeres.

Luego el capitan començo a preguntar por mexico diziendo donde esta mexico? esta lexos de aqui?

Dixeronle no esta lexos esta andadura de tres dias es vna ciudad muy populosa, y los

They said, "We know that the Otomis are very valiant and fierce fighters, yet all have been destroyed. They were unable to resist them; in the blink of an eyelid they destroyed them. What can we do? It will be well to receive them peacefully and take them as friends. That would be better than losing all our people." And so the lords of Tlaxcala agreed to receive them peacefully and take them as friends.

Then the lords and leaders went out with a great multitude of *tamemes* [bearers] loaded with all kinds of food. Reaching them, they greeted don Hernando Cortés peacefully.

He asked them, "Where are you from? Where do you come from?"

They said, "We are from the city of Tlaxcala, and we are coming to receive you because we are glad that you have come. You have reached our land; you are very welcome; this land where you are, which is called Quauhtexcallan, [52] is your home and land."

Today the city is called Tlaxcala, but before the Spaniards came it was called Texcallan.

Chapter Eleven, of how the Spaniards reached Tlaxcala, then called Texcallan.

The lords and leaders of Tlaxcala introduced the Spaniards into their society, receiving them peacefully, and then they took them straight to the royal palace, where they gave them lodging, and they treated them very well, with great diligence providing them with the necessary things. They also gave them [53] many of their maiden daughters, and they received them and used them as their women.

Then the Captain began to ask about Mexico, saying, "Where is Mexico? Is it far from here?"

They told him, "It's not far; it's a journey of three days. The city is very popu-

Auh in tlaxcalteca, ieppa mocha-
laniticatca, moqualancaitzticatca, mo-
tlavelitzticatca, mococoliticatca, aimel
mottaia, acā vel monepanoaia in cholo-
teca: Ipampa in quintenanaoatilique, inic
quinpoiomictizque:

quimilhuique. Ca cenca tlaveliloc, ca
toiaouh in chololtecatl iuhquin mexicatl ic
chicaoac, ca icniuh in mexicatl:

in o iuh quicacque in españoles: nimā ic
vmpa iaque in chololla, quinvicaque in
tlaxcalteca yoan in cempoalteca, moiau-
chi[fol. 16v]chiuhtiaque: in oacito nimā ie
ic tenotzalo, tetzatzililo, ixquichtin oal-
lazque in pipilti, in tlatoque, in teiacana, in
tiacaoan, yoan maceoalti, neteuitoal-
temaloc. Auh in ie ocenquizque ixquichtin, niman quioaltzatzacque in calacoaiā, in
izquicampa calacoa, nimā ie ic texixilioa,
temictilo, teviviteco, atle iniollo ipan catca
in Chololtecatl: amo mitica amo chimaltica quinnamicq̄ in Españoles, çan iuhquin
ichtacamictiloque, çan tlaixpopoiomictilti,
çan tlachtacamictilti, canel çan quintenanaoatilique in tlaxcalteca.

Now before this there had been friction
between the Tlaxcalans and the Cholulans.
They viewed each other with anger, fury,
hate, and disgust; they could come together on nothing. Because of this they put
[the Spaniards] up to killing them treacherously.

They said to them, "The Cholulans are
very evil; they are our enemies. They are
as strong as the Mexica, and they are the
Mexica's friends."

When the Spaniards heard this, they
went to Cholula. The Tlaxcalans and
Cempoalans went with them, outfitted for
war. When they arrived, there was a general summons and cry that all the noblemen, rulers, subordinate leaders, warriors,
and commoners should come, and everyone assembled in the temple courtyard.
When they had all come together, [the
Spaniards and their friends] blocked the
entrances, all of the places where one entered. Thereupon people were stabbed,
struck, and killed. No such thing was in
the minds of the Cholulans; they did not
meet the Spaniards with weapons of war.
It just seemed that they were stealthily and
treacherously killed, because the Tlaxcalans persuaded [the Spaniards] to do it.

Auh in ixquich muchioaia, muchi quioalmacaia, quioalilhuiaia, quioalcaquitiaia
in tlatolli in Motecuçoma. Auh in titlanti,
ixquich oalaci, ixquich vmpeoa, çan mocuitlacueptinemi, aoc quenman cactoc in
quicaqui, in caquitilo tlatolli: auh in ie ixquich tlacatl maceoalli, ça mâcomanti-

And a report of everything that was happening was given and relayed to Moteucçoma. Some of the messengers would be
arriving as others were leaving; they just
turned around and ran back. There was no
time when they weren't listening, when
reports weren't being given. And all the

naturales della son valientes y grādes con-
quistadores en todas partes hazen conquista.

Los tlaxcaltecas y chololtecas no eran
amigos tenian entre si discordia, y como
los querian mal dixeron mal dellos a los españoles para que los maltratasen, dixerōlos
que eran sus enemigos y amigos de los
mexicanos y valientes como ellos; los españoles oydas estas nueuas de cholollan
propusieron de tratarlos mal, como lo hizieron

partieron de tlaxcalla todos ellos y con
muchos Cempoaltecas y tlaxcaltecas que
los acōpañaron todos con sus armas de
guerra, llegando todos a chololla: los chololtecas no hizieron cuenta de nada ni los
recibierō de guerra ni de paz estuuieronse
quedos en sus casas desto tomarō mala
opinion [fol. 16v] dellos los españoles y
coniecturaron alguna traicion
    començaron luego a llamar a vozes a los
principales y señores y toda la otra gente
para que viniesen a donde estauā los españoles y ellos todos se iuntaron en el patio
del gran cu de Quetzalcoatl: estando alli
iuntos los españoles afrontados de la poca
cuenta que auian hecho dellos: entraron a
cauallo auiendo tomado todas las entradas
del patio, començaron a lancearlos y mataron todos quatos pudieron y los amigos
indios de creer es que matarō muchos mas.
Los chololtecas, ni lleuaron armas offensiuas ni deffensiuas sino fueronse desarmados
pensando que no se haria lo que se hizo:
desta manera murieron mala muerte,

Todas estas cosas que acontecieron,
luego que acontecieron: los mensajeros de
Motecuçoma se las venian a dezir: todo el
camino andaua lleno de mensajeros de aca
por alla, y de alla por aca, y toda la gente
aca en mexico y donde venian los españoles en todas las comarcas andaua la

lous, and its inhabitants are brave and great
conquerors; they make conquests everywhere."

The Tlaxcalans and Cholulans were not
friends, there was discord between them,
and as they wished them ill they said bad
things of them to the Spaniards so they
would treat them badly. They told them
that they were their enemies and friends
of the Mexica, and valiant like them.
When the Spaniards heard such news of
Cholula they decided to treat them badly,
as they did.

They all departed from Tlaxcala, with
many Cempohualans and Tlaxcalans accompanying them, all with their weapons
of war. When they all reached Cholula,
the Cholulans took no notice of anything;
they received them with neither war nor
peace, but stayed in their houses. From this
the Spaniards conceived a bad opinion of
them and conjectured some treason.
    Then they began to cry out loudly to
the leaders and lords and all the other people [of Cholula] to come to where the
Spaniards were, and they all assembled in
the square of the great cu [temple] of Quetzalcoatl. When they were together there,
the Spaniards, affronted by the little notice
they had taken of them, entered on horseback, having secured all the entrances to
the square, and began to put them to the
lance, killing as many as they could, and it
is to be believed that the friendly Indians
killed many more. The Cholulans bore
neither offensive nor defensive weapons,
but went unarmed, thinking that what was
done would not be done, so that they died
a bad death.

As soon as all these things happened,
Moteucçoma's messengers came to tell
him of them; the whole road was full of
messengers from here to there and there to
here, and all the people here in Mexico
and in the districts where the Spaniards
were coming went about very agitated and

nemi, ça achcan mocomonia, ça iuhquin tlallolini, ça iuh[fol. 17]quin tlalli xoxo-quivi, [54] ça iuhquin tlaixmalacachivi, mavizcuioac.

common people went about in a state of excitement; there were frequent disturbances, as if the earth moved and ⟨quaked⟩, [54] as if everything were spinning before one's eyes. People took fright.

Auh in ommicoac cholollan: nimā oalpeuhque in ie ic vitze Mexico, ololiuhtivitze, tepeuhtivitze, teuhtli, quiquetztivitze: in intepuztopil, in intzinacantopil iuhquin tlapepetlaca: auh in intepuzmaquauh, iuhquin atl monecuiloa, iuhquin tlacacalaca in intepuzvipil, in intepuzquacalala. Auh cequintin vel much tepuztli motquitivitze, tetepuztin muchiuhtivitze, pepetlacativitze: ic cenca valmomavizçotitiaque, ic cenca oalmotlamauhtilitiaque: ic cenca mauhcaittoia, ic cenca imacaxoia. Auh in imitzcuinoan iacativitze, quiniacantivitze iniacac icativitze, iniacac onotivitze, hiicicativitze, intenqualac pipilcativitz.

And after the dying in Cholula, [the Spaniards] set off on their way to Mexico, coming gathered and bunched, raising dust. Their iron lances and halberds seemed to sparkle, and their iron swords were curved like a stream of water. Their cuirasses and iron helmets seemed to make a clattering sound. Some of them came wearing iron all over, turned into iron beings, gleaming, so that they aroused great fear and were generally seen with fear and dread. Their dogs came in front, coming ahead of them, keeping to the front, panting, with their spittle hanging down.

### 12

Inic matlactli omume capitulo: vncan mitoa in quenin Motecuçoma, quioa ce tlacatl vei pilli: yoā oc cequintin miequintin pipilti in quinnamiquito Españoles: yoan in tlein ic tlatlapaloque, inic quitlapaloque Capitan, in itzalan iztactepetl, yoan popocatepetl./.

[fol. 17v] Auh in Moteucçoma: nimā ie ic quimonioa, quimonixquetza in pipilti, quiniacana in tzioacpopocatzin, yoan oc ceq̇ntin cenca miequintin itechiuhcaoan cōnamiquito, intzalan in popocatepetl, yoan iztactepetl, vncan in quauhtechcac, quimōmacaque teucuitlapanitl, quetzalpanitl, yoā teucuitlacozcatl.

Auh in oquimōmacaque iuhquin yixvetzca, cenca papaqui, ahavia, iuhquin cooçomatzitzquia in teucuitlatl, iuhquin

Twelfth chapter, where it is said how Moteucçoma sent a great nobleman along with many other noblemen to go to meet the Spaniards, and what their gifts of greeting were when they greeted the Captain between Iztactepetl and Popocatepetl.

Thereupon Moteucçoma named and sent the noblemen and a great many other agents of his, with Tzihuacpopocatzin as their leader, to go meet [Cortés] between Popocatepetl and Iztactepetl, at Quauhtechcac. They gave [the Spaniards] golden banners, banners of precious feathers, and golden necklaces.

And when they had given the things to them, they seemed to smile, to rejoice and be very happy. Like monkeys they grabbed

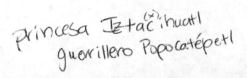

gente muy alborotada y desasosegada parecia que la tierra se mouia todos andauā espātados y atonitos.

[fol. 17] Y como vieron [55] hecho en cholula aq̄l estrauo, [56] los españoles con todos los indios sus amigos venian gran multitud en esquadrones con grā ruydo y con gran poluoreda y de lexos resplandecian las armas y causauan gran miedo en los que mirauan ansimismo ponian gran miedo los lebreles que trayan consigo que eran grandes, trayan las bocas abiertas las lenguas sacadas y yvan carleando ansi ponian gran temor en todos los que los vian.

upset. It seemed that the earth moved; everyone went about shocked and stunned.

After they had [55] wrought that havoc [56] in Cholula, the Spaniards with all their Indian friends came in a great multitude, in squadrons, with much noise and dust, and their weapons gleamed from a distance, arousing great fear in those who were looking. Likewise the greyhounds they brought with them inspired great dread, for they were large, with their mouths open and tongues hanging out, and they went along panting, and thus they inspired great fear in all who saw them.

24

12

Capitulo .12. de como Motecuçoma enbio a vno mu [57] principal suyo con otros muchos principales que fueron a recebir a los españoles y hizieron vn gran presente al capitan en medio de la sierra neuada del [58] bulcan.

[fol. 17v] Quando supo Motecuçoma, que los españoles auian partido de cholula y que yuan camino de mexico, despacho luego a vn principal suyo el mas principal de su corte que se llamaua tzioacpupuca y con el muchos otros principales y otra mucha gente para que fuesen a recebir a los españoles y diolos vn presente de oro que lleuasen. Partieronse de mexico y toparonse con los españoles entre las dos sierras que es la sierra neuada: y el bulcan

Chapter Twelve, of how Moteucçoma sent a high leader [57] of his, with many other leaders, who went to receive the Spaniards, and gave a great present to the Captain between the snowy peak and the [58] volcano.

When Moteucçoma learned that the Spaniards had departed from Cholula and were on their way toward Mexico, he immediately dispatched one of his leaders, the most important in his court, called Tzihuacpopoca, and many other leaders with him, and many other people, to go to receive the Spaniards, and he gave them a present of gold to take. They departed from Mexico and came up against the Spaniards between the two mountains, that is, the snowy peak and the volcano.

vncan motlatlalia, iuhquin iiztaia, iuhq̃n
cecelia yiollo: canel iehoatl in cenca cami-
qui, quipoçaoa, quiteucivi, quipitzonequi
in teucuitlatl. Auh in teucuitlapanitl quihi-
iauhtivitze, quitlatlavitzotivitze, qui-
moottititivitze, iuhquin tlapopoloca, in
tlein quimolhuia in popolochcopa.


Auh in iquac oquittaque Tzioacpopocatzin: quitoque. Cuix iee hin in
Motecuçoma: Quimilhuique, in intlan
mantivitze, in intlachixcaoan, in tlaxcal[fol.
18]teca, cempoalteca, inic quimōichtaca-
tlatlanique: conitoque ca amo ie iehoatl
totecuiioane. Inin tzioacpopocatzin, qui-
mixiptlatica in Motecuçomatzin:
quilhuique. Cuix ie te in tiMotecuçoma? Conito. Ca nehoatl in namote-
chiuhcauh in niMotecuçoma.
Auh nimā quilhuique. Nepa xiauh,
tleica in titechiztlacavia, ac titechmati, amo
vel titechiztlacaviz, amo vel toca timo-
caiaoaz, amo vel titechquamanaz, amo vel
titechixmamatiloz, amo vel titechichchi-
oaz, amo vel titechixcuepaz, amo vel
titechixpatiliz, amo vel titechtlacuepiliz,
amo vel titechixpopoloz, amo vel titech-
ixmimictiz, amo vel titechixçoquiviz, amo
vel titechixçoquimatocaz! amo tehoatl ca
vnca in Motecuçoma, amo vel techne-
tlatiliz, amo vel minaiaz! campa iaz? cuix
tototl, cuix patlaniz? cuinoço⁶¹ tlallan qui-
quetzaz yiovi, cuix cana ca tepetl coionqui
yitic calaquiz [fol. 18v] ca tiquittazque, ca
amo maca ixco titlachiezque, ticcaquizque
in itlatol, itenco titlacaquizque,

the gold. It was as though their hearts were
put to rest, brightened, freshened. For gold
was what they greatly thirsted for; they
were gluttonous for it, starved for it, pig-
gishly wanting it. They came lifting up the
golden banners, waving them from side to
side, showing them to each other. They
seemed to babble; what they said to each
other was in a babbling tongue.
And when they saw Tzihuacpopocatzin,
they said, "Is this one then Moteucçoma?"
They said it to the Tlaxcalans and Cempoalans, their lookouts, who came among
them, questioning them secretly. They
said, "It is not that one, o our lords. This is
Tzihuacpopocatzin, who is representing
Moteucçoma."
[The Spaniards] said to him, "Are you
then Moteucçoma?" He said, "I am your
agent Moteucçoma."
Then they told him, "Go on with you!
Why do you lie to us? What do you take
us for? You can't lie to us, you can't fool
us, ⟨turn our heads⟩, flatter us, ⟨make
faces at us⟩, trick us, confuse our vision,
distort things for us, blind us, dazzle us,
throw mud in our eyes, put muddy hands
on our faces. It is not you. Moteucçoma
exists; he will not be able to hide from us,
he will not be able to find refuge. Where
will he go? Is he a bird, will he fly? Or⁶¹
will he take an underground route, will he
go somewhere into a mountain that is hol-
low inside? We will see him, we will not
fail to gaze on his face and hear his words
from his lips."

alli los recibieron y presentaron el presente de oro que lleuauan y segun que a los indios les parecio por las senales esteriores que vieron en los españoles holgaronse y regozijaronse mucho con el oro mostrando que lo tenia es [59] mucho

y como vieron el principal, tzioac-pupuca: preguntaron a los que con ellos venian Tlalcaltecas, [60] y Cempoaltecas secretamente si era aquel Motecuçoma? Y dixeronles. Que no! Que no era el, que era vn principal suyo que se llama, tzioac-pupuca!

y despues preguntaron al mismo principal si era el Motecuçoma? Y dixo que si! que era el Motecuçoma:

y dixeronle. Vete de ay que mientes! que no eres Motecuçoma piensas de engañarnos? Piensas que somos algunos nescios, no nos podras engañar. [fol. 18] Ni Motecuçoma se nos podra asconder por mucho que haga, aunque sea ave y aunque se meta debaxo de tierra no se nos podra asconder de verle avemos y de oyr avemos lo que nos dira.

There they received them and gave them the present of gold that they brought, and according to the external signs that the Indians saw in the Spaniards, it seemed to them that they were pleased and greatly rejoiced over the gold, for they held it in [59] great esteem.

And when they saw the leader Tzihuac-popoca, they secretly asked the Tlax-calans [60] and Cempohualans who were coming along with them if that was Mo-teucçoma. They told him no, that it was not him, that it was a leader of his named Tzihuacpopoca.

And afterward they asked the leader himself if he was Moteucçoma, and he said that yes, he was Moteucçoma.

Then they told him, "Go on with you, you're lying. You aren't Moteucçoma. Do you think you can deceive us? Do you think we are a lot of simpletons? You can't deceive us. Nor can Moteucçoma hide himself from us, whatever he should do; though he should be a bird, or though he should go beneath the earth, he will not be able to hide from us. We are going to see him and hear what he tells us."

25

26

ic çan contelchiuhque, atle ipan conittaque ic çan onnenpoliuh in oc çequi in
intenamic, in intetlapalol: ic nimā quioal-
melauhtivetzque in melaoac vtli.

13

Inic matlactli omei capitulo vncā mitoa
in quenin Motecuçoma: quimioa oc cequintin tetlachivianime inic quītlachiviz-
quia Espanoles[62] yoan in tlein vtlica impan
muchiuh.

Auh ie no centlamantique titlanti; iehoan in tlaciuhq̄ in nanaoalti, yoan tletlenamacaque, no ic iaca, no ic iaque
in tenamiquizque: auh aoccā vel mo-
chiuhque, aoccan vel teittaque, aocmo
tlaipantilique, aocmo teipantilique, aocmo
onieoatque:

çan ie ce tlaoanqui vtlica ica ommotzo-
tzonato, quimonamictito, ica onmixtilque-
tzato: inic quittaq̄ iuhquin chalcatl ic omo-
chi[fol. 19]chiuh, mochalcachichiuh,
mochalcanenequi: iuhquin tlaoāqui,
mivincanenequi, motlaoācanenequi: chicuei çacamecatl ic melilpi, quimixnamicti-
vitz hiiacac icativitz in Españoles.

Auh çan inca ieoac: quimilhui. tle noma
amaxtivitze in nicā? tlen oc anquinequi? tle
noma quichioaznequi in Motecuçoma?
cuix quin omozcali? cuix quin axcan ie
momauhticapul? ca otlatlaco, ca ocon-

Therefore they just scorned and disregarded him, and so another of their meet-
ings and greetings came to naught. Then
they went straight back the direct way [to
Mexico].

Thirteenth chapter, where it is said how
Moteucçoma sent other sorcerers to cast
spells on the Spaniards,[62] and what happened to them on the way.

Another group of messengers—rainmakers, witches, and priests—had also
gone out for an encounter, but nowhere
were they able to do anything or to get
sight of [the Spaniards]; they did not hit
their target, they did not find the people
they were looking for, they were not suf-
ficient.

They just came up against a drunk man
in the road; they went to meet him and
were dumbfounded at him. The way they
saw him, he seemed to be dressed as a
Chalcan, feigning to be a Chalcan. He
seemed to be drunk, feigning drunkenness.
On his chest were tied eight grass ropes.
He came quarreling with them, coming
ahead of the Spaniards.

He ranted at them, saying to them,
"What are you still doing here? What
more do you want? What more is Moteucçoma trying to do? Did he come to his
senses yesterday? Has he just now become

Y luego con afrenta embiaron aquel principal y a todos [fol. 18v] los que con el avian ydo y ellos se boluieron a mexico y contaron a Motecuçoma lo que avian pasado con los españoles

Then with insults they dismissed that leader and all who had gone with him, and they returned to Mexico and told Moteucçoma what had happened with the Spaniards.

## 13

Capitulo .13. de como Motecuçoma enbio otros hechizeros contra los españoles y de lo que los acontecio en el camino.

Como supo Motecuçoma que ya venian los españoles camino de mexico embiolos al encuentro muchos satrapas de los ydolos agoreros y encantadores y nigromāticos para que con sus encantamientos y hechizerias los empeciesen y maleficiase y no podieron hazer nada, ni sus encantamientos los pudieron enpecer ni aun llegaron a ellos, porque antes que llegasen a ellos toparon con vn borracho en el camino y no pasaron adelante

parecio[fol. 19]les que era vn indio de los chalco[63] pareciales que estaua borracho traya ceñido a los pechos ocho cabestros o sogas hechas de heno como de esparto y venia de hazia donde estauan los españoles y llegando cerca dellos començo con gran enojo a reñirlos y dixoles

para que porfyays vosotros otra uez de venir aca? Que es lo que quereys? Que piensa Motecuçoma de hazer? Agora acuerda a despertar? Agora comiença a temer? y a errado! ya no tiene remedio!

Chapter Thirteen, of how Moteucçoma sent other sorcerers against the Spaniards and what happened to them on the way.

When Moteucçoma learned that the Spaniards were already on their way to Mexico, he sent to meet them many satraps of the idols, soothsayers, enchanters, and necromancers, so that with their enchantments and sorceries they would harm and bewitch them. But they were unable to do anything, nor could their enchantments harm them, nor did they even reach them, because before they did they ran across a drunk man in the road, and they got no farther.

It seemed to them that he was an Indian from Chalco,[63] and he seemed to them to be drunk. Tied to his chest he wore eight reins or ropes made of grass, like esparto grass, and he was coming from the direction where the Spaniards were. When he got close to them, with great annoyance he began to scold them, saying,

"Why do you persist in coming here again? What is it that you want? What does Moteucçoma intend to do? Has it occurred to him to wake up now? Now is he beginning to be afraid? He has already

cavili [64] in maceoalli, ca otlacaixpolo teca omoquavitec, ca teca omoquimilo, [65] ca teca omavilti, ca teca omocacaiauh.

Auh in o iuh quittaque in, in o iuh quicacque itlatol, oc nen itlan aqui, in quimocnotlatlauhtilia, quitlalilitivetzque ichiel itlalmomoz, yoan içacapepech, çan nimā aocmo vmpa quioalittac: tel çan nenpanca in ommotlalica, in vncan oc nen quitlalmomuztica:

çan ie iuhquin icamac ommaquique, [66] ie vncan quimaoa, quintequiaia, iuhquin motiti[fol. 19v]tzatlatoa: quimilhui. Tleçānen in nican amicativitze aoquic iez in Mexico, ie ic cēmāia, nepa xivia, aocmo vncā, tla xommocuepacan, tla xontlachiacan in Mexico, tlein ie mochioa: in iuh ie mochioa.

Nimā ic oallachixque, oallachixtivetzque, in quioalitta ie tlatlā in ixquich teucalli, in calpulli, in calmecatl, yoan in ixquich mexico calli, yoan iuhquin ma ie cuel necaliva.
Auh in o iuh quittaque in tlaciuhque, iuhquin canin ia, iniollo, aocmo onnaoatque, iuhquin aca itla quintololti: quitoque inin ca amo totech monequia in tiquittazque, ca ie itech monequia quittaz in Motecuçoma, in otiquittaque: ca amo çan aca, ca iehoatl in telpuchtli Tezcatlipuca:

niman ic poliuh, aocmo quittaque. Auh in titlanti aocmo tenamiquito, aocmo tevic quiçato, ça vncā oalilotque in tlaciuhque, in tletlenamacaque, quinonotzaco in Motecuçoma: oalnepanixtiaque [fol. 20] in achto iaque in Tzioacpopocatzin.

a great coward? He has done wrong, he has ⟨abandoned⟩ [64] the people, he has destroyed people, [he has hit himself on the head and wrapped himself up in relation to people], [65] he has mocked people and deceived them."

When they had seen this and heard what he said, they made an effort to address him humbly; they quickly set up for him a place to attend to him, an earthen platform with a straw bed, but he absolutely would not look at it. In vain they had set out for him the earthen platform they had tried to make for him there.

[It was as though they entered his mouth]; [66] he scolded them, greatly scolded them with angry words, saying to them, "What is the use of your coming here? Mexico will never exist again, it [is gone] forever. Go on with you; it is no longer there. Do turn around and look at what is happening in Mexico, what is going on."

Then they looked back, they quickly looked back, and saw all the temples, the calpulli [buildings], the calmecacs, and all the houses in Mexico burning, and it seemed as though there were fighting.

And when the rainmakers had seen that, their hearts seemed to fail them, they were silent, as though someone had forced something down their throats. They said, "What we have seen was needed to be seen not by us but by Moteucçoma, for that was not just anyone, but the youth Tezcatlipoca."

Then he vanished, and they saw him no more. And after that the messengers did not go to encounter [the Spaniards], did not move in their direction, but the rainmakers and priests turned back there and came to tell Moteucçoma. They came together with those who had first gone with Tzihuacpopocatzin.

porque a hecho muchas muertes iniustas a destruido muchos, a hecho muchos agrauios y engaños y burlas.

made his mistakes! Now there is no remedy! For he has brought about many unjust deaths and destroyed many. He has committed much abuse, deceit, and cheating."

Como vieron este hombre: los encantadores temieron mucho y prostraronse delante del, començaron a rogarle y hizieron vn monton de tierra como altar y echaron heno verde encima para que se sentase y el como hombre enojado ni quiso sentarse ni mirarle, ni hazer lo que le rogauā: por demas hizieron el altar o asiento, mas antes, se enojo mas brauamente: y mas reciamente los reñia con grandes vozes y gran denuedo les dixo

[fol. 19v] por demas aveys venido! Nunca mas hare cuenta de mexico para siēpre os dexo, no tendre mas cargo de vosotros ni os amparare: apartaos de mi: lo que quereys no se puede hazer! bolueos y mirad hazia mexico:

y ellos boluieronse a mirar hazia mexico: y vieron que todos los cues ardian, y los calpules y calmecates, y todas las casas de mexico: pareciolos que auia gran guerra dentro en la ciudad de mexico.

Como vierō aquello los encantadores desmayaron grandemente, y no podieron hablar palabra hizoseles vn nodo en la garganta: esto acontecio en la cuesta que suben hazia tlalmanalco:

hecho esto desaparecio aquel que les hablaua y boluiendo en si dixeron: esto que emos visto conbenia que lo viera Motecuçoma y no nosotros. Este que nos a hablado no es persona humana, es el dios Tezcatlipuca: estos mensajeros no curaron de yr mas adelante, sino boluierō a dar relacion a Motecuçoma de lo que auia pasado:

When they saw this man, the enchanters were greatly afraid and prostrated themselves before him. They began to pray to him, and they made a mound of earth as an altar and cast green grass on top for him to sit on. But he as an angry man would not sit down there nor even look at it, nor do what they asked him to do. In vain they made the altar or seat; instead he grew more fiercely angry and scolded them more strongly, saying to them loudly and with great vehemence,

"You have come in vain! I will never again take notice of Mexico, I leave you forever; I will take care of you no longer, nor defend you. Go from me. What you want cannot be done! Turn and look toward Mexico."

Then they turned to look toward Mexico, and they saw that all the *cus* [great temples] were burning, and the *calpules* [calpulli ceremonial centers] and *calmecates* [calmecacs, houses of instruction], and all the houses of Mexico. It appeared to them that there was a great war inside the city of Mexico.

When the enchanters saw that, their hearts failed them; they got a lump in their throat and could not speak. This happened on the slope going up toward Tlalmanalco.

After this, the person who had spoken to them disappeared and, coming to their senses, they said, "It would be fitting if Moteucçoma had seen what we have seen, not us. The one who has spoken to us is not a human being, he is the god Tezcatlipoca." These messengers thought no more of going on, but returned to give an account to Moteucçoma of what had happened.

Auh in oacico iehoantin titlantin, iuh quipovilique in Motecuçoma in iuh mochiuh in iuh quittaque. In motecuçoma, in o iuh quicac, ça oaltolo ça oaltolotimotlali, oalquechpilo, oalquechpilotimotlali, aocmo oalnaoat, çan ontlanauhtimotlali, vecauhtica in iuhqui ontlapolo,

ça ixquich inic quinoalnanquili: quinoalilhui, Quennel mocechtle[67] ca ie ic toncate, ca ie otictomacaque, cuix cacah tepetl tictlecavizque: auh cuix ticholozque ca timexica, cuix nellaontimaliviz in mexicaiutl, motolinia in icnoveve, in icnoilama: auh in piltzintli, in aia quimati, campa neviquililozque, quēnel, quēçannel nen, quēnoçonel, campanel, ca ie tictomacaticate in çaço tlein, in çaço quenami in ticmaviçozque.

And when the messengers got there, they told Moteucçoma what had happened and what they had seen. When Moteucçoma heard it, he just hung his head and sat there, not saying a word. He sat like someone on the verge of death; for a long time it was as though he had lost awareness.

He answered them only by saying to them, "What can be done, o men of unique valor?[67] We have come to the end. We are resigned. Should we climb up in the mountains? But should we run away? We are Mexica. Will the Mexica state flourish [in exile]? Look at the sad condition of the poor old men and women, and the little children who know nothing yet. Where would they be taken? What answer is there? What can be done, whatever can be done? Where are we to go? We are resigned to whatever we will see, of whatever nature."

## 14

Inic matlactli onnavi capitulo, vncan mitoa in quenin Motecuçoma tlanaoati in motzatzaquaz vtli inic amo vel aciquivi Españoles, in nicā mexico.

[fol. 20v] Auh in Motecuçoma, oc nen tlanaoatica in quitzatzaquazque in vtli, in vchpantli, quimetecaque in oallamelauhticac nicā Mexico: auh ie vmpa quimontlachieltiaia, in ipan vtli iaticac, calacticac tetzcucu.

Auh in vncan quimetepātzacca: niman quimatque, quittaque in çan oquitzatzacque, atle ipan conittaque, caanque, veca

Fourteenth chapter, where it is said how Moteucçoma gave orders for the roads to be closed so that the Spaniards could not get to Mexico here.

And in a vain attempt Moteucçoma ordered that the roads and highways be closed off in various places. They planted magueys in the road coming straight to Mexico here, directing them [instead] onto the road going into Tetzcoco.

And where they had closed the road with a wall of maguey, [the Spaniards] immediately recognized it, they saw that they

venidos los mensajeros a la presencia de Mo[fol. 20]tecuçoma: oydo lo que dixeron entristeciose mucho, estaua cabizbaxo. no hablaua, estaua enmudecida casi fuera de si:

Once the messengers had come into Moteucçoma's presence and he had heard what they said, he was greatly saddened. He sat with his head down; he did not speak, but was struck dumb and almost unconscious.

a cabo de rato, dixolos: pues que emos de hazer varones nobles? ya estamos para perdernos, ya tenemos tragada la muerte! no emos de subirnos a alguna sierra ni emos de huyr! Mexicanos somos, ponernos emos a lo que viniere por la honrra de nuestra generacion mexicana: pesame de los viejos y viejas y de los niños y niñas que no tienen posibilidad ni discrecion para valerse donde los escaparan sus padres! Pues que emos de hazer? Nacido somos venga lo que viniere.

After a while, he said to them, "Well, noble lords, what are we to do? We are about to be lost. We are already reconciled to our deaths. We will not climb some mountain or run away! We are Mexica, we will face what should come for the honor of our Mexica stock. I grieve for the old men and women, and for the little boys and girls who lack the possibility and discretion to take care of themselves. Where can their parents find escape for them? What are we to do, then? We are born [exist as we are]; let come what may."

28

14

Capitulo .14. de como Motecuçoma mãdo cerrar los caminos por que los españoles no llegasen a Mexico.

[fol. 20v] Auiendo oydo Motecuçoma todas estas cosas, y viendo que venian los españoles derechos a mexico, mando cerrar los caminos, por donde aviã de venir, mando plantar magueyes en los caminos, y mando que los lleuasen hazia Tetzcucu;

los españoles conocieron el cerramiento de los caminos, y tornaronlos abrir, y echarõ por ay los magueyes, con que estauã cerrados,

Chapter Fourteen, of how Moteucçoma ordered the roads closed so that the Spaniards would not reach Mexico.

After Moteucçoma had heard all these things, seeing that the Spaniards were coming straight to Mexico, he ordered the roads closed. He ordered magueys planted in the roads they would have to pass, and he ordered them to direct them toward Tetzcoco.

But the Spaniards recognized the closing of the roads and opened them up again, casting aside the magueys with which they were closed.

conxoxopeuhque, quioalchichitotzque, veca ica ommamaiauhque in metl:

vncā cochque amaquemecan, nimā ie ic vitze, tlamelauhtivitze, quimelauhtivitze in vtli, acico in cuitlaoac, çan oc no vncan cochque: in oquincentlalique tlatoque, in izquican tlatocachioa inic chināpaneca in Suchmilco in cuitlaoac, in mizquic: çan ie no ivi in quimilhuique, in iuh quimilhuique chalcatlatoque. [69] Auh in iehoanti [fol. 21] chinanpaneca tlatoque, çan nimā no intlan oncalacque.

Auh in o iniollo vmpachiuh, in Españoles: niman ic oalolinque ommotlalico in itztapalapan: niman ie no ic quinnotza, quinnenotzallani in tlatoque: Nauhtecutli mitoa. In itztapalapan, Mexicatzinco, culhoacan, Vitzilobuchco: çā ie no ie in quimilhuique, inic quintlatoltique (in o iuh mito). Auh çanno ivian, iocuxca intlan oncalacque in Españoles.

Auh in Motecuçomatzin, amo tlanaoatiaia inic aca quiniauchioaz, inic aca iauiotica quinnamiquiz, aiac iauiotica quinnamiquiz, çan tlanaoatiaia, inic amo çan tlacomachozque, [71] ça cenca inca nechioaloz.
Auh in iquac y, in nican Mexico, ça iuhquin cactoc, aocac oalquiça, aocac oalquiztica. In tenanhoan aocmo oaltequixtitlani, ça chichipaoaticac in vtli, ichpelpul icac, ça ichpeliuhticac [fol. 21v] in vtli, ça iuhquin tlalchipacpan, aocac ixtlapal iauh, aocac tlaxtlapaloa, necacaltemaloc, ça ixcavilo in tlaocuialo: quitoaia in macevalli. Ma iuhtie, ma motelchioa, tle oc iez in anquichioa, ca ie timiquizā, ca ie tipolivizque, ca ie toconchixticate in tomiquiz.

had just blocked it, and they disregarded it. They took the magueys, kicked them far away, sent them flying, hurled them far off to the side.

They spent the night at Amaquemecan, then came straight on along the road and reached Cuitlahuac, where they also spent the night. They assembled the rulers from each of the kingdoms among the chinampa people: Xochimilco, Cuitlahuac, Mizquic. They told them what they had told the rulers of Chalco. [69] And the rulers of the chinampa people also submitted to them.

And when the Spaniards were satisfied, they moved on this way and made a halt in Itztapalapan. Then they summoned, had summoned the rulers there as well, called the Four Lords, of Itztapalapan, Mexicatzinco, Colhuacan, and Huitzilopochco. They talked with them in the same way they had spoken to [the chinampa people] (as was said). And they too peacefully submitted to the Spaniards.

Moteucçoma did not give orders for anyone to make war against them or for anyone to meet them in battle. No one was to meet them in battle. He just ordered that they be strictly obeyed [71] and very well attended to.

And at this time there was silence here in Mexico. No one went out any more; mothers no longer let [their children] go out. The roads were as if swept clean, wide open, as if at dawn, with no one crossing. People assembled in the houses and did nothing but grieve. The people said, "Let it be that way; curses on it. What more can you do? For we are about to die and perish, we are awaiting our deaths."

dormieron en Amaquemecan, y otro dia partieron de alli, y llegaron a Cuitlaoac, en el pueblo de cuitlaoac. Don hernando cortes embio a llamar, todos los señores que estan en chipan, [68] que so xochimilco, Mizquic: y todos los pueblos de la chinā-pan, alli los hablo diziendo: los la razon de su venida esta platica: oyeron los de tlal-manalco, en Amaquemecā, y rescibieron de paz a Don hernādo Cortes, segun dizen alli los hablo: y tanbien todos se mostrarō de paz estos pueblos de la chināpan,

de alli se partieron, para ytztapalapā pueblo que dista de mexico dos leguas llegados alli Dō hernādo cortes hizo juntar a los principales que se llamā Nauhtecutli, que son ytztapalapan, [70] [fol. 21] Mexica-tzinco, Coloacan. Vitzilupuchco, alli los hablo de la manera que a los otros: ellos se mostrarō de paz y hablaron como amigos

Motecuçoma en todo esto ninguna cosa de guerra proueyo: ni mando que los hi-ziesen enojo ninguno, mas antes proveyo que fuesen proueydos de todo lo necesario, hasta que llegasen a mexico.

Estando los españoles en ytztapalapā ninguno de los mexicanos fue a uerlos, ni osauā salir de sus casas ni andar por los caminos todos estauā amedrentados de lo que auian oydo que los españoles auiā hecho por el camino todo: estauan es-perando la muerte, y desto hablauā entre si diziendo que avemos de hazer vaya por donde fuere ya es venido el tiempo en que emos de ser destruidos esperemos aqui la muerte.

They slept the night in Amaquemecan; the next day they departed from there and reached Cuitlahuac. In the settlement of Cuitlahuac don Hernando Cortés sent to summon all the lords who are in the *chinampa*[68] territory, that is, Xochimilco, Mizquic, and all the settlements of the *chinampa* country. There he spoke to them, telling them why he had come. The people of Tlalmanalco heard this speech in Amaquemecan, and received don Hernando Cortés peacefully. According to what is said, he spoke to them there. And also all these settlements of the *chinampa* country showed their peaceful intent.

From there they departed for Itztapala-pan, a settlement two leagues distant from Mexico. On their arrival there, don Her-nando Cortés assembled the leaders called the Nauhteuctli [four lords], of Itztapa-lapan,[70] Mexicatzinco, Colhuacan, and Huitzilopochco. There he spoke to them in the same manner as to the others; they showed their peaceful intentions and spoke as friends.

During all this time Moteucçoma nei-ther took warlike measures nor ordered that they cause [the Spaniards] any annoy-ance; rather he decreed that they be pro-vided everything necessary until they should reach Mexico.

While the Spaniards were in Itztapala-pan, none of the Mexica went to see them, nor did they dare come out of their houses or go about the roadways. They were all intimidated by what they had heard that the Spaniards had done all along the way. They were awaiting death, and they spoke of it among themselves, saying, "What are we to do? Let it take its course; the time has come when we are to be destroyed. Let us await death here."

Inic caxtolli capitulo: vncan mitoa in quenin Espanoles, vmpa vallevaque in Itztapalapan inic acico mexico.

Auh niman ie ic oalolini in ie ic oalcalaquizque nican Mexico; niman ie ic mocecencaoa, moiauchichioa; moolpia, vel quiilpia in iniautlatqui: niman ie iehoantin in incavallos: niman ie ic motetecpana, mocuecuētilia, movivipana, mocecēpantilia.

Auh nauhteme in cavallos in iacattivitze, in atto vitze, in teiacantivitze, in teiacac onotivitze, in te [fol. 22] in teiacana;[74] mocuecueptivi, ommocuecueptivi, onteixnamictivi, havic tlachixtivi, nanacaz. tlachixtivitze, noviampa onitztivi in cacaltzalan,[75] tlaixtotocativitze, onacotlachixtivi in tlapanco;

no iehoan in chichime in imitzcuinoan, iacattivitze, tlatlanecutivitze, neneciuhtivitze, nêneneciuhtivitze;

yioca icativitz, iacattivitz, icel icativitz in quachpanitl quiquechpanoa, quitlatlavitzotivitz, quimamalacachotivitz, havic quitlatlaztivitz, mochichicauhtivitz, moquichquetzivitz, vel mocolotilia, mocoloquetztivitz, mocolonectivitz;

quioaltoquilitivi tepuzmaquaveque, pepetlauhtivitz, in intepuzmaquauh, pepe-

Fifteenth chapter, where it is said how the Spaniards came from Itztapalapan when they reached Mexico.

Then they set out in this direction, about to enter Mexico here. Then they all dressed and equipped themselves for war. They girded themselves, tying their battle gear tightly on themselves and then on their horses. Then they arranged themselves in rows, files, ranks.

Four horse[men] came ahead, going first, staying ahead, leading.[74] They kept turning about as they went, facing people, looking this way and that, looking sideways, gazing everywhere between the houses,[75] examining things, looking up at the roofs.

Also the dogs, their dogs, came ahead, sniffing at things and constantly panting.

By himself came marching ahead, all alone, the one who bore the standard on his shoulder. He came waving it about, making it spin, tossing it here and there. It came stiffening, rising up like a warrior, twisting and turning.

Following him came those with iron swords. Their iron swords came bare and

29

30

[fol. 21v] Capitulo .15. de como los españoles, partieron de ytztapalapan, para entrar en mexico.

Partieron los españoles de Itztapalapan, todos adereçados a punto de [72] guerra, y en su ordenança, por esquadrones: fueron algunos de a cavallo, delante a descubrir, si auia alguna celada; lleuauā tanbien los lebreles delante yua en la retaguardia Don hernādo cortes con otros muchos españoles todos armados y en su ordenança, tras ellos yua el vagaxe y la artille [73] en sus carretones yuan muchos indios de guerra. Con todas sus armas muchos Tlaxcaltecas y vexotzincas desta manera ordenados en[fol. 22]traron en mexico.

En todo lo restāte desde [76] capitulo, no se dize otra cosa, sino la orden que lleuauan los españoles: y los yndios amigos, quando entraron en mexico.

Chapter Fifteen, of how the Spaniards departed from Itztapalapan to enter Mexico.

The Spaniards departed from Itztapalapan all outfitted for war and ordered by squadrons. Some horsemen went ahead to see if there was some ambush; they also took the greyhounds ahead. Don Hernando Cortés went in the rear guard with many other Spaniards, all armed [72] and in order. After them went the baggage and the artillery [73] on its carriages. Many Indian warriors went along, with all their arms, many Tlaxcalans and Huexotzinca. In this order they entered Mexico.

In all the rest of this [76] chapter, nothing is said except the order that the Spaniards and the Indian allies kept when they entered Mexico.

petlacativitz, quiquequechpanoa, quiquequechpanotivitze, inchichimal, quauhchimalli, eoachimalli.

Inic vntlaman[fol. 22v]titivitze, inic
vmpantitivitze cavallos temamativitze,
imiichcavipil, imeeoachimal intetepuz-
topil, yoan intetepuzmaquauh inquezpā
pipilcativitz in cavallosme, cocoiolloque,
coioleque, coiollotivitze iuhquin xaxa-
maca in coiolli, tlaxamacan coiolli in caval-
losti; in mamaça pipitzca, tlapipitzca, cenca
mitonia, iuhquin atl intechpa temo: auh in
intepopuçoquillo chachapaca tlalpan, iuhquin amulli chachapani; auh inic nenemi
cenca tlatiticuitza, tlatetecuitza: tlacoco-
motza, iuhquin tlatemotla, niman co-
coioni, cocomolivi in tlalli in vncan qui-
quetza imicxi, yioca momamana in vncan
quiquequetztivi in imicxi, in inma.

Iniquepantin tepuztlavitoleque, tepuz-
tlavitoloani inmac onotivitz in tepuztlavitolli, tlaeiecotivitze, tlatlaieecotivitze,
quiiixcatzitztivitze. Auh in cequintin quiquechpanoa, quiquequechpanotivitze [fol.
23] in tepuztlavitolli: auh in inmicon inio-
motlan pipilcatiuh, inciacacpa quiquiztiuh,
vel tetentiuh, cahcacatzcatiuh in mitl, in
tepuzmitl, imiichcavipil, intlanquac
ahacitiuh, vel titilaoac, vellatepizçotl, ixachi titilacpopul, iuhquin tepetlatl: auh in
intzontecon ic quimilivi çanno ie in ich-
cavipilli, yoan inquequetzal imicpac con-
quequetztivi, xexeliuhtiuh,
momoiaoatiuh.

Inic nappantin çanno iehoantin in cavallotin, çan ie no iuhqui in innechichioal in
iuh omito.

Inic macuillamantli iehoātin in matlequiquiceque, in matlequiquiçoani,
quiquequechpanoa in matlequiquiztli; cequintin quitecativitze. Auh in iquac in
ocalaquico in vei tecpan, in tlatocan; quitlazque, quitlatlazque in matlequiquiztli, ie
oncuecueponi, ie oncuecuepoca, xixitica,
tlatlatzini, oaoalaca, poctli moteca, poctli

gleaming. On their shoulders they bore
their shields, of wood or leather.

The second contingent and file were
horses carrying people, each with his cotton cuirass, his leather shield, his iron
lance, and his iron sword hanging down
from the horse's neck. They came with
bells on, jingling or rattling. The horses,
the deer, neighed, there was much neigh-
ing, and they would sweat a great deal;
water seemed to fall from them. And their
flecks of foam splatted on the ground, like
soapsuds splatting. As they went they made
a beating, throbbing, and hoof-pounding
like throwing stones. Their hooves made
holes, they dug holes in the ground wherever they placed them. Separate holes
formed wherever they went placing their
hindlegs and forelegs.

The third file were those with iron
crossbows, the crossbowmen. As they
came, the iron crossbows lay in their arms.
They came along testing them out, bran-
dishing them, ⟨aiming them⟩. But some
carried them on their shoulders, came
shouldering the crossbows. Their quivers
went hanging at their sides, passed under
their armpits, well filled, packed with arrows, with iron bolts. Their cotton upper
armor reached to their knees, very thick,
firmly sewn, and dense, like stone. And
their heads were wrapped in the same cotton armor, and on their heads plumes
stood up, parting and spreading.

The fourth file were likewise horse-
[men]; their outfits were the same as has
been said.

The fifth group were those with harquebuses, the harquebusiers, shouldering
their harquebuses; some held them [level].
And when they went into the great palace,
the residence of the ruler, they repeatedly
shot off their harquebuses. They exploded,
sputtered, discharged, thundered, ⟨dis-
gorged⟩. Smoke spread, it grew dark with

moteteca, poctica tlaioa [fol. 23v] in poctli centlalli momana cētlalli moteca: inic xoquiiac teixivinti, teiolmoiauh:

auh ça tlatzacutiuh, tetzinpachotiuh in iautachcauh in ma iuhqui tlacateccatl momati in iautlatoani, in iautecani, cololhuitivi, quitepevitivi, quitzcactitivi, quitlamatilitivi, quitzatzacutivi in itiacaoan, in itlavicecaoan, in imananquilloā, [77] in ma iuhqui quaquachictin, in ma iuhqui otomi in ichicavilloā, in inechicaoalhoan, in inetlaquechilhoan, in itlaxilloan altepetl, in iiolloan, in itetzonoan:

niman ie ixquich in aoa tepeoa, in tlateputzcatl, in tlaxcaltecatl, tliliuhquitepecatl, in vexotzincatl: tlatoquilitivitze, moiauhchichiuhtivitze imiichcavipil, inchichimal, intlatlavitol, inmimicon tetentiuh, cacacatzcatiuh in totomitl, cequi chichiquilli, cequi tihpontli, cequi itzmitl: momamantivi, motenvitec[fol. 24]tivi, motenpapavitivi, tocuileuhtivi, tlatlanquiquiztivi, moquacuecuechotivi.

Auh in cequintin tlamama, itacamama, cequintin tlaixquamama, cequintin tlaelpanmama, cequintin tlacacaxvia, cequintin tlaoacalhuia, cequintin tlatompiavia, cequintin tlaquimilhuia, manoço tlaquimilmamama, cequintin quivilana in vevei, in totomaoac tlequiquiztli, quauhtemalacac oonotiuh, quicavatztivitze.

smoke, everyplace filled with smoke. The fetid smell made people dizzy and faint.

And last, bringing up the rear, went the war leader, thought to be the ruler and director in battle, like [among us] a *tlacateccatl*. Gathered and massed about him, going at his side, accompanying him, enclosing him were his warriors, those with devices, his [aides], [77] like [among us] those with scraped heads [*quaquachictin*] and the Otomi warriors, the strong and valiant ones of the altepetl, its buttress and support, its heart and foundation.

Then all those from the various altepetl on the other side of the mountains, the Tlaxcalans, the people of Tliliuhquitepec, of Huexotzinco, came following behind. They came outfitted for war with their cotton upper armor, shields, and bows, their quivers full and packed with feathered arrows, some barbed, some blunted, some with obsidian points. They went crouching, hitting their mouths with their hands and yelling, singing in Tocuillan style, whistling, shaking their heads.

Some bore burdens and provisions on their backs; some used [tump lines for] their foreheads, some [bands around] their chests, some carrying frames, some board cages, some deep baskets. Some made bundles, perhaps putting the bundles on their backs. Some dragged the large cannons, which went resting on wooden wheels, making a clamor as they came.

37

38

39

40

41

## 16

Inic caxtolli occe capitulo: vncā mitoa in quenin Motecuçoma pacca, iocuxca quinnamiquito Españoles, in vmpa xoluco, in axcan ie vmpa mani ical albarado, in anoço vncan quitoa Vitzillan.

Sixteenth chapter, where it is said how Moteucçoma went in peace and quiet to meet the Spaniards at Xoloco, where the house of Alvarado is now, or at the place they call Huitzillan.

Auh in ie iuhqui in oacico xoluco, in ie vncan tlantimani ie vncan iaquetivitz.[78] Niman ie ic muchichioa, mocencaoa in Motecuçomatzin inic tenamiquiz: yoan oc cequintin veveintin tlatoque in tlaço[fol. 24v]pipilti, in itlatocaiovan, in ipilloan: nimā ie ic vi tenamiquizque, xicalpechtica cōmamāque in tlaçosuchitl, in chimalsuchitl, in iollosuchitl inepantla icatiuh in izquisuchitl, in coztic iiesuchitl, in cacaoasuchitl, icpacsuchitl, in suchineapantli: yoā quitqui in teucuitlacozcatl, chaiaoac cozcatl, cozcapetlatl.

And when they [the Spaniards] had come as far as Xoloco, when they had stopped there,[78] Moteucçoma dressed and prepared himself for a meeting, along with other great rulers and high nobles, his rulers and nobles. Then they went to the meeting. On gourd bases they set out different precious flowers; in the midst of the shield flowers and heart flowers stood popcorn flowers, yellow tobacco flowers, cacao flowers, [made into] wreaths for the head, wreaths to be girded around. And they carried golden necklaces, necklaces with pendants, wide necklaces.

Auh ie vncan in vitzilla ontenamic Motecuçomatzin, niman ie ic contlamamaca in iautachcauh, in intepachocauh iauquizque, coxochimacac, concozcati in cozcatl, consuchicozcati, consuchiapan, conicpacsuchiti: niman ie ic ixpan contequilia in teucuitlacozcatl, in izquitlamātli tenamiconi, tenamictli in ica oiecauh, cequi cōcozcati:

And when Moteucçoma went out to meet them at Huitzillan, thereupon he gave various things to the war leader, the commander of the warriors; he gave him flowers, he put necklaces on him, he put flower necklaces on him, he girded him with flowers, he put flower wreaths on his head. Then he laid before him the golden necklaces, all the different things for greet-

## 16

[fol. 24] Capitulo .16. de como Motecuçoma salio de paz a rescebir a los Españoles, adonde llaman xoluco, que es el aceꝗa que esta cabe las casas de albarado o vn poco mas aca que llamā ellos vitzillā.

En llegando los españoles a aquel rio que esta cabe las casas de albarado que se llama Xoluco, luego Motecuçoma se aparejo para yrlos a recebir cō muchos señores y principales y nobles para recebir de paz y con honrra a Don hernando cortes y a los otros Capitanes tomaron muchas flores her[fol. 24v]mosas y olorosas hechas en sartales y en guirnaldas y compuestas para las manos y pusieronlas em platos muy pintados y muy grādes hechos de calabaças, y tanbien lleuaron collares de oro y de piedras.

Llegando Motecuçoma a los españoles a lugar[79] que llamā vitzillan que es cabe el hospital de la conception, luego alli el mismo Motecuçoma puso vn collar de oro y de piedras al capitan Don hernādo cortes y dio flores y guirnaldas a todos los demas capitanes

aviendo dado el mismo Motecuçoma este presente como ellos lo vsauā hazer, luego Don hernando cortes pregunto al

Chapter Sixteen, of how Moteucçoma came out peacefully to receive the Spaniards at the place called Xoloco, which is the canal next to the house of Alvarado, or a little farther this way, what they call Huitzillan.

When the Spaniards reached that river next to the house of Alvarado, called Xoloco, Moteucçoma equipped himself to go receive them, along with many lords, leaders, and nobles. In order to give don Hernando Cortés and the other captains a peaceful and honorable reception, they took many beautiful and fragrant flowers, in chains, wreaths, and arrangements for the hands, and they put them in very large and well-painted dishes made of gourds. They also took necklaces of gold and fine stones.

When Moteucçoma reached the Spaniards, at the place[79] they call Huitzillan, near the Hospital of La Concepción, there Moteucçoma himself put a necklace of gold and fine stones on Captain don Hernando Cortés, and gave flowers and garlands to all the other captains.

After Moteucçoma himself had given this present, as they were accustomed to do, don Hernando Cortés asked Moteuc-

Nimā quioalilhui in Motecuçoma. Cuix amo te? cuix amo ie te? ie te in timotecuçoma:

quito in Motecuçoma, ca quemaca ca nehoatl: nimā [fol. 25] ie ic vel ommoquetza conixnamictimoquetza, connepechtequilia, [80] vel ixquich caana, motlaquauhquetza: inic contlatlauhti, quilhui.

Totecuioe oticmihiovilti, oticmociavilti, otlaltitech tommaxitico, o itech tommopachiviltico in Matzin, in motepetzin mexico, o ipan tommovetzitico in mopetlatzin, in mocpaltzin, in o achitzinca nimitzōnopielili, in onimitzonnotlapielili, ça oiaque in mōtechiuhcaoan in tlatoque: in Itzcoatzin, in veve Motecuçoma, in Axaiaca, in Tiçocic, in Avitzotl, in o cuel achic mitzommotlapielilico, in oquipachoco in atl, in tepetl in Mexico: in incuitlapan, inteputzco in ovalietia in momaceoaltzin, cuix oc vallamati in imonica, in inteputzco, ma ceme iehoantin quitztiani quimaviçotiani, in nehoatl in axcan nopan omochiuh in ie niquitta, in ça imonica, inteputzco totecuioan [fol. 25v] camo çan nitemiqui, amo çā nicochitleoa, amo çan niccochitta, amo çan nictemiqui ca ie onimitznottili, mixtzinco onitlachix, ca ononnentlamatticatca in ie macuil in ie matlac, in vmpa nonitztica, in quenamican in otimoquixtico in mixtitlan in aiauhtitlan: anca iehoatl inin quiteneuhtivi in tlatoq͞ in ticmomachitiquiuh in matzin, in motepetzin: in ipā timovetzitiquiuh in mopetlatzin, in mocpaltzin in tioalmovicaz. Auh in axcan ca oneltic, otioalmovicac, oticmihiovilti, oticmociavilti, ma tlaltitech ximaxiti, ma ximocevitzino, ma xoconmomachiti in motecpancaltzin, ma xicmocevili in monacaiotzin, ma tlaltitech maxitican in totecuioan.

ing people. He ended by putting some of the necklaces on him.

Then [Cortés] said in reply to Moteucçoma, "Is it not you? Is it not you then? Moteucçoma?"

Moteucçoma said, "Yes, it is me." Thereupon he stood up straight, he stood up with their faces meeting. He bowed down deeply to him. [80] He stretched as far as he could, standing stiffly. Addressing him, he said to him,

"O our lord, be doubly welcomed on your arrival in this land; you have come to satisfy your curiosity about your altepetl of Mexico, you have come to sit on your seat of authority, which I have kept a while for you, where I have been in charge for you, for your agents the rulers—Itzcoatzin, the elder Moteucçoma, Axayacatl, Tiçocic, and Ahuitzotl—have gone, who for a very short time came to be in charge for you, to govern the altepetl of Mexico. It is after them that your poor vassal [myself] came. Will they come back to the place of their absence? If only one of them could see and behold what has now happened in my time, what I now see after our lords are gone! For I am not just dreaming, not just sleepwalking, not just seeing it in my sleep. I am not just dreaming that I have seen you, have looked upon your face. For a time I have been concerned, looking toward the mysterious place from which you have come, among clouds and mist. It is so that the rulers on departing said that you would come in order to acquaint yourself with your altepetl and sit upon your seat of authority. And now it has come true, you have come. Be doubly welcomed, enter the land, go to enjoy your palace; rest your body. May our lords be arrived in the land."

mismo Motecuçoma? y Motecuçoma respondio, yo soy Motecuçoma y entonce humillose delante del capitan haziendole gran reuerencia y enyestose luego de cara a cara. El capitan cerca del y començole a hablar desta manera.

O señor nuestro seays muy bienvenido aveys llegado a vuestra tierra a v̄ro pueblo y a vuestra casa mexico! Aveys venido a sentaros en vuestro trono y vuestra silla el qual yo en v̄ro nombre he poseydo algunos dias otros señores ya son muertos le tuvieron ante que yo: el vno que se llamaua Itzcoatl, y el otro [fol. 25] Motecuçoma el viejo, y el otro Axaiacatl, y el otro Tiçocic, el otro Auitzutl. Yo el postrero de todos e venido a tener cargo y regir este v̄ro pueblo de mexico todos emos traydo a cuestas a vuestra republica y a vuestros basallos los defuntos ya no pueden ver ni saber lo que pasa agora: pluguiera a aquel por quien viuimos que alguno dellos fuera viuo y en su presencia aconteciera lo que acontece en la mia, ellos estan absentes. Señor n̄ro ni estoy dormido ni sonādo con mis ojos veo vuestra cara y vuestra persona dias a que yo esperaua esto, dias a que mi coraçon estaua mirādo a aquellas partes donde aveys venido aveys salido dentre las nubes y dentre las nieblas lugar a todos ascondido, esto es por cierto lo que nos dexaron dicho los reyes que pasaron que auiades de boluer a reynar en estos reynos y que auiades de asentaros en v̄ro trono, y a [81] v̄ra silla agora veo que es verdad lo que nos dexarō dicho. Seays muy bienvenido trabaxos abreys pasado veniendo tan largos caminos [fol. 25v] descansad agora aqui esta v̄ra casa y vuestros palacios: tomaldos y descansad en ellos con todos vuestros capitanes y conpañeros que an venido con vos.

çoma himself [if it was he], and Moteucçoma replied, "I am Moteucçoma." Then he prostrated himself before the captain, doing him great reverence, and then he raised himself face to face with the captain, very close to him. He began to speak to him in this fashion:

"O our lord, you are very welcome. You have reached your land, your settlement, your home Mexico. You have come to sit on your throne and seat, which I have possessed for some days in your name. Other lords, now dead, had it before me; one was named Itzcoatl, another Moteucçoma the elder, another Axayacatl, another Tiçocic, another Ahuitzotl. I have come last of all to rule and have charge of this your settlement of Mexico. We have all borne your commonwealth on our backs. Your deceased vassals can no longer see or know what is happening now. Would to the Giver of Life that one of them were alive now, and in his presence would occur what is occurring in mine; but they are absent. Our lord, I am not asleep or dreaming; with my eyes I see your face and your person. For some time I have been expecting this, for some time my heart has been looking in the direction from which you have come, having emerged from within the clouds and mists, a place hidden to all. This is surely what the kings who are gone left announced, that you would come to rule these realms and that you would assume your throne and seat. [81] Now I see that what they left announced is true. You are very welcome; you have undergone great travails in coming such a long way; rest now. Here are your home and your palaces; take them and rest in them with all your captains and companions who have come with you."

Auh in ontzonquiz in itlatlatlauhtiliz Motecuçoma concaquiti in Marques: niman ic concaquiztili connaoaittal[fol. 26]hui in Malintzin. Auh in ocōcac in Marques in itlatol in motecuçoma: niman ie quioalnaoatia in Malitzin [82] quinoalpopolotz: quioalito in ipopolochcopa.

Ma moiollali in Motecuçoma, macamo momauhti, ca cenca tictlaçotla, ca axcan uel pachiui in toiollo, ca tiquiximati in ticcaqui, ca ie ixquich cavitl in cenca tiquittaznequi in ixco titlachiaznequi. Auh inin ca otiquittaque, ie otioallaq̃ in ichan in Mexico, iuian quicaquiz in totlatol:

niman ie ic imatitech conanque, ie ic quivicatiuitze, quitzotzona inic quinextilia in intetlaçotlaliz. Auh in Españoles quiitta, quicecemitta, icxitlan ompepeoa, ontletleco, oaltetemo inic quitta.

Auh in tlatoque izquintin in itlan mantiaque. Inic ce, Cacamatzin, Tetzcucu tlatoani. Inic vme, Tetlepāquetzatzin: tlacuban tlatoani. Inic ei, Itzquauhtzin [fol. 26v] tlacochcalcatl: tlatilulco tlatoani. Inic navi, Topantemoctzin, tlatilulco itlatlatlalicauh catca, in Motecuçoma in ommantiaque. Auh in oc cequintin pipiltin tenochca in Atlixcatzin, tlacatecatl, in tepeoatzin, tlacochcalcatl, Quetzalaztatzin, Ticociaoacatl, Totomotzin, hecatēpatiltzin. Quappiatzin: inn anoc Motecuçoma camo çã motlatique, minaxque, quitlauelcauhque.

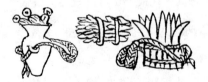

And when the speech that Moteucçoma directed to the Marqués had concluded, Marina reported it to him, interpreting it for him. And when the Marqués had heard what Moteucçoma had said, he spoke to Marina [82] in return, babbling back to them, replying in his babbling tongue,

"Let Moteucçoma be at ease, let him not be afraid, for we greatly esteem him. Now we are truly satisfied to see him in person and hear him, for until now we have greatly desired to see him and look upon his face. Well, now we have seen him, we have come to his homeland of Mexico. Bit by bit he will hear what we have to say."

Thereupon [the Spaniards] took [Moteucçoma] by the hand. They came along with him, stroking his hair to show their good feeling. And the Spaniards looked at him, each of them giving him a close look. They would start along walking, then mount, then dismount again in order to see him.

And as to each of the rulers who went with him, they were: first, Cacamatzin, ruler of Tetzcoco; second, Tetlepanquetzatzin, ruler of Tlacopan; third, the Tlacochcalcatl Itzquauhtzin, ruler of Tlatelolco; fourth, Topantemoctzin, Moteucçoma's storekeeper in Tlatelolco. These were the ones who went. And the other Tenochca noblemen were Atlixcatzin, the Tlacateccatl; Tepehuatzin, the Tlacochcalcatl; Quetzalaztatzin, the Ticocyahuacatl; Totomotzin; Ecatenpatiltzin; and Quappiaztzin. When Moteucçoma was made prisoner, they not only hid themselves and took refuge, they abandoned him in anger.

44

A cabo de dezir Motecuçoma su platica, y Marina declarola a Don hernando cortes, como Don hernando cortes vuo entendido lo que auia dicho Motecuçoma. Dixo a Marina

dezilde a⁸³ Motecuçoma que se consuele y huelque⁸⁴ y no aya temor que yo le quiero mucho y todos los que comigo vienen, de nadie recibira daño emos recebido grā contento en verle y conocerle lo qual emos deseado muchos dias a, ya se a cumplido nuestro deseo emos venido a su casa mexico despacio nos hablaremos:

luego don hernādo cortes tomo por la mano a Motecuçoma, y se fueron ambos juntos a la par para las casas reales.

Los señores que se hallaron presentes con Motecuçoma fueron los siguientes: el señor de Tetzcuco que se llamaua Cacamatzin; el segundo el señor de tlacuba se llamaua Tetlepanquetzatzin, El tercero el que gouernaua en el tlatilulco que se llamaua Itzquauhtzin:⁸⁵ [fol. 26] El quarto, el mayordomo de Motecuçoma, que tenia puesto en el tlatilulco que se llamaua topātemoctzin. Estos fueron mas principales sin otros muchos menos principales mexicanos, que alli se hallaron; el vno de los quales se llamaua Atlixcatzin Tlacatecatl: el otro se llamaua Tepeoatzin Tlacochcalcatl, otro se llamaua Quetzalaztatzin ticociaoacatl, otro se llamaua Totomochtzin hecatempatiltzin, otro se llamaua Quappiatzin: Todos estos quando fue preso Motecuçoma les desāpararon y se ascondieron.

When Moteucçoma had finished giving his speech, Marina interpreted it for don Hernando Cortés. When don Hernando Cortés understood what Moteucçoma had said, he said to Marina,

"Tell⁸³ Moteucçoma to console himself, relax,⁸⁴ and not be afraid, for I and all who are coming with me like him very much; he will receive no harm from anyone. It has given us great pleasure to see him and make his acquaintance, as we have wished to do for a long time now. Our desire has been fulfilled, and we have come to his home, Mexico. We will speak at leisure."

Then don Hernando Cortés took Moteucçoma by the hand, and they went together, side by side, toward the royal palace.

The lords who were present with Moteucçoma were the following: the lord of Tetzcoco, named Cacamatzin; second, the lord of Tacuba, named Tetlepanquetzatzin; third, the governor in Tlatelolco, named Itzquauhtzin;⁸⁵ and fourth, the majordomo that Moteucçoma had placed in Tlatelolco, named Topantemoctzin. These were the highest leaders, in addition to many other Mexica leaders of lower rank who were present, one of whom was named Atlixcatzin, Tlacateccatl; another named Tepehuatzin, Tlacochcalcatl; another Quetzalaztatzin, Ticocyahuacatl; another named Totomochtzin Ecatempatiltzin; another named Quappiatzin. When Moteucçoma was taken prisoner all these abandoned him and hid themselves.

Inic caxtolli omume capitulo: vncan mitoa in quenin Españoles quivicatiaque Motecuçoma inic calaquito vei tecpā: yoan in tlein vmpa mochiuh.

Auh in oacito tecpan, in ocalaquito: çan niman vel quitzizquique, [86] vel quixpixtinenca, amo connixcaoaia in Motecuçoma, innehoan Itzquauhtzin: auh in oc cequintin çan oalquizque.

Auh in ie iuhqui: [fol. 27] niman ie uevetzin [88] in tlequiquiztli, iuhquin tlayxneliui, avic viloa, tlaixmoiaoa, tlachichitoca, iuhquin tlacica, çan oquiuhquin netequipacholo, iuhquin nenanacavilo, iuhquin tlen mach onnettitilo, mauiztli oonoc, iuhquin mochi tlacatl quitollo yiollo: çān oc iuh onioac, nemamauhtilotoc neihiçavilotoc, necuicuitiuechotoc, necochmamauhtilotoc.

Auh in otlatvic, niman ie ic motzatzilia in ixquich intech monequi, in iztac tlax-

Seventeenth chapter, where it is said how the Spaniards went with Moteucçoma to enter the great palace, and what happened there.

And when they had reached the palace and gone in, immediately they seized [86] Moteucçoma and kept close watch over him, not letting him out of their sight, and Itzquauhtzin along with him. But the others were just [allowed to] come back out.

And when this had happened, then the various guns were fired. [88] It seemed that everything became confused; people went this way and that, scattering and darting about. It was as though everyone's tongue were out, everyone were preoccupied, everyone had been taking mushrooms, as though who knows what had been shown to everyone. Fear reigned, as though everyone had swallowed his heart. It was still that way at night; everyone was terrified, taken aback, thunderstruck, stunned.

And when it dawned, everything [the Spaniards] needed was proclaimed: white

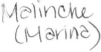
Malinche (Marina)

17

[fol. 26v] Capitulo .17. de como los españoles con Motecuçoma llegaron a las casas reales: y de lo que alli paso.

Desque los Españoles llegaron a las casas reales con Motecuçoma: luego le detuuieron consigo nunca mas de [87] dexaron apartar de si, y tambien detuuieron consigo a Itzquauhtzin gouernador del tlatilulco: a estos dos detu[fol. 27]uieron consigo, y a los demas dexaron a yr:

y luego soltaron todos los tiros de polbora que trayā, y con el ruydo y humo de los tiros: todos los indios que alli estauan se pararon como atordidos, y andauā como borrachos: començaron a yrse por diuersas partes muy espantados: y ansi los presentes como los absentes cobrarō vn espanto mortal

dormieron aquella noche: y otro dia luego muy de mañana, començose a pregonar de parte del capitan, y de parte de Motecuçoma que se truxesen todas las cosas necesarias para los españoles, y para los cauallos. Y motecuçoma ponia mucha

Chapter Seventeen, of how the Spaniards arrived at the royal palace with Moteuccçoma and what happened there.

As soon as the Spaniards arrived at the royal palace with Moteucçoma, they detained him there with them and never again let him [87] away from them. They also detained with them Itzquauhtzin, governor of Tlatelolco. They detained these two and let the rest go.

Then they discharged all the firearms they had along, and with the noise and smoke of the shots all the Indians who were there stood still as if stunned and went about like drunk people; in fright they began to go in various directions. And thus both those present and those absent conceived a mortal fright.

They slept [in the palace] that night, and the next day, very early in the morning, it began to be proclaimed on behalf of the Captain and of Moteucçoma that all of the things needed for the Spaniards and for the horses should be brought. Moteucçoma

calli, totollaleoatzalli,[89] totoltetl, chipaoac
atl, in quauitl, in tlatlatilquauitl, in tecolli,
in apaztli, in petzcaxitl, in apilloli, in
tzotzocolli, in tlatzoionilcaxitl, in ie ixquich in çoquitlatquitl: iehoatl uel
tlanaoatica in Motecuçomatzin. Auh in
quinoalnotzaia pipilti, aocmo qui-
tlacamatia, ça quallani, aocmo iuic quiça,[90]
aocmo [fol. 27v] iuic onui, aocmo moca-
qui: auh tel amo ic xiccaoalo, maco in ixquich itech monequi in qualoni, in ioaloni,
ioan in atl, in maçatlaꝗlli.

Auh inn o uel motlalique: nimā ie ic
quintemolia in Motecuçomatzin in ixquich in itetzō in altepetl, in tlauiztli, in
chimalli, cenca quimatataquilia, cēca qui-
mauiztemoa in teucuitlatl. Auh in
Motecuçomatzin: niman ie ic quiniacan-
tiuh in Españoles, cololhuitiui, quite-
peuitiui, innepantla icatiuh, tlaiacac
icatiuh, quitzitzizquitiui,[93] caantiui. Auh
in onacique in tlatlatilcali:[94] itocaiocan,
teucalco: niman ie ic oallaquixtilo in ixquich in petlacotl, in quetzalapanecaiutl, in
tlauiztli, in chimalli, in teocuitlacomalli in
incozqui diablome, teucuitlaiacametztli, in
teocuitlacotzecoatl,[95] in teocuitlama-
temecatl, in teocuitlaixquaamatl:

niman ie ic tla[fol. 28]ixcoleoalo in itech
chimalli in teucuitlatl: yoan in itech in ixquich tlaviztli: auh in ie muchi omocoleuh
in teucuitlatl, ie ic contlecavia, cōtle-
quechia, contlemina in ixquich nepapan
tlaçotli muchi tlatlac. Auh in teucuitlatl
quixaxantecaque in Españoles: auh in chalchivitl in quexquich quiqualittaque, quicuique: auh in oc cequi chalchivitl, çan
quinamuxque in tlaxcalteca: yoan noviā
nenque, quixaqualotinenque in novian
tlatlatican, tlatlatilcali,[96] tlatlatiloian,
muchi quicuique in ixquich in quittaque,
in quiqualittaque.

tortillas, roast turkeys,[89] eggs, fresh water,
wood, firewood, charcoal, earthen tubs,
polished bowls, water jars, large clay pitch-
ers, vessels for frying, all kinds of earthen-
ware. Moteucçoma himself ordered it. But
when he summoned the noblemen, they
would no longer obey him, but grew
angry. They no longer performed their
duty to him,[90] no longer went to him; no
longer was he heeded. But he was not
therefore forsaken; he was given all he
needed to eat and drink, and water and
deer fodder [for the Spaniards].

And when [the Spaniards] were well
settled, right away they interrogated Moteucçoma about all the stored treasure of
the altepetl, the devices and shields. They
greatly prodded him, they eagerly sought
gold as a thing of esteem. And then Moteucçoma went along leading the Spaniards. They gathered around him, bunched
around him; he went in their midst, leading the way. They went along taking hold
of him,[93] grasping him. And when they
reached the storehouse,[94] the place called
Teocalco, then all the ⟨shining things⟩
were brought out: the quetzal-feather head
fan, the devices, the shields, the golden
disks, the necklaces of the devils, the
golden nose crescents, the golden leg
bands,[95] the golden arm bands, the golden
sheets for the forehead.

Thereupon the gold on the shields and
on all the devices was taken off. And when
all the gold had been detached, right away
they set on fire, set fire to, ignited all the
different precious things; they all burned.
And the Spaniards made the gold into
bricks. And they took as much of the
green-stone as pleased them; as to the rest
of the green-stone, the Tlaxcalans just
snatched it up. And [the Spaniards] went
everywhere, scratching about in the hiding
places, storehouses,[96] places of storage all
around. They took everything they saw
that pleased them.

diligencia en que truxesen todas las cosas necesarias: y los piles y achcauhtles, y otros officiales a quien concernia a⁹¹ esta prouision ne⁹² querian obedecer a Motecuçoma ni llegarse a el pero con todo esto proueyan de todo lo necesario

desque se vuieron aposentado los españoles y concertado todo su repuesto, y [fol. 27v] repusado, començaron a preguntar a Motecuçoma por el tesoro real para que dixese donde estaua y el los lleuo a vna sala que se llamaua Teucalco donde tenian todos los plumajes ricos, y otras joyas muchas de pluma y de oro y de piedras: y luego los sacaron delante dellos

començaron los españoles a quitar el oro de los plumajes, y de las rodelas, y de los otros atauios del areyto que alli estauan, y por quitar el oro destruyeron todos los plumajes, y joyas ricas, y el oro fundierōlo y hizieron barretas: y las piedras que les parecieron bien tomaronlas: y las piedras baxas y plumajes todo lo tomaron los indios de tlaxcalla, y escudriñarō los españoles toda la casa real: y tomaron todo lo que les parecio bien.

put much effort into seeing that all the necessary things were brought, but the *piles* [noblemen] and *achcauhtles* [headmen] and other officials concerned with⁹¹ these provisions did not want to obey Moteucçoma or⁹² to approach him. But for all that they provided everything necessary.

As soon as the Spaniards had found lodging and all been resupplied, and they had rested, they began to ask Moteucçoma about the royal treasure so that he would tell them where it was, and he took them to a hall named Teocalco, where they had all the rich feather-pieces and many other jewels of feathers, gold, and fine stones. And then they got them out in their presence.

The Spaniards began to remove the gold from the feather-pieces, shields, and other dancing accoutrements that were there, and in order to remove the gold they destroyed all the feather-pieces and rich jewels. They melted the gold and made it into bars, and they took the stones that seemed good to them. The Indians of Tlaxcala took all the less precious stones and the feathers. The Spaniards scrutinized the entire palace and took everything that seemed good to them.

48

50

49

Inic caxtolli omei capitulo: vncan mitoa, in quenin Españoles calaquito in ipilchan Motecuçoma: auh in tlein vmpa muchiuh.

Niman ie ic vi in vel itlatlatiaia Motecuçoma in vmpa mopia in vel itech iaxca in motecuçoma: itocaiocan Totocalco [fol. 28v] iuhquin mocecenquetza, iuhquin yioiolipan, iuhquin moquequetzotzona, iuhquin iiztaia iniollo.⁹⁷ Auh in onacito, in oncalacque tlatlatiloian, iuhquin tlacecēmana, novian aactivetzi, iuhquin mihicultia, mihicolia: nimā ie ic oallaquixtilo in vel ixcoian yiaxca, in vel ineixcavil, in vel itonal, mochi tlaçotlanqui, in chaiaoac cozcatl, in machoncotl, in teucuitlamatemecatl, yoan in matzopetztli, teucuitlaicxitecuecuextli, yoan in xinvitzolli⁹⁸ tlatocatlatquitl, yoā in iacaxivitl, yoan in ixquich in oc cequi in itlatqui in amo çan tlapoalli muchi quicuique, moch intech compachoq̄ moch cōmotechtique, moch cōmotonaltique. Auh in ococoleuhque in ixquich in teucuitlatl; in ontlacocoleoaloc, niman ie ic quicentlalia itoalco, itoalnepantla in ixquich in tlaçohivitl.

Auh [fol. 29] in ie iuhqui in o mochi munechico in teucuitlatl. Nimā ie ic quīoalnotza, quīoalnenotzallani in ixquichtin in pipiltin in Malintzin: tlapanco oalmoquetz, atenanticpac: Quitoa. Mexica xioalhuian ca cenca ie tlaihiovia in Españoles: xiqualcuicā⁹⁹ in tlaqualli, in chipaoac atl, yoan in ixquich monequi, ca ie tlaihiovia, ie quiciavi, ie quihiovia, ie mociavi, ie mihiovia: tleica in amo anoallaznequi? ic neci ca anqualani.

Auh in Mexica çā nimā aocmo motlapaloaia in ma onvian, cenca momauhtiaia, mauhcaçonequia mihiçaviaia, cenca maviztli onoc, maviztli moteteca, aocac tlaxtlapaloa, ça iuhq̄n tequani vnca,

Eighteenth chapter, where it is said how the Spaniards went into Moteucçoma's personal home, and what happened there.

Thereupon they went to the place where Moteucçoma stored his own things, where all his special property was kept, called Totocalco. It seemed that they ⟨all bunched together⟩, were struck [with hope], patted one another on the back of the neck, their hearts brightening.⁹⁷ And when they got there and went into the storage place, they seemed to disperse in all directions, quickly going in everywhere, as though covetous and greedy. Thereupon [Moteucçoma's] own personal property was brought out, belonging to him alone, his own portion, all precious things: necklaces with pendants, arm bands with quetzal feathers, golden arm bands, bracelets, golden bands with shells for the ankles, and the turquoise diadem,⁹⁸ insignia of the ruler, and the turquoise nose rods, and other things without number belonging to him. They took all of it; they appropriated it, assigned and apportioned it to themselves. And when they had taken off each and every piece of the gold, when it had been detached, then they assembled all the precious feathers in the courtyard, in the middle of the courtyard.

And when the collection of all the gold was completed, thereupon Marina summoned to her, had summoned, all the noblemen. She stood on a flat roof, on a roof parapet, and said, "Mexica, come here, for the Spaniards are suffering greatly. Bring⁹⁹ food, fresh water, and all that is needed, for they are suffering travail, are tired, fatigued, weary, and exhausted. Why is it you do not want to come? It is a sign that you are angry."

But the Mexica no longer at all dared to go there. They were greatly afraid; they were limp with fear; they were taken aback. Fear greatly prevailed; it spread about. No one dared come out. It was as

[fol. 28] Capitulo .18. de como los Españoles entraron en las proprias casas de Motecuçoma; y de lo que alli paso.

Hecho lo arriba dicho procurarō de saber de la recamara de Motecuçoma y el los lleuo a su recamara que se llamaua totocalco que quiere dezir [fol. 28v] la casa de las aues: yuan los españoles muy regocijados por pensar que alli hallarian mucho oro: y llegando luego sacaron toda la recamara del mismo Motecuçoma donde auian muchas joyas de oro y de plata y de piedras preciosas y todo lo tomaron, y los plumajes ricos quitaronlo todo el oro y las piedras, y pusieron las plumas en medio del patio para que las tomassen sus amigos:

y luego mādo el capitan Don hernādo cortes por medio de Marina que era su interprete la qual era vna india q̄ sabia la lengua de castilla y la de mexico que la tomarō en yocatan esta començo a llamar a vozes a los Tecutles, y piles mexicanos para que viniessen a dar a los españoles lo necesario para comer,

y nadie osaua venir delante dellos ni llegarse a ellos, todos estauā atemorizados y espantados, embiauālos lo necesario para comer, y los que lo lleuauā, yuā temblando en poniendo la comida no parauā mas alli luego se yuan casi huyendo.

Chapter Eighteen, of how the Spaniards entered Moteucçoma's private home, and what happened there.

When the above had been done, [the Spaniards] attempted to find out about the special storehouse of Moteucçoma, and he took them to his storehouse, named Totocalco, which means "bird house." The Spaniards went along very joyfully, thinking that they would find much gold there; on arrival they took everything out of Moteucçoma's own storehouse, where there were many precious items of gold, silver, and precious stones, and they took it all. They removed all the gold and stones from the rich feather-pieces and put the feathers in the middle of the courtyard for their friends to take.

Then Captain don Hernando Cortés gave orders through Marina, who was his interpreter—she was an Indian woman who knew the languages of Castile and Mexico; they took her in Yucatan. She began to call loudly to the Mexica *tecutles* [lords] and *piles* [nobles] to come to give the Spaniards the necessary food.

But no one dared to come into their presence or approach them; they were all terrified and frightened. They sent them the necessary food, but those who carried it went trembling; when they put the food down, they tarried no longer, but immediately left, almost fleeing.

51

52

ça iuhquin tlalli mictoc: tel amo ic mocaoa, amo ic netzotzonalo in concaoa in ixquich intech monequi, ça in mauhcac [100] in concaoaia, çan momamauhtitivi, ça onmomauhcatlaloa [fol. 29v] in ontlacaoa. Auh in ocontepeoato valnetlalolo, vallachichitoca, tlacica, tlaviviioca.

though a wild beast were loose, as though it were the deep of night. Yet there was not for that reason a halt or hesitation in delivering everything [the Spaniards] needed, but they delivered it fearfully, [100] they went in fear, they ran in fear as they went to deliver it. And when they had spilled it on the ground, everyone came running back in a flash, panting and trembling.

## 19

Inic caxtolli onnavi capitulo: vncan mitoa in quenin Españoles, quinnaoatique Mexica; inic quichioazque in ilhuiuh Vitzilobuchtli: auh inin amo ixpan muchiuh in Capitan; ca iquac in vmpa ia atenco inic acico Panphilo de narbayez.

Nineteenth chapter, where it is said how the Spaniards ordered the Mexica to hold the festivity of Huitzilopochtli. But when this happened the Captain was not present, for at that time he went to the coast because of the arrival of Pánfilo de Narváez.

Auh çatepan, niman ie ic quitlani in iilhuiuh Vitzilobuchtli, in quenami ilhuiuh, quimaviçoznequi quittaznequi, in quenami, in quenin muchioa: nimā ie ic tlanaoatia in Motecuçoma, in aquique vel oconcalaqui itechiuhcaoan, quioalquixtiaia in tlatolli. Auh in ovalquiz tlatolli in vmpa caltzacutica motecuçoma: niman ie ic quiteci in oauhtli chicalutl in cioa, mocexiuhçauhque, vncā in teu[fol. 30]itoalco, oalquizque in Españoles, cenca omocecencauhq̄ in ica iautlatquitl, moiauchichiuhque, moquichchichiuhque, intlan quiquiça, intzalan quiquiça, quiniaiavaloa, quincecemitta, imixco tlatlachia in teci cioa. Auh in ie iuhqui in oquimonittaco, nimā ie ic calaqui in vei tecpan, iuh ma-

And afterward [Pedro de Alvarado] requested the festivity of Huitzilopochtli, wanting to see and behold how his festivity was and what sorts of things were done. Thereupon Moteucçoma gave the orders; those of his subordinates who could still enter [where he was] brought out the announcement. And when the announcement came out from where Moteucçoma was detained, then the women who had fasted for a year ground up the amaranth, the fish amaranth, in the temple courtyard. The Spaniards came out well adorned in battle equipment, outfitted for war, arrayed as warriors. They passed among the grinding women, circling around them, looking at each one, looking upon their

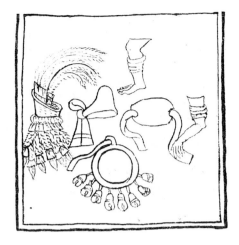

53

54

19

[fol. 29v] Capitulo .19. de como los españoles mandaron a los yndios hazer la fiesta de Vitzilobuchtli: esto fue en absencia del capitan quando fue al puerto por la venida de Panphilo de narbayez.

Chapter Nineteen, of how the Spaniards ordered the Indians to hold the festivity of Huitzilopochtli; this was in the absence of the Captain, when he went to the port because of the arrival of Pánfilo de Narváez.

Auiendose partido el capitan Dō hernando cortes, para el puerto a recebir a Paphilo de narbayez, dexo en su lugar a Don pedro de albarado con los españoles que quedaron aqui en mexico: el qual en absencia del capitan persuadio a Motecuçoma para que mādasse hazer la fiesta de Vitzilobuchtli, porque querian ver como hazian aquella solēnidad. Motecuçoma mando que se hiziesse esta fiesta para dar cōtento a los españoles aparejaronse ansi los satrapas como los principales, para hazer la fiesta.

[fol. 30] En toda esta letra que se sigue, no se dize otra cosa, sino la manera como hazian la estatua de Vitzilobuchtli, de masa, de diuersas lecūbres y como la pintauan, y

When Captain don Hernando Cortés departed for the port to receive Pánfilo de Narváez, he left in his place, with the Spaniards who remained here in Mexico, don Pedro de Alvarado, who, in the absence of the Captain, encouraged Moteucçoma to order the festivity of Huitzilopochtli to be held, because they wanted to see how they performed these ceremonies. Moteucçoma ordered this festivity to be held to give pleasure to the Spaniards. Thus the satraps, as well as the leaders, prepared themselves to hold the festivity.

In all this subsequent text, nothing else is said except the way they made the statue of Huitzilopochtli from the dough of various vegetables, how they painted it, how

chiztic: quilmach iquac temictizquia intla
miec tlacatl cenquiçani toquichtin.


Auh in ie oacic ilhuitl in toxcatl, teu-
tlacpa in quipeoaltia in quitlacatilia in
inacaio, quitlacatlaliaia, quitlacatla-
chieltiaia, quitlacanextia. Auh inin
quinacaiotiaia çan tzoalli, ie in michi-
oauhtzoalli, tlacopepechpan in quitlaliaia,
ie in vitzitzillacutl, yoā nacaztlacutl.


Auh in ie utlacat, nimā quiquapotonia,
yoan quichioa, ixtlā tlatlaan, yoan icoana-
coch xivitl in tlaçalolli: auh in icoa[fol.
30v]nacoch itech pipilcac in vitznaoaiotl,
teucuitlatl xoxopiltic, tlaxoxopiltectli, yoā
yiacapilol, mitl; Teucuitlatl in tlachiuhtli,
tlatzotzontli, yoan tlateantli, tlacanaoalli,
tlateicuilolli: no itech pilcaia moteneoa
vitznaoaiutl, ixtlan tlatlaan; inic ixtlan tlatlaan, vncan icac texutli, yoan têcuxtli yoā
icpac conquetza ivitzitzilnaoal; nimā con-
toquilia, itoca anecuiutl, hivitl in tlachichi-
oalli, mimiltic, achitzin vitztic, achi tzim-
pitzaoac: nimā ie [101] in tozpololli
icuexcochtlan in contlalilia itech pilcac
tziuhcuexpalli, yoā itzitzicaztilma, tlatlil-
palli: macuilcan in tlapotonilli, quauhtlachcaiotica, quimolololotica, yoan in itilma
in tlani quimoquentia, tzotzontecomaio,
oomicallo: auh in pani quimolpilia, yoan
ixicul: inic tlacuilolli tlaquaquallo, ca much
vncā [fol. 31] icuiliuhtoc in tzontecomatl,
nacaztli, iollotli, cuitlaxculli eltapachtli, to-
chichi, macpalli, xocpalli, yoan imaxtli:
çan in maxtlatl, vellaçotlanqui: auh in
itlamachio inic no tlaquaquallo inic tla-
quittli: auh in ivei[maxtli] [102] çan amatl, iehoatl in quaoamatl, inic patlaoac cemmatl:
auh inic viac cempoalli, inic tlacuilolli texoacaxilqui, [103] auh in iquezpan quima-
manticatca iacatecpaio: in iezpan çan amatl

faces. And when they were through looking at them, they went into the great palace. It [later] became known, according to
what is said, that they would have killed
people at that time if many of the men had
congregated.

And when the feast day of Toxcatl had
arrived, toward sunset they began to give
human form to [Huitzilopochtli's] body.
They formed it like a person, they made it
look like a person, they gave it a person's
appearance. And what they made his body
of was just dough of amaranth seed, fish
amaranth seed. They placed it on a platform of sticks, "hummingbird sticks" and
"ear sticks."

And when it had become like a person,
then they put feather-down on his head
and painted his face, making his face
striped, and they [put] serpent earplugs on
him, with turquoise glued on them. And
from the serpent earplugs hung rings of
thorns, made of gold, like toes, cut like
toes. And his nose rod was an arrow, made
of hammered gold, set with stones,
thinned and with stones scattered on it.
Also from it hung what is called the *huitz-
nahuayotl* [ring of thorns]. It was ⟨painted
with stripes⟩ on the surface, and the manner of its being painted on the surface was
with blue and yellow. On his head they
placed his hummingbird totem. They followed that with what is named an *aneuc-
yotl,* arranged of feathers, cylindrical, a bit
pointed, a bit pointed at the bottom.
Then [101] they placed at the back of his neck
a ⟨ball of yellow parrot feathers⟩, from
which hung a boy's lock of neck-hair. And
he had a cloak of nettles, colored black,
feathered in five places with eagle down,
that he gathered about himself. Below he
wore a cape covered with skulls and bones,
and above he wrapped himself also in a
sleeveless jacket, painted in *tlaquaquallo*
[chewed-up] style, for there were painted
all severed heads, ears, hearts, entrails, liv-
ers, lungs, hands, and feet. And he had a

como la cōponian, y como despues ofre-
cian delante della, muchas cosas.

they arranged it, and how afterward they
offered many things before it.

catca, tlapalli inic tlacuilolli, inic tla-
ezicuilolli: iacatecpaio, çanno amatl in tlachioalli, çanno iuhqui inic tlacuilolli, tla-
ezicuilolli, yoan ichimal ietica otlatl in
tlachioalli, otlachimalli, nauhcan tlapotonilli, quauhtlachcaiotica, hivichachapan-
qui, moteneoa: Tevevelli, auh chimalpaio,
çanno iuhqui in ezpanitl inic tlacuilolli;
yoan navi imiuh ic quicentzitzquia in ichimal [fol. 31v] yoan iopochmacuex imac
pilcac, coiotomitl in tlavipantli, yoan itech
pilcatica amatl tlaxoxotlalli.

Auh in otlatvic in ie ilhuiuh ipan, in
ioatzinco ie ic quixtlapoa in ivic mone-
toltia, ixpan oncenpanti quitlenamaquilia
ixpan quimana in izquican ventli in tlacatlaqualli, in tzoalilacatzolli. Auh in iquac
in, aocmo quitlecavique, aocmo cacoquix-
tique in itepeioc: auh in ixquich tlacatl in
telpopochtequioaque iuhquin nececēque-
tzalo, iuhquin inioiolipā [104] in ilhuitlazque,
in ilhuitlamatizque, inic quintlattitizque,
quintlamaviçoltizq̄, quintlaixtlatizque, in
Españoles:

tlatotoca, netlalolo, vmpa itztioa in
teuitoalco, inic vmpa necocololoz. Auh in
ocecenquixoac: nimā ie ic peoalo, ie ic
vmpeoa in cuico yoan necocololoz. Auh
in mocenpoalçauhque, yoan [fol. 32] yoan
in mocexiuhçauhque nepanixtinemi: in
tetzaqua imoocoquauh, in aquin quiçaznequi ic quitlaieiecalhuia in ocoquavitl:
auh in aquin maxixaz quitlalitiuh icuechi, [105] yoan iaztaxel. Auh in aquin çan
niman atlatlacamati, in amo tetlaçaltoca in

simple loincloth, but his loincloth was very
precious. It too had the *tlaquaquallo* motif
woven into its design. His large loincloth [102] was just of paper, paper from tree
bark, a *braza* wide and twenty long,
painted with a blue ⟨striped design⟩. [103]
And at his hips he carried his blood banner,
just of paper, with a flint knife at the point
[of the staff]; it was painted with [red]
color, painted like blood. And the flint
knife at the point was likewise made of
paper, painted the same way, painted like
blood. And the shield he had was made of
strong reeds, a reed shield, feathered in
four places with eagle down, sprinkled
with feathers. It is called a *tehuehuelli*. And
it had a shield banner, painted like the
blood banner. And he held four arrows together with his shield. And from his left
arm hung an arm band, arranged of coyote
fur, and from it hung strips of paper.

And when it had dawned and was already the day of his festivity, very early in
the morning those who had made vows to
him unveiled his face. Forming a single
row before him they offered him incense;
each in his place laid down before him offerings of food for fasting and rolled amaranth dough. And at this time they no longer took him up or raised him to the top of
his temple. And it was as though all the
youthful warriors had gathered together
and had hit on the idea [104] of holding and
observing the festivity in order to show the
Spaniards something, to make them marvel and instruct them.

Everyone ran and scurried in the direction of the temple courtyard for the snake-
dancing there. And when all had assembled, singing and snake-dancing began.
Those who had fasted for twenty days and
those who had fasted for a year ⟨went
about jointly⟩. Their pine rods detained
people; they brandished the pine rods at
anyone who tried to leave. Anyone who
needed to [leave to] relieve himself put
down his net cape [105] and his forked

59

61

60

62

aquen tlatta, vel ic quicuitlavitequi, qui-
metzvitequi, caculhuitequi, caliticpa con-
topeoa, conchiccanaoa, conixiquetza,
mihixiquetztiuh, nanacazitztiuh aiac temac
naoati;

cenca iehoā tlamamauhtiaia, tla-
mauhtiaia, cemimacaxoa, cemimacaxtin
catca in iachvan vitzilobuchtli in
mocexiuhçauhque. Auh in tlaiacatia in
vevei tachcavan, in veveichiva tel huel
quiçaia, amo quintzacuiliaia: auh in ie ixquich telputzintli, in cuexpaltzine in
cuexpaltzitzineque, yoan in tzotzocoleque,
in tepallamani, in yiaque: in moteneoa [fol.
32v] in telpuchiaque,[106] in ce ic nemi, in
ce cacitinemi, in anoço vme cacitinemi no
quintzaquaia: quimilhuiaia, vmpa xiviā on
nocne, anquiteittitia, amotech itto.

heron-feather ornament ⟨as a signal⟩.
When anyone absolutely would not obey,
[would not accept punishment], was inso-
lent, because of that they beat him soundly
on the back, the thighs, the shoulders.
They shoved him outside the precinct,
they threw him out, pushing him so he fell
flat on his face; he went out on his face, on
his ear. No one in [their] hands made a
sound.

The helpers of Huitzilopochtli, those
who had fasted for a year, inspired great
and general fear, they were respected by
all, they were persons of universal authority. Those who went in the lead [of the
dance], the great leaders, who had done
great things, were able to pass, and they did
not detain them. But as to all the youths,
those with a lock of hair behind the head
and those with the jar-shaped headdress,
who had taken a captive with the help of
others, ⟨the leaders⟩, called youth ⟨lea-
ders⟩,[106] who had gone and taken one or
perhaps two captives, they also detained
them, saying to them, "Get along with
you, rascals, you are showing [bad] things
to people, they are taking an example
from you."

20

Inic cempoalli capitulo: vncā mitoa in
quenin Espanoles quinmictique, quimixtlatique in Mexica, in quilhuiquixtiliaia
Vitzilobuchtli in vncā mitoaia Teuitoalco.

Auh in ie iuhqui, in ie ilhuitlamacho, in
ie netotilo in ie cuico, in ie cuicoanolo: in
cuicatl, iuhquin xaxamacatimani. In ie
inmā, in otlainmantic inic temictizque in
Espanoles: niman ie ic oalquiça omoiau-

Twentieth chapter, where it is said how
the Spaniards killed and annihilated the
Mexica who were celebrating the feast of
Huitzilopochtli at what they call the Teo-
ithualco [Divine Courtyard, Courtyard of
the Gods, temple courtyard].

When things were already going on,
when the festivity was being observed and
there was dancing and singing, with voices
raised in song, the singing was like the
noise of waves breaking against the rocks.

[fol. 31v] Y estando en ella haziendo vn grā areyto, muy ricamente adereçados: [fol. 32] todos los principales en el patio grāde del cu de Vitzilobuchtli donde estaua la ymagen hecha de masa de bledos, y muy ricamente atauiada con muchos ornamentos: los quales estan en la letra esplicados, y otras cerimonias que se ponen en todo este capitulo.

During [the ceremonies] all the leaders, very richly costumed, were performing a great dance in the great square of the *cu* of Huitzilopochtli where the image made of amaranth dough was, very richly decorated with many ornaments, which are explained in the text, as well as other ceremonies that are included throughout this whole chapter.

63

64

65

## 20

[fol. 32v] Capitulo .20. de como los españoles hizieron gran matança en los yndios estando haziendo la fiesta de Vitzilobuchtli en el patio del mismo Vitzilobuchtli.

Los españoles al tiempo que les parecio convenible salieron de donde estauan y tomaron todas las puertas del patio por que no saliese nadie y otros entraron con sus armas: y començaron a matar a los que estauā en el areyto y a los que tañian los

Chapter Twenty, of how the Spaniards performed a great slaughter of the Indians while they were celebrating the festivity of Huitzilopochtli in the square of that same Huitzilopochtli.

At the time that seemed opportune to them, the Spaniards came out from where they had been and took all the gates to the square so that no one could get out. Others entered with their weapons and began to kill those who were in the dance. They cut

chichiuhque, ocontzatzaquaco, in izquicampa quixoaia, calacoaia, in quauhquiiaoac tecpantzinco, acatl yiacapan,
Tezcacoac. Auh in ocōtzatzacque: no iz-
quicā momanque, aocac vel hoal[fol.
33]quiça.



Auh in ie iuhqui; nimā ie ic calaqui in
teuitoalco in temictizque: in intequiuh in
temictique çan tlacxipāvia imeevachimal,
cequi intotopchimal, yoan intetepuzmaquauh: niman ie ic quiniaoaloa in mi-
totia, nimā ie ic vi in vevetitlan, nimā
quimavitecque in tlatzotzona oalcocoton
vmexti in imacpal çatepan quiquech-
vitecque veca vetzito in iquech: nimā ie
muchintin texixili tepuztopiltica, yoan
teviviteque, tepuzmaquauhtica: cequintin
quincuitlaço, niman valmotoxaoa in in-
cuitlaxcol, cequintin quinquatzatzaianque,
vel quitzeltilique in intzontecon, vel
itzeltix in intzōtecō. Auh in cequintin
quimaculhuitecque, oalcacamatlapan,
oaltzatzaian in innacaio: cequintin quin-
cotzvivitecque, cequin quinmetzvivitec-
que, cequintin quimitivitecque, nimā
moch [fol. 33v] oalmotoxaoa in incuitlax-
cul. Auh in aca oc nen motlaloa in icui-
tlaxcul ça quivilana, iuhquin xoxoquiova
in momaquiztiznequi, aoc campa vel hui:
auh in aquin quiçaznequi, vmpa quioal-
huitequi, quivalxixili.



Auh cequintin, tepantli quitlecavique,
tel huel momaquixtiq̄: cequintin calpulco
cacalacque vmpa momaquixtique. Auh in
cequintin intlan momaq̄xtique, intlan
cacalacque in o vel micque, çan momic-
canenequia, vel momaquixtique: auh in
aca oc mopoçaoa[107] in conitta, conixili.
Auh in imezço in tiacavan iuhquin atl ic
totocac, iuhquin aalacatoc, yoan xoquiiac
eoatoc in eztli. Auh in cuitlaxcolli iuhquin

When it was time, when the moment had
come for the Spaniards to do the killing,
they came out equipped for battle. They
came and closed off each of the places
where people went in and out: Quauhquiahuac, Tecpantzinco, Acatliyacapan,
and Tezcacoac. And when they had closed
these exits, they stationed themselves in
each, and no one could come out any
more.
When this had been done, they went
into the temple courtyard to kill people.
Those whose assignment it was to do the
killing just went on foot, each with his
metal sword and his leather shield, some of
them iron-studded. Then they surrounded
those who were dancing, going among the
cylindrical drums. They struck a drum-
mer's arms; both of his hands were severed. Then they struck his neck; his head
landed far away. Then they stabbed everyone with iron lances and struck them with
iron swords. They stuck some in the belly,
and then their entrails came spilling out.
They split open the heads of some, they
really cut their skulls to pieces, their skulls
were cut up into little bits. And some they
hit on the shoulders; their bodies broke
open and ripped. Some they hacked on the
calves, some on the thighs, some on their
bellies, and then all their entrails would
spill out. And if someone still tried to run it
was useless; he just dragged his intestines
along. There was a stench as if of sulfur.
Those who tried to escape could go nowhere. When anyone tried to go out, at
the entryways they struck and stabbed him.
But some climbed up the wall and were
able to escape. Some went into the various
calpulli temples and took refuge there.
Some took refuge among, entered among
those who had really died, feigning death,
and they were able to escape. But if someone took a breath[107] and they saw him,
they stabbed him. The blood of the warriors ran like water; the ground was almost
slippery with blood, and the stench of it

cortaron las manos, y las cabeças y dauan destocadas, y de lançadas a todos quātos topauan, y hizieron vna mantāça muy grande y los que acudian a las puestas huyendo alli los matauā

algunos saltauā por las paredes algunos se metian en las capillas de los cues alli se echauā y se fingian muertos corria la sangre por el patio, [fol. 33] como el agua quando llueue: y todo el patio estaua sembrado de cabeças, y braços, y tripas, y cuerpos de hombres muertos y por todos los rincones buscauā los españoles a los que estauan biuos para matarlos:

como salio la fama deste hecho por la ciudad comēçaron a dar voz diziendo alarma! Alarma! y luego a estas vozes se junto gran copia de gente todos con sus armas y començaron a pelear cōtra los españoles

off the hands and heads of those who were playing instruments. They stabbed and lanced everyone they encountered, performing a very great slaughter. Those who ran fleeing to the gates were killed there.

Some leaped over the walls. Some went into the chapels of the *cus*, where they lay down and played dead. Blood ran in the square like water when it rains. The whole square was strewn with heads, arms, intestines, and dead bodies. The Spaniards searched in all the corners for those alive, to kill them.

When word of this deed got out into the city, they began to call out, saying, "To arms! To arms!" At this shouting a large number of people assembled, all with their weapons, and they began to fight against the Spaniards.

66

67

68

tlavilani. Auh in Españoles, novian nemi in tlatemoa in calpulco, novian ontlaxiltivi in tlatemoa, in açaca vmpa minaia, novia nen[fol. 34]que, quixaqualotinenque in izquican calpulco in tlatemoque.

Auh in omachoc: niman ie ic tzatzioa. Tiacavane mexicae vallatotoca, ma nechichioalo in tlaviztli, in chimalli, in mitl, vallacivi, vallatotoca, ie miqui in tiacaoan; ommicque, onixpoliuhque, ommixtlatique: Mexicae tiacaoane. Nimā ie ic tlacavaca, ie ic tzatzioa, netenviteco; iciuhca valnechicaovac in tiacavan iuhquin nececenquetzalo in mitl in chimalli quiitqui. Nimā ie ic necalioa, quimōmina in ica tlatzontectli, in ica tlacochtli, yoan in minacachalli, [108] yoan in tlatzontectli, itzpatlacio in contlaça: iuhquin cozpul ommoteca in acatl, in impan Españoles.

rose, and the entrails were lying dragged out. And the Spaniards went everywhere searching in the calpulli temples, stabbing in the places where they searched in case someone was taking shelter there. They went everywhere, scratching about in all the calpulli temples in searching.

And when it became known [what was happening], everyone cried out, "Mexica warriors, come running, get outfitted with devices, shields, and arrows, hurry, come running, the warriors are dying; they have died, perished, been annihilated, o Mexica warriors!" Thereupon there were war cries, shouting, and beating of hands against lips. The warriors quickly came outfitted, bunched together, carrying arrows and shields. Then the fighting began; they shot at them with barbed darts, spears, and tridents, [108] and they hurled darts with broad obsidian points at them. A cloud of yellow reeds spread over the Spaniards.

69

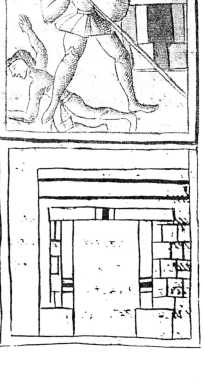

70

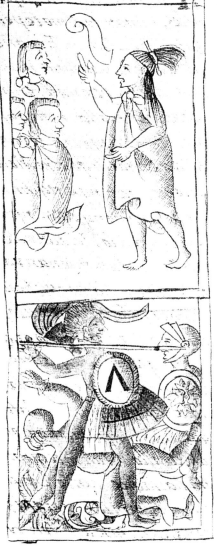

71

72

Inic cempoalli oce capitulo: vncan mitoa iancuican peuh iauiotl, inic quimicalque Mexica in Españoles in nican mexico.

[fol. 34v] Auh in iehoantin Españoles: niman valmotepetlatzatzacque. Auh in Españoles no quinvalmina in Mexica in ica tepuzmitl, yoan ic quinvalmotla in tlequiquiztli. Auh niman tepuztli contlatlalilique in Motecuçoma: auh in ixquichtin tiacavan in omicque: nimā ie ic tequixtilo, teçaçaco, teiiximacho. Auh in tenanvan in tetaoan tlachoquiztleoa techoquililo, nechoquililo, oc inchachan quinvicaca, çatepan quinoalhuicaque in Teuitvalco, quincentlalique: vmpa quincentlatique, cecni in itocaiocan: Quauhxicalco. Auh in cequintin tlatlaque çan tetelpuchcali.[111]

Auh in ie oncalaquiz tonatiuh, in oc achiton tonatiuh: niman ie ic valtzatzi in Itzquauhtzin, tlapanco valtzatzi: quioalito. Mexicae, Tenuchcae, Tlatilulcae, amech[fol. 35]tlatlauhtia in amo tlatocauh, in Tlacatecutli in Motecuçoma: quioalitoa. Ma quicaquican in Mexica, ca amo titenamicvan, ma motlacavaltican,[115] ma momana in mitl in chimalli, motolinia in icnoveve, in icnoilama in cuitlapilli, in atlapalli in aiamo quimati in moquequetza, in movilana, in coçultentoc, in vapaltentoc, in aiamo quimomachitia: ipampa conitoa in amotlatocauh. Camo titenamicvan, ma netlacaoaltilo, ca ocontepuziotique, tepuztli icxic ocontlatlalilique:

Auh in oconito in, nimā ie ic conchachalatza, conaoa, çan ie ilhuice tlavelcui in Mexica qualani, ce ilhuice poçoni: conilhuia. Tlein quioalitoa Motecuçoma nocne? amo ce yioquichoan?[116] Nimā ie ic tlacaoaca, niman ic maantimoquetz in tlacaoaca: nimā ie ic onvetzi in mitl in tlapanco. Auh in Motecuçomatzin yoan Itzquauhtzi, quinchi[fol. 35v]malcaltia in Españoles in ma quinminti in Mexica.

Twenty-first chapter, where it is said how the war first began, when the Mexica battled with the Spaniards here in Mexico.

And then the Spaniards fortified themselves. From there the Spaniards shot at the Mexica with iron bolts and fired guns at them. And then they placed Moteucçoma in irons. And then all the warriors who had died were retrieved, taken to places, and identified. And wailing arose from the mothers and fathers, crying and weeping over them. First they took them to their various homes, and afterward they brought them to the temple courtyard and assembled them there. They burned them in a particular place called Quauhxicalco. But some were burned only at the various youths' houses.[111]

And when the sun was setting, while there was still a little sunlight, then Itzquauhtzin cried out; from a roof terrace he cried out, saying, "O Mexica, o people of Tenochtitlan and Tlatelolco, your ruler the Tlacateuctli Moteucçoma addresses you, saying, 'Let the Mexica hear: we are not their match, may they be dissuaded [from further fighting].'[115] May the arrows and shields of war be laid down. The poor old men and women, the common people, the infants who toddle and crawl, who lie in the cradle or on the cradle board and know nothing yet, are all suffering. This is why your ruler says, 'we are not their match; let everyone be dissuaded.' They have placed him in irons, they have put irons on his feet."

And when he had finished saying this, the Mexica railed against him, reproaching him. They grew angry and began to fall into a ranting rage. One of them, boiling over and ranting, said to him, "What does Moteucçoma say, you rogue? Aren't you one of his men?"[116] Then there was a clamor, an increasing clamor, and then arrows fell on the roof. But the Spaniards held their shields over Moteucçoma and Itzquauhtzin lest the Mexica's arrows should hit them.

[fol. 34] Capitulo .21. de como començo la guerra entre los mexicanos y los Españoles en mexico.

[fol. 34v] Como començo la guerra entre los indios[109] y los españoles. los españoles se fortalecieron en las casas reales en[110] el mesmo Motecuçoma: y tanbien con Itzquauhtzin el gouernador del tlatilulco, los indios los cercaron, y los combatian reciamente: los Españoles se deffendian con los tiros de poluora y ballestas y escopetas y haziā gran daño en los indios: y luego hecharon crillos a Motecuçoma: y tanbien los indios començaron a enterrar los que auian sido muertos en el patio por los españoles por cuya muerte se hizo gran llanto en toda la ciudad, porque eran gēte muy principal los que auian muerto enterraronlos diuersas partes[112] segun sus ritos el mesmo dia y a la puesta del sol.

Itzquauhtzin gouernador del Tlatilulco, subiose sobre los tlapancos de casa[113] real: y començo a dar vozes diziendo A mexicanos a tlatilulcas mirad que el señor Motecuçoma vuestro rey os ruega que se ceseys[114] de pelear y dexeys las armas porq̄ estos hombres son muy fuertes mas que nosotros: y si no dexays de darles guerra recibira gran daño todo el pueblo porque ya an [fol. 35] atado con hierro a v̄ro rey.

Chapter Twenty-one, of how the war between the Mexica and the Spaniards began in Mexico.

How the war between the Indians[109] and the Spaniards began: the Spaniards fortified themselves in the royal palace with[110] Moteucçoma himself and also with Itzquauhtzin, the governor of Tlatelolco. The Indians surrounded them and battled them fiercely. The Spaniards defended themselves with artillery, crossbows, and muskets, and did the Indians great damage. Then they put Moteucçoma in irons, and also the Indians started burying those whom the Spaniards had killed in the square, for whose death a great wail went up in all the city, because those who had died were of very high rank. They buried them in[112] different places according to their rites that same day at sunset.

Itzquauhtzin, governor of Tlatelolco, went up on the *tlapancos* [roof terraces] of the[113] royal palace and began to shout, saying, "O Mexica, o Tlatelolca, consider that the lord Moteucçoma your king implores you to cease[114] fighting and lay down your weapons, because these men are very strong, stronger than us. If you do not stop making war on them, the whole people will be greatly harmed, because they have already tied your king with iron."

Oydas estas voces por los mexicanos y tlatilulcas: començaron entre si a brauear y maldezir a Motecuçoma diziendo. Que dize el puto de Motecuçoma? Y tu vellaco con el, no cesaremos de la guerra: luego comēçaron a dar alaridos y a tirar saetas y dardos hazia donde estaua el que hablaua, junto con Motecuçoma: y los españoles arodelaronlas ansi no recibieron daño.

When the Mexica and Tlatelolca heard these shouts, they began to rage against Moteucçoma and curse him among themselves, saying, "What does this faggot Moteucçoma say? And you're a wretch along with him. We will not halt the war." Then they started giving war cries and shooting arrows and darts toward where the speaker was, together with Moteucçoma. But the Spaniards covered them with shields and they received no harm.

Inic cenca qualanque in Mexica; iehica ca vel quimixtlatique in tiacaoan in ainnemachpan in quinpoiomictique, in amo ivivi ic concauhque quiiaoalotinemi in tepancalli: [117] tlatlapia in aҫaca onichtacacalaqui, in aҫaca conichtacacalaquia tlaxcalli; ҫan niman ic ommotzacu in ixquich in omacoia, ҫan nimã aocac tle concaoaia: iuhquin quincuitlaoatzque. Auh in aquique oc nen xonexcaia, tlamatzoaia, motlamaceviaia, in ichtacatzin cõmacaia in tlaqualtzintli: intla oittoque, intla oittaloque, niman vncã quinmictia, vncan quintlatlatia, aҫo quincuexcochvitequi, anoҫo quintetepachoa.

Cequintin mexica ceppa ittaloque, quicalaquiaia totomitl: iehoantin tlanexotlaque, in ca cequintin [fol. 36] oncalaqui ichtaca, ic cenca netlaquauhnaoatiloc inic vellapieloz, vel mopiaz in izqui vtli yoan in izqui acalutli, vel necuitlaviloa vel ixpialoia. Auh in quicalaquiaia totomitl tequitque intlaivalhoã in calpixque aiutzintepecatl yoan chinantecatl: niman vncan ihiotl quiz, nimã vncã intequiuh vetz, acaloco in quimõcuexcochvivitecque, vitzantica,

ҫan monetechvia in tenuchca, yoan ҫan iliviz in quintzitzquia in tequitque; quitoaia. Ca iehoatl in: nimã ic conmictia. Auh intla aca conittaia ichopilotenteuh: niman quicuitivetzi, conmictia: quitoa, ca no iehoatl in oncalactinemi in contlatlamaca in Motecuҫoma: yoan intla aca quitta, quimolpilia tequitcaaiatl, no quicuitivetzi, quitoa: ca no iehoatl in tlapalpul, in tetzauhtlatolli quitquitinemi, cõcalaquia, in conitta motecuҫoma. Auh in oc nen momaquixtiz[fol. 36v]nequi, in quintlatlauhtia: quimilhuia. Tle amai me-

The reason the Mexica were very angry was that [the Spaniards] had entirely annihilated the warriors and killed them treacherously, without warning. They did not neglect to surround the palace; [117] they kept watch at various places where someone might enter by stealth, where someone might secretly deliver bread. Everything that had been being given to them was completely blocked off, absolutely no one delivered anything any more. It was as though they were drying out their innards. And as to those who would try to give them news and inform them, or gain their favor by giving them a bit of food, if they were seen and detected, then they killed them there, they disposed of them, by striking them on the nape of the neck or stoning them.

Once some Mexica were seen delivering arrows fitted with birds' feathers; they let it out that some [others] were secretly getting in. Therefore strict orders were given that good watch should be kept, that each road and canal should be well guarded. Great care was taken to keep a good lookout. And those who had taken in the arrows were doing their duty, sent by the stewards of Ayotzintepec and Chinantlan. Then and there they took their last breaths, their task came to a conclusion. At the canal they struck them on the napes of their necks with heavy pointed sticks.

There was internal strife among the Tenochca, and it was without reason that they seized those who were performing duties, saying "This is the one," and then killing him. And if they saw a crystal lip plug on someone, they hastened to seize him and killed him, saying, "He too is one of those who go inside and give provisions to Moteucҫoma." And if they saw someone who had tied about him a thin tributeworker's cloak, they hurried to seize him too, saying, "This is another wretched fellow who goes about carrying scandalous

Tenian gran rauia contra los españoles porque mataron a los principales y valientes hobres a traycion: y por tanto tenian cercadas las casas reales que a nadie dexauan entrar ni salir ni meter ningun bastimento, por que muriessē de hambre: y si alguno metia secretamente comida a algunos de los de dentro los de fuera en sabiendolo le matauā: Supieron los de fuera que algunos mexicanos entrauan alla, y metian saetas secretamente. Y luego pusieron grā diligencia en guardar que nadie entrarse,[118] ni por tierra ni por agua, y a los que hallaron culpados de auer [fol. 35v] metido algo mataronlos,

They were greatly enraged against the Spaniards because they killed the leaders and brave men [warriors] treacherously. Hence they kept the royal palace surrounded, letting no one go in or out or take in any provisions, so that they would die of hunger. If anyone secretly gave food to someone on the inside, when those outside learned of it they would kill him. Those on the outside learned that some Mexica were going in there, secretly taking in arrows. Then they increased their diligence in keeping watch so that no one should enter,[118] neither by land nor by water, and those whom they found guilty of having taken something in they killed.

y luego se leuanto gran rebuelta entre los mexicanos vnos acusauā a otros de auer entrados[119] y ansi matauan muchos en especial[120] los seruiçiales o pajes de Motecuçoma, que trayā beçotes de cristal que era particular librea o señal de las[121] de la familia de Motecuçoma: y tambien a los que trayan mantas delcadas que llamā ayatl, que era librea de los pajes de Motecuçoma: a todos los acusauā, y dezian. Que auiā entrado a dar comida a su señor, y a dezir lo que pasaua fuera y a todos los matauā: y de alli adelāte vuo grāde vigilancia que nadie

Then a great confusion arose among the Mexica, some accusing others of having gone in,[119] so they killed many, especially[120] the servants or pages of Moteucçoma, who wore crystal lip plugs, which were a particular livery or sign of those[121] of Moteucçoma's family, as well as those who wore thin cloaks called *ayatl,* which were the livery of Moteucçoma's pages. They accused them all, saying that they had gone in to give food to their lord and tell what was happening outside, and they killed them all. From then on there was great

xicae, camo no nehoatl: conilhuia, ca no tehoatl nocne, amo titequitqui: niman ic vncan cōmictia ça teixpipia, ça motecuitlavitinemi, ça imix intequiuh, ça tepipia in mexica: ca miequintin in tlapictli quitzacutiaque in ixpopoiomictiloque in amo vel intlatlacul quitzacutiaque. Auh in oc cequinti tequitque motlatique, minaxque, aocmo moteittitiaia, aocmo motenextiliaia, aocmo tevic quiçaia, cenca momauhtiaia, mauhcaçonequia, miinaxtinenca, inic amo temac vetzizque.

Auh in iquac oquincaltzacque in Españoles: çan chicomilhuitl in quincalicalque. Auh in caltzacuticatca cempoalilhuitl omei: auh izquilhuitl in, in acalotli motatatacac, mopapatlauh, movevecatlano, motetepexiq̄tz novian movicantlali, moovitili in acalotli: Auh in vtli [fol. 37] ipā, neteteñantiloc, tenamitl motetecac, netetenantlaliloc, mooviuicantlali in caltzalātli:

auh in ie iuhqui.

and harmful tales, who takes them in to Moteucçoma when he goes to see him." And he who would try to save himself would implore them, saying, "O Mexica, what are you doing? I am not one of them." They told him, "You are one of them, you rogue, you are not doing duty." Then and there they killed him. They were just keeping watch on everyone, going about being careful about everyone; they kept their eyes peeled, the Mexica just watched everyone. They punished many for invented things, who were treacherously killed; they punished them for wrongdoings not their own. And others doing duty work hid themselves, went to shelter, no longer showed themselves to anyone or let themselves be seen, no longer came out among people. They were greatly afraid, limp with fear; they went about taking refuge so that they would not fall into someone's hands.

And when they had the Spaniards closed in their buildings, they fought them for only seven days. They were shut in for twenty-three days, and during each of these days the canals were excavated, widened, deepened, and the sides made steeper. Everywhere the canals were made more difficult to pass. And on the roads, various walls were built, walls were laid here and there. Walls were set up and the passageways between houses made difficult.

And when this was done . . .

entrase y ansi todos los de la casa de Motecuçoma se huyerō y ascondieron por que
no les matassen.

Dieron bateria los mexicanos a los españoles siete dias y los tuuieron cercados
veynte y tres dias: y este tiempo ensan-
charon y ahondaron las aceças, y atajaron
los caminos con paredes y hizieron grandes
baluartes para que no pudiessen salir los españoles por ninguna parte.

vigilance that no one should enter. And so
all those of Moteucçoma's house fled and
hid so they would not be killed.

The Mexica assaulted the Spaniards for
seven days and kept them surrounded for
twenty-three, and during this time they
widened and deepened the canals and
blocked the roads with walls, and made
great bulwarks so that the Spaniards would
not be able to get out anywhere.

73

74

75

76

77

Inic cempoalli omume capitulo: vncā
mitoa in quenin machiztico in ie vitz capitan don hernādo Cortes inic oalmocuepaia
mexico.

In omachiztico in ie vitz in Capitan
tepeiacacpa in quiçaco, miequintin in quinoalhuicac in Españoles yoan cenca miequintin in tlaxcalteca yoā in cempoalteca
vel miequintin vel ixachin, vel ixachintin,
vel tonac, vel tonaque: amo çaniuh vallaque, valiauiaque, valmotlaviztitiaque,
valmoiauchichiuhtiaque, inchichimal, in-
mamaquauh, inmamavitzoc quiquequeque-
quechotivitze, teuhtli quioalq̄tztiaque,
omach iixtlaliuhque omach yixtenexiuh-
que, omach moca tlalloaque,¹²² omach
teteuhquimiliuhque, ça moca tlaltin,
omach cocotztlaloaq̄, [fol. 37v] cenca oalmotlaloa, cenca oalhuicini, motzatza-
tzilitivi: quitotivi. vallatotoca tlaxcaltecae,
cempoaltecae.

Auh in Mexica monaoatique, inic amo
quinmottitizque, çā motlatizque, mi-
naiazque, iuhquin tlalli mictimotecac,
aocac naoati, tel hoallachielotoc in tla-
tzacuilcamac, yoan tepancamac, yoan
tlacoiocco achi quicocoionique in tepantli,
inic vmpa ontlachie: çan iehoan in oten-
oaque, in otentli quitocatoque in iuh quichiuhque: auh in calnepantla onoque amo
iuh quichiuhque. Auh intla quimittani in
cana quexquichtin mani, tepeuhtimani, in
tiacaoan, ca iniol iuh tlamatizquia in Españoles: ca in mexica iehoan quipeoaltia,
iehoan quitzintia, iehoan inpeoal in iauiotl.

Twenty-second chapter, where it is said
how it became known that Captain don
Hernando Cortés was on the way here,
coming back to Mexico.

It became known that the Captain was
on the way here, coming from the direction of Tepeyacac; he brought many Spaniards and a great many Tlaxcalans and people of Cempoallan. There were very
many, a great number, an abundance and
multitude. They did not come in their ordinary garb, they came to do battle, with
their devices and their war gear, their
shields, their war clubs, their strong
pointed sticks that they came shouldering.
They came stirring up dust, with their
faces all covered with earth and ash, full of
dirt,¹²² wrapped in dust, dirty. They came
running very fast, making great haste,
shouting as they went, saying, "Everyone
is running along, o Tlaxcalans, o Cempoalans!"

And the Mexica told one another that
they would not show themselves to them,
but hide themselves and take shelter, as
though it were the middle of the night. No
one made a sound, but everyone was looking out from doorway openings, openings
in walls, and holes where they had pierced
the walls a little in order to see out from
there. Only those who had places at the
side of the road, which followed the road-
side, did this; those who lived in the interior of house complexes did not. If the
Spaniards had seen how many warriors
there were in places, piled together, they
would have realized that the Mexica
would start and commence the battle, that
it would be on their initiative.

22

[fol. 37] Capitulo .22. de como llego la
nueua de como El capitan don hernando
cortes auiendo vencido a Panphilo de nar-
baez boluia ya para mexico: con otros muchos Españoles que de nueuo auian
venido.

Estando las cosas como arriba se dixo:
vino nueua como el capitan Don hernando
cortes, venia con muchos Españoles, y con
muchos indios de Cempoalla, y de Tlaxcalla: todos armados, y a punto de guerra y
con gran priesa: y los mexicanos concer-
taron entre si, de abscondense, todos: y no
los salir a recebir ni de guerra ni de paz: y
los españoles con todos los demas amigos,
fueronse derechos; hazia las casas reales,
donde estauan los Españoles.

Y los mexicanos todos estauan mirando
y ascōdidos, que no los viesen: los Españoles. Y esto hazian por dar a entender
que ellos no auian començado la guerra:
y como entro el Capitan con toda la otra
gente en las [fol. 37v] casas reales començaron a soltar todos los tiros en alegria de
los que auian llegado, y para atemorizar a
los contrarios: y luego començaron los
mexicanos a mostrarse y a dar alaridos y a
pelear contra los españoles, echando saetas,
y dardos cōtra ellos: y los Españoles ansimismo començaron a pelear tirar saetas y
tiros de polbora, fueron muertos muchos
de los mexicanos tirauan los españoles
todos sus tierras [123] muy certeros que nūca
hereauan tiro que no matase con el: y
como vieron los mexicanos el daño que
recibian de parte de los Españoles començaron a culebrar para escaparse de los tiros:
y andar de lado.

Chapter Twenty-two, of how news
came that Captain don Hernando Cortés
had bested Pánfilo de Narváez and was already returning in the direction of Mexico
with many Spaniards who had newly arrived.

With things being in the state said
above, news came that Captain don Hernando Cortés was coming in great haste
with many Spaniards and many Indians of
Cempohuallan and Tlaxcala, all armed and
ready for war. The Mexica agreed among
themselves that they would all hide and
not come out to meet them, either with
hostilities or in peace. The Spaniards with
all of their friends went straight toward the
royal palace, where the Spaniards were.

The Mexica were all looking, hidden so
the Spaniards would not see them. They
did this to let it be understood that they
had not begun the war.

When the Captain and all the other
people entered the palace, they began to
fire the guns to show their joy over those
who had arrived and to inspire fear in the
enemy. Then the Mexica began to show
themselves, let out war cries, and fight
against the Spaniards, hurling arrows and
darts at them, and the Spaniards likewise
began to fight, shooting arrows and firearms. Many Mexica were killed; all of the
Spaniards' shots were very well aimed;
there was never a shot [123] that failed to kill
someone. When the Mexica saw the damage they were receiving from the Spaniards, they began to zigzag to escape the
guns, and to go sideways.

Auh in ie iuhqui in ocalaquito vei tecpan: niman ie ic quitlatlaça in tlequiquiztli:
auh in ie iuhqui, nimā ie ic oalquiça [fol.
38] quioalixtia in micalizque; nimā ie ic
tlacaoaca, ie ic necalioa: nimā ie ic muchioa in iauiotl, niman ie ic tlaiecolo onvetzi in mitl, in tetl, in impan Espanoles.
Auh in iehoātin Españoles: quioallaça in
tepuzmitl, yoan in tlequiquiztli, miec tlacatl minaloc yoan tlequiquizviloc: in tlate-
puztlavitolhuiani, vel quixcatzitta in mitl,
vel ipan quitlachialtia in mitl in aquin
quiminaz: auh in tepuzmitl inic iauh iuhquin quiquinacatiuh, iuhquin çoçolo-
catiuh, cenca çoloni: auh atle çannen
quiça in mitl, moch temina, mochi
nalquiça in teitic: yoan in tlequiquiztli, vel
tepan quiiacatia, vel tepan contlachialtia.
Auh in iquac vetzi, vellaltitech viloa, vellaltitech nepacholo, iuhquin pepechtli
neteco, amo tenemachpan in tepā iauh,
amo quiteimachitia in temictia, in quezqui
ipan iauh vel izqui miqui: in iquac imo-
vi[fol. 38v]can vetzi, in aço imixquac, in
anoço incuexcochtlan, anoço iniollopan,
anoço imelchiquipan, anoço imitipan, in
anoço vel inxillan: auh intla çan īmetzpan,
anoço imacolpan vetzi, amo nimā ic
miqui, amo ic oviti, çan tel vmpati. Auh in
oquittāq mexica in iuh vetzi tlequiquiztli
yoan in tepuzmitl, ça avic vivi, iuhquin
ixtlapalhuiui, tlatlaxtlapaloa cenca vel motlachielia, vel mimati.

Auh in ie iuh navilhuitl necalioa: in tiacaoan tlecoque, iehoan in tlatzonanti, in
tlapepenti, in tlaviceque, in imixco ca iauiotl, muchintin tlecoque in icpac teucalli,
vme vepantli quitlecavica, yoan miec in
aoaquavitl, mimimiltic; itoca, teuquavitl in
quitlecavique, in impan quioallaçazquia.

Auh nimā ie ic tleco in Españoles quitlecavia in teucalli, tlatlamātitivi, cuecuen-
titi[fol. 39]vi in Españoles: tlaiacantivi in
matlequiquiceque, cencā tlamach in tleco,
amo mamana, quitlaztivi in matlequiquiz-

And when they had entered the great
palace, they fired the guns. When this happened, then [the Mexica] came out to face
them and fight. Then there was a clamor as
the battle was joined, as war was waged.
Weapons were brandished; arrows and
stones fell on the Spaniards. But the Spaniards shot back with iron bolts and guns;
many people were hit by bolts and guns.
The crossbowman aimed the bolt well, he
pointed it right at the person he was going
to shoot, and when it went off, it went
whining, hissing, and humming. And the
arrows missed nothing, they all hit someone, went all the way through someone.
The guns were pointed and aimed right at
people. When they were fired, everyone
went down, was pressed to the ground; the
people lying there were like a mattress. It
came upon people unawares, giving no
warning when it killed them. However
many were fired at died, when some dangerous part was hit: the forehead, the nape
of the neck, the heart, the chest, the stom-
ach, or the whole abdomen. But if only
their thighs or shoulders were hit, then
they did not die of it, nor were their lives
put in danger, but they healed. And when
the Mexica saw how the guns and iron
bolts were shot, they just went back and
forth, as though crossing this way and that;
everyone went from side to side, being
very alert and careful.

When the fighting had gone on for four
days, the warriors, those who had been
chosen and picked out as best, those who
possessed devices, whose countenances
showed the spirit of war, all those climbed
up on top of the temple. They took up
two large beams and many round oak logs
called "god wood" that they were going to
hurl down on [the Spaniards].

Thereupon the Spaniards climbed up on
the temple. They went in separate units, in
rows. Those with harquebuses went ahead.
Very gently did they climb, not getting agitated; as they went they fired the harque-

Dieron convate quatro dias arreo a las casas donde estauā los Españoles: y despues destos quatro dias: los capitanes mexicanos escogierō muchos soldados viejos y hombres valientes: y subieronse sobre v̄ cu el que estaua mas cerca de las casas reales, y subieron alla, dos vigas rollizas para desde alli echarlas sobre las casas reales y hundirlas para poder entrar.

[fol. 38] Visto esto los españoles, luego subieron al cu con mucha orden, y lleuauan sus escopetas y vallestas començārō a subir muy despacio y tirauā con los [124] vallestas y escopetas a los de árriba en cada rencle yua delante vn escopetero: y luego vn soldado con espada y rodela, y luego vn alabardero por esta orden: yvan subiēdo al cu y los de arriba echauā los maderos por las gradas del cu abaxo, pero ningun daño hizieron a los españoles. Y llegando a lo alto del cu, comēçarō a herir y matar a los que estauan arriba,

They gave battle against the houses where the Spaniards were for four days straight. After these four days the Mexica captains chose many veteran soldiers and brave men, who climbed up on a *cu*, the one that was closest to the royal palace, and they hoisted two round beams up there, to hurl them down onto the palace in order to cause it to collapse so that they could enter.

When the Spaniards saw this, they immediately climbed up the *cu* in close order, carrying their muskets and crossbows. They began to go up very slowly, shooting the [124] crossbows and muskets at those above. In each row a musketeer went ahead, then a soldier with sword and shield, and then a halberdier. In this order they went climbing up the *cu*. Those above hurled the timbers down the steps of the *cu*, but they did no damage to the Spaniards. Reaching the top of the *cu*, they started striking and killing those who were up there.

78

79

tli, ic tlamotlativi, tlaōcaiotitivi, in tepuz-
tlavitoloani, in tlatepuzmiviani, tlaiecaiotia
in tepuzmaquaveque, in tlanauhcaiotitivi,
tepuztopileque, tzinacātopileque.

Auh in tiacaoan oc nen valmomamanaia
in quioallaça quavitl, in tomaoac aoaquavitl in impā Españoles: çan quichimal-
topeoa, çan niman aoctle onievat. Auh in
opanvetzito in Españoles: nimā ie ic
tevivitequi, yoan texixili, tetzotzopitza.
Auh in tiacaoā niman ie ic valmotepeoa in
itlamamatlaioc teucalli, iuhquin tlilazcatl
valmotepeoa. Auh in Espanoles vel mochintin quinteucalhuique in ixquichtin
tlecoca in tiiacaoan, vel mochinti [fol. 39v]
moteucalhuique, niman aocac maquiz.
Auh in ontemictico, niman ie ic callacq̄
valmotzatzacutivetzque. Auh inin muchiuh ie tlaqualizpan:

auh in ie iuhqui nimā ie ic teiximacho,
teçaçaco: auh in ie muchintin oçacoque in
moteucalhuiq̄: nimā ie ic tetlatilo in tetelpuchcali. [126]

buses at things. Second went the crossbowmen, those who shot crossbows.
Third went those with swords. Fourth
went those with iron lances, staffs shaped
like a bat [halberds].

And when the warriors were trying to
arrange themselves to hurl the logs, the
thick oak logs, down on the Spaniards,
they just pushed them aside with their
shields, it did no good at all. And when the
Spaniards got on top, they struck, stabbed,
and jabbed at people. Thereupon the warriors threw themselves down to the land-
ings of the temple; like black ants they
threw themselves down. And the Spaniards cast down from the temple every one
of the warriors who had climbed up. They
cast down absolutely all of them; not a one
escaped. And when they had finished the
killing, they went into [the palace] and
quickly shut themselves in. And this all
happened at mealtime.

After this, [the dead] were identified and
removed; when all those who had been
cast down from the temple had been
removed, they were burned in the various
youths' houses. [126]

80

81

y muchos dellos se desperauā [125] por el cu abaxo, finalmente todos murieron los que auian subido al cu tornaronse los españoles a su fuerte y barrearonse muy bien.

Los mexicanos enterraron a los que alli murieron porque toda era gente principal y de mucha cuēta en la guerra.

Many of them threw themselves off headlong, [125] and finally all who had climbed the *cu* died. The Spaniards returned to their fort and barricaded themselves very well.

The Mexica buried those who died there, because they were all leading people, of great weight in the war.

82

## 23

Inic cempoalli vmei Capitulo vncan mitoa in quenin Motecuçoma, yoan ce vei pilli tlatilulco micque: auh in innacaio quivallazque iquiiaoaioc [127] in calli in vncan catca Españoles.

Auh ie iuh navilhuitl neteucalhuiloc in quimontlaçaco in Motecuçoma, yoan Itzquauhtzin, omicque, atēco itocaiocan, Teoaioc: ca vncan catca in ixiptla aiotl, tetl in tlaxixintli, iuhquin aiotl ipan mixeuhtica in tetl.

Auh in oittoque, in oi[fol. 40]ximachoque in ca ie Motecuçomatzin, yoan Itzquauhtzin: in Motecuçomatzin niman quioalnapalotiquizque, quioalhuicaque in vncan itocaiocan Copulco: niman ie ic quiquaquauhtlapachoa, niman ie ic contlemina, contlequechia: niman ie ic cuecuetlaca in tletl, iuhquin tetecuica, iuhquin nenenepiloa tlecueçalutl, iuhquin tlemimiiavatl moquequetza, in tlenenepilli: auh in inacaio Motecuçoma, iuhquin tzotzoiocatoc, yoan tzoiaia inic tlatla.

Auh inic tlatlac, çan tlavelpan, aocmo cenca teiollocopa: cequi caoa: quitoa. Inin tlapalpul: cemanaoac in otlamamauhtiaia, cemanaoac in ooalimacaxoia, cemanaoac in o ivic valnemamauhtiloia, valneiçaviloia: in iehoatl in, in aquin çā tepitzin, inic quiiiolitlacoaia, niman contlatlatiaia, miec in tlapictli oquitzacuilti in amo nelli in çan tlatol[fol. 40v]chichioalli: yoan oc miectin in caoaia, quiquinacaia, ôoiovaia, moquaquacuecuechoaia.

Auh in Itzquauhtzin conacalhuito, acaltica conanato in inacaio, inic caxitico nican tlatilulco, cenca motlaocultique, cenca icnoioac in iniollo, teixaioviton, aiac ma cavaia, aiac in ma quitelchioa: quitoaia. Oquihiovi in tlacatl, in tlacuchcalcatl in Itzquauhtzin, ca ivan otlaihiovi, yoā omotolini in Motecuçoma, quexquich oquihiovi in topampa in vmpa otivallaque, otioalitztiaque in ixquich cavitl in ocatca in

Twenty-third chapter, where it is said how Moteucçoma and a great nobleman of Tlatelolco died, and the Spaniards threw their bodies out at the entryway [127] of the house where they were.

Four days after people had been cast down from the temple, [the Spaniards] removed [the bodies of] Moteucçoma and Itzquauhtzin, who had died, to a place at the water's edge called Teoayoc [Place of the Divine Turtle], for an image of a turtle was there, carved in stone; the stone represented a turtle.

And when they were seen and recognized as Moteucçoma and Itzquauhtzin, they hastened to take Moteucçoma up in their arms and brought him to the place called Copolco. Then they placed him on a pile of wood and set fire to it, ignited it. Then the fire crackled and roared, with many tongues of flame, tongues of flame like tassels, rising up. And Moteucçoma's body lay sizzling, and it let off a stench as it burned.

And when it was burning, some people, enraged and no longer with goodwill, scolded at him, saying, "This miserable fellow made the whole world fear him, in the whole world he was dreaded, in the whole world he inspired respect and fright. If someone offended him only in some small way, he immediately disposed of him. He punished many for imagined things, not true, but just fabricated tales." And there were many others who scolded him, moaning, lamenting, shaking their heads.

But Itzquauhtzin they put in a boat; they took his body in a boat until they got him here to Tlatelolco. They grieved greatly, their hearts were desolate; the tears flowed down. Not a soul scolded him or cursed him. They said, "The lord Tlacochcalcatl Itzquauhtzin has suffered travail, for he suffered and was afflicted along with Moteucçoma. What tribulations he endured on our behalf in the past, during

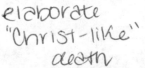

*elaborate "Christ-like" death*

[fol. 39v] Capitulo .23. de como Motecuçoma y el gouernador del Tlatilulco fueron echados muertos fuera de la casa donde los españoles estauā fortalecidos.

Chapter Twenty-three, of how Moteucçoma and the governor of Tlatelolco were thrown dead outside the house where the Spaniards were fortified.

Despues de lo arriba dicho, quatro dias andados despues de la matança que se hizo con el cu, hallaron los mexicanos muertos a Motecuçoma, y al Gouernador del Tlatilulco echados fuera de ¹²⁸ las casas reales cerca del muro dōde estaua vna piedra labrada como galapago que llamauā Teoayoc:

y despues que conocieron los que los [fol. 40] hallaron que eran ellos dieron mādado, y alçaronlos de alli, y lleuaronlos a vn oratorio que llamauā Copulco, y hizieronlos alli las cerimonias que solian hazer a los difuntos de gran valor: y despues los quemaron como acostumbrauan, hazer a todos los señores y hizieron todas las solemnidades que solian hazer en este caso al vno dellos que era Motecuçoma le enterraron en mexico, y al otro en el tlatilulco

algunos dezian mal de Motecuçoma porque auia sido muy cruel:

los del tlatilulco llorauan mucho a su gouernador porque era muy bienquisto.

After the above-said, four days after the killing at the cu, the Mexica found Moteucçoma and the governor of Tlatelolco dead, thrown outside ¹²⁸ the royal palace close to the wall where there was a stone carved like a tortoise that they called Teoayoc.

After those who found them recognized who they were, they gave orders to have them removed and took them to an oratory that they called Copolco. There they performed for them the ceremonies customary for the dead of great reputation. Afterward they burned them as they customarily did all the lords, and performed all the ceremonies that they usually performed in such cases. One of them, Moteucçoma, they buried in Mexico, and the other in Tlatelolco.

Some spoke ill of Moteucçoma because he had been very cruel.

The people of Tlatelolco mourned their governor greatly because he was very well liked.

Motecuçoma: niman ie ic quichichioa in tecpanitl, yoan oc cequi amatlatquitl ic quichichiuhque: yoan quitlamamacaque: auh niman ic quivicaque in quitlatito in teuitvalco, itocaiocan: quauhxicalco: cenca tlamaviztililiztica inic tlatlac [fol. 41] in inacaio.

Auh iuh navilhuitl necalioac, ça onchicomilhuitique in caltzacuticatca in Españoles. Auh in oacic chicomilhuitl: oc valquizque ommotlachielito, ommotlatlachielito, vmpa onacito in maçatzintamalco; concuito ovatl, valxiloiotia, çan coniaucuito in toquizvatl, cenca çan oniciuhtivia, çan tequitl onacito: nima ic valcalactivetzque; auh in onquizca ie vmmotzcaloa, ie vncalaqui in tonatiuh.

all of Moteucçoma's time!'' Then they outfitted him, equipping him with the lordly banner and other items of paper, and they gave him provisions. Then they took him and burned him in the temple courtyard at the place called Quauhxicalco. It was with great splendor that his body was burned.

After four days of fighting, for seven days the Spaniards were just enclosed in the house. But when the seven days were past, they came back out for a while to take a look, looking around here and there; they went as far as Maçatzintamalco. They gathered stalks of green maize, beginning to form ears. They just gathered the maize leaves as one does in war, going in great haste. Hardly had they got where they were going when they quickly went back into the building. When they had come out the sun was already off to one side, about to set.

83

Despues de algunos dias que estauan cercados los españoles, y que cada dia les dauan guerra vn dia salierō de su fuerte algunos dellos, y cogieron de los mahizales maçorcas de mahiz, y cañas de mahiz, y tornaronse a su fuerte.

After the Spaniards had been surrounded for several days, and every day they offered them battle, one day some of them sallied forth from their fort and collected from the maize stands ears and stalks of maize, then returned to their fort.

84

85

86

87

Inic cempoalli onnavi Capitulo: vncan mitoa in quenin Españoles yoan in tlaxcalteca quizque, choloque in mexico ioaltica.

Auh in ovaliovac in oacic ioalnepantla. nimā ie ic quiça in Españoles: ommotenque, yoan in ie ixquich tlaxcaltecatl: in españoles iacattivi, auh in tlaxcalteca tlatoquilitivi, tlatzinpachotivi, iuh[fol. 41v]quin ma intenanoan, intzacuilhoan muchiuhtivi, quivicatiaque quauhtlapechtli contecatiaque in acaloco in ipan ompanotiaque:

in iquac in aoachquiauhtimani, aoachtzetzeliuhtimani, aoachpixauhtimani, oc cequi in vel companavique acalotli Tecpantzinco, Tzaputla Atenchicalco. Auh in oacito mixcoatechialtitlā [129] inic nauhcan acaloco: ie vncan ittoque, in ie quiça: ce atlacuic civatl, in quimittac: niman ie ic tzatzi: quito. Mexica, xioalnenemican, ie quiça, ie navalquiça in amoiaovan: nimā no ce tlacatl tzatzic in icpac vitzilobuchtli vel tepan motecac in itzatziliz, ixquich tlacatl quicac: quito. Tiacavane, mexicae, ie onquiça in amoiauoan, vallatotoca in acalchimalli, yoan in vtli ipan.

Auh in ocacoc: nimā ie ic tla[fol. 42]caoaca: nimā ie ic tlatzomoni in acalchimaleque, totoca, tequitlaneloa, macalhuitequi, macalhuitectivi, tlamattivi mictlantonco, macuilcuitlapilco: auh in acalchimalli, necoc in impan valmonamic, in impan valmopic, in tenuchca imacalchimal, yoā in tlatilulca imacalchimal; yoan cequintin icxipā iaque, nonoalco tlamelauhque, tlacupampa itztiaque, quiniacatzacuilizquia: nimā ie ic contlaça in acalchimalleque in tlatzontectli in impā in Españoles: necoccampa necoc in valhuetzi in tlatzontectli. Auh in iehoantin Españoles, no quinvalmina in Mexica, quivallaça in tepuzmitl, yoan in tlequiquiztli necoc micoa: minalo in Españoles, yoan tlaxcalteca: minalo in Mexica.

Twenty-fourth chapter, where it is said how the Spaniards and Tlaxcalans came out and fled from Mexico by night.

When night had fallen and midnight had come, the Spaniards came out. They formed up, along with all the Tlaxcalans. The Spaniards went ahead, and the Tlaxcalans went following, bringing up the rear, like their wall of protection. [The Spaniards] went carrying a wooden platform [or platforms]; they laid it down at a canal and crossed over on it.

At this time it was drizzling and sprinkling, the rain was gently dripping down. They were able to cross some other canals, at Tecpantzinco, Tzapotla, and Atenchicalco. But when they got to Mixcoatechialtitlan, [129] at the fourth canal, there they were seen coming out. It was a woman fetching water who saw them; then she shouted, saying, "O Mexica, come running, your enemies have come out, they have emerged secretly!" Then another person shouted, on top of [the temple of] Huitzilopochtli; his crying spread everywhere, everyone heard it. He said, "O warriors, o Mexica, your enemies are coming out, let everyone hasten with the war boats and on the roads!"

When it was heard, there was a clamor. Everyone scrambled; the operators of the war boats hastened and paddled hard, hitting one another's boats as they went in the direction of Mictlantonco and Macuilcuitlapilco. The war boats came upon them from both directions; the war boats of the Tenochca and the war boats of the Tlatelolca converged on them. And some people went on foot, going straight to Nonoalco, heading toward Tlacopan to try to cut them off there. Then the war-boat people hurled barbed darts at the Spaniards; from both sides the darts fell on them. But the Spaniards also shot at the Mexica, shooting back with iron bolts and guns. There were deaths on both sides. Spaniards and Tlaxcalans were hit, and Mexica were hit.

[fol. 41] Capitulo .24. de como los Españoles, y Tlaxcaltecas: salierō huyendo de mexico, de noche.

Despues que los Españoles, y los amigos que con ellos estauan se hallaron muy apretados ansi de hābre como de guerra vna noche salieron todos de su fuerte, los españoles delante, y los indios Tlaxcaltecas detras, y lleuauā vnas [fol. 41v] puentes, hechas con que se pasauā las acequias,

quando esto acontecio lluuia mansamente, pasaron q̄tro acequias: y antes que pasasen las demas salio vna muger a tomar agua, y violos como se yuan: y dio vozes diziendo a mexicanos, ya v̄ros enemigos se van: esto dixo tres o quatro vezes. Luego vno de los que velauan, començo a dar vozes desdel cu de Vitzilobuchtli, en manera que todos le oyeron dixo. A valientes hombres, ya an salido v̄ros enemigos, començad a pelear que se van.

Chapter Twenty-four, of how the Spaniards and Tlaxcalans left Mexico fleeing at night.

After the Spaniards and the friends who were with them saw themselves sorely pressed by hunger as well as battle, one night they all came out of their fort, the Spaniards ahead, the Tlaxcalan Indians behind. They carried some bridges already made, with which they crossed the canals.

When this happened, it was raining gently. They crossed four canals, but before they could cross the rest a woman went out to fetch water and saw that they were going; she shouted, saying, "O Mexica, your enemies are leaving!" She said this three or four times. Then one of those who were standing watch started shouting from the *cu* of Huitzilopochtli, so that everyone heard him, saying, "O brave men, your enemies have come out; begin the fight, for they are leaving."

Como oyeron todos esta voz, començaron a dar alaridos: y luego començarō arremeter ansi por tierra como por agua acudieron a vn lugar que se llamaua Mictlantonco, macuilcuitlapilco: alli atajaron a los españoles, los mexicanos de vna parte, los tlatilulcanos de otra alli, començaron a pelear contra los españoles: y los españoles contra ellos ansi fueron muertos y heridos de ambas partes muchos.

Y llegando los españoles a vna [fol. 42] acequia que se llamaua Tlaltecaiocā como no podieron pasarla todos, y los dauā guerra por todas partes: los indios Tlaxcaltecas cayeron en la acequia, y muchos de los españoles y las mugeres que con ellos tantos cayeron que la acequia se hinchio y

When they all heard this shout, they began to give war cries, and then they started attacking, both by land and by water. They ran to a place called Mictlantonco Macuilcuitlapilco; there they headed off the Spaniards, the Mexica from one direction, the Tlatelolca from the other, and there they began to fight against the Spaniards and the Spaniards against them. Thus many were killed and wounded on both sides.

When the Spaniards reached a canal named Tlaltecayocan, because they could not all get across and they were being attacked from all sides, the Tlaxcalan Indians fell in the canal, along with many of the Spaniards, and the women who were with them. So many fell in that the canal filled

Auh in Españoles in oacique in tlalteca-
ioacan in vncan in tultecaacalo[fol. 42v]co:
vncan iuhquin motepexivique, motepe-
xitenque, mochintin vncā onvetzque, ommotepeuhque in tlaxcaltecatl, in Tliliuhquitepecatl, yoan in Españoles, yoā in
cavallome, cequi cioa: vel ic ten in acalotli,
vel ic tzoneuh. Auh in ça tlatzacutiaque, ça
tlacapan, ça nacapan in onquizque, in
vmpanoque.

Auh in oacito petlacalco, in oc ce vncan
icaca acalutli, çan ivian, çan matca, çan tlamach, çan tlamatzin in onquizque, in ipan
quauhtlapechtli, vncan patito, vncan
imihio quicuique, vncā moquichquetzque.
Auh in oacito popotlan, otlatvic, otlanez,
ie oquicheuhtivi, ie veca motlamatilitivi.


Auh nimā ie ic quimicaoatztivi, quimo-
lolhuitivi, intech icativi in Mexica, quim-
aantivi in tlaxcalteca yoā in Españoles
mictivi: auh no mictilo in Mexica in tla-
ti[fol. 43]lulca, necoc micoatiuh, tlacupan
quinquixtique in quintoca. Auh in oquin-
quixtito Tiliuhcan, xocotlihiovican, vncan
in xoxocotla, vncan in iaumic in chimal-
pupuca, in ipiltzin Motecuçoma: in ipan
quiçato mintoc, tlatzōtectica, yoan vivitec-
toc, çā ie no vncan in mic, Tlaltecatzin,
tepanecatl tecutli in quiniacanaia, in quin-
tlaixtlatitivia, quimotlaxilitivia, quim-
otequilitivia, quimoquechilitivia in Españoles:


nimā ie ic companavique in Tepçolatl
(ce atoiatontli) vmpanoque, onapanoque,
in vncan Tepçolac, nimā ic ontlecoque in
acueco, ommotlalito otoncalpulco, quauh-
tenaniotoc, quauhtenametoc in itvalli:
vncā mocevique, mocecevique, yoā vncan
ihiiocuique, imihio quicuique, vncan
patito, vncā quinnamiquico in teucalhuiacan in valteiacan.

When the Spaniards reached Tlalte-
cayoacan, where the Tolteca canal is, it
was as though they had fallen off a preci-
pice; they all fell and dropped in, the Tlaxcalans, the people of Tliliuhquitepec, and
the Spaniards, along with the horses, and
some women. The canal was completely
full of them, full to the very top. And those
who came last just passed and crossed over
on people, on bodies.

When they reached Petlacalco, where
there was yet another canal, they passed
gently, slowly, gradually, with caution, on
the wooden platform. There they restored
themselves, took their breath, regained
their vigor. When they reached Popotlan,
it dawned, light came. They began to go
along with spirit, they went heading into
the distance.

Then the Mexica went shouting at
them, surrounding them, hovering about
them. They captured some Tlaxcalans as
they went, and some Spaniards died. Also
Mexica and Tlatelolca were killed; there
was death on both sides. They drove and
pursued [the Spaniards] to Tlacopan. And
when they had driven them to Tiliuhcan,
to Xocotliiyohuican, at Xoxocotla, Chimalpopoca, son of Moteucçoma, died in
battle. They came upon him lying hit by a
barbed dart and struck [by some hand
weapon]. At the same place died Tlaltecatzin, a Tepaneca lord who had been guiding the Spaniards, pointing out the way for
them, conducting them, showing them the
road.

Then they crossed the Tepçolatl (a small
river); they forded and went over the
water at Tepçolac. Then they went up to
Acueco and stopped at Otoncalpolco,
[where] wooden walls or barricades were
in the courtyard. There they all took a rest
and caught their breath, there they restored themselves. There the people of
Teocalhueyacan came to meet them and
guide them.

los que yuan detras, podieron pasar la
acequia sobre los muertos:

llegaron a otra aceǫa que se llama petlacalco, y pasaron con harta dificultad
aviendola pasado alli se rehizieron todos, y
se recogieron, y llegarō a otro lugar que se
llama puputla, ya q̄n ¹³⁰ amanecia:

y los mexicanos seguiālos con gran grita:
los españoles con algunos Tlaxcaltecas,
yuan juntos por su camino adelante, y peleando los vnos con los otros, siguieronlos
hasta cerca de tlacuban, hasta vn lugar que
se llama Tiliuhcan: y alli mataron al señor
de tlacuba que era hijo de Motecuçoma.
Tanbien aque ¹³¹ murio vn principal que se
llamaua Tlaltecatzin, y otro se llamaua
Tepanecatl [fol. 42v] tecutli, todos yuan
guiando a los españoles, y los enemigos los
mataron.

llegaron los españoles a vn lugar que llamauā Otonteocalco alli ¹³² se recogieron
en el patio, y se refocilaron porque los indios mexicanos ya se auian buelto a coger
el cāpo: alli los llegaron a recebir de paz; los
otomies del pueblo de teucaluiacā y los dieron comida.

up, and those who came behind we[re]
to cross the canal on top of the dea[d].

They reached another canal, nam[ed]
Petlacalco, and crossed it with great difficulty. Having crossed it, they all reorga-
nized themselves, collected their strength,
and reached another place called Popotla
when ¹³⁰ dawn was already coming.

The Mexica followed them with great
shouting. The Spaniards, with some Tlaxcalans, went ahead together on their way,
each side fighting with the other. They
followed them as far as close to Tacuba, to
a place called Tiliuhcan, and there they
killed the lord of Tacuba, who was a son of
Moteucçoma. Here ¹³¹ died also a leader
named Tlaltecatzin, and another named
Tepanecatl teuctli. All of them were going
along guiding the Spaniards, and the enemies killed them.

The Spaniards reached a place called
Otonteocalco; there ¹³² they took shelter
in the courtyard and regained their
strength, because the Mexica Indians had
already gone back to pick up the spoils.
There the Otomis of the settlement of
Teocalhueyacan approached them to receive them peacefully, and they gave them
food.

88

89

25

[fol. 43v] Inic cempoalli ommacuilli capitulo, vncā mitoa in quenin Teucalhuiacan tlaca, ivian, iocuxca quīnamiquico in Españoles yoan quinmacaque in tlaqualli, in iquac choloque mexico.

Tlacatecutli itoca, otoncoatl in ipiltoca, in valteiacā, in vncan quicavaco tlaqualli, iztac tlaxcalli, totolin, totollalevatzalli, [133] totollaapoçonilli, totoltetl, yoa cequin ioioli in tutultin, yoan cequi nochtli contecaque ixpan in capitan: quitoque. Oanquimihioviltique, oquimociaviltique in totecuiovan in teteu, ma mocevitzinocan, ma tlaltitech maxitican, ma mihiocuitican:

nimā quinoalnāquili in Malintzin: quito. Notechiuhcavan, quimitalhuia in Capitan:

Twenty-fifth chapter, where it is said how the people of Teocalhueyacan came in peace to meet the Spaniards, when they fled from Mexico, and gave them food.

Tlacateuctli was the [official] name and Otoncoatl the personal name of the leader of those who came there to deliver food. They laid down before the Captain white tortillas, turkey hens, roast turkey, [133] boiled turkey, eggs, and some live turkey hens, as well as some tuna-cactus fruit. They said, "You are doubly welcome; may our lords the gods rest, may they lie down and catch their breath."

Then Marina answered them, saying, "My good men, the Captain says, 'Where

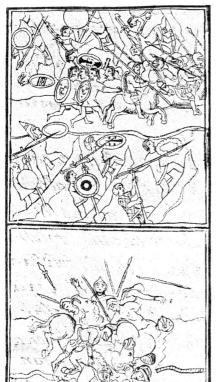

25

[fol. 43v] Capitulo .25. de como los de Teucalhuiaca salieron de paz y con bastimentos a los españoles, quando yuan huyendo de Mexico.

Chapter Twenty-five, of how the people of Teocalhueyacan came out peacefully and with provisions for the Spaniards when they went fleeing from Mexico.

Estando los españoles en este aposēto arriba d̄ho vinieron los otomies de teucalhuiacan con su principal que se llamaua Otoncoatl: y truxeron comida a los españoles que estauan muy necesitados dieronlos muchas tortillas y gallinas asadas y

With the Spaniards lodged as said above, the Otomis of Teocalhueyacan came with their leader, named Otoncoatl, bringing food to the Spaniards, who were in great need. They gave them many tortillas, roasted and stewed fowl, and other kinds

campa vallaque, campa inchan: nimā quilhuique. Ma quimocaquiti in totecuio; ca
[fol. 44] vmpa tivallaque in ichantzinco in
Teucalhuiacan, ca titeucalhuiaque: nimā
quioalito in Malintzin. Ca ie qualli otech-
mocnelilique, vmpa tiazque in muztla,
vmpa ticuchizque.

Auh nimā vel iquac in o tlatlavizcalli
ieoac, in otlatlalchipaoac in teçacoc, in
çaçacoque in ie ixquich Tlaxcaltecatl, in
cempoaltecatl, yoan in Españoles, in motepexivique in tultecaacaloco, yoan in petla-
calcu, anoço mictlantonco: acaltica in
teçaçacoc, aztapilla, aztapiltitlan, tulla, tul-
itic in quimamaiavito, quimōtzotzoponti-
tlaçato, inca vmmamaiavito, yoan in cioa
quintlatlaçato, pepetlauhtivi, cuztique,
coztalanpopul, coztemiloltique [135] in cioa,
muchintin quinpepetlauhq̄ quintla-
cuicuilique, quintlatepevilique, quin-
petztoccauhque. Auh in Espanoles [fol.
44v] nonqua quintetenque, quin-
vivipanque, ie on tolcellome, ie ō meztal-
lome, ie on acaxilome ie on tolcellutl innacaio; yoan quinçaçacaque in mamaça in
temamani intoca cavallome.

Auh in ixquich in intlatqui in tlamamal-
chichiuhtiuh muchi namoieloc, muchi
maceoaloc, in aquin çaço tlein ipan
oquiçato quicuitivetzi, quimotechtia,
quimomamaltia quitqui in ichan, yoan vel
ipan nemimictiloc in ixquich in çaço tlein
oquimauhcacauhtiquizque yoan miec in
iaūtlatquitl in vncan namoieloc in tomaoac
tlequiquiztli in matlequiquiztli, yoan cequi
vncan tepeoac, vncan tepeuh in tlequi-
quiztlalli, in tepuzmaquavitl, in tepuztopilli in tzinacantopilli, in tepuztlavitolli,
in tepuzmitl: yoā no vncan maceoaloc in
tepuzquacalalatli, in tepuzvipilli, in tepuz-
matlavipilli, in [fol. 45] eoachimalli, in
tepuchimalli, in quauhchimalli: yoan

have they come from, where is their
home?' " Then they said to her, "May our
lord hear: We have come from Teocalhueyacan, which is his home; we are people of Teocalhueyacan." Then Marina replied, "Very well, and many thanks. We
will go there tomorrow and stay the
night."

And then just as dawn broke and day-
light came, [bodies] were removed. They
[the Mexica] removed all the Tlaxcalans,
Cempoalans, and Spaniards who had fallen
into the Tolteca canal and at Petlacalco or
Mictlantonco. They were removed in
boats. They went and flung them out in
the stands of white rushes, among the
white rushes, in the stands of reeds, in the
midst of the reeds, forking them with
spears, flinging them away. They also
threw down the women, naked, yellow,
⟨yellow all over⟩;[135] they stripped all the
women, took everything from them,
spilled out what they had, left them lying
bare. But the Spaniards they laid out in a
separate place, arranging them in rows.
They were [like] tender reed sprouts, new
maguey sprouts; their bodies were [like]
sprouting reeds and rushes. They also
removed the people-bearing deer named
horses.

And the goods that they had gone carrying with them were all picked up and acquired by others. Anyone who came upon
anything whatever rushed to take and appropriate it, loading it on his back and taking it home, and there was great fighting
over whatever they had gone leaving behind in fear, and much war gear was taken:
cannon, harquebuses, and some of it lying
strewn about—gunpowder, swords, iron
lances, halberds, crossbows, crossbow
bolts. And also they acquired there iron
helmets, iron cuirasses, coats of mail,
leather shields, metal shields, wooden
shields. And they acquired there gold in
bricks, golden disks, and gold dust, and
gilded necklaces with pendants.

cozidas: y otras maneras de comida: y hablaron al capitan Don hernando cortes,
saludandole de paz y rogandole que des-
cansasen y comiesen:

of food, and they spoke to Captain don
Hernando Cortés, greeting him peacefully
and asking that they should rest and eat.

y entonce el capitan los hablo por la lengua de Marina india, preguntandoles donde [134] eran ellos dixeron que eran del
pueblo de Teucaluiacan. Luego informado
el capitan de que tan lexos estaua su
pueblo, dixoles mañana yremos a dormir a
v̄ro pueblo ellos hizieron gracias, porque
queria yr a su pueblo

Then the Captain spoke to them with
the Indian woman Marina as interpreter,
asking them where they were from. [134]
They said that they were from the settlement of Teocalhueyacan. Then when the
Captain was informed how far their settlement was, he told them, "tomorrow we
will go to sleep the night at your settlement." They expressed their thanks because he wished to go to their settlement.

93

auiendo llegado el capitan con los españoles: y los amigos a este fuerte ya d̄ho.
[fol. 44] Los mexicanos començaron a
sacar la gente ansi españoles como Tlaxcaltecas, y cempoaltecas que se auiã ahogado
en el acequia que se llamaua Toltecaacaloco, y en la que se llamaua petlacalco y
en la que se llamaua Mictlantonco sacaronlos: y despojaronlos y echaronlos desnudos
por entre las espadañas y jūzias para que alli
las [136] comiesen las aues y los perros: a los
españoles a otra parte los echaron por si
conozian que eran barbados, y teniã los
cuerpos muy blancos,

tanbien los cauallos que se auian
ahogado, y todas las cargas que lleuauan
todo lo desbarataron, y lo robaron: y todas
las armas que hallaron las tomaron: los tiros
de polbora tanbien los tomaron, y derra-
maron toda la polbora que auia, [fol. 44v]
tomaron muchas escopetas, y muchas vallestas y muchas espadas y muchas alabar-
das, y muchos capacetes, y cosoletes, y
cotas, y muchas dargas, [137] y lanças, y mu-

After the Captain with the Spaniards and
the friends had reached this fort that was
mentioned, the Mexica began to remove
the people, Spaniards as well as Tlaxcalans
and Cempohualans, who had drowned in
the canal named Toltecaacaloco and in the
one named Petlacalco and in the one
named Mictlantonco. They took them
out, stripped them, and threw them naked
among the reeds and rushes so that the
birds and dogs would eat them [136] there.
They threw the Spaniards in another place,
separately. They recognized that they were
bearded and had very white bodies.

They also dispersed and stole [what was
on] the horses that had drowned and all the
loads they carried; they took all the weapons they found; they also took the firearms
they found and spilled out all the powder
there was. They took many muskets,
crossbows, swords, halberds, helmets,
corselets, coats of mail, long shields, [137]
lances, and round shields. Here they also
took much gold in small bars, in vessels,

vncan momaceuh in teucuitlatl in tlaxan-
tectli, yoan teucuitlacomalli, yoan teucuitlatl tlaxaqualolli, yoan in chaiaoac cozcatl
teucuitlaio.

Auh in ie ixquich in otlanamoieloc,
nimā ie ic onnetepeoalo in atlan, netla-
tetemolilo, cequintin tlamatemoa, cequintin tlacxitemoa.

Auh inic quizque in iacattiaque, ie vel
quizque: auh in ça tlatzacutiaque, iehoantin in motepexivique in matlanvique,
mochintin micque vel iuhqui tlacatepetl
motlali monenepanotoque, çan mo-
netechmictique, mihiomictīq̄:


auh in ie iuhqui in vncā acueco, in on-
cochque, oc veca iovan oc vellavizcalpan
in meuhq̄, in mochichiuhque, in moiauh-
chichiuhque, in ōmaaquique in iautlatquitl: niman ie ic oneoa, onolini, ōmo-
tema. Auh in mexica quimicavatztivi [fol.
45v] quimoiovitivi, aocmo intech onaci,
ça vecapa quimitztivi ça quinvecapavitivi,
ça quinnachcapavitivi. Auh in onacique
cecni, itocaiocan calacoaian, tlamimiloltic-
pac, tlacpactonco, in vncā tecuecuentla,
vncā ōtemictitiquizque ontexixilque,
amo quimimachitique in vncan tlaca, in
calacoaian tlaca, amo innemachpan in mictiloque, intech motlavelquixtique, intech
mellelquixtique. Auh in ontemictique:
nimā ie ic ontemo in tlani, connamiqui in
tlalpechtli, in ixtlaoatontli: itoca, Tiçapan:
niman ie ic ontleco Teucalhuiacan.

And when they were through taking
things, everyone scattered in the water,
searching; some searched with their hands,
some with their feet.

When they [the Spaniards] were coming
out, those who went in the lead were able
to get through, but those who came behind were the ones who fell in, who fell in
the water. They all died. It was truly like a
mountain of people that was formed. They
lay pressed against one another, killing and
smothering one another.

While this went on, [the Spaniards] at
Acueco kept sleeping. It was still very dark,
still dawn when they arose and readied
themselves, dressing for war, donning their
war gear. Then they made their departure,
got started on their way, put themselves in
order. And the Mexica went clamoring at
them, yelling at them; they no longer
caught up to them, but went looking toward them from afar, dealing with them
from afar, from a good distance. And when
the Spaniards reached a certain place called
Calacoyan, on top of a rounded hill, up on
the little eminence, where there were rows
of rocks, they started killing and stabbing
people. They did not give notice to the
people of Calacoyan; unexpectedly they
were killed. [The Spaniards] took out their
rage on them, vented their wrath on them.
When they had done the killing, they
went down below, encountering some flat
land, a little plain called Tiçaapan; then
they went up to Teocalhueyacan.

chas rodelas: aqui tanbien tomaron mucho oro en barretas em basijas y oro en poluo, y muchas joyas de oro, y de piedras:

començaron luego a buscar por todas las acequias lo que auia caydo de los despojos, ansi de los viuos como de los muertos:

los españoles que yuan en la uanguardia solos se saluaron con los indios que yuā con ellos, y los que yuā en la retaguardia todos murieron ansi indios como indias y los españoles y todo el fardaje se perdio,

dormieron los españoles que se escaparon en vn lugar que se llamaua acueco, y de alli muy de mañana se partieron: y los mexicanos yuan en su seguimiento dandoles grita desde lexos. llegādo a vn lugar que se llamaua Calacoaian que esta ençima de los cerros destruyeron todo aquel bueblo dezendicrō hazia los llanos que se llamaua Tiçapan: [fol. 45] y luego començaron a subir hazia el pueblo de Teucalhuiacan.

and in gold dust, and much jewelry of gold and fine stones.

Then they began to search through all the canals for what spoils had fallen in, from the living as well as from the dead.

Only the Spaniards who went in the vanguard saved themselves, along with the Indians who went with them; everyone in the rear guard died, Indian women as well as men and the Spaniards, and all the baggage was lost.

The Spaniards who escaped slept the night in a place named Acueco, and they left there very early in the morning. The Mexica went pursuing them, shouting at them from afar. Reaching a place named Calacoyan, which is on top of the hills, they destroyed that whole settlement. They went down toward the plains [to a place] named Tiçaapan, and then they began to climb toward the settlement of Teocalhueyacan.

Inic cempoalli onchiquacencapitulo, vncan mitoa in quenin Españoles acito Teucalhuiacan: auh in quenin quinpaccacelique vmpa tlaca.

In teucalhuiacan oncalacq̄ onmocacaltemato in otōcal[fol. 46]pulco, çan cuel in onacito, aiamo vel nepantla tonatiuh: auh in onacique, ça temac: moch mocencauh in ixquich qualoni in totoli .&. cenca quinpapaquiltique, çan ivian intlan oncalacque, ixquich quinmacaia in ixquich quimitlaniliaia, in maçatlaqualli, in atl, in tlaolli, in elotl, in eloxoxouhqui, in elopaoaxtli, in elotlaxcalli, in xilopaoaxtli, in eloixcalli, in elotamalli: yoan in aiotlatlapanalli, quintlanenectiaia, quintlanenequiltiaia, quimōmocniuhtique, onmocniuhtlaque.

Auh in tliliuhquitepeca, vncā vallaque, quimōneloco in teucalhuiaque: iehica ca in tliliuhquitepeca incotonca ioan invaniolque in teucalhuiaq̄ in tliliuhquitepeca, inquizcā iniolcan, inquechtetzon yionocan in teucalhuiacan, vncā quizticate,

vncā mononotzque vncan quicemitoque, vncā quicentlalique in intlatol, qui-

Twenty-sixth chapter, where it is said how the Spaniards reached Teocalhueyacan, and how the people there received them gladly.

When they entered Teocalhueyacan, they went to arrange themselves in various buildings of the Otomi calpulli ⟨temple⟩; they got there quickly, before high noon. When [the Spaniards] arrived, all the food—turkeys, etc.—was prepared and at hand. They made [the Spaniards] very happy, joining them peacefully, giving them everything they asked them for: deer fodder, water, shelled maize, fresh ears of maize—raw, cooked, made into tortillas, baked, made into tamales—cooked tender maize, and gourds broken into pieces. They kept offering them various things, they made friends with them, they became friends.

And the people of Tliliuhquitepec came there to mingle with the Teocalhueyacan people, because the people of Tliliuhquitepec had split off from the people of Teocalhueyacan and were their relatives. Teocalhueyacan was the birthplace, the foundation site of the people of Tliliuhquitepec, the place from which they came.

There they consulted together, agreed, stated as one, said jointly, and arranged an

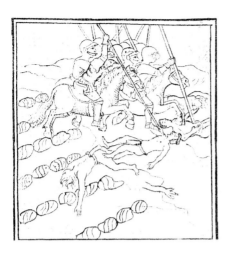

26

[fol. 45v] Capitulo .26. de como los Españoles llegaron al pueblo Teucalhuiacan y
del buen tratamiento que alli los hizieron.

Llegados los Españoles al pueblo de
Teucalhuiacan ante [138] mediodia [fol. 46]
fueron muy bien recebidos por los otomies
cuyo era aquel pueblo, y dierōlos luego
mucha comida la qual les tenian aparejada
regocijaronlos y recrearonlos mucho ansi a
ellos como a todos los que con ellos yuan,
y tambien a los cauallos dandolos quanto
auia menester, y ellos tenian

los otomies de tlaxcaltecas [139] que se escaparon de la guerra conozieronse con los
de Teucaluiacan porque eran todos pa-
rientes y desde [140] pueblo de Teucaluiacan
auian ydo a poblar a Tlaxcalla:

y luego todos ellos juntos se hablaron
para saludar al capitan, y a los españoles:
luego todos juntos fuero a hablar al capitan, y a los otros capitanes diziendolos que
aquella era su casa y su pueblo: y ellos eran
sus basallos, tanbien se quexaron al capitan
del mal tratamiento que les auian hecho
a [141] Motecuçoma, y los mexicanos cargan-
dolos mucho tributo, y muchos trabaxos y
dixeronlos que si los dexaua que mas mal

Chapter Twenty-six, of how the Spaniards reached the settlement of Teocalhueyacan, and the good treatment they received there.

The Spaniards, arriving at the settlement
of Teocalhueyacan before [138] midday, were
very well received by the Otomis to
whom that settlement belonged, and then
they gave them much food that they had
ready for them. They entertained them
well, [the Spaniards] as well as all those
who went with them, also giving the
horses whatever they needed, if they
had it.

The Tlaxcalan Otomis [139] who escaped
from the battle got to know the people of
Teocalhueyacan because they were all relatives, and it was from this [140] settlement of
Teocalhueyacan that they had gone to settle Tlaxcala.

Then all of them spoke together about
greeting the Captain and the Spaniards,
and then they all went together to speak to
the Captain and the other captains, telling
them that this was their home and their
settlement, and they were their vassals.
They also complained to the Captain of
the bad treatment that Moteucçoma and
the Mexica had given them, [141] loading
them down with much tribute and great

ne[fol. 46v]panvique, contlamāvique in
innenonotzal, inic quinamicque, inic quī-
tlatlauhtique in capitan in teutl, yoan in
ie mochintin teteu, ca omaxitico in in-
chantzinco in nicā teucalhuiacan, ca nican
tictotlatlauhtilia, tictociauhquechilia in
timaceoalhoā, in titeucalhuiaque, yoan in
Tliliuhquitepeca; yoan ma quimocaquiti in
totecuio. Ca in motecuçoma yoā in mexicatl, ca cenca otechtolini, otechtlaciavilti,
vel toiacacpa oquiquixti in netoliniliztli; [142]
ca ixquich in in techtequitia in tlacalaquili: [143] auh inin ca totecuio ca totlatocatzin.
Auh intla techmocavilitiquiça catlacatl in
mexicatl, vellavaliloc, intla techmocavi-
litiquiçaz, intla movecavitiz, in oalmovicaz
in valmocueptzinoz, aotechtlamique,
aotechpopoloque in Mexicatl: ca vel huei
tlavaliloc, ca vel quimaxilti inic tlaueliloc.

Auh in ocōcaqui[fol. 47]ti in Malintzin
in tlatolli in capitan: nimā quinoalhui.
Macamo motequipachocā camo nive-
caoaz, iciuhca nioallaz, iciuhca niquin-
matiquiuh, nican tlatoloz, nican tlatoloian
iez, popoliviz in Mexicatl, macamo amech-
iolitlacocan.

Auh in o iuh quicaque in teucalhuiaque
cenca papacque, ic aatlamatque, ic cuecue-
notque, iz [144] ic moquetzque, ic
moiehoatocaque, quimolhuiltocaque, ilhuiz iuhquin mocacaq [146] ilhuiz iuhquin
aatlamati, iuhquin vncā motlatlalia iniollo
monelchiuhque, ie om ma nelli iuh momatque. Auh inic iuhqui in ocuchque oc
veca iovan in ie tlapitzalo, in quipitza
quauhtlapitzalli, quavilacapitztli, yoan tla-
tzotzonalo, iautlatzotzonalo:

ie ic neeoalo, meeva in Españoles, ne-
chichivalo: Auh in ie iuhqui, ie ic oneoalo
neutemalo, pepexocatiuh in vtli: nimā ic
onacito in tepu[fol. 47v]tztzla, aia vel
quēman oc qualcan in ommotlalito, çan

agreement to meet with and address the
Captain, the god, and all the gods. "They
have arrived here in Teocalhueyacan,
which is their home. Here we address and
greet them, we their subjects, we of Teocalhueyacan and those of Tliliuhquitepec,
and may our lord hear. Moteucçoma and
the Mexica have greatly afflicted and exhausted us, they have afflicted us in extreme measure. [142] [Moteucçoma] assigns
us all this tribute, [143] for he is our lord and
ruler. And if [the Spaniards] go and leave
us, the Mexica are inhuman, very fierce; if
they go and leave us, if it is a long time
before they come back and return, will not
the Mexica have finished us off and destroyed us? For they are very fierce, exceeding in viciousness."

And when Marina had reported what
they said to the Captain, he replied to
them, "Let them not be concerned, I will
not be gone long, I will quickly come back
and find my way to them. Here the judgment will take place, here will be the place
of judgment. The Mexica will be destroyed, let them not cause you grief."

And when the people of Teocalhueyacan heard this, they rejoiced greatly; they
grew proud and presumptuous because of
it, they rose up, [144] thinking themselves
preferred and fortunate. Even more than
seeming satisfied [146] and proud, they
seemed to be consoled, they were convinced, they thought it true. And this to
the extent that when [the Spaniards] had
gone to sleep, far into the night wind instruments were being played, wooden
flutes and wooden fifes, and there was
drumming, war drumming.

⟨While the drumming was still going
on⟩ people got up, the Spaniards arose and
got outfitted. When this was done, the departure took place; the group formed on
the road, and the road was full to overspill-

tratamiento les auian de hazer porque eran crueles y inhumanos [fol. 46v] mexicanos:

como Marina vuo d̄ħo al capitan lo que los otomies deziā: Dixoles el capitan. No tengays pena aūq̄ me vaya que yo boluere presto y hare que esta sea cabecera y no sea subjecta a mexico y destruyere a los mexicanos.

Como oyeron estas palabras los otomies de Teucalhuiacan consolaronse mucho, y cobraron presumcion, y argullo [145] para reuelarse de los mexicanos:

y los españoles dormieron aquella noche alli; y otro dia ante que amanesciese aparejaronse para partirse, y tomaron el camino de Tepotzotlan llegaron a aquel lugar antes de mediodia. Como los de Teputzotlan los vieron que yuan a su pueblo: començaron luego todos a huyr metieronse en los mōtes y ascondieronse por las barrācas no quedo nadie en el pueblo que recibiese a los españoles, ninguna cosa lleuaron consigo dexaron todas sus haziendas solamente saluaron sus personas porque tuuieron gran miedo que las auiā [fol. 47] de matar: y los españoles entraronse en las casas principales o palacios del señor en aquel pueblo dormieron aquella noche todos jūtos y todos estauā con gran temor de que viniesen sobre ellos los enemigos:

otro dia en amaneciendo almorçaron de lo que hallaron por las casas del pueblo. Despues que vuieron almorçado partieronse y por el camino donde yuan: yuan tras ellos: los mexicanos dādoles grita y si

afflictions, and they told them that if they left them they were going to give them more bad treatment, because the Mexica were cruel and inhuman.

When Marina had told the Captain what the Otomis said, the Captain told them, "Don't be concerned; although I'm going, I will return quickly, and I will see to it that this [settlement] will be a head town and not subject to Mexico, and I will destroy the Mexica."

When the Otomis of Teocalhueyacan heard these words, they were greatly consoled, and they gained the presumption and pride [145] to rebel against the Mexica.

The Spaniards slept there that night. The next day before dawn they prepared themselves to depart and took the road to Tepotzotlan; they reached that place before midday. When the people of Tepotzotlan saw that they were going to their settlement, they all immediately began to flee. They went into the mountains and hid themselves in the ravines; no one stayed in the settlement to receive the Spaniards. They took nothing with them; they left all their property and saved only their persons, because they were greatly afraid that they were going to kill them. The Spaniards entered the main residence or palace of the lord in that settlement. They slept all together that night, and all were in great fear that the enemy would fall upon them.

The next day at dawn they breakfasted on what they found in the houses of the settlement. After breakfast they left, and on the road where they were going the Mexica went behind them, shouting at them.

achi quitocatiaque: auh in teputzoteca niman ic tzomonque olinque, ic choloque, quauhtla calacque: cequintin tepetl quitlecavique; cequintin atlauhtli, çan inpan macauh in Espanoles, aiac inca muchiuh: iehica ca cenca vei in intepololiz, ipampa mochololtique, mocholtique: çan ixquich in innacaio quimaquixtique: auh in ixquich in intlatqui quitepeuhtiquizque, çaniuh tlacauhtiquizque: tecpan in oncalacque, ommotepancaltemato, vncā cochque, çan cenietivi, çan cemololiuhtivi, çan centepeuhtivi: iehica ca çan mauhcavi, çan momauhtitivi.

Auh in otlatvic, in ie achi qualcā: niman ie ic tlatlaqua, quiqua in inneuhca: in ommoneuhcaiotique, in oconquaque in inneuhca: nimā ic oneuh[fol. 48]que, ie ic vtlatoca, quimicavatza, ça veca, ça vecapa, ça quinvalhuecapavia, in quinvalicavatza. Auh intla ça acame motlapaloa in intech onaci, iuhquin aquimōtlatoltia in ꝗnvalixili, çan ic cen vi in quimixili, aocmo valmocuecuetzoa aocac quiça aocac quiquixtia in quixili:

nimā ic onacito in citlaltepec, ommotecato, çāno tlalcaviloque, amo quinmochieltique in maceoalti. Auh in tiacaoan, in vncā tlaca, in chaneque, aocmo valmixmana, ça motlatia, itla quimotoctia, aço tenopalli, aço metl, aço tlatepevalli, anoço texcalli: iehica ca amo ixnamiquiztin, no vncā cochque.

Auh in otlatvic, ie achi qualcan, ie tlatotonie, in ie tlaiamania: niman ie ic tlatlaqua, niman ie ic no ceppa vmpeoa, ommiquania xoloc: çan ie no ivi, inpan macauh, aocac in manel ça çe[fol. 48v]ton, quinmochielti, vel cacactivetz in calli, aiac in ma ivic quiz: tlacpac in motlatique, icpac in tepetl xoloc: noviampa valla-

ing. Then they reached Tepotzotlan. It was not yet late, still in good time, when they stopped; they had proceeded only a short distance. Then the people of Tepotzotlan scrambled about, started moving, ran from them, and went into the woods. Some climbed up the mountains, some [hid in] ravines. [Everything] was left to the Spaniards. No one attended to them; because of their great destruction of people, they ran off and fled, saving nothing but their bodies. They left all their property scattered about, abandoning things just as they were. [The Spaniards] went into the palace, arranged themselves there, and slept there, all together, gathered together, bunched, because they went in fear, frightened.

And when it dawned and the time was opportune, then they ate their breakfast, and when they had breakfasted they departed. As they went on their way, [the Mexica] shouted at them, just coming after them at a distance, shouting at them from afar. But if some of them dared come near them, as though they were going to engage them in talk, [the Spaniards] stabbed them. Those who were stabbed were gone forever. They moved no more; no one came to save those who were stabbed.

Then they got to Citlaltepec and made a halt. Also there things were left abandoned for them; the people did not await them. And the warriors who were from there no longer presented themselves, but hid, taking refuge behind something, a rock cactus, or a maguey, or a mound of earth, or a crag, because [the Spaniards] were irresistible. There too they spent the night.

And when it dawned and the time was opportune, when it was warm and pleasant, they ate; then they got on their way again and moved to Xoloc. In the same way it was left in [the Spaniards'] hands. No one, not a single person, awaited them. The houses were entirely empty; no one at all came out toward them. They hid

alguno se acercaua a los españoles, luego le matauā

fueron derechos al pueblo de citlaltepec: y como vierō los de Citlaltepec que yuan alla, los Españoles ascondieronse ningun recibimiento les hizieron comieron de lo que hallaron por las casas, y dormieron alli aquella noche, y de mañana almorçaron: aviendo almorçado partieronse.

Y llegaron al pueblo que se llama Xoloc los de aquel pueblo, todos huyeron, y nadie oso esperar todos se subieron al cerro que se llama xoloc, y alli se ascondierō, y todos tuuieron gran temor. [fol. 48v] Los españoles dormieron alli aquella noche:

If someone drew close to the Spaniards, right away they killed him.

They went straight to the settlement of Citlaltepec, and when the people of Citlaltepec saw that the Spaniards were headed there, they hid themselves and did not receive them at all. They ate what they found around the houses. They slept there that night, and in the morning took breakfast; having breakfasted, they left.

They reached the settlement called Xoloc, and the inhabitants all fled; no one dared await them. They all climbed the hill called Xoloc and hid there. They were all greatly afraid. The Spaniards slept there that night.

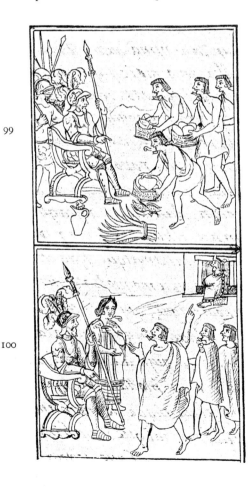

99

100

101

102

chielo, acã motlatique tlapechian, tlaco-
mulco, anoço atlauhco, ie quimacacia, ie
quinmauhtia, in ma amo quimimachititi in
iniauvan, in maca innemachpan inpã val-
choloti.

above, on top of Mount Xoloc, from
which one looks out in all directions. They
did not hide anywhere on plains, in gullies,
or in ravines, apprehensive and afraid lest
their enemies spring upon them without
warning, unawares.

 

Auh in otlatvic in ie iazque, in ie
oneoazque, in ie onolinizque: niman ie ic
tlatlaqua; ie ic vmpeoa, necoc omac
onotivi; in mamaça in intemamacaoan, intoca cavallome: auh in ixquich tlamama
çan tlatic onotivi, ololiuhtivi. Auh in on-
tlanque in vi; nec contlequechia, contlemina, contlecavia in otonteucalli, yoan
in ixquich teucalli, in incal tlatlacateculo,
nec tlatla, cuecuetlaca: in tlecueçallutl, in
tlenenepilli, in tlecocomochtli [fol. 49]
poctlevatoc, poctli mantoc, poctli moteca.
Auh in iquac ie iativi, quimicavatztivi in
maceoaltin, çan vecapa:

niman ic ommotlalito in Aztaquemecan:
icxitlan itzintlã in iehoatl tepetl Aztaque-

And when dawn came and they were
about to go, make their departure, and
break camp, then they ate and got on their
way. On both sides of the road came their
people-bearing deer, called horses, and all
those who bore burdens went gathered together inside [the rows]. And just as they
were going they set fire to, ignited, and
burned the Otomi temple and all the other
temples, houses of demons. Then they
burned and crackled, there were tongues
of flame and smacking sounds; smoke
rose, hung about, spread out. And as they
went off, the people shouted at them, but
from afar.

Then they made a halt at Aztaquemecan, at the foot and base of Mount Az-

103

104

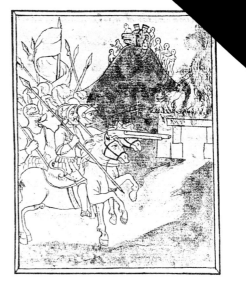

105

y otro dia muy de mañana, como vuieron almorçado, partieronse los españoles,
yuan por el camino, en dos rencles, los de
cauallo: y todos los de a pie, y los que
lleuauā cargas, yuan en medio de los de
cauallo, y de camino: quemaron todas las
casas de los demonios, que hallaron a
mano, porque eran paxizas, y como las
casas ardia. Espantauanse los que lo vian
yendo por su camino adelante los españoles: yuan tras ellos dandoles grita los
maceoalles de aquellos [fol. 49] lugares,
pero no osauan llegarse:

The next morning very early, after
breakfasting, the Spaniards left. The horsemen went along the road in two files, and
all the footmen and those who carried
loads went on the road in the middle of the
horsemen. They burned all the houses of
demons that they found at hand, because
they were of thatch, and when the houses
started burning, those who saw it were
shocked. As the Spaniards went ahead on
their way, the *macehuales* of those places
went behind them shouting at them, but
dared not approach.

aquel dia llegaron al pueblo que se llama
aztaquemecan, este es vn monte alto po-

That day they reached the settlement
called Aztaquemecan, where the people

...lalique tlatzintlan:
...to, no tlacpac, olol-
...vncan icac otonteucalli,
...mato, çanno impan ma-
... acito in maceoaltin,
...in calli, cacactivetz in

taquemecan. They established themselves
there below, at a place called Çacamolco.
Also there was a rounded hill above, and
an Otomi temple stood there. They set
themselves up in the houses there. Likewise the place was left to them, the people
were gone when they arrived; the houses
everywhere lay silent and abandoned.

## 27

Inic cempoalli onchicume capitulo
vncan mitoa in quenin Mexica intech acito
in Españoles inic quinteputztocaia.

Twenty-seventh chapter, where it is
said how the Mexica caught up to the
Spaniards when they were following after
them.

No vel iquac in onacito Mexica in
quiniacatzacuilizquia: in ommotecato
mexica itzintlan tepetl itoca Tona. Auh in
otlatvic nec mo[fol. 49v]cencaoa in Espanoles tlatlaqua: no ivi mexica mocecencaoa tlatlaqua, aatli pinolatl quiy: cequintin
tlacpac tlecoque, iautlachixque, iau-
tlapixque, quimonitztoque in quēmā
oneoazque, in quenman onolinizque in
Españoles: vel imix intequiuh in ontlachix-
ticate.

Also at the very same time, the Mexica
got there, wanting to intercept [the Span-
iards]; they established themselves at the
foot of the mountain named Tonan. When
dawn came, the Spaniards readied themselves and ate, and the Mexica likewise
readied themselves and ate and drank; they
drank a maize and chia beverage. Some
climbed to the top [of the mountain] and
looked out for the enemy, observed the
enemy, looking to see when the Spaniards
would break camp and make their departure; those who were watching kept their
eyes peeled.

Auh in ie iuhqui in ie olini in ie utlatoca
in Espanoles: niman ie ic valtzatzi in iautlachixque: quivalitoa. Mexicae ie iauh in
amoiaouh, ticcencaoa, ticcecencaoa,
ticemolini, ticenvi, aiac mocauhtiaz. Auh
in oquicacque nec netlalolo, tlaixquiquiça,
tlatotoca.

And when the Spaniards were getting
going, were on the road, then the lookouts
shouted down, saying, "O Mexica, your
enemies are going! We must prepare ourselves, each and every one, we must all get
going and be on our way; no one must stay
behind." And when they heard this, everyone ran, scurried back and forth, hastened.

blado los españoles les subieron al monte, aposentaronse en la falda del monte en vna poblacion que se llama Çacamulco, que esta en vn collado, aposentaronse en vn cu de los otomies: Tanbien los habitadores, de aquel pueblo, se huyeron; y dexaron el pueblo.

are settled on a high mountain. The Spaniards climbed up the mountain toward them and lodged on its lower slopes in a town called Çacamolco, which is on a hill. They lodged in a *cu* of the Otomis. The inhabitants of that settlement also fled and abandoned the settlement.

106

### 27

Capitulo .27. de como los mexicanos llegaron adonde estauan los españoles siguiendo el alcance.

Estando los españoles en este pueblo: llegaron grã numero de mexicanos con proposito de acabarlos y asentaronse cerca de vna cuesta que se llama Tona, que q̃re [fol. 49v] dezir n̄ra madre embiaron luego espias los mexicanos para que espiasẽ a los españoles para que viesen quãdo començasen a caminar

y como começaron los españoles a caminar las espias dieron vozes a los mexicanos diziendoles como ya los españoles se yuan. Oydo esto: luego [147] mexicanos començaron a marchar tras ellos;

Chapter Twenty-seven, of how the Mexica, in pursuit, arrived where the Spaniards were.

While the Spaniards were in this settlement, a great number of Mexica arrived with the intention of finishing them off. They took up a position close to a hill called Tonan, which means "our mother." Then the Mexica sent spies to keep watch on the Spaniards and see when they should take the road.

When the Spaniards started on their way, the spies cried out to the Mexica telling them that the Spaniards were already leaving. When they heard this, the [147] Mexica immediately began to march after them.

los españoles como los vieron yr tras si con gran priesa entendieron querian pelear, y pararonse y pusieronse en orden de guerra: y los mexicanos como eran muchos tomaron en medio a los españoles començaron a combatirlos de todas partes: y los españoles mataron muchos mexicanos y tlatilulcanos por quanto se arrojaron

The Spaniards, seeing them coming behind them in great haste, understood that they wanted to fight, and stopped and placed themselves in battle order. Because there were many of the Mexica, they surrounded the Spaniards and began to fight them on all sides. The Spaniards killed many Mexica and Tlatelolca because they

Auh in oquinvalittaque in Españoles: quinvalmochialtique, ic oalmomanque in quinnamiquizque, vel quinnemilia in quenin vel quinchivazque. Auh in ie iuhqui nec quinxopiloa, quincuitlaxeloa [fol. 50] in quexquich calitic momantiquiz, nec texixilioa, tetzotzopitzalo, vel vncan tonacamicque in mexica in tlatilulca, çan quimōmomacato, inmac ommotlaçato, çã conmotoquilique in miquiztli, ça quezquin in tematitlampa quiz in amo mic: auh in veca manca, in tevecapavitimanca amo micque. Auh in ontemictique in imellel onquiz in Españoles: niman ie ic vi, quinteputzvitivi in ixquichtin tlamama. Ca aocac quinmati in campa cochque in iquac: vncan in in valmocuepato, in quimonicxicaoato, quimonteputzcaoato in Españoles.

Auh in ie iuhqui: nimā ie ic teiiximacho in tiacaoan in omicque, in oxixilioaque, vncan quintlatique in ixquichtin: auh in intecullo quipepena, in imomio quinenechicoaia, coololoaia, çatepā [fol. 50v] contocaia, contlaltocaia.

Auh in izquilhuitico in Mexico inic calaquico in Españoles: ipā ce hecatl in cemilhuitlapoalli: auh in xiuhtonalli ce acatl, oc muztla tlamatlactiz Quecholli: auh in cemilhuitique vme calli: vel iquac in tlamatlacti quecholli: auh in oacic, tlami quecholli in vel ilhuitl: niman ie ic quioaltoquilia in Panquetzaliztli, cempoalilhuitl: nimā quivaltoquilia Tititl no cempoalilhuitl; niman quivaltoquilia Izcalli tlami, no cempoalilhuitl: nimā iquac valmotlalia macuililhuitl moteneoa Nemontemi: auh in ontzonquiz macuililhuitl: nimā ic vmpcoa in Atl cavalo, anoço quavitl eoa, vncā xiuhquitzquilo, vncan peoa in iancuic xivitl, no cempoalli: nimā quioaltoqui[fol. 51]lia tlacaxipeoaliztli no cempoalli: niman quivaltoquilia Toçoztontli, no cempoalli: niman quivaltoquilia vei teçoztli, no cem-

And when the Spaniards saw them coming, they waited for them, they set themselves up to encounter them, considering well how they would be able to handle them. When it was time, they charged at them; all who had been in the houses rushed out among them, stabbing and piercing. Mexica and Tlatelolca died there in great abundance. They simply gave themselves to them, they hurled themselves into their hands, they pursued death. There were only a few who escaped death at their hands. But those who stayed far away, who kept dealing with them from afar, did not die. And when the Spaniards had done the killing and vented their wrath, they went off, with all the bearers following behind. No one knows where they spent the night at that time. There [the Mexica] turned back; they stopped tracking the Spaniards and left them behind.

At this point the warriors who had died, who had been stabbed, were identified, and they burned them all there. They picked among their ashes, collecting their bones and piling them up. Afterward they buried them, buried them in the ground.

Here are the days that passed after the Spaniards entered Mexico on the day count One Wind and the year count One Reed, one day before the tenth day of [the month of] Quecholli. When they had been here a day, it was Two House, exactly the tenth day of Quecholli. And on the very day that the end of Quecholli arrived, Panquetzaliztli followed after it, for twenty days; then Tititl followed it, also for twenty days; then Izcalli, the end [of the year], followed, also for twenty days. Then at that time were put five days called Nemontemi, and at the end of the five days began Atl cahualo, or Quahuitl ehua, when the year is taken hold of and the new year begins, also twenty days; then followed Tlacaxipehualiztli, also twenty; then followed Toçoztontli, also twenty; then

mucho en los españoles; y ansi murieron muchos dellos y fueron ahuyentados: auiendo vencido, los españoles, esta batalla prosiguierō su camino y de alli adelāte no siguierō los mexicanos.

Estuuieron los españoles desde que entraron en mexico hasta que salieron dozientos y treynta y cinco dias: y estuuieron en paz y amistad con los indios ochenta [fol. 50] y cinco [149] dias,

quando los españoles vuieron vencido la batalla arriba dicha luego tomaron su camino para Tlaxcalla, y entrādo en el termino de Tlaxcalla: los mexicanos se boluieron buscaron entre los muertos las personas señaladas, que auian sido muertos, y hizieronles sus exequias, y quemaron sus cuerpos, y tomaron las cenizas: y boluieronse a mexico, diziēdo que los Españoles auian huydo, que nunca mas auian de boluer

como los españoles, vuieron entrado en los terminos de tlaxcalla segun la relacion de los españoles: que alli se hallaron los principales de Tlaxcalla ansi hombres como mugeres salieron a recebirlos con mucha comida lleuaronlos a su ciudad lleuando a cuestas los que no podiā andar y curando a los heridos y llegados a la ciudad de Tlaxcalla les hizieron muy buen tratamiēto, y se compadescieron y lloraron por el desastre que les auia [fol. 50v] acontescido, y por los muchos que quedaron muertos en mexico, ansi los españoles como los indios Tlaxcaltecas.

Curaronse los españoles, y esforçaronse ē la ciudad de Tlaxcalla por mas de medio año y eran muy pocos para tornar a dar guerra a los mexicanos:

en este medio tiempo llego a tlaxcalla vn fran<sup>co</sup> hernandez español con trecientos soldados españoles y con muchos cauallos y armas y tiros de artilleria y municion con esto tomo animo el capitan don hernando cortes y los que con el estauā que auian escapado de la guerra para tornarse aparejar y boluer a conquistar a mexico.

hurled themselves at them so, and thus many died, and they were put to flight. Having won this battle, the Spaniards continued on their way, and from there forward the Mexica did not follow them.

From the time the Spaniards entered until they left, they were in Mexico 235 days, and for 85 days [149] they were in peace and friendship with the Indians.

When the Spaniards had won the battle mentioned above, they set their course for Tlaxcala, going into the Tlaxcalan jurisdiction. The Mexica went back, looking among the dead for those who were celebrated; they performed their funeral rites for them, burned their bodies, took the ashes, and returned to Mexico, saying that the Spaniards had fled and were never going to return again.

According to the reports of the Spaniards who were there, when they had entered the jurisdiction of Tlaxcala, the important people of Tlaxcala, men as well as women, came out to receive them with much food. They took them to their city, carrying on their backs those who could not walk, and treating the wounded. Upon reaching the city of Tlaxcala they treated them very well; they grieved and wept over the disaster that had befallen them and for the many who had been left dead in Mexico, Spaniards as well as Tlaxcalan Indians.

The Spaniards healed their wounds and gathered strength in the city of Tlaxcala for more than half a year. There were too few of them to give battle to the Mexica again.

During this interval a Francisco Hernández, Spaniard, arrived in Tlaxcala with three hundred Spanish soldiers and many horses, weapons, pieces of artillery, and munitions. With this, Captain don Hernando Cortés and those who were with him, having escaped from the war, took courage to outfit themselves again and conquer Mexico back.

poalli: niman quivaltoquilia Toxcatl no cempoalilhuitl: ie vncan ixpoliuhque Tia-caoan in xaxamacaque, in mexica in mi-coac: nimã quivaltoquilia Etzalqualiztli, no cempoalilhuitl: niman quivaltoquilia Tecu-ilhuitontli, ie vncan in quizque, vel ipan in ilhuitl in quizque in Españoles, in moio-alpoloque, amo tenemachpan, amo iuh catca teiollo inic quizque ioaltica. Auh inic mocempoa in izquilhuitique matlacpoalli oçe, oncaxtolli: [148] auh in tocnioan catca chicunapoalilhuitl oncaxtolli. Auh in toiaovan catca vmpoalilhuitl: [149]

Auh in o iuh iaque in Españoles: iuh nemachoc in ca o ic cen iaque, in ca ic cen oiaque, aocmo cepa valmocuepazque, aocmo [fol. 51v] ceppa imiloch quichi-oazque: niman ie no ceppa ic tlachichivalo, tlacencavalo in diablome inchan: tlatlach-panoc, tlacuicuivac, moquiquixti in tlalli.

followed Huei toçoztli, also twenty; then followed Toxcatl, also twenty days. At this time the warriors who were cut to pieces perished; many Mexica died. Then fol-lowed Etzalqualiztli, also twenty days; then followed Teucilhuitontli. At this time the Spaniards came out, right on the day of the festivity; they disappeared by night, with-out anyone being aware. People had not realized they would come out at night. The total of all the days that passed is 235. [148] They were our friends for 195 days, and our enemies for 40 days. [149]

And when the Spaniards had gone, it was thought that they had gone forever, that they would never come back, never make a return. Then again the homes of the devils were fixed up and ornamented; they were swept and cleaned out, and the earth was removed.

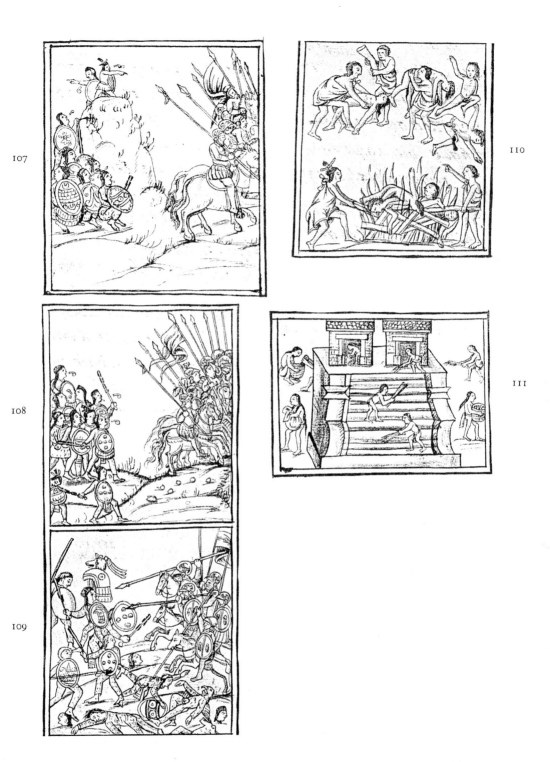

107

110

108

109

111

Inic cempoalli onchicuei capitulo: vncan mitoa in quenin Mexica vei ilhuitl quichiuhq̄ in iquac oquizque Españoles vncan mexico.

Auh in oacic vei tecuilhuitl: oc ceppa, ie no ceppa ilhuiquixtique in Mexica, vncā cempoaltica. In ixquich in imixiptlavan, in impatilloan in diablome, ie no ceppa quin-cecencauhque, quintlaquentique, quin-quequetzallotique, quincocozcatique, quimonaaquique xiuhxaiacatl, yoan quinquequentia in teuquemitl, in quetzal-que[fol. 52]mitl, in tozquemitl, quauh-quemitl. Auh inin tlatquitl in monec, quipiaia in vevei pipiltin:

Twenty-eighth chapter, where it is said how the Mexica celebrated a great festivity when the Spaniards left Mexico.

And when Huei teucilhuitl arrived, again, once again the Mexica celebrated a feast day, on the twentieth day. Again they ornamented and clothed all the images and representations of the devils. On each of them they placed precious feathers, neck-laces, and turquoise masks, and they dressed them in gods' garments, quetzal-feather garments, yellow parrot-feather garments, eagle-feather garments. And the great noblemen kept all this gear that was used.

niman quioaltoquilia in Tlasuchimaco, no cempoaltique: nimā quivaltoquilia in xocotl vetzi, no cempoaltique. Auh in Ochpaniztli ic nappoaltique. Teutl eco: ic macuilpoaltique. Tepeilhuitl chiquacem-poaltique. Quechulli ic chicōpoaltique: vncan cexiuhtizquia y, intlacatle mu-chivani, intlacamo iani. Panquetzaliztli, chicuepoaltique. Atemuztli, chicunappoal-tique. Tititl matlacpoaltique. Izcalli tlami, ic matlacpoalli oce: nican in muchioa in Nemontemi, macuililhuitl. Atl cavalo, matlacpoalli omume, anoço Quavitl eoa. Tlacaxipeoaliztli, matlacpoalli omei. Toçoztontli matlacpoalli onnavi. Vei to-çoz[fol. 52v]tli, ic caxtolpoalli omume.¹⁵⁰ Tecuilhuitontli, ic caxtolpoalli omei: vncan cexiuhtico y, inic micque tul-tecaacaloco.

Auh in ie no ceppa quiçaco, in ie no ceppa tiquimittaque ce xivitl, ipā matlac-

Then followed Tlaxochimaco, during which they also spent twenty days; then followed Xocotl huetzi, also twenty days. And with Ochpaniztli they spent the fourth twenty; with Teotl eco the fifth twenty; Tepeilhuitl the sixth; Quecholli the seventh. At this point [the Spaniards] would have spent a year if nothing had happened and they had not gone away. Panquetzaliztli was the eighth; Atemoztli, the ninth; Tititl, the tenth; Izcalli, the end, the eleventh; here Nemontemi took place, five days. Atl cahualo or Quahuitl ehua, the twelfth; Tlacaxipehualiztli, the thir-teenth; Toçoztontli, the fourteenth; Huei toçoztli, the seventeenth;¹⁵⁰ Teucilhui-tontli, the eighteenth. At this point a year had passed since [the Spaniards] had died at the Tolteca canal.

And when they appeared again, when we saw them again, in Izcalli, it had been a

[fol. 51v] Capitulo .28. de la primera fiesta que hizieron los mexicanos despues que los Españoles salieron de noche desta ciudad.

Chapter Twenty-eight, of the first festivity that the Mexica celebrated after the Spaniards left this city by night.

Quando los Españoles salierō de mexico y fueron a tlaxcalla era en el mes que se llama Tecuilhuitontli que comiença a dos de Junio y llegado el mes siguiente que ellos llamauan Vey tecuilhuitl: que comiença a veynte y dos de junio como ya estauā algo descansados de la guerra pasada, hizieron muy gran fiesta a todos sus dioses y sacaron todas las estatuas dellos y atauiaronlas con sus ornamentos y con muchos quetzales de pluma rica y pusieronlas sus caratolas de torquesas hechas de mosayco: esto hizieron agradeziendo a sus dioses porque los auiā [fol. 52] librado de sus enemigos.

Luego se sigue el otro mes suyo que se llama Tlaxochimaco que comiença a doze de Julio: Tras este se sigue el mes que llaman Xocotl vetzi que comiença primero dia de agosto. Tras este se sigue el mes que llamā Ochpaniztli que es a veynte de agosto. Tras este se sigue el mes q̄ llaman Teutleco que comiença a diez de setiembre. Tras este se sigue el mes que llamā Tepeiluitl, que caye a treynta de setiembre. Tras este se sigue el mes que llaman. Quecholli que comiença a veynte de otubre. Luego se sigue el mes que se llamā Panquetzaliztli que comiença a nueue de nuuiembre. Luego se sigue que llamā Atemuztli que comiença a veynte y nueue de nuuiembre. Luego se sigue el mes que se llama Tititl que comiença a diezinueue de deziembre. Tras este se sigue el mes que llamā yzcalli que comiençaua [151] a ocho de henero: y luego se sigue cinco dias que

When the Spaniards left Mexico and went to Tlaxcala, it was the month called Teucilhuitontli, which begins on the second of June. When the following month, which they call Huei teucilhuitl, beginning the twenty-second of June, had come, now that they were somewhat rested from the past war, they celebrated a very great festivity for all of their gods. They took out all their statues of them and decorated them with their ornaments and with many *quetzales* of rich feathers, and put on them their masks of turquoise mosaic. They did this in gratitude to their gods for having freed them from their enemies.

Then follows another month, called Tlaxochimaco, beginning the twelfth of July; after this follows the month they call Xocotl huetzi, beginning the first day of August. After this follows the month they call Ochpaniztli, on the twentieth of August; after this follows the month they call Teotl eco, beginning the tenth of September. After this follows the month they call Tepeilhuitl, which falls on the thirtieth of September. After this follows the month they call Quecholli, beginning the twentieth of October. Then follows the month they call Panquetzaliztli, beginning the ninth of November. Then follows [the month] they call Atemoztli, beginning the twenty-ninth of November. Then follows the month called Tititl, beginning the nineteenth of December. After this follows the month they call Izcalli, which would begin [151] the eighth of January; and then

poalli oce, ipan in Izcalli: quauhtitlan in quiçaco, ommotlalico in Tlacuban çan onchicomilhuitico: niman iaque vmpoaltito. Auh ie no ceppa quiçaco, çan quiztiquizque quauhtitlampa itztiaque: çan tequitl ontemictitiquizque in tlaliztacapan y iztacalla: tlatilulca in micque, achi vel centzontli in mic.

Auh in tecentlatalhui, in ie topan nenonotzaloc, no vmpoaltica ipan toxcatl: ie vel ic oxivitl in tiacaoan micque in teuitvalco, in Toxcatica./.

year and eleven twenties [since they left]. It was at Quauhtitlan that they appeared; they made a halt at Tlacopan, where they stayed only seven days; then they went away for forty days. When they appeared again, they only came by quickly, going in the direction of Quauhtitlan. All they did was kill some people in passing at Tlaliztacapan and Iztaccalla; those who died were Tlatelolca; close to four hundred died.

And when they had had full discussions and consultations about [their plans for] us, it was another forty days, in Toxcatl, with which it had been fully two years since the warriors died in Toxcatl in the temple courtyard.

## 29

[fol. 53] Inic cempoalli onchicunavi capitulo: vncan mitoa in quenin valla Totomoniztli, inic micque nicā tlaca: in itoca vei çavatl, in iquac oquizque Españoles in Mexico.

Auh in aiamo totech moquetza in Españoles: achtopa momanaco vei cocoliztli,

Twenty-ninth chapter, where it is said how, at the time the Spaniards left Mexico, there came an illness of pustules of which many local people died; it was called "the great rash" [smallpox].

Before the Spaniards appeared to us, first an epidemic broke out, a sickness of pus-

ellos llamauā Nemontemi que quiere dezir dias valdios o aciagos, los quales no contauan con el año: y luego comen[fol. 52v]çaua otro año en el mes que llamauan Quauitl Eua que començaua segundo dia de hebrero. Luego se sigue el 2º mes que llaman Tlacaxipeoaliztli que comiença a veynte y vno de hebrero. Luego se sigue el 3º mes que se llama Toçoztontli que comiença a .15. dias de março. Luego se sigue el 4º mes que se llama Vey toçoztli que comiença a .3. dias de abrir en este mes salieron los españoles huyendo de mexico: En el año pasado.

En este año boluierō algunos dellos vinieron por la uia de Quauhtitlan y llegaron hasta tlacuba, y no estuuieron mas de siete dias: y luego se boluieron y dende a quarenta dia boluieron otra uez, y destruyeron algunos lugares mataron mas de quatrocientos hombres que eran maceoales del Tlatilulco. Y dende a quarenta dias se contaron dos años de su uenida boluieron todos en el mes que se llamaua Toxcatl.

follow five days that they called Nemontemi, meaning useless or unlucky days, which they do not count with the year. Then began another year with the month they called Quahuitl ehua, which began the second day of February. Then follows the second month, which they call Tlacaxipehualiztli, beginning the twenty-first of February; then follows the third month, called Toçoztontli, which begins the fifteenth day of March; then follows the fourth month, called Huei toçoztli, which begins the third day of April. It was in this month [sic] that the Spaniards left Mexico fleeing, the year before.

In this year some of them returned, coming by way of Quauhtitlan, and reached Tacuba [Tlacopan]. They were there only seven days; then they went back, but after forty days they returned again and destroyed some settlements, killing more than four hundred men who were *macehuales* of Tlatelolco. Forty days after that, it had been two years since they came. They all returned in the month called Toxcatl.

112

29

[fol. 53] Capitulo .29. de la pestilencia que vino sobre los yndios de viruelas despues que los españoles salieron de mexico.

Chapter Twenty-nine, of the pestilence of smallpox that broke out among the Indians after the Spaniards left Mexico.

totomonaliztli, ipan tepeilhuitl in tzintic, in tetech motecac vevei tepopul: cequi vel pepechtic, novian in motecac in teixco, in teicpac, in teelpan .&. vellaixpolo, vel miequintin ic micque, aoc vel nenemia, ça onoca in imonoian in incuchian, aoc vel moliniaia, aoc vel mocuechiniaia, aoc vel mocuecuetzoaia, aoc vel monacacicteca, aoc vel mixtlapachtecaia, aoc vel maquetztitecaia. Auh in iquac mocuechiniaia, cenca tzatzia: cenca tlaixpolo, in pepechtic, in pepechiuhqui in çaoatl, vel miec tlacatl, ic momiqui[fol. 53v]li, yoã miequintin çan apizmicque, apizmicoac, aocac motecuitlaviaia, aocac teca muchivaia.

Auh in cequintin çan veveca in intech motlali in çavatl, amo cenca quimihioti, amo no miequintin ic micque: yoã miec tlacatl ic itlacauh in ixaiac, ichachaquachiuhque, iacachachaquachiuhque, cequītin yixcueponque, ixpopoiotque:

iquac in manca inin totomonilliztli, vel epoalilhuitl, epoaltonal in quiz in cuetlan, in neemachoc, in iolioac: ie chalcopa vatztia[152] in totomoniliztli, yoã miec inic cocototzauh: amo tel ic cen cocototzauh. In momanaco Teutl eco: auh in cuetlanito ipan in Panquetzaliztli: vncan vel caxavaque in Mexica, in tiacaoan.

Auh in ie iuhqui: nimã ie vitze, valolini in Españoles in vmpa Tetzcoco: quauhtitlam[fol. 54]pa in quiçato ommotlalico Tlacuban: nec vncan motequimaca, vncã moxeloa: in Pedro de Aluarado, itequippã muchiuh in vtli vallaticac tlatilulco. Auh in Marques coioacan motlalito: auh itequiuh muchiuh in marques: auh in vtli in acachinanco vallaticac tenuchtitlan, in moma marques ca vei oquichtli in tenuchcatl vei tiacauh:

tules. It began in Tepeilhuitl. Large bumps spread on people; some were entirely covered. They spread everywhere, on the face, the head, the chest, etc. [The disease] brought great desolation; a great many died of it. They could no longer walk about, but lay in their dwellings and sleeping places, no longer able to move or stir. They were unable to change position, to stretch out on their sides or face down, or raise their heads. And when they made a motion, they called out loudly. The pustules that covered people caused great desolation; very many people died of them, and many just starved to death; starvation reigned, and no one took care of others any longer.

On some people, the pustules appeared only far apart, and they did not suffer greatly, nor did many of them die of it. But many people's faces were spoiled by it, their faces and noses were made rough. Some lost an eye or were blinded.

This disease of pustules lasted a full sixty days; after sixty days it abated and ended. When people were convalescing and reviving, the pustules disease began to move in the direction of Chalco.[152] And many were disabled or paralyzed by it, but they were not disabled forever. It broke out in Teotl eco, and it abated in Panquetzaliztli. The Mexica warriors were greatly weakened by it.

And when things were in this state, the Spaniards came, moving toward us from Tetzcoco. They appeared from the direction of Quauhtitlan and made a halt at Tlacopan. There they gave one another assignments and divided themselves. Pedro de Alvarado was made responsible for the road coming to Tlatelolco. The Marqués went and established himself in Coyoacan, which became his responsibility, along with the road coming from Acachinanco to Tenochtitlan, for the Marqués considered the Tenochca great and valiant warriors.

Ante que los españoles que estauan en Tlaxcalla viniesen a conquistar a mexico dio vna pestilencia de viruelas en todos los indios en el mes que llamauā Tepeiluitl, que es al fin de setiembre desta Pestilencia, murieron muy muchos indios tenian todo el cuerpo, y toda la cara: y todos los miembros tan llenos y lastimados de viruelas que no se podian bullir ni menear de vn lugar ni boluerse de vn lado a otro: y si alguno los meneaua dauā vozes esta pestilencia mato gentes sin numero muchos murieron de hambre porque no auia quien podiese hazer comida,

los que escaparon desta Pestilencia quedaron con las caras ahoyadas: y algunos los ojos quebrados.

Duro la foerça desta Pestilencia sesenta dias, y despues que fue afloxando en mexico fue hazia chalco

acabādose esta Pestilencia en mexico [fol. 53v] Vinieron los Españoles que ya estauan en tetzcuco, y boxaron la laguna y vinieron por quauhtitlan hasta Tlacuba y alli se repartieron en capitanias y se posieron en diuersas estācias A don Pedro de albarado le cupo el camino que va de Tlacuba derecho al Tlatilulco: el capitan dō hernando cortes se puso en coyoacā y guardaua el camino que va de coyovacan a mexico.

De hazia la parte del Tlatilulco se començo primero la guerra en vn lugar que se [153] nextlatilco y llegaron peleando hasta el lugar que se llama nonoalco donde esta agora vna yglesia que se llama Sanct Miguel; y los Españoles se retruxeron no ganarō nada en esta escaramuça: Tambien el capitan Don hernando cortes acometio por su parte [154] a los mexicanos, por el camino que se llama acachinanco: y los mexicanos resistianlos grandemente.

Before the Spaniards who were in Tlaxcala came to conquer Mexico, a pestilence of smallpox struck among all the Indians in the month they called Tepeilhuitl, which is at the end of September. Very many Indians died of this pestilence; they had their whole bodies, faces, and limbs so full of pocks and damaged by them that they could not stir, or move out of their place, or turn from one side to the other. If someone moved them, they would cry out. This pestilence killed innumerable people. Many died of hunger, because there was no one who could prepare food.

Those who escaped from this pestilence were left with their faces pitted, and some lost eyes.

The force of this pestilence lasted sixty days, and when it began to slacken off in Mexico, it went toward Chalco.

When this pestilence was ending in Mexico, the Spaniards, who were already in Tetzcoco, arrived. They skirted the lake and came by Quauhtitlan as far as Tacuba, and there they divided themselves into captaincies and took up various stations. Don Pedro de Alvarado was assigned the road going from Tacuba straight to Tlatelolco; Captain don Hernando Cortés positioned himself in Coyoacan and guarded the road going from Coyoacan to Mexico.

The war began first toward the direction of Tlatelolco, in a place [called] [153] Nextlatilco, and in the battle they went as far as the place called Nonoalco, where now there is a church called San Miguel, but the Spaniards retired without gaining anything in this skirmish. Captain don Hernando Cortés also attacked the Mexica in his sector, [154] by the road called Acachinanco, and the Mexica resisted them strongly.

auh in nextlatilco, anoço iliacac, vel
vmpa achto iaupevaco, niman acitiuetzico
in nonoalco in quinvaltocaque tiacavan,
aiaac mic in mexica: niman ic moteputztique in Españoles. In tiacavan in acaltica
tlaecoa, in acalchimaleque quimōmina: in
immiuh, ontzetzelivi in impan Españoles:
niman ic calaque. Auh in Marques niman
ie ic quivallaça in invicpa tenuchca quivaltoca in vtli in acachināco: miecpa valmi-
calia, auh connamiqui in Mexica.

And it was right in Nextlatilco, or in
Ilyacac, that war first began. Then [the
Spaniards] quickly reached Nonoalco, and
the warriors came pursuing them. None of
the Mexica died; then the Spaniards retreated. The warriors fought in boats; the
war-boat people shot at the Spaniards, and
their arrows sprinkled down on them.
Then [the main force of the Mexica]
entered [Nonoalco]. Thereupon the Marqués sent [his men] toward the Tenochca,
following the Acachinanco road. Many
times they skirmished, and the Mexica
went out to face them.

113

114

115

116

[fol. 54v] Inic cempoalli ommatlactli capitulo vncan mitoa in quenin Españoles quixinque imacal vmpa tetzcocu, inic tepevaco nican mexico.

Auh in ovalla imacal tetzcocu matlactetl omume, çan oc much vmpa mocenten in acachinanco, niman vncā valmiquani in Marques in acachinanco: nimā ie ic quitlatemolitinemi in campa vel calaquiz acalli, in campa ie melavaticac acalotli, in aço vecatlan, in acanoço vecatlan inic amo cana macanaz: auh in acalotli in cocoltic, in cuecuelpachtic, amo vel vncan quicalaquique,

vntetl in acalli in concalaquique, concuitlaviltequiltique in vtli xolloco vallamelauhticac: auh ceppa quīcentlatalhuique, quicemitoque, inic quincentlaxilizque mexica in quincentlatalhuizque: nec motec[fol. 55]pana, quivica in tlequiquiztli quiniacantivitz in quachpanitl, çan niman amo mamana, amo momocivia, tlatzotzontivitze, yoan tlapitztivitze yoan quavilacapitztli.

Auh in vntetl acalli, çan ivian onotivitz, çan cectlapal in vallonotia in acalli: auh in oc cectlapal atle valla in acalli, iehica ca calla, nec iativitze, necalivativitz, necoc micoa, necoc tlamalo. Auh in oquittaque in tenuchca in çoquipan onoque: nec motlaloa, momauhcatlaloa, tetlan tlaano in pipiltzitzinti, çan atlan in vi, cematl mantiuh in macevalli, tlachoquiztleva. Auh in acaleque quimacaltenque in impilhoantzitzin, quintlanelhuia, quintequitlanelhuia, aoc tle ma itla conmocuilique, çā moch conmauhcacauhtiquizque, intlatquitzin, çan much vmpa contepeuhtiquizque. Auh in toiaovan tlanamoxtivi, [fol. 55v] quicuitivi in tlein ipan oquiçato, in tlein oquipantito quicui, quimotquilia in aço tilmatli, in aço quachtli, in anoço tlaviztli, in anoço teponaztli in anoço vevetl.

Thirtieth chapter, where it is said how the Spaniards constructed boats in Tetzcoco in order to come to make a conquest here in Mexico.

When their twelve boats had come from Tetzcoco, at first they were all assembled at Acachinanco, and then the Marqués moved to Acachinanco. He went about searching where the boats could enter, where the canals were straight, whether they were deep or not, so that they would not be grounded somewhere. But the canals were winding and bent back and forth, and they could not get them in.

They did get two boats in; they forced them down the road coming straight from Xoloco. Once they had a general consultation and decided to send their whole force against the Mexica. Then they lined themselves up, carrying the guns. A cotton banner came ahead. They were not at all excited or perturbed. They came beating drums and blowing [trumpets] and wooden fifes.

And the two boats came gradually, keeping on one side. On the other side no boats came, because there were houses there. They came ahead, fighting as they came; there were deaths on both sides, and on both sides captives were taken. When the Tenochca who lived in Çoquipan saw this, they fled, fled in fear. The little children were taken along with the others. They just went into the water; the water was full of people, and a wail arose. And those with boats put their children in them and poled them along, working vigorously. They took nothing at all with them, they just left all their poor property in fear, they just scattered everything in their haste. And our enemies went snatching things up, taking whatever they came upon. Whatever they hit on they carried away, whether cloaks, lengths of cotton cloth, warriors' devices, log drums, or cylindrical drums.

[fol. 54v] Capitulo .30. de como los vergantines que hizieron los Españoles: en
Tetzcuco, venieron sobre mexico. Estos
vergantines se labraron en Tlaxcalla y los
indios los truxeron ē pieças a cuestas hasta
la lengua [155] donde se armaron

Estando los españoles en tlaxcalla labraron doze vergantines y ante q̄ los ar-
masen truxeronlos en pieças los indios
hasta tetzcuco y alli los armaron en-
clauaron y brearon los quales hechos; y
puesta en ellos la artilleria: entraron en
ellos los españoles que para esto estauā
asinados y vinieron por la laguna hasta vn
desembarcadero que se llama Acachinanco
que es cerca de mexico en aquel derecho
de Sancto antonio yglesia, [156] que esta cerca
de las casas de albarado y el capitan don
hernando cortes: luego se metio en los vergantines, y començaron a sondar el agua
para descubrir el alto que auia por donde
auian de andar los vergatines:

como vuieron descubierto los caminos
por donde podiā andar los vergantines, pu-
sierōse a gesto de guerra en los mesmos
vergantines con determinacion [fol. 55] de
destruyr a los mexicanos y luego puestos
en orden con su bandera delante y tocando
su atambor y pifano començaron a pelear
contra los mexicanos

y muchos de los mexicanos que tenian
las casas dentro en el agua como començo
la guerra por el agua començaron a huyr cō
sus hijos y con sus mugeres algunos lleuauā
a cuestas a sus hijos y otros en canoas.
Todas sus haziendas xauan [157] en sus casas y
los indios que ayudauan a los españoles en-
trauā en las casas que dexauan y robaban
quanto hallauan

Chapter Thirty, of how the brigantines
that the Spaniards made in Tetzcoco came
against Mexico. These brigantines were
built in Tlaxcala, and the Indians carried
them in pieces on their backs to the
lake, [155] where they were assembled.

While the Spaniards were in Tlaxcala,
they built twelve brigantines, but before
assembly the Indians carried them in pieces
to Tetzcoco, and there they assembled
them, nailing them together and caulking
them. When they had been finished and
the artillery placed in them, the Spaniards
assigned to them boarded and came by the
lake to a landing place called Acachinanco,
which is close to Mexico, in the vicinity of
the church of San Antonio, [156] close to the
houses of Alvarado. Then Captain don
Hernando Cortés went into the brigantines, and they began to sound the water to
discover the depth where the brigantines
would have to go.

When they had found ways by which
the brigantines could go, they took a warlike stance in these brigantines, determined
to destroy the Mexica. Then, arranged in
order, with their banner at the front and
playing their fife and drum, they began to
fight against the Mexica.

When the battle began on the water,
many of the Mexica who had their houses
in the water began to flee with their wives
and children. Some carried their children
on their backs, others in canoes. They
left [157] all their belongings in their houses,
and the Indians who were helping the
Spaniards went into the houses they had
left and stole whatever they found.

Auh in tlatilulca vmpa tlaiecoque in çoquipan, acalchimaltica: auh in xolloco in oacico in vncan tenamitl onoca, in onepātla in quitzacutoca vtli: in tlequiquiztli vei, ic quimotlāq, aiamo xitin in iancuican vetz; auh inic vppa, xitin: auh inic expa, iequene vel tlaltitech ia: auh inic nappa iequene vel ic cen tlaltitech ia in tenamitl.

Auh in ontetl acalli quinnamictiuh in acalchimaleque, necaliva in atlan. Auh in tlequiquiztli imacaliacac tetentiuh: auh in vnca tetzavatoc acalli, in vncan tecpichauhtoc; vmpa inpan contlaça [fol. 56] miec tlacatl ic mic: niman aaquetztivetzi, nenecuiliuhtivetzi, papachiuhtivetzi: çan ie no ivi in tepuzmitl in aquin vel quimottilia, aocmo quiça, niman miqui, vncan quihiovia.

Auh in o vel quittaque Mexica, in o vel quinemiliq in iuh vetzi tlequiquiztli, yoā in tepuzmitl, aocac motlamelauhcaquetza, ça

The Tlatelolca fought in Çoquipan, in war boats. And in Xoloco [the Spaniards] came to a place where there was a wall in the middle of the road, blocking it. They fired the big guns at it. At the first shot it did not give way, but the second time it [began to] crumble. The third time, at last [parts of] it fell to the ground, and the fourth time finally the wall went to the ground once and for all.

And the two boats [of the Spaniards] went along contending with the war boatmen; there was skirmishing in the water. A gun went in the prow of each of their boats, and where the [Mexica] boats were close together and assembled, they fired on them; many people died from it. [When hit, each boat] quickly lifted its prow, wavered, and sank. Likewise when they took good aim at someone with the iron bolts, he did not escape; immediately he died, he expired.

But when the Mexica had been able to see and judge how the guns hit, or the iron bolts, they no longer went straight, but

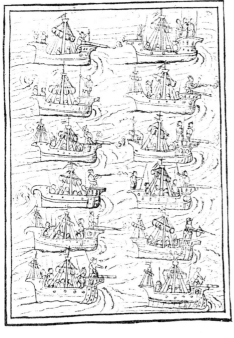

[fol. 55v] Tanbien los indios del tlatilulco, andauan alli peleando con sus canoas: Como llegaron los españoles, adonde estauan atajada, vna acequia cō albarrada, y pared desbarataronla con el artilleria,

Also the Indians of Tlatelolco went about there fighting with their canoes. When the Spaniards reached the place where a canal was blocked with a barricade or wall, they knocked it down with the artillery.

y pasaron dos vergantines començaron a pelear con los que estauan defendiendo la acequia los españoles que yuā en los vergantines tornaualos la artilleria hazia donde estauan mas espesas las canoas y hazian gran daño en los indios con la artilleria, y escopetas.

Visto esto los mexicanos començaron apartarse, y a guardarse del artilleria, yendo culebreādo con las canoas: y tambien quando vian algun tiro que soltauā agaçapauāse, en las canoas: y començaron a retraerse hazia las casas, y ansi quedo desocupado el camino

Two brigantines went through and began to fight with those who were defending the canal. The Spaniards who were in the brigantines aimed the artillery at where the canoes were thickest; they did great damage to the Indians with the artillery and muskets.

Seeing this, the Mexica began to draw back and protect themselves from the artillery, going zigzagging with the canoes, and also when they saw that they were about to fire one of the cannon, they crouched down in the canoes. They began to retreat toward the houses, so that the road was left empty.

avic vivi, tlatlaxtlapaloa, ça ixtlapalhuivi. Auh in iquac ie no quitta in ie vetziz in vei tlequiquiztli, tlaltech viloa, tlaltech neteco, nepacholo. Auh in tiacavan cacalacti-vetzque in caltzalan chipavatimoquetz in vtli, in vchpantli, ça iuhquin chipacpul icac.

Auh niman onacico in vitzillan, in oc ce vncã onoc tenamitl: auh miequintin itlan mopachotoca, quimotoctitoca in tenamitl: achitonca vncan ommacã, ontzo[fol. 56v]tzon in imacal, vncan achitonca on-vecavaque in oquic conchichiuhque tlequiquiztli.

went back and forth, going from one side to the other, zigzagging. Also, when they saw that the big gun was about to go off, everyone hit the ground, spread out on the ground, crouched down, and the warriors quickly went in among the houses. The road cleared off; the highway was as if swept clean.

Then [the Spaniards] reached Huitzil-lan, where there was another wall. Many [Mexica] lay crouching at it, hiding behind the wall. For a little while [the Spaniards'] boats were grounded. They were there for a short time while they adjusted the guns.

llegaron los españoles a vn lugar [fol. 56] que se llama vitzillan que es cerca de la yglesia de sanct Pablo, alli estaua otro paredon hecho, y a las espaldas del, estauan muchas gentes de los mexicanos alli se detuuieron algo los vergantines entre tanto que adereçauan la artilleria pa derrocar al paredon.

The Spaniards reached a place called Huitzillan, which is near the church of San Pablo. Another barrier had been erected there, and behind it were many of the Mexica. The brigantines halted there for a time while they adjusted the artillery to knock down the barrier.

121

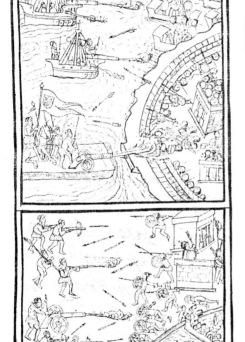

119

120

Inic cempoalli ommatlactli oce capitulo: vncan mitoa in quenin Españoles ic valietiaque in vergantines, quinvaltocaque in acaltica nenca in quinnamiquito: nimā ic valquizque itech acico in ixquich calli.

Thirty-first chapter, where it is said how the Spaniards came with the brigantines, pursuing those who were in boats. When they were done contending with them, they drew close and reached all the houses.

Auh in oconchichiuhque: nimā ie ic quivalmotla in tenamitl: auh in tenamitl, nimā tzatzaian, cuitlaxeliuh. Auh inic vppa vetz; nimā tlaltitech ia in tenamitl, vevelocac, vmpet, oncoion: niman no iuhquin chipacpul moquetz vtli. Auh in tiacavā in tenantitlan onoca, nimā ic valxitinque, valnetlalolo, nemauhcaquixtilo. Auh [fol. 57] in ixquich nepapan tlacatl: niman iciuhca contetentivi in acalotli, niman iciuhca conixmana tetica, xantica yoan cequi quavitl inic tlaatzopque.

And when they had finished adjusting [the guns], they shot at the wall. The wall then ripped and broke open. The second time it was hit, the wall went to the ground; it was knocked down in places, perforated, holes were blown in it. Then, like the other time, the road stood clear. And the warriors who had been lying at the wall dispersed and came fleeing; everyone escaped in fear. And then all the different people [who were on the side of the Spaniards] quickly went filling in the canals and making them level with stones, adobes, and some logs, with which they closed off the water.

Auh in ie iuhqui, in ommatzop acalotli: niman ie ic valeoa in cavallome, aço matlacteme, ontlaiavaloco, ontlamalacachoco, ommocovitzoco, ommotevilacachoco: ie no ceppa centlamantli valevaque in cavallome, quinvalcuitlapāvitiaque. Auh cequintin tlatilulca calactivetzque in tecpan catca in ichan motecuçoma: niman ic valmauhcaquiçaia, quimonmonamictico in cavallostin: ce quixilico in tlatilulca. Auh in oquixilico, oc vel can in itepuztopil: niman quimacuilito in icnivan, icuitlapan quioalmaiauhque, quivaltzineuhque: auh in otlalpan vetzico mec [158] quivivitequi, concuex[fol. 57v]cochvivitecque, oncan ommic.

And when the canals were stopped up, some horse[men] came, perhaps ten of them; they came going in circles, spinning, turning, twisting. Another group of horse[men] came following behind them. And some Tlatelolca who had quickly entered the palace that had been Moteucçoma's residence came back out in alarm to contend with the horse[men]. They lanced one of the Tlatelolca, but when they had lanced him, he was able to take hold of [the Spaniard's] iron lance. Then his companions took it from [the Spaniard's] hands, throwing him on his back and unhorsing him. When he fell to the ground, they [158] struck him repeatedly on the back of the neck, and he died there.

[fol. 56v] Capitulo .31. de como los de los vergantines, auiendo oxeado las canoas; que los salieron por la laguna: llegaron a tierra junto a las casas.

Chapter Thirty-one, of how the brigantines, having scattered the canoes that went out against them on the lake, came to land next to the houses.

## 122

Despues que los Españoles, adereçaron sus tiros, tiraron al paredō con ellos: y de los primeros tiros, arroynaronle todo, y de los segundos tiros, dieron con el en el suelo, y los soldados indios que estauan detras el paredō: luego echaron a huyr, y los indios amigos, luego cegaron la acequia para pasar adelante con piedras, y adoues, y tierra, y maderos,

desque tuuieron llana la acequia: luego vinieron los de a caballo, y entraron en la ciudad, y alancearō los que pudieron de los indios: y tor[fol. 57]naronse a salir: y luego entraron otros de a caballo, y hizieron lo mismo, y los indios, acogianse a las casas reales. Tambien alancearō a algunos indios entre los quales, fue alanceado vn indio del Tlatilulco, y asio de la lança con que estaua atrauesado: y otros sus compañeros asieron. tanbien della y quitarōsela al de a cauallo, y con ella le mataron y derrocaron del cauallo:

y luego se juntaron los españoles y ētraron dentro, del en vn patio q̃ llamaua Quauhquiaoac y lleuauā consigo vn tiro grueso y asestarōle. Este [159] lugar estaua vna aguila de piedra grande y alta como vn estado de hombre: y por eso llamauan aquel patio Quauhquiyauac de la vna parte del aguila estaua vn tigre de piedra tambien y de la otra vn oso, tanbien de piedra: y los capitanes de los indios ascondiãse detras de ocho colunas de piedra que alli estauan y

After the Spaniards had adjusted their cannon, they shot at the barrier with them. With the first volley they ruined it all, and with the second they knocked it to the ground. Then the Indian soldiers who were behind the barrier began to flee, and the friendly Indians filled in the canal with stones, adobe, earth, and timbers in order to be able to go forward.

When they had the canal filled up level, the horsemen came and entered the city, lancing the Indians that they could, then they came back out, and other horsemen entered and did the same; the Indians took refuge in the royal palace. They also lanced a group of Indians, among whom was one from Tlatelolco who seized the lance with which he was pierced, and others among his companions also grabbed hold of it and took it from the horseman, and with it they killed him and unhorsed him.

Then the Spaniards assembled and entered a courtyard they called Quauhquiahuac; they took with them a heavy cannon and aimed it. [In] [159] this place there was a large eagle of stone, as high as a man standing, and for that reason the courtyard was called Quauhquiahuac. On one side of the eagle was a tiger, also of stone, and on the other a bear [sic], also of stone. The captains of the Indians hid themselves behind eight stone columns

Niman ie ic quioalcentlaça, oalcemolini in Españoles: nimā ic onacico in quauh-quiiavac. Auh in tomaoac tlequiquiztli quivicativi, intlatqui ietiuh, contecaque in quauhquiiavac. (Auh inic moteneoa quauhquiiaoac, ca vncan icaca in quauhtli, tetl in tlaxixintli, vel cennequetzalli inic quauhtic, inic vecapan: auh quitzatzacu-timani, in centlapal icaca ocelutl: auh in centlapal icaia cuitlachtli, çanno tetl in tlaxintli). Auh in ie iuhqui in vevei tiaca-van, oc nē quimotoctiticaca in tetlaque-tzalli: auh in tetlaquetzalli ompantli, nepan chicuei. Auh in coacalli itlapāioc, no teten-toque in tiacavan, motlatlapantenque aocac ixtlapal iauh in tiia[fol. 58]cavan.

Auh in Españoles çā niman amo mamana: auh in oquitlazque tlequiquiztli cenca tlaiovac, poctli motecac. Auh in quimotoctitimanca in tetlaquetzalli, netla-loloc yoan in ixquichtin tlapanco onoca valmotepeuhque veca netlaloloc, nec qui-vallecavia in tlequiquiztli contecaco temalacatitlan: auh in icpac vitzilobuchtli, oc nē tlapiaia, quivitequia in teponaztli, iuhquin ontetemi quivitequi teponaztli: auh nimā ic ontlecoque vmentin Es-pañoles, vmpa quimonvivitequito: auh in oquimonvivitequito inca valmaiauhque, quinvalchicanauhque:

auh in quaquachictin in ixquichtin in tiacavan in acaltica tlaiecoaia, muchintin valquizque, vallalvacaquizque: auh in te-tlanelhuia in telpopotzitzinti, çan iehoātin in quivalhuivicaque in [fol. 58v] acalli. Auh in ie iuhqui in tiaiacavan, nec qui-mottilia in caltzalantli vellatotoca, vel ne-tzatzililo: quitoa. Tiacavane, ma val-latotoca:

auh in ie iuhqui, in oquittaque in Es-pañoles in ie impan monamiqui in ie quin-totona,[160] nimā ic mocototztlalique, moteputztique, vel totoca, motlaloa necoccampa in valminaloia in tlatzontec-tica, yoan necoccampa in valtepacholo, quin vmpa xolloco patito, imihio

Then the Spaniards sent everyone, they all moved together; they reached Quauh-quiahuac [Eagle Gate]. As they went they took the cannon and its gear and set it down at Quauhquiahuac. (The reason it is so called is that an eagle stood there, carved of stone, some seven feet tall, and enclos-ing it were a jaguar standing on one side, and a wolf standing on the other, likewise carved in stone.) And when things were in this state the great warriors tried to take shelter behind the stone pillars; there were two rows of them, eight altogether. And the roof of the Coacalli was also full of warriors. None of them ventured to cross into the open.

And the Spaniards did not move at all; when they fired the cannon, it grew very dark, and smoke spread. Those who had been taking shelter behind the stone pillars fled; all who had been lying on the roof jumped down and ran far away. Then they brought the cannon up and set it down at the round stone [of gladiatorial sacrifice]. On top of [the temple of] Huitzilopochtli they were still trying to keep watch, beat-ing the log drums, as though the air were full of them. Then two Spaniards climbed up and struck [the drummers]; after they had struck them they cast them aside, threw them down.

And those with scraped heads, all the warriors who were fighting in boats, came onto dry land, and only the youths who poled the others conducted the boats. And at this point the warriors inspected the pas-sageways, with much running and shout-ing, saying, "O warriors, let everyone come running!"

When things were in this condition, the Spaniards saw that they were upon them, pursuing them,[160] and then they hunched down and retreated, running fast and flee-ing. From both sides there was shooting [at the Spaniards] with barbed darts, and stones were thrown from both sides. Then

mucha otra gente estaua encima de la casa que estaua armada sobre las colūnas

that were there, and many other people were on top of the house that rose above the columns.

y los españoles tiraron con el tiro grueso que lleuauan consigo a aquel edificio que estaua alli y con el trueno [fol. 57v] y con el humo los que estauan abaxo, se espantaron y echaron a huyr, y los de arriba se echaron de alli abaxo, y todos huyeron, lleuaron el tiro mas adelante hazia el patio del Vitzilobuchtli, donde estaua vna grāde piedra redonda como muela de molino; y sobre el cu de Vitzilobuchtli estauan vnos satrapas, sentados tañendo vn teponaztli, y cantando, y aunque vian lo que pasaua, no cesaua de tañer, y cātar; y subieron dos españoles, y mataronlos echaronlos por las gradas abaxo del cu.

Como los españoles entrauan por la ciudad, vinieron los indios diestros que andauan en las canoas, y saltaron en tierra començaron a llamar a otra gente para inpedir a los españoles la entrada:

The Spaniards fired the heavy cannon that they had with them at that building that was there, and with the thunderous sound and the smoke those who were below took fright and began to run away, and those above hurled themselves down, and they all fled. They took the cannon farther ahead in the direction of the square of Huitzilopochtli, where there was a large round stone like a millstone. Some satraps were seated on the *cu* of Huitzilopochtli, playing a *teponaztli* and singing, and though they saw what was happening, they did not stop playing and singing. Two Spaniards climbed up, killed them, and threw them down the steps of the *cu*.

As the Spaniards entered the city, the Indians skilled with canoes came and landed; they began to summon other people to prevent the Spaniards' entry.

como vieron los españoles a los indios que veniā sobre ellos con gran inpetu, y que los desbaratauā, recogeronse, y començaron a retraerse, y los indios peleauan reciamente: los españoles se recogeron a su estancia que llamauā acachinanco, y dexaron el tiro en el patio de Vitzilobuchtli, y

When the Spaniards saw the Indians coming against them with great impetus and dispersing them, they regrouped and began to withdraw, and the Indians fought fiercely. The Spaniards retreated to their base, called Acachinanco, leaving the cannon in the courtyard of Huitzilopochtli.

quicuito, vmpa valmomanato: niman ie ic valnecuepalo. Auh in iehoantin Españoles, niman ic no mocuepa motlalito in aca-chinanco: auh in tlequiquiztli vncan qui-cauhtiquizque in temalacatitlan; niman conanque in tiacavan, quitototza quimaia-vito atlan, tetamaçolco quitztiltitiaque.

they went to Xoloco to mend, catch their breath, and re-form, and then they came back. And then the Spaniards went back again and stayed in Acachinanco. In their haste they left behind the cannon on the round stone. Then the warriors took it; they quickly pushed it in the direction of Tetamaçolco and threw it in the water.

de alli lo tomaron los indios, y le echaron en vna agua profunda que llamauā Tetamaçulco, que esta cabe [fol. 58] el monte que se llama Tepetzinco, donde estan los baños.

The Indians took it from there and threw it into deep water at the place they called Tetamaço!co, which is near the mountain called Tepetzinco, where the baths are.

## 32

[fol. 59] Inic cempoalli ommatlactli omume capitulo: vncan mitoa in quenin Mexica valmauhcaquizque in vncan imaltepeuh ipan in quimimacazque Españoles.

Auh in iquac in, in tenuchca valcalacque in nican tlatilulco, tlachoquiztleoa, tlatzatziztleoa, ixachi in imixaio cioatzitzinti: auh in toquichtin quinvivicatze in incicivaoā in aca quiquechpanoa in ipiltzin: nimā iquac in quicauhque in imaltepeuh ça cemilhuitl. Auh in tlatilulca ie ne vmpa itztivi in tenuchtitlan in micalizque.

Auh in ie iuhqui in Pedro aluarado: ie ne vmpa quivallaz in iliacac, in ivicpa nonoalco, aiatle vel quichiuhque, iuhquin tetitech onevaco; iehica ca in tlatilulca cenca mochicauhque, necoc in tlaiecoloc, vtli ipan, yoan atlan [fol. 59v] in acalchimaltica; in omoxixiuhtlati in aluarado, nimā ic mocuep, motlalito in tlacuban: auh çan iviptlaioc in quivalcentlazque in acalli in acachto valla, can oc ontetl: auh çatepā muchi cēquiça in caltenco nonoalco ommotemato: niman ie ic oalquiça in tlalhoacapā, in tlalhoacpan: nima ie ic quivaltoca opitzactli, in calla icac, quivaliollotia.

Auh in vncan valquizque Españoles ocactivetz, aocac tlacatl oquiz in maçevalli. Auh in tzilacatzin vei tiacauh cenca oquichtli: nimā ic quivallaz, etetl in quitqui iteuh, vevei tepopul mamalacachtic ie in tenaiocatetl, anoço iztac tetl, [162] centetl imac ietiuh, vntetl ichimaltitlan ietiuh, niman ie ic quintoca quimontepevato atlan, qui[fol. 60]mōtoxavàto in Españoles, ça atlan in oniaque, vel aaietixque in ontetemoque

(Auh inin Tzilacatzin otomitl catca inic tiacauh, ipampa in tlaotonxintli, iehica amo imixco tlachiaia in iniaovan in manel

Thirty-second chapter, where it is said how the Mexica left their altepetl in fear and came here when they dreaded the Spaniards.

And at this time the Tenochca came entering into Tlatelolco here, weeping and shouting. Many were the tears of the women; the men came accompanying their women, and some of them carried their children on their shoulders. In just one day they abandoned their altepetl. But the Tlatelolca still went to Tenochtitlan to fight.

And at this point Pedro de Alvarado hurled his forces at Ilyacac, toward Nonoalco, but they could do nothing; it was as though they had hit against a stone, because the Tlatelolca made great efforts. There was fighting on both sides of the road and in the water with war boats. When Alvarado tired, he returned and established himself in Tlacopan. But just two days later they sent out all the boats; at first only two came, then afterward all of them, and formed beside the houses in Nonoalco. Then they came onto dry land, and then they began to follow the narrow road between the houses; they came toward the center of them.

When the Spaniards landed it fell silent; not one of the people came out. But then Tzilacatzin, who was a great warrior and very valorous, hurled three stones he was carrying, huge round stones, wall stones or white stones;[162] he had one in his hand and two on his shield. Then he went pursuing the Spaniards, scattering them, forcing them into the water. They went right into the water; those who went down in the water got thoroughly wetted.

(This Tzilacatzin had the warrior [rank] of Otomi, for which reason he wore the Otomi hairstyle, so he looked down on his

[fol. 59] Capitulo .32. de como los mexicanos se rendieron y començaron a salirse de la ciudad por miedo de los Españoles.

Chapter Thirty-two, of how the Mexica gave up and began to leave the city for fear of the Spaniards.

Despues de las cosas arriba dħas, los indios mexicanos, huyeron para Tlatilulco, dexando a la ciudad de mexico, en poder de los españoles: y los indios del tlatilulco, acudieron a mexico, a hazer guerra a los españoles:

y don pedro de albarado, que estaua todos aquellos dias, peleando contra los del tlatilulco, en aquella estancia que llaman yliacac, cabe nonoalco, no hizo ninguna cosa, porque los del tlatilulco, se defendieron muy bien por tierra, y por el agua: como vio albarado que no aprouechaua con ellos nada desconfiado: boluiose a tlacuba, y dende a dos dias los españoles vinieron cō todos los vergantines junto a las casas del tlatilulco y dos de los vergatines fueron hazia el barrio que se llama nonoalco y oxearon de por alli todas las canoas de guerra y saltaron en tierra començaron de entrar por entre las casas en concierto [fol. 59v] de guerra todos los indios, se apartaron, ningunos [161] salio contra ellos,

como nadie osaua, yr contra los españoles, vn valiente hombre vezino del tlatilulco que se llamaua tzilacatzin, salio contra los españoles, y a pedradas mato algunos dellos, porque tenia grā fuerça en el braço, y salieron otros tras, el hizieron retraer a los españoles. y boluieron al agua, hazia donde tenian los vergantines:

y aquel tzilacatzin tenia sus armas, y sus diuisas, como otomih, y con su ferocidad espantaua: no solamente los indios amigos

After the things mentioned above, the Mexica Indians fled toward Tlatelolco, leaving the city of Mexico in the hands of the Spaniards, and the Indians of Tlatelolco headed for Mexico to give battle to the Spaniards.

Don Pedro de Alvarado, who was fighting during all these days against the Tlatelolca in the place they call Ilyacac, near Nonoalco, achieved nothing, because the Tlatelolca defended themselves very well on land and on water. When Alvarado saw that he was getting nowhere with them, giving up hope he returned to Tacuba. Two days later the Spaniards came against them with all the brigantines, next to the houses of Tlatelolco. Two of the brigantines went toward the district called Nonoalco and chased away all the war canoes; they went on land and began to enter among the houses in military formation. The Indians all kept at a distance; no one [161] came out against the Spaniards.

Because no one dared to go against them, a brave man, a citizen of Tlatelolco named Tzilacatzin, sallied forth against the Spaniards and by casting stones killed some of them, for he had great strength in his arm. Others came out behind him and made the Spaniards retreat. They returned to the water, toward where they had the brigantines.

This Tzilacatzin had weapons and insignia in the style of an Otomi, and with his ferocity he frightened not only the Indian

Españoles, amo tle impan quimittaia, vel tlacenmamauhtiaia: in iquac in quittaia in Tzilacatzin, niman mocototztlaliaia in toiaovan: auh cenca quitemoaia, inic quimictizque, in aço quitepuzmivizque, in anoço quitlequiquizvizque. Auh in Tzilacatzin, çā mixpoloa inic amo iximachoz: in quenman tlaviztli in ommaquiaia, itenpilol compiloaia, yoan iteteucuitlanacoch yoā conmocozcatia in icozqui chipoli, çan tlapouhtiuh in itzontecon, neztiuh inic otomitl: auh in quēmanian çanio in ichcavipil canactontli inic [fol. 60v] ommoquaquimiloa. auh in q̄manian inic mixpoloa cōmaquiaia ihuitzoncalli, quatzone quauhtlalpiloni icuexcochtlampa tentiuh, ic tlalpitiuh iehoatl inic tetlepantlaxoia, iuhquin tetlepantlazqui ipā quiztiuh, quintlaieiecalhuitiuh in tetlepantlazque iteteucuitlamatemecauh necoccampa in ietiuh yiocanixti ietiuh in imac: auh in teucuitlamatemecatl cuecuenio auh no ie in icxic ieietiuh, cotzeoatl, teucuitlacotzeoatl çan petlanqui.)

enemies, even though they be Spaniards, thinking nothing of them. He inspired general fear. When our enemies saw Tzilacatzin, they would hunch down. They strove greatly to kill him, whether shooting him with iron bolts or with guns. But Tzilacatzin disguised himself in order not to be recognized. Sometimes he would put on [his own] device, with his lip pendant and his golden earplugs, and he would put on his shell necklace. He would go with his head uncovered, showing that he was an Otomi. But sometimes he put on only cotton upper armor and covered his forehead with a little narrow cloth. Sometimes to disguise himself he put on a feather hairpiece or wig, with eagle feathers tied at the back of the neck. This was the way in which those who threw people in the fire were attired; he went about looking like one of them, imitating them. He had golden arm bands on both sides, on both arms, shimmering, and he also had shining golden bands on the calves of his legs.)

de los españoles: Pero tanbien a los mismos españoles, y los españoles ponian gran diligencia por matarle, pero el disfraçauase cada dia por que no le conoziesen a las vezes, yua la cabeça descubierta como otomi, y otras vezes armauase, con armas de algodon. y otras vezes, se ponia la cabellera, de manera que no le viesen ni conoziesen

friends of the Spaniards, but also the Spaniards themselves. The Spaniards went to great lengths trying to kill him, but each day he disguised himself so that they would not know him. Sometimes he went with his head uncovered as an Otomi; other times he donned cotton armor, and other times he put on a hairpiece so that they would not see him or know him.

130

133

131

132

134

Auh nīma imuztlaioc in ie no cuel ceppa quiçaco in imacal conacanaco nonoalco, aiauhcaltitlā: auh niman no quiçaco in tlacxipanvia yoan in ie ixquich tlaxcaltecatl yoan otomitl, vel tonac in quintepevitivitze in Españoles. [fol. 61] Auh in oacico nonoalco: nimā ie ic tlaiecolo, necaliva, vel motetemman in tlaiecoliztli in iauiotl, necoc in micoaia ixquich minaloa in iniaovan, no ixquich in mexicatl, necoc ivi, necocolo, iuh cemilhuitl, iuh ioac in necalioac.

Çan vmen in vevei tiacaoā in amo mitzacuiliani, in atle inpan quimitta in iniaovā catca, in amo quitlaçotlaia in innacaio. Inic ce tlacatl itoca Tzoiectzin. Inic vme itoca, Temoctzin: auh ic teeca in omoteneuh in Tzilacatzin.

Auh in omoxiuhtlatique in Españoles, in avel quinchioa, in avel quinpetla in Mexica: niman ic iaque, calacque, vel imellel acic, quincuitlapanvitivi in intlavilanalhoan.

Then the next day they came again and grounded their boats at Nonoalco, at Ayauhcaltitlan. Also those who go on foot and all the Tlaxcalans and Otomis came, a great abundance of them. The Spaniards came herding them ahead of them. And when they got to Nonoalco, there was fighting and skirmishing; the scene filled with combat and battle. There were deaths on both sides; equal numbers of the Mexica and their enemies were hit. Thus on both sides there were wounded, and the fighting went on day and night.

There were only two great warriors who did not hide their faces, who thought nothing of their enemies, who did not place value on their bodies. The first was named Tzoyectzin and the second Temoctzin. A third was the already mentioned Tzilacatzin.

When the Spaniards tired, when they were unable to do anything with the Mexica, unable to penetrate them, they went away. They entered [their quarters] in very low spirits, their auxiliaries following after them.

## 33

[fol. 61v] Inic cempoalli ommatlactli omei capitulo vncan mitoa in quenin chinanpaneca in Suchmilca, cuitlavaca, yoan in Itztapalapaneca, yoan oc cequintin vallaque in quinpalevizquia mexica

Auh ceppa muchiuh in iehoantin suchmilca, cuitlaoaca mizquica, colhoaque, Mexicatzincatl, Itztapalapanecatl, vallaivaque, quinonotzaco in quauhtemoc-

Thirty-third chapter, where it is said how the chinampa people, those of Xochimilco, Cuitlahuac, Itztapalapan, and others, came as though to help the Mexica.

Once it happened that the people of Xochimilco, Cuitlahuac, Mizquic, Colhuacan, Mexicatzinco, and Itztapalapan sent messengers who came to talk with

[fol. 60v] Otro dia los españoles, hizieron lo mismo, vinieron en los vergantines, cō muchos amigos indios, al mismo barrio de nonoalco: començaron a pelear con los del tlatilulco, y trauose reciamente la batalla, y pelearon todo el dia, hasta la noche: y murierō muchos indios, de ambas partes,

y señalaronse alli, entonce tres indios del tlatilulco muy valientes: el vno llamauan tzoyectzin, y el otro llamauā [fol. 61] Temoctzin, y el tercero tzilacatzin que se dixo ya:

como vieron los españoles, que venian la noche: y no ganauan nada, boluieronse a sus estancia, con los indios sus amigos.

The next day the Spaniards did the same thing; they came in the brigantines with many Indian friends to the same district of Nonoalco. They began to fight with the Tlatelolca; the battle was fierce, and they fought all day long until night. Many Indians died on both sides.

Three very valiant Indians of Tlatelolco distinguished themselves there at that time: the one called Tzoyectzin, another called Temoctzin, and the third Tzilacatzin, who was already mentioned.

When the Spaniards saw that night was coming and they were gaining nothing, they returned to their base with their Indian friends.

135

136

33

[fol. 61v] Capitulo .33. de como los chinanpaneca que son xuchmilco, cuitlaoac, Itztapalapan &. venieron en ayuda de los mexicanos.

Estando las cosas en la disposicion que arriba se dixo: vinieron a socorrer a los mexicanos, y tlatilulcanos, q̃ todos estauā fortalecidos en el tlatilulco, los chinanpanecas que es Xochmilco Cuitlaoac, miz-

Chapter Thirty-three, of how the Chinampaneca, who are from Xochimilco, Cuitlahuac, and Itztapalapan, etc., came in succor of the Mexica.

With things in the state told above, the Chinampaneca, who include Xochimilco, Cuitlahuac, Mizquic, Itztapalapan, Mexicatzinco, etc., came to give aid to the Mexica and Tlatelolca, who were all forti-

tzin, yoā in oc cequintin in tlatoque, in tiacavan; quimilhuico. Nopiltzintzine ca achitzin ic ticpalevico in atl, in tepetl, aço velitiz ca çan ic ixtlavico in intlatol in tlatoque, in oc vmpa tlapia, canel nican onoque in tlatoque, [163] ca ovallaque, ocenquiçaco in quauhtli ocelutl in acaltica: ca quil axcā quicentlaçaz in toiaouh.

Auh in ie iuhqui in oconitoque in intlatol, in ontlanonotzque [fol. 62] niman ie ic quimilhuia. Ca ie qualli, oanmotlacnelilique oanquimihioviltique, oanquimociaviltique ma xicmopalevilican in altepetl, ma tlaieiecavi: [164]

niman ie ic quintlauhtia, quinmaca in tlaviztli, in chimalli, yoan quincacacavatique, cecenxicalpechtli in quinmacaque cacaoatl: nimā ie ic quimilhuia. tlacueleoatl, tla tlaieiecavi tiacaoane, ca ie vitze in toiaovan, nima ie ic vi in titlanti in vmpa onoque in cuitlavaca in quinvalhuicaque. Auh in oiaque niman ic maantimoquetz in tlacavaca in izquican vtlica: niman ie ic necalioa.

Auh in iehoantin in, in Suchimilca niman ie ic no icavaca, yoan macalhuitequi: amo ma techpalevique, çan nimā ie ic tenamoia, quinnamoxque in cioatzitzinti, yoan in pipiltzitzinti, yoan in ilamatzitzin [fol. 62v] niman cequintin vncan ꝙnmictique vncan ihiotl quiz. Auh in oc cequintin amo quinmictique, çan ivian acalco quimontemovique.

Auh in ie iuh quichioa in in ie tenaoalpoloa: niman ic tzatzique in tequivaque, quitoque. Mexicae tlein ie quichioa in, tlaveliloque? ma vallatotoca; niman ie ic tlacavaca, quintoca acaltica. Auh in nonovalco in onoca in ixquich acalli: nimā ic muchi vmpa mocemitquic, much vmpa ia inic tlantoca: nimā ic quintzacuilico in Suchmilca: niman ie ic temictia, texixili, teviviltequi. Auh cequintin çan quimacique: auh vel muchintin, vncā micque, vel oncan mixtlatique. Auh in ixquichtin

Quauhtemoctzin and other warrior rulers, saying to them, "My lords, we have come to give a little help to the altepetl. Perhaps in this way the words of the rulers who are still in charge there will come true, for the rulers [i.e., other prominent people] are here, [163] the eagle and jaguar warriors have come assembled in boats. It is said that now they will repel all our enemies."

And when [the messengers] had had their say and [the Mexica] had consulted, they said to them, "Very well, we thank you. You are doubly welcome here. Do help the altepetl, let an attempt be made." [164]

Then they made them presents, giving them devices and shields, and they gave them cacao, giving a broad gourd of cacao to each. Then they said to them, "Come on, let the attempt be made, o warriors, for our enemies are coming!" Then the messengers went where the Cuitlahuac people were whom they had brought. And when they went, the clamor grew everywhere on the road. Then there was fighting.

But these Xochimilco people, though then they too set up a clamor and hurled themselves in their boats, did not help us at all, but started snatching people. They snatched the women and little children and also the old women; then they killed some of them there and they expired. The others they did not kill, but, uncontested, lowered them into boats.

And when they were doing this, destroying people in stealth, those on duty shouted out about it, saying, "O Mexica, what are these rogues doing? Let everyone come running!" Then there was a clamor, and they pursued them in boats. All the boats lay at Nonoalco, from whence they were all taken and went in pursuit. Then they intercepted the Xochimilco people and started killing, spearing and striking. Some they only took captive, but all died there, were annihilated. And they gave up

quic, Itztapalapan, mexicatzinco _eta_. Y venidos hablaron al señor de mexico que se llamaua Quauhtemoctzin, y a los otros principales, que con el estauan, y los capitanes hablaronle diziendo: señor n̄ro venimos a socorreros en esta necesidad, y para esto somos ēbiados de n̄ros mayores para pagar la deuda que deuemos: y para esto emos traydo, y estan aqui presentes los mejores soldados que entre nosotros ay para que ayuden por agua y por tierra.

Oydo esto el señor de mexico, y los demas dixeron en .m.d. tenemos lo que los señores hazen de embiaros para n̄ra ayuda aparejaos [fol. 62] para pelear,

y luego dieronlos armas para con que peleasen, y dieronlos mucho cacao: y luego los pusieron en el lugar donde auian de pelear. Y puestos en sus lugares todos començaron a pelear:

y los de xochmilco començaron a robar para las casas donde estauan, solamente las mugeres, y niños y viejas, y mataron algunas mugeres y niños y viejas, y otros metieron en las canoas para lleuarlos como esclauos.

Algunos soldados de los mexicanos, vieron lo q̄ pasaua, y dieron aviso a los capitanes: y luego fueron contra ellos por agua y por tierra y començaron a matar en ellos y a prenderlos a todos los destruyeron y mataron, y de las mugeres y niños y viejas que auian captiuado, y el robo no lleuaron nada.

Los españoles se recogieron a sus estācias, despues de la pelea

y a los de xuchmilco y cuitlaoac y mexicatzinco y Itztapalapā _eta_. Que captiuaron lleuaronlos delante de Quauhtemoctzin que estaua en vn lugar que se llamaua yacaculco donde esta agora vna yglesia de sanctana en el Tlatilulco y dixeron a Quauhtemoctzin y Maieoatzin la traycion que hazian los de xuchmilco [fol. 62v] y cuitlaoac:

y el Maieoatzin señor de Cuitlaoac reprehendio a aquellos q̄ auian hecho mala

fied in Tlatelolco. On arrival they spoke to the lord of Mexico, called Quauhtemoctzin, and to other leaders who were with him. The captains addressed him, saying, "Our lord, we have come to aid you in this time of necessity, and we have been sent for this purpose by our elders to pay the debt we owe. For this purpose we have brought the best soldiers we have among us, who are present here, to help on water and on land."

Hearing this, the lord of Mexico and the others said, "We appreciate what the lords are doing in sending you in our succor. Prepare yourselves to fight."

Then they gave them weapons to fight with, and they gave them much cacao, and then they put them in the place in which they were to do battle. Once in their places, they all began to fight.

But the Xochimilca began to rob around the houses, where there were only women and children, and old women. They killed some of the women and children and old women and put others in the canoes to carry off as slaves.

Some Mexica soldiers saw what was going on and advised the captains. Then they went against them by water and by land and began to kill some of them and take captives. They destroyed and killed them all, and of the women and children and old women they had captured, and the plunder, they got away with nothing.

After the battle the Spaniards retired to their quarters.

[The Mexica] took the Xochimilca, Cuitlahuaca, Mexicatzinca, people of Itztapalapan, etc., whom they had captured before Quauhtemoctzin, who was in a place called Yacacolco, in Tlatelolco, where now there is a church of Santa Ana. They told Quauhtemoctzin and Mayehuatzin of the treachery performed by the Xochimilca and Cuitlahuaca.

And Mayehuatzin, lord of Cuitlahuac, reprimanded those who had done the bad

in quimacique, çā muchtin vncan quin-
cauhq̄ aiac vicoc in cioatzitzinti.

Auh in iquac ie iuh muchioa in, ni[fol.
63]man ic mocototztlalique in Españoles.

Auh in iuh quimolhuica, in iuh qui-
chivazquia xochimilca, çan ic technaoal-
polozquia: auh in ixquichtin quimacique
in suchimilca: in Cuitlavaca .&. niman ie ic
quinvica, quintototza in vmpa Iacaculco,
in axcan ie sant Ana; vmpa icaca in Quauhtemoctzi, yoan in Maiehoatzin, cuitlaoac
tlatoani (ca nican ipan muchiuh in iauiotl).

Auh in oaxivaque contlapalotimani in
Maiehoatzin: conilhuia. Nicauhtzine,
moiolicatzin: auh in maiehoatzin, quin-
valilhuia. In antlapalpopul cuix namech-
cuicuitlavi, tle oamaxque. Auh in
quauhtemoctzin niman quioalilhui in
Maiehoatzin. Nicauhtzine ma ximotlacotili:[165] auh in Maiehoatzin: niman ie ic tla-
mictia, navi in cōmicti in imaceoalhoan:
no navi in conmicti in Quauh[fol. 63v]-
temoctzin. Auh in çatepan in ac onaaqui in
mamalti, oallanavatiloc inic mictilozque
novian in inteteupan tlatlacateculo, vel
novian tepanixque in mamalti.

Auh çatepā ie ic qualani in Mexica: quitoque. Ca nican totlan onoc, technelotoc
in suchimilcatl in ie nican chanchiva, amo
nel vmpa contlalia in itlatol. Auh inin ça ti-
quincaoa, çan popolivi: auh in ie iuhqui, in
o vel motzōtec, niman ie ic teçaçaco in cioatzitzinti, in ilamatzitzin yoā in ie
tlapalivi, muchintin mimictiloque, aocac
mocauhque, ca iuhquin quimontla-
tolevito, quimoncuitlachivito in ovallaque
in techpalevizquia xochmilcatl, in cuitlaoacatl.

Auh niman iquezquilhuioc, ontetl in
acalli quiçaco, vncan in iiauhtenco; çan
mixcavico in Españoles, ioatzinco in
quiçaco, aiaac tlacatl, çan oc val[fol.

there all [the Mexica people] whom they
had taken captive; none of the women
were taken away.

When this happened, the Spaniards
retired.

What the Xochimilco people had told
themselves they would do was just to destroy us by stealth. And [the Mexica] hur-
riedly took all the people of Xochimilco,
Cuitlahuac, etc., whom they had captured
to Yacacolco, where [the church of] Santa
Ana is now; there stood Quauhtemoctzin
and Mayehuatzin, the ruler of Cuitlahuac
(for he was here during the time that war
was waged).

Those who had been captured greeted
Mayehuatzin, saying to him, "Take it
slowly, my lord." But Mayehuatzin replied
to them, "You wretches, did I invite you?
What have you done?" Then Quauhtemoctzin said to Mayehuatzin, "My lord,
please do your service."[165] Then he offered sacrifices, killing four of his subjects;
Quauhtemoctzin also killed four. Afterward it was ordered that whoever was included among the captives was to be killed
in the temples of the demons all around;
they all had an equal part in the captives.

Afterward the Mexica were angry over
it all, saying, "The Xochimilco people live
here among us, mixed with us, and make
their homes here; are they not telling tales
there [in Xochimilco]? Well then, we
abandon them, they can just perish."
When this judgment had been made, the
women, the old women included, and the
able-bodied men were apprehended, and
were all killed; not a one remained, because the people of Xochimilco and Cuitlahuac told false tales on them, and
worked against them when they came saying they wanted to help us.

Then some days after that, two boats appeared at Iyauhtenco, with only Spaniards
in them. It was very early morning when
they appeared; there was no one else with

obra: y Quauhtemoctzin dixo al Mayeoatzin, herm.º haz tu officio, castiga esos que
an pecado: luego el Mayeoatzin començo a
matar en ellos, y el Quauhtemoctzin le
ayudo mataron cada vno dellos quatro y a
todos los demas que auian capituado: los
mexicanos mandaronlos matar en los cues
de los ydolos murieron en todos los cues de
los [166] muchos cues.

Por esta causa los mexicanos tomaron
gran enojo contra los de xuchmilco: y dixeron estos de xuchmilco moran entre
nosotros y espiannos y auisan a los de su
pueblo de lo que nosotros hazemos mue-
ran! y como aviendo determinado de
matarlos todos começarõ a sacarlos de sus
casas hombres y mugeres viejos, y viejas: y
a todos los mataron sin dexar nadie por
odio de aquellos que auian hecho la trayciõ
so color de ayudar

dende a dos o tres dias vinieron dos vergantines por hazia la parte del Tlatilulco
que se llama yiauhtenco, y vinieron en
ellos españoles solos sin ningunos indios
otros y como arribaron luego saltaron en
tierra: en tierra luego comença[fol. 63]ron
a pelear arrojar saetas y pelotas: y los soldados del tlatilulco agaçapauanse y ascondianse detras de las paredes y de las casas y
los capitanes estauan mirando quando seria
t̄po començaron a dar grita para começar
la pelea.

deeds. Quauhtemoctzin said to Mayehuatzin, "brother, do your duty, punish those
who have sinned." Then Mayehuatzin
began to kill some of them, and Quauhtemoctzin helped him. Each one killed
four of them, and the Mexica ordered that
the rest be killed in the *cu*s of the idols.
They died in all the *cu*s of the many that
there were. [166]

Because of this the Mexica conceived a
great anger against the Xochimilca, saying,
"These Xochimilca dwell among us and
spy on us and advise the people of their
settlement what we are doing. Let them
die!" Having decided to kill them all, they
began to pull them out of their houses,
men and women, old men and old
women, and they killed them all, leaving
no one, out of hate for those who had
committed treachery under the pretext of
giving aid.

Two or three days later, two brigantines
came toward the part of Tlatelolco called
Iyauhtenco; the Spaniards came in them
alone, without any Indians. When they arrived, they came to land, and on land they
began to fight, shooting crossbow bolts
and musket balls. The soldiers of Tlatelolco crouched and hid themselves behind
the walls and the houses; the captains,
looking for when it would be time, began
to call out for the battle to begin.

137

64]mixcavitiaque. Auh in ie iuhqui in oconacanque imacal: niman ie ic vallalhoacaquiça: auh in ovallalhoacaquizque niman ie ic micaltivitze, tlatlequiquizvitivitze, tlatepuzmivitivitze. Auh in tiacavan cēca mopachoa tenantitlan, yoā quimototoctitimani in calli anoço tepantli. Auh in iautlachixqui vel yix itequiuh in canin neovaz: auh in ie qualcā in ie inman, niman ie ic tzatzi: quitoa. Mexicae ma ie cuel.

them, they came by themselves. At this point they grounded their boats and came on dry land, and once on dry land they came skirmishing, shooting guns and iron bolts. And the warriors crouched very low at the walls, taking the houses or walls as shelter. And the sentinel kept his eyes peeled for where they would rise up. And at the right moment, when it was time, he cried out, saying, "O Mexica, up and at them!"

138

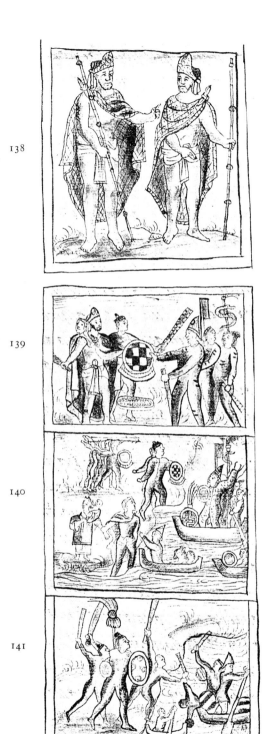

139

140

141

142

143

144

## 34

Inic cempoalli ommatlactli onnavi capitulo: vncan mitoa in quenin iehoantin Mexica tlamaque in quimacique Españoles caxtolti.

Thirty-fourth chapter, where it is said how the Mexica took captives, capturing fifteen Spaniards.

Mexicae ma ie cuel: niman ie ic tlacaoaca, yoan tlapitzalo yoan chimallaça in iautlachixqui: niman ie ic quintoca in Españoles, quimaiauhtivi yoã quimantivi, caxtoltin in anoque in Españoles: nimã ic quin[fol. 64v]oalhuicaque: auh in imacal nimã ic quitzinquixtique, anepantla contecato.

"O Mexica, up and at them!" Then there was a clamor and blowing of wind instruments, and the sentinel brandished his shield. Then they pursued the Spaniards; they went knocking them down and taking them. Fifteen Spaniards were taken, and then they brought them back. And [the Spaniards] withdrew their boats, stationing them out on the water.

Auh in oquimaxitico caxtoltin omei in vncan miquizque itoca: tlacuchcalco: nimã ie ic quinpepetlaoa, much quincuilique in iniautlatqui, yoã in imichcavipil, yoan in ixquich in intech catca, moch quintepeoaltique: niman ie ic tlacoti quinmictia: auh in imicnioan quinvalitztoque anepantla.

And when they had gotten the eighteen [sic] to where they were to die, called Tlacochcalco, they stripped them. They took away from them all their war gear and their cotton upper armor, and they made them drop everything that was on them to the ground. Then they performed their office and killed them; their companions watched from out on the water.

Auh ceppa quicalaquique vntetl in imacal in vmpa xocotitlã: in oconacanque, nimã ie ic vmpa itztivi in incalla xocoteca. Auh in Tzilacatzin, yoan oc cequintin tiacaoan; in oquimittaque in Españoles: niman intech oalietiquizque, quinoallalochtocaque, quintepachotivi, atlan quintepeoaco in Españoles.

Once they got two of their boats into [the canal] at Xocotitlan. When they had beached them, then they went looking into the house sites of the people of Xocotitlan. But Tzilacatzin and some other warriors who saw the Spaniards immediately came out to face them; they came running after them, throwing stones at them, and they scattered the Spaniards into the water.

Auh ie no ceppa quioalhuicaque in imacal in vncan coionacazco inic tlaie[fol. 65]cozque, inic micalizque. Auh in oacico niman ic valquizque cequintin Españoles, quinvaliacan in Castañeda xicotencatl:

Another time they brought their boats to Coyonacazco to fight and give combat. And when they got there, some Spaniards came out, with Castañeda Xicotencatl leading them; he had on a [device of] a

[fol. 64] Capitulo .34. de como los yndios mexicanos prendieron quinze Españoles.

Chapter Thirty-four, of how the Mexica Indians captured fifteen Spaniards.

Dezian los capitanes. Ea pues mexicanos Ea pues mexicanos: luego començaron todos a tocar sus trompetas y a pelear con los Españoles y lleuauā de vencida a los españoles y prendieron quinze Españoles: y los Españoles huyeron con los vergā[fol. 64v]tines a lo alto de la laguna:

y a los presos quitaron las armas y despojaronlos, y lleuaronlos a vn cu q̄ se llama Tlacuchcalco alli los sacaronlos[167] los coraçones delante del ydolo que se llamaua Macuiltotec y los otros españoles estauan mirando desde los vergantines como los matauan.

The captains said, "Into the fray, Mexica! Into the fray, Mexica!" Then they all began to blow their trumpets and do battle with the Spaniards. They defeated them and captured fifteen Spaniards, and the Spaniards fled in the brigantines to the deep part of the lake.

They stripped the captives of their weapons and clothes and conducted them to a *cu* called Tlacochcalco. There they took out their hearts[167] before the idol called Macuiltotec. From the brigantines the other Spaniards were watching them kill them.

Otra uez vinieron dos vergantines al barrio que se llama Xocotitlan y como llegaron a tierra saltaron en tierra por el barrio adelante peleando: y como vio aquel capitan indio que se llamaua Tzilacatzin q̄ entrauan peleando acudio a ellos con otra gente que le siguio y peleādo los echaron de aquel barrio: y los hizieron acoger a los vergantines.

Otra uez vinieron dos vergatines al barrio que se llama Coionacazco y saltaron en tierra: los Españoles y començaron a pelear venia alli por capitan Rodrigo de [fol. 65] castañeda començaron a echar saetas: y

Another time two brigantines came to the district called Xocotitlan, and when they touched land they disembarked, fighting their way into the district. When that Indian captain called Tzilacatzin saw that they were entering doing battle, he met them with others who followed him; battling, he ejected them from that district and made them take refuge in the brigantines.

Another time two brigantines came to the district called Coyonacazco; the Spaniards disembarked and began to do battle. Rodrigo de Castañeda served as captain; they began to shoot crossbow bolts, and

iquetzaltemal ietinemi. [168] Nimā ie ic val-
latepuzmivia: auh ça ce in minoc ixquac,
niman ic momiquili: iehoatl in valtemi in
Castañeda. Auh in tiacaoā itech ietiquiz-
que, atlan quinnemitique, quintetepa-
choque: auh vncā miquizquia in castañeda:
auh ça acaltitech pilcatia inic quivicaque
xocotitlan.

Auh centetl acalli onoca tetenanteputzco, vncā in colivi tetenamitl: auh in oc
centetl acalli vmpa onoca in totecco: in
ipan vtli tlamelaoa Tepetzinco, çan tlatla-
pixtoca in atlan. Auh in ie ioa quivica.

Auh iquezquilhuioc ie no ceppa tech-
centlatalhui in Españoles: nec vitze, ie qui-
oalmottilique in quavecatitlan vtli, in oallamelauhticac iztanamacoian. Auh in
vncan in quauecatitlan in vtli [fol. 65v] ca-
moiauhque. Auh in ixquich tlaxcaltecatl,
in aculhoacatl, in chalcatl: niman ie ic catzupa in acalutli: yoan in ocamoiauhque
vtli: contlaça in xamitl, yoan in calquavitl,
in tecoc in tlaixquatl in tlaquetzalli, in
quāmimilli, in acatl quicuitlalpia in con-
tepeoa atlan. Auh in iquac in omotzop nec
valmotema in Españoles, cencā ivian in
iativitze, quiniacana in quachpanitl, tlapitztivitze, tlatzotzontivitze. Auh imi-
campa onotivitze in ie ixquich tlaxcaltecatl, yoan in ie ixquich altepeoa, cenca
muchicava moquaquacuecuechoa, meel-
tzotzona in tlaxcalteca, cuica, no cuica in
mexica necoccampa cuico, queoa in çaço
tlein quilnamiqui, ic mellaquaoa muchioa.

Auh in oacico tlalhoacan [171] in tiacaoā
vel nepacholo, vel mopachoa [fol. 66] vel
netlatilo, quitetetzontlaliaia, quichixtoque
in quemman teevitiloz. in quenman quica-
quizque tzatziliztli. in teevitiliztli: auh in
otzatzioac. Mexicae, ma ie cuel iehoatl:
niman ic quivalixti, in Tlapanecatl heca-

quetzal-feather ball. [168] Then they shot
iron bolts in this direction; just one person
was hit, in the forehead, and then he died.
The one who made the shot was Castañeda. And the warriors quickly went to
face them, they made them go into the
water, they stoned them. Castañeda was
about to die there, but he just hung onto a
boat, so that they took him to Xocotitlan.

And one boat was at Tetenantepotzco,
where the walls curve, and another boat
was at Totecco, on the road going straight
to Tepetzinco. They just lay keeping
watch on the water, and as it grew dark
they took them away.

A few days after that the Spaniards had
another conference about us. Then they
came and inspected the road at Quauhecatitlan that comes straight to Iztanama-
coyan. At Quauhecatitlan they widened
the road by removing water; all the Tlaxcalans and people of Acolhuacan and
Chalco filled in the canal. To widen the
road they threw in adobe, laid down house
beams, door lintels, pillars, and round logs,
and scattered bundles of reeds in the water.
And when it was filled in the Spaniards
came in formation. They came very
slowly, with the standard leading them,
playing wind instruments and beating
drums. Behind them came all the Tlaxcalans and the people of all of the altepetl.
The Tlaxcalans were very spirited, shaking
their heads, beating their chests, singing.
The Mexica sang too; there was singing on
both sides. To give themselves encouragement they sang whatever came to mind.

When they got to Tlilhuacan, [171] the
warriors crouched far down and hid themselves, hugging the ground, waiting for the
war cry, when there would be shouting
and cries of encouragement. When the cry
went up, "O Mexica, up and at them!" the
Tlappanecatl Ecatzin, a warrior of Otomi

castañeda mato a vno cō vna saeta y saltaron con el ciertos soldados indios y dieron con el en el agua y estuuieron a punto
de matarle si no que se escapo asido de vn
vergantin

Castañeda killed someone with a bolt.
Some Indian soldiers leaped upon him,
knocked him into the water, and were on
the point of killing him, if he had not escaped by grasping at a brigantine.

Estaua otro vergantin de los Españoles
en el lugar que se llama Tetenanteputzco
cerca de aquella yglesia que se llama sācta
lucia, otro vergantin estaua en el barrio que
se llama Totecco que es cabe la yglesia de
Concepcion: estos vergantines estauan en
el agua aguardando tp̄o estauan todo l[169]
dia alli, y a la noche se yuan

Another of the Spaniards' brigantines
was in the place called Tetenantepotzco,
close to the church called Santa Lucía. Another brigantine was in the district called
Totecco, which is next to the church of
Concepción. These brigantines were in
the water biding their time; they were
there all[169] day long, and at night they
went away.

y dende a tres o quatro dias determinaron entre si los españoles de darnos
guerra por alli. Entrarō por el camino que
se llama Quauecatitlan que va derechos[170]
hazia dōde venden la sal yuā tantos yndios
y españoles que no cabian por el camino
porque de vna parte y de otra auia agua y
echaron tierra y adoues y maderos para
poder mejor pasar y como vuieron en-
sāchado el camino luego comēçaron a entrar por el camino en orden de guerra con
su bandera delāte [fol. 65v] y tocando el
tambor y pifano y venian tras ellos todos
los yndios de tlaxcalla y de otros pueblos,
que eran amigos: entranron los españoles
con mucha fantasia que no tenian en nada a
los mexicanos y los Tlaxcaltecas, y otros
indios amigos yvan cātando: y tambien los
mexicanos cātauan de la misma manera,
segun q̄ solian hazer en las guerras,

Three or four days later, the Spaniards
decided to give us battle there. They entered along the road called Quauhecatitlan,
which goes straight[170] toward where salt is
sold. There were so many Indians and
Spaniards going along that they did not fit
in the road, because there was water on
both sides. They threw in earth, adobe,
and timber in order to be able to get by
better, and when they had widened the
road, they began to come in by the road in
order of battle, with their banner ahead,
playing the fife and drum. Behind them
came all the Indians from Tlaxcala and
from the other settlements that were
friendly. The Spaniards entered with much
display of despising the Mexica, and the
Tlaxcalans and the other Indian friends
went singing. The Mexica too sang in the
same manner as they used to in the wars.

y como llegaron a vn barrio que se llama
Tliloacan que es agora Sanct m̄īn: los soldados Tlatilulcanos estauan ascondidos y
agaçapados por temor del artilleria: esperando la pelea y la grita de sus capitanes
que mandasen pelear y como oyeron el
mandato, luego aremetio a los españoles
aquel capitan Tlatilulcano q̄ se llamaua
Tlappanecatl hecatzin y comēço a dar

When they reached a district called Tlilhuacan, which is now San Martín, the
Tlatelolca soldiers were hidden and
crouched down for fear of the artillery,
awaiting the battle and the shout of their
captains ordering them into the fight, and
when they heard the command, the Tlatelolca captain called Tlappanecatl Ecatzin
rushed at the Spaniards and began to shout,

tzin, otomitl, inca ommomotlac: quito. Tiiacavane tlatilulcae! ma ie cuel, aquique in in Tenime, xivalnenemican: niman ic ica ce maiavito in Español, tlalli ic quivitec: iehoatl in valiacattivia in quimaiavito in quivaliacatitivia. Auh in oquimaiavito: nec convilanato in Español.

rank, faced [the Spaniards] and threw himself at them, saying, "O Tlatelolca warriors, up and at them, who are these barbarians? Come running!" Then he went and threw a Spaniard down, knocking him to the ground; the one he threw down was the one who came first, who came leading them. And when he had thrown him down, he dragged the Spaniard off.

## 35

Inic cempoalli oncaxtolli capitulo: vncan moteneoa, in quenin ie no ceppa tlamaque mexica in quimacique Españoles, in iuh mopouhque in axivaque Españoles, ontecpātli ommatlactli omei: yoā no miequin tlaxcalteca, Tetzcuca, chalca, xuchmilca. Auh in quenin muchtin, vncā quinmictique in imixpan inTeuoan catca./.

[fol. 66v] Auh in ie iuhqui in ixquichtin tiiacavan, nec quivalcentlaça in omopachotoca, caltzalantli quivaltotocatiquizque. Auh in Españoles in oquittaque ça iuhquin tlavāque: niman ie ic tlamalo, miequintin in axivaque in tlaxcalteca, in aculhoaque, in chalca, in xuchmilca .&. vel tonacatlamaloc, tonacamicoac, vel atlan quin-

Thirty-fifth chapter, where it is told how the Mexica took captives again—according to the count of the Spaniards they captured, there were fifty-three, as well as many Tlaxcalans and people of Tetzcoco, Chalco, and Xochimilco—and how they killed all of them before their former gods.

And at this point they let loose with all the warriors who had been crouching there; they came out and chased [the Spaniards] in the passageways, and when the Spaniards saw it they [the Mexica] seemed to be intoxicated. Then captives were taken. Many Tlaxcalans, and people of Acolhuacan, Chalco, Xochimilco, etc.,

vozes esforcando [172] a los suyos y aferro con vn español yn dio con el en tierra y tomaronle los otros soldados que yuan con este Tlappanecatl hecatl.

encouraging [172] his followers. He came to grips with a Spaniard and knocked him to the ground, and the other soldiers who were with this Tlappanecatl Ecatl took him prisoner.

## 35

[fol. 66] Capitulo .35. de como los mexicanos prendieron otros españoles mas de cincuenta y tres y muchos Tlaxcaltecas, Tetzcucanos, chalcas, xuchmilcas y a todos los mataron delante los ydolos.

Chapter Thirty-five, of how the Mexica captured more Spaniards, more than fifty-three, and many Tlaxcalans, Tetzcoca, Chalca, and Xochimilca, and killed them all before the idols.

[fol. 66v] Trauose vna batalla muy recia en este dia: de manera que los mexicanos como borrachos se arrojaron contra los enemigos, y captiuaron muchos de los Tlaxcaltecas, y chalcas, y tezcucanos, y mataron muchos dellos, y peleando y hizieron saltar a los españoles en las acequias y a todos los indios sus amigos parose con esto

This day the battle was very fierce, so that the Mexica hurled themselves as if drunk against the enemy. They captured many of the Tlaxcalans, Chalca, and Tetzcoca, and killed many of them. In the battle they forced the Spaniards and all their Indian friends to leap into the canals. With all this the road turned so muddy that it was unpassable. [173]

nemitique in Españoles, yoā in ie ixquich
tlacatl: auh in vtli vel petzcauhtimoquetz,
aoc vel nenemoa, ça nepepetzcolo, ça
neaalaoalo.


Auh in mamaltin tevivilano. Ie vncan
in, in axioac in vandera, vncan anoc; iehoantin caciq̄ in Tlatilulca: vncan in macic,
in ie axcan sanct Martin moteneoa: çan atle
ipā quittaque, amo ōnecuitlaviloc. Auh in
oc cequintin tematitlampa quizque: vmpa
quimōciauhcavato in col[fol. 67]hoaca-
tonco, acalotenco, vmpa valmomanato.


Auh nimā ie ic quinvica in mamaltin in
vmpa iacacolco, tetototzalo, quimolol-
huitivi in immalhoan, in aca chocatiuh, in
aca cuicatiuh, in aca motenvitectiuh. Auh
in onteaxitiloc iacaculco: nimā ie ic tevi-
pano, tevipanolo, ceceniaca oniatimani in
mumuzco, in vncan tlamictilo, iacattiaq̄ in
Españoles, coniacatique: auh ça vntlatzac-
uique, ontlatoquilique in ixquichtin al-
tepeoaque. Auh in ontlamictiloc, nec
quinquaquauhço in intzontecon in Españoles: no quiçoçoque in cavallosme
intzōtecon, tlatzintlan in quitecaque: auh
in intzontecon Españoles tlacpac in onoca,
in çoçotoca, tonatiuh quixnamictoca. Auh
in ixquich nepapan tlacatl, amo quinço-
çoque in intzontecō in veca tlaca. auh in

were captured. A great abundance were
captured and killed. They made the Spaniards and all the others go right into the
water. And the road became very slippery;
one could no longer walk on it, but would
slip and slide.

And the captives were dragged off. This
was where the banner was captured; that is
where it was taken. It was the Tlatelolca
who captured it, at the place now called
San Martín. They thought nothing of it,
they did not take care of it. The other
[Spaniards] escaped; [the Mexica] harried
them as far as Colhuacatonco, at the edge
of the canal, where they re-formed.

Then they took the captives to Yacacolco, hurrying them along, going along
herding their captives together. Some
went weeping, some singing, some went
shouting while hitting their hands against
their mouths. When they got them to
Yacacolco, they lined them all up. Each
one went to the altar platform, where the
sacrifice was performed. The Spaniards
went first, going in the lead; the people of
all the different altepetl just followed,
coming last. And when the sacrifice was
over, they strung the Spaniards' heads on
poles [on the skull rack]; they also strung
up the horses' heads. They placed them
below, and the Spaniards' heads were
above them, strung up facing east. But

el camino todo lodoso que no podian
andar por el [173]

aqui prendieron muchos españoles y
lleuauālos arrastrando en este lugar tomaron a los españoles vna bādera donde
esta la yglesia de sāc m̄ī: y los Españoles
huyeron y siguieronlos hasta el barrio que
llaman Coloacatonco alli se recogieron

Here they captured many Spaniards and
dragged them away. In this place, where
the church of San Martín is, they took a
banner from the Spaniards. The Spaniards
fled, and they pursued them as far as the
district they call Colhuacatonco, where
they took refuge.

y los indios boluieron a coger el campo
y tomaron sus captiuos y pusieronlos en
procesion todos maneatados pusieron delante los [174] a los españoles: y luego a los
Tlaxcaltecas, y luego a los demas indios
captiuos y lleuaronlos al cu que llamauā
mumuzco alli los mataron vno a vno
sacando los coraçones primeramente mataron a los españoles: y despues a todos los
yndios sus amigos: auiēdolos muerto pusieron las cabeças [fol. 67] en vnos palos delante de los ydolos todas espetadas por las
sienes las de los españoles mas altas: y las de
los otros indios mas baxas y las de los cauallos mas baxas murieron en esta batalla Cincuenta y tres españoles y quatro cauallos:

The Indians went back to pick over the
field of battle. They took their captives and
put them in procession, all with their
hands bound. They put the Spaniards [174] in
front, then the Tlaxcalans, then the other
captive Indians. Taking them to the *cu*
they called Momozco, they killed them
there one at a time, removing their hearts.
First they killed the Spaniards, then all
their Indian friends. After killing them
they put their heads on some poles before
the idols, all pierced through the temples,
with those of the Spaniards highest, those
of the Indians lower, and those of the
horses yet lower. Fifty-three Spaniards and
four horses died in this battle.

149

150

151

axioaque Españoles ontec[fol. 67v]pantli
onmatlactli omei, yoan nauhtetl cavallos:


auh tel novian tlatlapielo, necalioa: amo
ic mocaoa in tlapieliztli, in novian tech-
iaoalotinemi in xuchmilca in acaltica,
necoccampa tlamalo, necoccampa micoa.


Auh in ixquich macevalli, cenca tlaihi-
oviaia maianaia, miec in mapizmiquili
aocmo quia in qualli atl, in ecatl, ça tequixquiatl in quia ic miec tlacatl momiquili,
yoã miec tlacatl ic tlaelli quitlaz ic mic:
yoan much qualoc in cuetzpalin, in
cuicuitzcatl, yoan Eloçacatl, yoan in
tequixquiçacatl: yoan quiquaquaque in
tzumpanquavitl, yoan quiquaquaque in
tzacuxuchitl, yoan in tlaquili, [175] yoan in
cuetlaxtli yoan in maçaeoatl, quitletle-
oatzaia, quimooxquiaia quitototopotzaia,
quitotoponiaia inic quiquaia yoã [fol. 68]
in tetzmetl, yoan in xantetl quitetexoaia:
aoctle iuhqui inic tlaihioviloc, temamauhti
in tzaqualoc, vel tonac in apizmic: auh çan
ivian techvalcaltechpachotiaque, çan iviã
techololalique.

they did not string up the heads of all the
various [other] people from far away.
There were fifty-three of the Spaniards
they captured, along with four horses.

Nevertheless, watch was kept everywhere, and there was fighting. They did
not stop keeping watch because of [what
had happened]. The people of Xochimilco
went about in boats surrounding us on all
sides; there were deaths and captives taken
on both sides.

And all the common people suffered
greatly. There was famine; many died of
hunger. They no longer drank good, pure
water, but the water they drank was salty.
Many people died of it, and because of it
many got dysentery and died. Everything
was eaten: lizards, swallows, maize straw,
grass that grows on salt flats. And they
chewed at colorin wood, glue flowers,
plaster, [175] leather, and deerskin, which
they roasted, baked, and toasted so that
they could eat them, and they ground up
medicinal herbs and adobe bricks. There
had never been the like of such suffering.
The siege was frightening, and great numbers died of hunger. And bit by bit they
came pressing us back against the wall,
herding us together.

[fol. 67v] en todo esto no cesaua la guerra, por el agua matauãse vnos a otros por las canoas,

In this whole time the battle did not cease on the water, those of each side killing the others in canoes.

y auia gran hambre entre los mexicanos y grande enfermedad porque bebian del agua de la laguna: y comian sauandixas lacartixas y ratones eta. Porque no les ẽtrauan ningun bastimento y poco a poco fueron acorralando a los mexicanos cercandolos de todas partes.

There was great hunger among the Mexica, and much sickness, because they drank water from the lake and ate vermin, lizards, mice, etc., because no supplies reached them. Bit by bit they went penning the Mexica in, surrounding them on all sides.

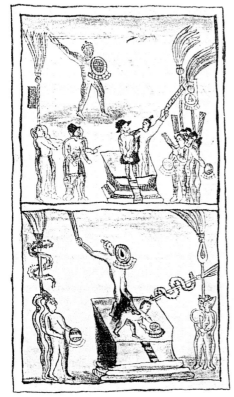

152

153

154

## 36

Inic cempoalli oncaxtolli oce capitulo; vncan mitoa in quenin Españoles iancuican calaquico tianquizco in nican tlatilulco.

Auh ceppa muchiuh nauhteme in cavallos in calaquico tianquizco. Auh in ocalaquico, nec tlanaoatl quitoca, tianquiztentli quitoca in tiiacavan quinxixiltivi, mieꝗntin in micque concuitlaxeloco in tianquiztli: iquac iancuican quittaco in tianquiztli: niman ic iaque, ic moteputztique. Auh in tiacaoan intech motlapaloque quintocaꝗ: auh in iquac calaquico iancuican tianquizco amo tene[fol. 68v]machpan, amo quiteimachitique:

auh yoan nimā iquac quitlatique in teucalli, contleminque: auh in ocontleminque nec cuetlan, cenca veca eoac in tletl, in tlenenepilli, iuhquin ihicoioca tletl yoan cuecuetlani. Auh in oquittaque in ie tlatla in teucalli: niman ie ic nechoquililo, nechoquiztlapalolli: iuh nemachoc in ca ie ontenamoieloz.

Auh vecauhtica in necalioac in tianquizco, vel tetemman in iauiotl, aiaxcā in quicauhque in tenamitl, in vncan in tenexnamacoiā Auh in vncan copalnamacoian, yoan atecocolecan, yoā in vncan xuchicalco in caltzalan, in calacoaia, vel ipā mantinenca in tiacavan in tenamitl. Auh in ixquich quauhquecholtecacalli in tianquiztli quiiavalotoc moch tenamitl mochiuh [fol. 69] miequintin tlapanco onoca in vallamotla, quioallaça in tetl, in mitl, oallatepachoa, vallamina, yoan moch mocuitlacoioni in quauhquecholtecacalli, achitoton quicoionique. Auh in iquac ie

Thirty-sixth chapter, where it is said how the Spaniards for the first time entered the marketplace here in Tlatelolco.

Once it happened that four horse[men] came and entered the marketplace. On entering they followed a circle, going around the edge of the marketplace. They went lancing the warriors, and many died. They came penetrating into the midst of the marketplace. That was the first time they saw it; then they turned around and went away. And the warriors were daring with them; they pursued them. And when they came into the marketplace for the first time, no one expected it, they gave no sign of it.

And then was also when they burned the temple, setting fire to it. When they had set it on fire, it flared up; the tongues of flame rose very high, and the fire seemed to crackle and roar. And when they saw the temple burning, there was weeping and people greeted one another tearfully; it was thought that plundering was to begin.

Fighting went on for a long time in the marketplace; it was full of combat. It was a long time before they abandoned the walls at Tenexnamacoyan, Copalnamacoyan, and Atecocolecan. And at Xochicalco, where ⟨the Spaniards⟩ were entering the passageways, the warriors went about on the walls everywhere. And all the houses of the Quauhquechollan people that surrounded the marketplace became a rampart. Many [warriors] who were on the roofs hurled down stones and arrows, stoning and shooting arrows from there, and they made holes in all the houses of the

[fol. 68] Capitulo .36. de la primera vez que los Españoles entraron en el tiãquez del tlatilulco.

Andando la guerra como arriba esta dicho, vn dia entraron quatro de cauallo en el tianquiz del tlatilulco y dieron vna buelta por todo el alrededor yvan alanceãdo a quantos topauan y mataron muchos soldados mexicanos: despues que dieron vna buelta atrauesaron por el medio del tianquiz, luego salieron huyendo y saltaron tras ellos muchos soldados tirandolos: esta entrada que hizieron fue supita que nadie penso q̃ osaran entrar

y el mesmo dia pusieron hoego al cu mayor que era de Vitzilobuchtli y todos se q̃mo [fol. 68v] en obra de dos o tres horas.

Chapter Thirty-six, of the first time the Spaniards entered the *tiánquiz* of Tlatelolco.

With the war going as said above, one day four horsemen entered the *tiánquiz* of Tlatelolco and took a turn all around it, lancing everyone they came upon, and they killed many Mexica soldiers. After going around once, they crossed the middle of the *tiánquiz,* then left fleeing. Many soldiers ran after them, shooting at them. This entry of theirs was unexpected, and no one thought that they would dare enter.

On the same day they set fire to the principal *cu,* which was Huitzilopochtli's, and it burned completely in about two or

155

Como vieron los mexicanos que se quemaua el cu començaron a llorar amargamente porque tomarõ mal aguero de uer quemar el cu:

y luego se trauo vna batalla muy recia dieron esta batalla casi v̄ dia y derrocaron los españoles vnos paredones o albarradas con el artilleria de donde los dauan guerra y despues de derrocados acogeronse a las casas de que estaua cercado del tianquiz y subierõ los soldados mexicanos sobre los tlapancos destas casas y de alli tirauan saetas y piedras: y los mexicanos agujeraron aquellas casas y hizieron dellas guaridas para valerse de los cauallos.

three hours. When the Mexica saw the *cu* burning, they began to weep bitterly, because they took it for a bad omen to see the *cu* burned.

Then there was a very fierce battle lasting almost a day. With the artillery the Spaniards demolished some large walls or barricades from where they were giving them battle. After they were demolished, they took refuge in the houses surrounding the *tiánquiz.* The Mexica soldiers climbed up on the *tlapancos* of these houses and from there shot arrows and threw stones; and the Mexica made holes in those houses [to shoot from], using them as shelters to protect them from the horses.

no valtetoca in cavallosme, in ie no quin-
xopiloznequi, in ie quiniacatzacuiliznequi:
vmpa cacalactivetzi in tiacavan.


Auh ceppa muchiuh in Españoles: acatl
yiacapan in valcalacq̄ nec tenamoielo,
nec teçaçaco in maceoaltzitzinti. Auh in
oquittaque in tiiacavan: nec quivallaça in
tiiacavan, vncan icativitz quachic: itoca
Axoquentzin quintocac in iiaovan,
quintetlaçalti, quinmalacacho: auh inin tiacauh vncā momiquili, vncan quitepuz-
miviq̄ yielpan, in quitlaxilique, yiollopan
in quitlaxilique tepuzmitl, iuhquin ne-
cochaano in[fol. 69v]ic ommomiquili: auh
nimā ic mocototztlalique in toiaovan.


Auh in vmpa in iacacolco: çanno ivi in
tlaiecolo, in Espanoles in tlatepuzmivia
tecpantivitze, quinpalevitivitze, quin-
tlamatilitivitze in nauhtecutli, quitzacu-
tivitze in vtli. Auh in tiacavan nec nepacholo, inic quincuitlaxelozque, ie
omm̄opiloa in tonatiuh. Auh in ie iuhqui
in ie vitze: cequintin tlapanco tlecoque in
toiaovan: auh in otzatzic, quito. hui tlaxcaltecae, xioalnenemican, nican cate in
amoiaovan: nec quivallaça in mitl, in
impan in mopachotoca, nec xitinque:


yiolic onacico in iacaculco vncā motetemmā in iauiotl: çan vncā ommotzotzo-
naco avel quinpetlaque in Tlatilulca, in
amac onoque quinvalmina, quinvaltepa-
choa aoctle in panoani, aoctle acuepana-
vaztli, ocaanque.

Quauhquechollan people, breaking out
little holes. And when the horse[men]
were pursuing people and trying ⟨to tram-
ple them⟩ and cut them off, the warriors
quickly went in there.

Once it happened that the Spaniards
came into Acatliyacapan; then people were
snatched, the poor commoners were taken
away. When the warriors saw it, they let
loose against them. Coming among the
warriors was a scraped-head named Axoquentzin. He pursued his enemies; he
made them let people go, he spun them
about. But this warrior died there; they hit
him with an iron bolt in the chest, they
shot an iron bolt into his heart. He died as
if he were stretching out when going to
sleep. Then our enemies retired.

And at Yacacolco likewise there was
fighting. The Spaniards who shoot the
iron bolts came in formation. The Four
Lords came helping them, accompanying
them, closing the road. And the warriors
crouched down in order to penetrate into
their midst. The sun was already low. And
as they were just about to come [out attacking the Spaniards], some of our enemies climbed on a roof and cried out, saying, "Hey, Tlaxcalans, come running, here
are your enemies!" Then they threw darts
down on those who had been crouched
there, and they dispersed.

Slowly [the Spaniards] reached Yacacolco; the battle was fierce there. They just
hit against a wall, they could not break
through the Tlatelolca. Those who were
on the other side of the water shot arrows
at them, threw stones at them. They were
not able to cross, not able to find a way
over.

Otra uez entraron los españoles: y los indios amigos en el tianquiz y començaron a robar y catiuar indios [fol. 69] Como vieron esto los soldados mexicanos salieron tras ellos y hizieronlos dexar la presa y aq̇ murio vn capitan señalado de los mexicanos que se llamaua Axuquentzin y luego se retruxeron los españoles que peleauā de la parte de san m̄īn aunque de las otras partes todavia peleauā los españoles y sus amigos:

vna capitania de soldados mexicanos hizieron vna celada para tomar a los españoles y sus amigos descuydados. Y dar sobre ellos a la pasada: y algunos soldados de Tlaxcalla que ayudauan a los españoles subieronse sobre los tlapancos y vieron la celada y dieron vozes a los demas para que acudiesen a pelear con los que estauan celada:[176] como vieron los de la celada que los auian visto huyeron y ansi pasaron aquel paso seguros para yr a su estancia

auiendo peleado todo el dia boluieronse los españoles sin romper a sus enemigos aquel dia porque los auian quitado las puentes de manera que no podieron pasar a los enemigos.

Another time the Spaniards and the Indian friends came into the *tiánquiz* and began to abduct and capture Indians. When the Mexica soldiers saw this, they went out after them and made them abandon their prey. Here an outstanding captain of the Mexica, called Axoquentzin, died. Then the Spaniards who were in the battle in the direction of San Martín withdrew, though on other sides the Spaniards and their friends continued to fight.

A company of Mexica soldiers set up an ambush to take the Spaniards and their friends by surprise and leap upon them as they passed by, but some soldiers from Tlaxcala who were helping the Spaniards climbed up on the *tlapancos* and saw the ambush. They shouted to the rest to come and do battle with those who were in the ambush.[176] When those in the ambush saw that they had been seen, they fled, and thus they safely passed that narrow place on the way to their quarters.

Having fought all day, the Spaniards went back without having routed their enemies that day, because they had removed the bridges so that they could not get at the enemy.

156

[fol. 70] Inic cempoalli oncaxtolli omume capitulo: vncan mitoa in q̄nin Mexica in cohuvitiaia in quitlatlapoaia in atl in ioaltica, in vncan catzupaia Españoles in tlaca.

Auh in toiaovan, catzuptivitze in acalutli. Auh in onoiaque [179] in iavme ie no ceppa quiquixtia in tetl inic otlaatzupca iaume: in otlatvic ie no ceppa iuhcan, in iuhcan catca ialhoa: muchipa iuh quichiuhque in vncā catzupaia in acalotli, in çan nimā quivalquixtiaia in tetl in quavitl .&. ic achi vecaoac in iauiotl, aiaxcan in quinvalpetlaque: auh in acalotli in, iuhq̄n vei tenamitl ipan momatia.

Auh in Españoles yoan in ixquich tlaxcaltecatl incentequiuh in vtli, in vei vtli iacacolco, yoan in tlilhoacan in atezcapan. Auh in iacaculco, in cuepopan, in apaoazcan, yoan atliceuhian inic [fol. 70v] iaticac aiacac, in totecco intequiuh muchiuh in xuchmilcatl, in cuitlaoacatl, in mizquicatl, in culhoacatl in Itztapalapanecatl, incē-tequiuh muchiuh in acaltica in tlaiecoaia.

Auh in atliceuhca, yoan aiacacalque in acaleque, in tlaminani, vel muchicaoa inic quinnamiqui, amo moquequetza, vel

Thirty-seventh chapter, where it is said how the Mexica kept making it hard for the Spaniards to pass, by night opening up the water [of the canals] where the Spaniards had filled them in by day.

And our enemies came filling in the canals. But when the enemy had gone, [179] [the Mexica] again removed the stone with which the enemy had filled them in. When dawn came, things were just as they had been the day before. They always did this where [the Spaniards] had filled in the canals, immediately taking back out the stone, wood, etc. In this way the war took somewhat longer, and the Spaniards were slow in breaking through them. These canals were considered to be like great walls.

The Spaniards and all the Tlaxcalans were jointly responsible for the road, the highway to Yacacolco and to Tlilhuacan and Atezcapan. And Yacacolco [itself], Cuepopan, Apahuazcan, and Atliceuhyan, going to Ayacac and Totecco, were made the responsibility of the people of Xochimilco, Cuitlahuac, Mizquic, Colhuacan, and Itztapalapan; it was their common responsibility to give battle in boats there.

And [181] the boatmen and archers of Atliceuhyan and Ayacac made great efforts to encounter [the Spaniards], they lost no

157

158

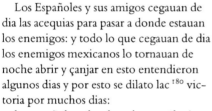

37

[fol. 70] Capitulo .37. de como de
noche abrianlas [177] los caminos del agua
que de dia los cerrauanlos [178] los españoles.

Chapter Thirty-seven, of how at night
they opened [177] the waterways that the
Spaniards closed [178] by day.

Los Españoles y sus amigos cegauan de
dia las acequias para pasar a donde estauan
los enemigos: y todo lo que cegauan de dia
los enemigos mexicanos lo tornauan de
noche abrir y çanjar en esto entendieron
algunos dias y por esto se dilato lac [180] victoria por muchos dias:

los españoles y los tlaxcaltecas cōbatian
por tierra vnos por la parte que se dize
yacalco y otros por la parte que se dize
Tliloacan, y otros por la parte que se dize
atezcapā, y de la parte del agua peleauan los
de xuchmilco y los de Cuitlaoac, y los de
Mizquic, y los de coloacan, y los de Itztapalapan,

y los tlatilulcanos del barrio de atliceuhyan, y los del barrio de ayacac resis-
tian por el agua no descansauan en la pelea
eran tan espesas las saetas [fol. 70v] y los
dardos que todo el ayre parecia amarillo:

y los capitanes de los mexicanos vno que
se llamaua Xiuhcozcatzin, y otro se llamaua Quaquauhtzī, y otro se llamaua Tezcacoatl, y otro se llamaua Tecpanecatl, y
otro se llamaua Vitzitzi, y otro se llamaua

By day the Spaniards and their friends
filled in the canals in order to get to where
the enemy was, but by night the Mexica
enemies opened up and dug out again everything they had filled in during the day.
They were at this for several days, and for
this reason victory [180] was long delayed.

On land the Spaniards and the Tlaxcalans would do combat, some in the area
called Yacacolco, others in the area called
Tlilhuacan, and others in the area called
Atezcapan. On the water those of Xochimilco, Cuitlahuac, Mizquic, Colhuacan, and Itztapalapan did battle.

The Tlatelolca of the districts of Atliceuhyan and Ayacac fought back on the
water, never resting from the battle. The
arrows and darts were so thick that the
whole sky seemed yellow.

The captains of the Mexica, one of
whom was called Xiuhcozcatzin, another
Quaquauhtzin, another Tezcacoatl, another Tecpanecatl, another Huitzitzin, and
another Itzcuintzin, who were all from the

moneneuhcavia, iuhquin tzetzelivi in tlatzontectli, iuhquin coatl motlamina
mopipiaçoa in mitl: in iquac atlatica quitlaça iuhquin cozpul ommoteca in impan
iaume:

auh in cequintin tiacaoan in Xiuhcozcatzin, quaquatzi, Tezcacoacatl, Tecpanecatl, Vitzitzin, Itzcuintzin: in iacaculca
vel ipan mantivia in calli; amo moqueque-
tzaia, amo quixiccavaia in Cioatzintli, in
piltzintli, aiaxcan in quimōcaltechpachoto
in oc ce acalotli itech in amaxac icac.

[fol. 71] [181] Auh ceppa muchiuh in vmpa
totecco, vmpa oalquizque in Españoles:
auh in onacico in vncan telpuchcalli icac:
itocaiocan. aiacac: niman contleminque.
 Auh in oc centetl in imacal in Españoles,
valcalac in vncan atliceuhian, yoā miec in
imacal in xuchimilca in quivalhuicaticalac.
Auh in tiiacauh in Temilotzin, tlacateccatl;
momuzco moquetzticac, quimonitzticac
in Españoles: auh in tiiacauh Coiovevetzin: in onaqui tlaviztli quauhtlocelutl;
cectlapal quauhtli cectlapal ocelutl acaltica
in valla tolmaiecampa in quivallaz: yoan
miec in acalchimalli, in quitlamatilitivitze:
quivalitotia. Tiacavane ma ie cuel iehoatl
ticcentlaça: nimā ie ic macalhuitequi. Auh
in oquittaque in Españoles: niman ic moteputztique, quintocaque; nec vallamelaoa in
atliceuhiā. Auh in imacal Españoles: nec
[fol. 71v] quitzinquixtia, contecato amanalco. Auh in Xuchimilca, miequintin inic
micque mitl: auh in ie iuhqui in oǫnto-
caque, oc ceppa valmomāque, nec quin-
valtoca in tiiacavan: in Coiovevetzin
quimotocti in mumuztli: nimā ic quīcuep
vel quimaxitito in vmpa icac telpuchcalli in
atliceuhian: ie no ceppa quivaltocaque in
coiovevetzin atlan conchololtico: ie no
cuele contlaz in telpuchotomitl, Itzpapalotzin inn oonaqui tlaviztli, nec ǫntoca,
iuhquin çoquitl quimololoa, vel quin-
tepeoato acaacalco: [183] niman ic iaque, ic
popolivito.

time, they were equal to them. It seemed
that barbed darts showered down; the arrows came in large bunches, ⟨as when a
serpent strikes⟩. When they threw darts
with the *atlatl*, a yellow mass seemed to
spread over the enemy.
 Some of the warriors of Yacacolco,
whose houses were right there—the Tezcacoacatl Xiuhcozcatzin, the Tecpanecatl
Quaquatzin, Huitzitzin, and Itzcuintzin—
lost no time. They did not abandon the
women and children. With difficulty they
pressed [the Spaniards] back to another
canal at Amaxac.
 Once it happened that the Spaniards appeared at Totecco, and when they got to
where the youths' house stood, at the place
called Ayacac, they set fire to it.
 And another of the Spaniards' boats
came into Atliceuhyan, and many boats of
the Xochimilco people came in along with
it. And the warrior Temilotzin, the Tlacateccatl, stood up on an altar platform facing
the Spaniards. And the warrior Coyohuehuetzin, who had put on an eagle-jaguar
device, eagle on one side and jaguar on the
other, came in a boat from the direction of
Tolmayeccan to repulse them. Many war
boats accompanied him. He came saying,
"O warriors, up and at them, let's all get
going!" Then they all ran to their boats.
And when the Spaniards saw them, they
retreated. [The Mexica] pursued them,
coming straight to Atliceuhyan. Then the
Spaniards withdrew their boats and stationed them at Amanalco. And many people of Xochimilco died from arrows. And
when they had chased them away, [the
Spaniards] reformed, and then the warriors
came pursuing them. Coyohuehuetzin
took cover behind an altar platform. Then
he turned them around and pushed them
all the way to where the youths' house
stood in Atliceuhyan. Again [the Span-
iards] came back pursuing Coyohuehuetzin, making him jump in the water. And
then again the youth of Otomi rank, Itz-

Itzcuītzin; estos todos eran del barrio de yacacolco todos estos deffendian las entradas por que no entrasen donde estaua recogida la gente mugeres y niños, y peleando con gran perseuerancia y hizieron retraer a los ya d̄hos de la parte de otra acequia que se llama Amaxac.

district of Yacacolco, defended the entryways so they would not come in where the women and children had taken refuge, and battling with great perseverance they made the above-mentioned retreat in the direction of another canal, called Amaxac.

[fol. 71] [181] Otra uez acometieron los españoles y lleuaron a vn lugar que se llama ayacac donde estaua vna casa grande que se llamaua Telpuchcalli posieron hoego a la casa

y v̄ vergantin de los españoles por el barrio que se llama atliceuhyan cō muchas canoas que les siguierō de los amigos y vn capitan que se llamaua Coioueuetzin mexicano, que traya vnas armas vestidas la mitad dellas era vna aguila, y la otra mitad de vn tigre vino en vna canoa de hazia la parte que se llama Tolmaiecan y seguianle muchas canoas con gente armada luego començo a dar vozes a los suyos que començasen a pelear: y luego començaron la pelea, y los españoles se retruxeron: y este capitan con los suyos los siguian [182] y retruxeronse hazia vn lugar que se llama atliceuhia: Tambien los vergantines se retruxeron hazia la laguna deste alcance morieron muchos Xochmilcanos. Otra uez [fol. 71v] tornaron los españoles encerraronse en vn cu que se llama Mumuztli, y otra uez boluieron tras los españoles hasta donde estaua Telpuchcalli que llaman Atliceuhian: boluieron otra uez los españoles tras los indios con coioueuetzin en el acequia: reboluio vn capitan mexicano que se llamaua Itzpapalotzin otomi hizo retraer a los españoles a los vergātines: entonce censo la batalla

Again the Spaniards attacked and reached a place called Ayacac, where there is a large house called a *telpochcalli;* they set fire to the house.

One of the Spaniards' brigantines was going through the district called Atliceuhyan with many canoes of the friends following it. A Mexica captain called Coyohuehuetzin, who had on some insignia that were half an eagle and the other half a tiger, came in a canoe toward the place called Tolmayeccan, many canoes full of armed men following him. Then he began to shout to his followers to begin to fight; then the battle began, and the Spaniards withdrew. This captain with his followers pursued [182] them, and they withdrew toward a place called Atliceuhyan. The brigantines also withdrew toward the lake. In this pursuit many Xochimilca died. Another time the Spaniards returned and shut themselves up in a *cu* called Momoztli. Again they turned and pursued the Spaniards to where the *telpochcalli* was, at the place called Atliceuhyan. The Spaniards again turned on the Indians with Coyohuehuetzin at the canal. A Mexica captain called Itzpapalotzin, an Otomi [in rank], turned and made the Spaniards retreat to the brigantines. Then the battle ceased.

Auh in cuitlaoaca in momatque ca omic, ca o tehoan mic, in intlatocauh in Maiehoatzin, cenca qualani: quitoaia, Ca oanquimictique in totlatocauh Xiqual[fol. 72]nextican, tleica in oanquimictique totlatocauh. Auh in Maiehoatzin in oquima in ca qualani, in imaceoalhoan: inic quitlaqualanilia: [184] nimā quilhui in Coiovevetzin. Nachcauhtzine, tla ce xiqualquetza in tachcavan in vel tzatzi, in tlatolchicaoac, in tozcachicaoac: niman ic quivalnotzque ce tequioa, itoca: Tlamaiocatl: nec quinaoatia in Maiehoatzin: quilhuia. Tla xoniauh, tla xiquimonilhui in cuitlaoaca: Cuitlavacae, onechoaliva in amotlatocauh in Maiehoatzin, xoconittacan nechca moquetzticac mumuzco. Auh in oquicacque cuitlaoaca, quivalitoque. Ca amo, ca oanquimictique: nec quimonilhuia. Ca amo miqui, vel, xocottacan ie in nechca icac: yoan quivalitoa, ca amo nimiqui, ma itla nechitlacalhuiti, in notēçac, in nochalchiuh, [fol. 72v] in notlaviz: auh in ocontzonquixti in itlatol, nec tlacaoaca: niman ie ic necalioa, nec quivaltoca. Auh in tianquizco in vmpa copalnamacoian, aiaxcan in mocauh, vncā vecaoac in iauiotl.

Auh ceppa tecentlatalhuique in toiaovan in Tliliuhquitepeca, atetemoleque: ie quimottilique in vpitzactli in calla quiztacac, yiovi catca ce pilli: itoca, Tlacatzin. Auh in ie calaqui in toiaovan: nec quintoca in tiiacaoan. Auh ce tlacatl tiacauh, tequioa, itoca Tlapanecatl, atezcapā ichan catca: nec quinoalnamiqui, nimā ic quicuitivetzque in toiaovan: auh in tiiacavan, nimā ipan

papalotzin, let go; he too had put on a device. Then he chased them, rolling them up like mud, scattering them into the boats. [183] Then they left and disappeared.

And the people of Cuitlahuac, who thought that their ruler, Mayehuatzin, had died, that he had died along with the others, were very angry, and said, "You have killed our ruler. Show him to us. Why have you killed our ruler?" But when Mayehuatzin found out his subjects were angry, [because it made him angry], [184] then he said to Coyohuehuetzin, "My elder brother, please get one of the war leaders who can shout, who has a strong voice." Then they summoned a seasoned warrior named Tlamayocatl, and Mayehuatzin gave him instructions, saying to him, "Go over there and say to the people of Cuitlahuac, 'O people of Cuitlahuac, your ruler Mayehuatzin has sent me. Look at him standing over there at the altar platform.' " When the people of Cuitlahuac heard it, they replied, "No, you have killed him." Then he said to them, "He is not dead. Look well at the person standing there." And [Mayehuatzin] replied, "I am not dead; may they not let my lip pendant, my green-stones, and my device come to harm." When he finished his statement, there was a clamor. Then fighting began, and [the enemy] came chasing [the Mexica]. In the marketplace, at Copalnamacoyan, the battle did not halt soon; it lasted a long time there.

Once our enemies, the people of Tliliuhquitepec and Atetemollan, had a conference about us. They had already seen a narrow roadway going among the houses, the passageway of a nobleman named Tlacatzin. When our enemies went in there, the warriors pursued them. And a warrior, a seasoned warrior named Tlappanecatl, from Atezcapan, came to face them. Then

y los del pueblo de Cuitlaoac pensando
que su señor que se llamaua Maieoatzin
quedaua muerto con los demas, y enoja-
ronse mucho contra los Mexicanos entre
los quales estaua señor dixeron por que
aveys muerto a n̄ro señor? Y su señor que
estaua viuo como supo que sus basallos estauan enojados hablo al capitan Coioueuetzin y dixole? Señor hermano bus [185] a
vno de sus soldados valientes que tenia
recia voz: y coioueuetzin llamo a vn capitan que se llamaua Tlamaiocatl y el señor
de cuitlaoac dixole, ve y di a mis basallos
que yo te embio para que les digas que
estoy biuo [fol. 72] y que mire aca y verme
an. Como aquel Capitan hablo a los de
cuitlaoac, y les dixo lo que les auia mandado el señor Maiehoatzin ellos no quisi-
eron creerle mas dixeron que le auian
muerto y que no era verdad lo que les
dezian y el otro respondio no es muerto
como pensays mirad [fol. 72v] y verleys
adonde esta viuo que alli se puso para que
le veays y hablo el señor de Cuitlaoac y
dixo mirad que no me perdays nada de mis
atauios y joyas y armas que viuo estoy.
Como dixo estas palabras el señor de Cuitlaoac luego los indios amigos de los españoles comencaron [186] a dar grita y a pelear contra los mexicanos y metieronlos
hasta dentro del tianquiz adonde se vende
el copal, y alli pelearon gran rato.

Otra uez entraron en consejo n̄ros
enemigos para acometernos y destruyrnos
en especial los otomies de tlaxcalla: y otros
capitanes muchos y determinaron de entrar
por vna calle que estaua junto donde es
agora sanct m̄īn: y la calle yva derecho a
vna casa de vn pilli Tlatilulcano que se llamaua Tlacatzin, y luego los salieron al encuentro los del tlatilulco vn capitan que se

The people from the settlement of Cuitlahuac, thinking that their lord named
Mayehuatzin was dead along with the rest,
grew very angry with the Mexica, among
whom their lord was. They said, "Why
have you killed our lord?" When their
lord, who was alive, heard that his vassals
were angry, he spoke to the captain Coyohuehuetzin, saying to him, "Lord brother,
seek out [185] one of your brave soldiers who
has a strong voice." Coyohuehuetzin summoned a captain called Tlamayocatl, and
the lord of Cuitlahuac told him, "Go and
tell my vassals that I am sending you to tell
them I am alive, and that they should look
this way and they will see me." When that
captain spoke to the people from Cuitlahuac and told them what the lord Mayehuatzin had ordered them, they would not
believe him, but said that they had killed
him and that what they were telling them
was not true. The other answered, "He is
not dead as you think; look and you will
see him where he is, alive, for he placed
himself there so you would see him." The
lord of Cuitlahuac spoke and said, "Watch
that you don't lose any of my adornments,
jewels, and insignia, for I am alive." When
the lord of Cuitlahuac said these words,
the Indian friends of the Spaniards began [186] to shout and combat the Mexica,
and they forced them inside the *tiánquiz*
where copal is sold; there the battle went
on for a long while.

Again our enemies, especially the Otomi of Tlaxcala along with many other captains, consulted about attacking and destroying us. They decided to enter along a
street that was next to where San Martín is
now; the street went straight to the house
of a Tlatelolco *pilli* called Tlacatzin. Then
the Tlatelolca went out to meet them, a
captain called Tlappanecatl going ahead,

ommotepeuhque, quinmintivi in toiaovan: nimã ic contetlaçaltito in cacica tiiacauh. Auh in toiaovan nec quivalmetzvitecque: vncã in inez[fol. 73]coaian: [187] niman ic iaque, ōmocacauhque in micali.

our enemies quickly seized him. But the warriors hurled themselves upon our enemies, shooting arrows at them, and then they made those who had captured the warrior let him go. But then our enemies hit him on the thigh [at the place where it is bled (in ritual bleeding)]. [187] Then they stopped fighting and left.

## 38

Inic cempoalli oncaxtolli omei capitulo: vncã mitoa in quenin españoles quitlalique quauhtematlatl, inic quinpoiomictizquia in tlatilulca.

Auh niman in iehoan Españoles, quitlalique in quauhtematlatl in mumuzticpac, inic quintepachozq̄ in macevaltin. Auh in oquicencauhque, in ie quitlaçazque, cenca cololhuitinemi, cēca ommapiloa, quinmapilhuia in macevalti, ommapiloa in vmpa omocenquixtiq̄ in amaxac, in ie ixquich macevalli, cenca quimōmottitia, ommaçoa in Españoles, inic impan contlaçazque conmaiavizque, in iuhqui quintematlavizque: nec quimalacachoa nec quitevilacachoa: nimã ic meoatiquetz in quauhtemalacatl in iquauhio. Auh in tetl [fol. 73v] amo vel vmpa ia in ipã macevalli, çan ie icampa iteputzco in vetzito tianquiztli xumolco.

Auh ic vncã mixnamicque in iuh nezque Españoles iuhquin mixmapilxixili, cenca chachalaca. Auh in quauhtematlatl mocuecuepa avic iaiauh, çan ivian motlamelauhcaquetztia: niman ic vel nez in iiacac catca in tematlatl cenca tomaoac in mecatl, inic mecaio: niman ic quitocaiotique quauhtematlatl:

auh ie no ceppa quicentlazque in Españoles: yoã in ixquich tlaxcaltecatl, nimã ie ic motecpana in iacaculco, yoan tecpancaltitlan yoan copalnamacoia: nimã ie vmpa atecocolecan quiniacana in ixquich techiaoalotoc, cencan ivian in onotiui.

Thirty-eighth chapter, where it is said how the Spaniards installed a catapult with which they were going to kill the Tlatelolca by stealth.

And then those Spaniards installed a catapult on top of an altar platform with which to hurl stones at the people. And when they had it ready and were about to shoot it off, they gathered all around it, vigorously pointing their fingers, pointing at the people, pointing to where all the people were assembled at Amaxac, showing them to each other. The Spaniards spread out their arms, [showing] how they would shoot and hurl it at them, as if they were using a sling on them. Then they wound it up, then the arm of the catapult rose up. But the stone did not land on the people, but fell behind the marketplace at Xomolco.

Because of that the Spaniards there argued among themselves. They looked as if they were jabbing their fingers in one another's faces, chattering a great deal. And the catapult kept returning back and forth, going one way and then the other; bit by bit it righted itself. Then it could be seen clearly that there was a stone sling at its point, attached with very thick rope. Then because of that they named it a "wooden sling."

And again they sent out the Spaniards and all the Tlaxcalans. Then they formed up at Yacacolco, Tecpancaltitlan, and Copalnamacoyan. Then at Atecocolecan [the Spaniards] led all those who surrounded us; very slowly they proceeded.

llamaua tlappanecatl que yua delante pero los que yuan con el arrojaronse sobre los enemigos con gran furia y tomaronles al capitan que lleuauan preso que se llamaua Tlappanecatl pero escapo con vna herida en vna pierna: y ceso la guerra por entonce.

but those who went with him hurled themselves at the enemy with great fury, and the captain called Tlappanecatl was captured and was being carried away prisoner, but he escaped, with a wound in a leg. For then the fighting stopped.

## 38

[fol. 73]Capitulo .38. del trabuco que hizieron los españoles, para conq̃star a los del Tlatilulco.

Como los indios mexicanos, todos estauan recogidos, en vn barrio que se llama Amaxac; y no los podian entrar: ordenaron de hazer vn trabuco, y armaronle encima de vn cu, q̃ estaua en el tianquiz, que llaman mumuztli:[188] y como soltaron la piedra, no lleuo adonde estaua la gente, cayo mucho mas atras, junto a la orilla del tianquiz,

Chapter Thirty-eight, of the catapult that the Spaniards made to conquer the Tlatelolca.

When the Mexica Indians had all taken refuge in a district called Amaxac and they could not get at them, they ordered a catapult to be built and set it up on top of a *cu* that was in the *tiánquiz*, called a *momoztli*.[188] When they launched a stone, it did not land where the people were but fell much farther back, next to the edge of the *tiánquiz*.

y como salio el tiro en vacio, començaron los españoles a reñir entre si.

Como vieron que por via del trabuco no pudian hazer nada determinaronse acometer al fuerte adonde estauan los mexicanos y pusieronse todos en ordenança ordenaron sus esquadrones y començaron a yr contra el fuerte y los mexicanos como los vieron yr ascondianse por miedo del artilleria y los españoles yuã [fol. 73v] poco a poco llegandose al fuerte muy bien ordenados y muy juntos.

As the shot hit nothing, the Spaniards began to argue among themselves.

When they saw that they could achieve nothing by means of the catapult, they decided to attack the stronghold where the Mexica were. They put themselves in proper order, arranging their squadrons, and began to move against the stronghold. When they saw them coming, the Mexica hid themselves for fear of the artillery, and the Spaniards went along bit by bit, in very good order and closely spaced, approaching the stronghold.

Auh in tiiacaoan valmomātivi, vel mochi-
chicaoa, vel moquichquetza, aiac tla-
cue[fol. 74]cuetlaxoa, aiac tlacioa-
tlamachtia: quitoa. Xioalnenemican
tiiacavane, aquique in tenitotonti, tlalhuicatotonti. Auh in tiiacavan avic vivi,
ixtlapalhuivi, aocac tlamelauhca icac, motlamelauhcaquetza

(auh miecpa motlacacuepaia in Españoles, amo monextiaia in iuh mochichioa nican tlaca: no iuh mochichioaia,
tlaviztli cōmaquiaia, tilmatli pani quimol-
piliaia, inic mixpoloaia, çan mote-
toctitivitz, çan ic quiteimachitia, in o aca
quiminque, nepacholo, tlaltech viloa,
cenca tlachialo, cenca mixpepetza [189] in
campa ie vallauh, in campa ie valitztiuh in
tepuzmitl, vel mimati, vel motlachielia in
tiiacaoan in Tlatilulca:)


Auh cencan yiolic in techxocotivi, in
techcaltechpachotivi. Auh in copalnamacoian in ipan vtli amaxac [fol. 74v]
cenca netech pachiuhtiuh in chimalli,
moquanamictiuh.
Auh ce tlacatl itoca catca Chalchiuhtepeoa, quimotocti tepantli, vncā in
amaxac. Auh in iehoatl in ca mexicatl
tlatilucatl: [190] auh cenca quimottilia in
cavallo inic quixiliz: auh in oquixil cavallo:
niman ic valmotzineuh in Español: niman
ic caantiquizque in icnivan, niman ic quinteputztique, çan much ieoātin in tiiacavan,
yoan in pipiltin, intech ietiquizq̄ nec imi-
campa quinteputztique, ic ie no ceppa
quinquetzato in copalnamacoian, in vncan
tenamitl onoca: nec ic onceceuh, viviloac,
cacalacoac.
Auh ceppa muchiuh in ixquich in techiaoalotoc: amo no iehoan in españoles:
cenqui[fol. 75]çato in vmpa Teteuhtitlan
oc ioan in momanato: nimā ie ic tlaatzupa,
catzupa in atezcatl in itoca Tlaixcuipā iuhquin moquequeztinemi ixquich tetl quitqui, ixquich quavitl, tlaquetzalli, tlaixquatl,

And the [Mexica] warriors came in formation, working up their spirits, taking a
manly posture; no one was faint of heart,
no one was like a woman. They said,
"Come running, o warriors! Who are
these little barbarians, these little backlanders?" And the warriors went this way and
that, sideways; no one stood straight, raised
up straight.

(And often the Spaniards changed their
appearance, not showing themselves. They
got themselves up as the local people do,
putting on devices, tying cloaks on to disguise themselves, hiding behind the others.
The only way they could be recognized
was when they shot someone. Then everyone crouched down and hit the
ground; everyone looked and searched
closely [189] to see where the iron bolt came
from, which way it was aimed. The Tlatelolca warriors were very alert, kept very
good watch.)

Very slowly they went along throwing
us back, pushing us against the wall. And at
Copalnamacoyan, on the Amaxac road,
the weapons clashed against one another,
there was a head-on encounter.
And in Amaxac a person whose name
was Chalchiuhtepehua took shelter behind
a wall. He was one of the Mexica from
Tlatelolco. [190] He looked closely at a horse
in order to spear it, and when he speared it,
the Spaniard was unhorsed. Then his companions quickly seized him. Then all the
warriors and noblemen went after them,
keeping close to them and following behind them. They forced them back again
to Copalnamacoyan, where the wall stood.
Then the fighting paused; everyone went
away and entered his quarters.
Once it happened that all those who
were surrounding us, not including the
Spaniards, went and assembled at Teteuhtitlan; it was still dark when they took
position. Then they began filling in the
waters, filling in a small lake called Tlaixcuipan. They seemed to go jostling one

[fol. 74v] Y vno de los mexicanos del tlatilulco que se llamaua chalchiuhtepeoa, pusose en celada, con otros soldados que lleuauan consigo com proposito de herir a los cauallos: y como llegaron los españoles adonde estaua la celada hizieron[191] a vn cauallo, luego el español cayo en tierra: y los mexicanos le tomaron, y luego salieron todos, porque salieron todos los mexicanos valientes que estauã en el fuerte y hizieron grã daño en ellos en los amigos de los españoles: y ansi se retruxeron. Otra uez al tianquez al lugar donde llaman Copalnamacoyan adonde estaua vn baluarte:

One of the Mexica of Tlatelolco, called Chalchiuhtepehua, laid an ambush, together with other soldiers he had with him, with the intention of wounding the horses. When the Spaniards reached the place of the ambush, they wounded[191] a horse; then the Spaniard fell to the ground, and the Mexica captured him. Then they all sallied forth, for all the brave Mexica who were in the stronghold came out, and they inflicted great damage on the Spaniards and their friends, and thus they withdrew again to the *tiánquiz,* to the place called Copalnamacoyan, where there was a bulwark.

despues desto todos los indios enemigos de los mexicanos que tenian cercados a los mexicanos concertarõ de cegar vna laguna que les haziã mucho embaraço para entrar al fuerte de los mexicanos llamauase esta laguna tlayxcuipã que estaua cerca donde esta agora la yglesia de sancta lucia: y ansi

After this all the Indians who were enemies of the Mexica and who had the Mexica besieged agreed to fill up a lake that was greatly impeding their access to the stronghold of the Mexica. This lake was called Tlaixcuipan and was close to where the church of Santa Lucía is now. Thus the

xamitl, tenacaztli .&. chachalacatinemi, teuhtli quiquetztinemi: in ipampa iuh quichiuhca, ca iuh quilnamiquia, iuh quimopictiaia, inic quinnamoiezque in macevalti in otentoque in onoque in ipan vtli tepeiacac iaticac.

Auh in oquittaque tiiacaoan in ie tlein quichioa, quimopictia: niman ie ic quinemilia in quenin vel quichioazque: auh in o vel quinemilique, niman ie ic ce vitz in acalli, cencā yiolic, in quitlanelhuitivitze, contecaco vtenco, amo valneztia in tlaviztli, çan vallapachiuh[fol. 75v]tia, ie no ce valla, çan ie no ivi in iiolic quivallanelhuitiaque: auh ie no ceppa valla vme in acalli ic onnauhtetix. Nimā ic valmevatiquetz vntetl quauhtli, ontetl ocelutl: inic ce quauhtli, iehoatl in Topātemoctzin: inic vme, iehoatl in Tlacutzin. Auh inic ce ocelutl iehoatl in Temilotzin: inic vme, iehoatl in Coiovevetzin: nimā ie ic oneoa: ce ocelutl, ce quauhtli, quintequitlanelhuia, iuhquin patlani acalli, vmpa tlamattiuh in teteuhtitlan in q̓niacacotonazque, in quinviltequizque. Auh in iquac oiaque ie no ceppa no contlazque in omentin no ce quauhtli, auh no ce ocelutl quintlacomotlazque: auh in iquac ie vi nec tlapitzalo, niman ie ic tenamoielo: auh ceq̓ntin nipa quiniacatzacuilico [fol. 76] in tiiacaoan.

Auh in oquittaque in toiaovan motlalozquia miec in atlan mic, in polacq̄ in illacque, ça netech ommotiliniaia, iuhquin aocmo quimati, ça iuhquin çoçotlaoa ça iuhquin chachapantivetzi, in oc nen motlaloznequi ça quauhcamac activetzi, tevivilano, omach moçoquineloque, omach moçoquipetzcoque, vel chachaquanque, vel popolacque, vel miec in ixpoliuh, oncan vel tonacamicoac: auh çayioppa in vncā ontonacamicque in toiaovan in nepapan tlaca: auh in iquac ommiquico in toiaovan, in imuztlaioc, ça cactimanca:

another, some carrying stone, some wood, pillars, door lintels, adobes, corner stones, etc. They went about chattering, raising the dust. The reason they did it was that it occurred to them and they imagined that they would plunder the common people who lived beside the road going to Tepeyacac.

And when the [Mexica] warriors saw what they were doing and what their intention was, they considered what they could do. And when they considered well, a boat was brought; they came poling it very slowly, stationing it at the side of the road. No warrior's device could be seen; everything was just covered over. Then another was brought; they came poling it slowly in the same way, and again two more boats were brought, making four. Then two eagle [warriors] and two jaguar [warriors] rose up. The first eagle was Topantemoctzin and the second Tlacotzin. The first jaguar was Temilotzin, and the second Coyohuehuetzin. Then they got started. They vigorously poled one jaguar and one eagle. The boats seemed to fly, heading for Teteuhtitlan to cut them off, to head them off. And when they had gone, again they dispatched two, also one eagle and one jaguar, to throw themselves into their midst. And when they went, wind instruments were played. Then people were plundered, but the warriors cut off some [of the enemy] on the other side.

When our enemies saw this, they tried to flee. Many died in the water, sinking and submerging, just pulling at one another, as though they had lost their senses and were fainting. They seemed to fall splattering; when they tried to flee they just fell between the logs. When they were dragged out they were completely covered with mud, slimy with mud, entirely drowned. A great many perished, there was a great abundance of deaths. This was the only time that the different [local] people who were our enemies died in great

otro dia muy de mañana cargaronse de pie- dras y de tierra y de adoues y de manera [192] [fol. 75] de las casas que rrocauā [193] y robarō todas las casas que estauan por alli cerca

visto los mexicanos lo que hazian los enemigos sacarō ascondidamente quatro canoas con gente de guerra quatro capi- tanes con ellos el vno que se llamaua Topantemoctzin, y el otro Tlacotzin, y el otro temilotzin, y el quarto que se llamaua Coioueuetzin. Como estuuieron a punto: començaron a remar reciamēte, y fueron contra los que cegauan la laguna dos canoas por la vna parte y otras dos por la otra.

[fol. 75v] Luego començaron a pelear, y muchos murierō, vnus en el agua, otros en tierra, otros echauā a huyr, y cayan entre los maderos, que auian puesto: y de alli los sacauā, arrastrando los mexicanos, llenos de lodo, murieron muchos en este recuentro aquel dia:

[fol. 76] Y otro dia luego los españoles, acometieron el fuerte, que era donde llamā amaxac, donde esta la yglesia de la Cōcep- cion: y pelearon gran rato, y finalmente llegaron adonde estaua el vagaxe de los mexicanos, y como lle[fol. 76v]garon a vna casa grande que se llama Techpuchcalli [195] adonde estaua mucha gente subieronse a las açoteas de aquella casa y todos los que estauan en la casa dieron consigo en el agua por huyr: y vn capitan que se llamaua Vi- tziloatzin con muchos soldados que estaua sobre los tlapancos comēçaron a restir [196] a los españoles poniendose por muro para que no pasasen adōde estaua el vagaxe: y los españoles arrojaronse contra ellos y comēçaron a matar en ellos y a destrozarlos y salieron otros soldados en fabor de aque- llos de manera que no podierō los es- pañoles pasar adonde queriā y retrux- eronse:

next day very early in the morning they loaded themselves up with stones, earth, adobe bricks, and wood [192] from the houses they had demolished, [193] and they robbed all the houses that were in that vi- cinity.

When the Mexica saw what the enemy was doing, they secretly got out four canoes full of warriors under four captains, one of whom was called Topantemoctzin, another Tlacotzin, another Temilotzin, and the fourth Coyohuehuetzin. When they were ready, they began to paddle [pole] with vigor, and with two canoes on one side, and the other two on the other, they went against those who were filling in the lake.

Then they began the battle, and many died, some in the water, some on land. Others started to flee and fell between the timbers that they had put in place. The Mexica dragged them from there, full of mud. Many died in the encounter of that day.

Then the next day the Spaniards at- tacked the stronghold, at the place they call Amaxac, where the church of Concepción is, and they fought for a long while, until finally they reached the place where the Mexica's baggage was. When they reached a large house called a *telpochcalli*, [195] where there were many people, they climbed up on the roof terraces of that house, and all who were inside the house threw them- selves into the water to get away. A captain called Huitzilhuatzin, with many soldiers who were on the *tlapancos*, began to re- sist [196] the Spaniards, making of themselves a barrier so they could not get to where the baggage was. The Spaniards hurled them- selves upon them and began to kill some of them and destroy them, but other soldiers sallied forth in their favor, so that the Spaniards could not get where they wanted to, and withdrew.

auh ic vallaque in Españoles in vncan amaxac, vel vmpa acito, in vmpa tlantoque in macevaltin, vel techiaoaloque, vel motetemmā in iauiotl, in vel vncā amaxac [fol. 76v] yoan ipan vtli in tepeiacac iaticac: nimā ic calaquito in telpuchcali:[194] moteneoa veican: iehica ca vncan monechicoaia in ixquich telpuchtli: niman ic tlecoque in tlapanco. Auh in ixquich maceoalli: niman ie ic ommotepeoa in icampa Telpuchcalli, nec atla onnetepevalo. Auh ce vei tiiacauh quachic itoca, Vitzilhoatzin tlapanco moquetz, icpac in telpuchcalli, oc iuhquin tenamitl muchiuh, oc ic achi contocac in macevalli. Auh in Españoles: nimā ic impā ommotepeuhque, impan ommotquique: niman ie ic quivivitequi, quitlatlapana, quitzeltilia: niman ic ie no ceppa quivallazque in tiiacaoan: auh niman ic quicauhtiquizque in tiiacauh: niman ic conanato, amo tel vel mic, nimā ic iaque, cactimoman.

Auh in diablome imixip[fol. 77]tlavan: vncan contlecavique, contlatlatique. Auh in tiiacavan, oc nen valmomantivi. tel amo ma quinmina in cioa: çan iehoantin in oquichicativitze:[197] auh in necacaoaloc ça achiton tonatiuh.

Auh inic navilhuitl çan ie no ivi in mochiuh cemolinque in toiaovan: in vmpa onoc macevalli vmpa tlamattivi in Españoles, cencan ivian in iativi. Auh in tiiacauh Tlacateccatl in Temilotzin, oc nen quinmopachiviaia, tepantli quimotocti Quauhtli ipan quizticac, itepuzmaquauh ieticac, inic quincotonazquia: auh in oquittac in aoccampa veli, nimā ic atlan valmomaiauh, axotlatiuh, cenca tlacavaca: vncan ie no ceppa motetemmā in iauiotl, çan vncan acito: vel cemilhuitl in manca iauiotl.

numbers there. And the day after our enemies had died, everything lay silent.

And at this time the Spaniards came to Amaxac; they reached the very place in which the common people lay in extremity. They fully surrounded us, and there was fierce battle, right in Amaxac and on the road going to Tepeyacac. Then [the Spaniards] went into the youths' house[194] called Hueican, because all the youths were gathered there, and then they climbed up to the roof. And then all the common people scattered behind the youths' house; then everyone scattered into the water. And one great warrior, a scraped-head named Huitzilhuatzin, stood up on the roof above the youths' house. He was like a bulwark, and the people followed him for a little while. But then the Spaniards fell upon them, and they struck him, breaking him apart, cutting him to pieces. Then [the Mexica] let loose with the warriors again and made them let go of the warrior [Huitzilhuatzin]. Then they took him; he was not quite dead. Then they went away, and there was silence.

Then [the Spaniards] set fire to and burned the images of devils there. The warriors still tried to keep in formation. But [the Spaniards] did not shoot the women, only those who came standing up as men.[197] When the fighting stopped, there was only a little sun.

And on the fourth day our enemies moved together in the same way. The Spaniards headed for where the common people were, going very slowly. And a warrior, the Tlacateccatl Temilotzin, tried to spy on them, taking shelter behind a wall. He was dressed as an eagle, and he had an iron sword with which he was going to cut them up. But when he saw that he could do nothing anywhere, he threw himself into the water, ripped into the water. There was a great clamor. Then there was fierce fighting again; it went no

y otro dia los españoles pegaron hoego aquella casa en la qual auia muchas estatuas de los ydolos los españoles peleauā contra los mexicanos ya dentro de su fuerte: y a las mugeres, y niños no los hazian mal sino a los hōbres que peleauan: aquel dia despartio la noche la pelea.

Y otro dia los españoles y todos los amigos començaron de [198] caminar hazia dōde estauan los mexicanos en su fuerte: y los mexicanos quiseron hazer [fol. 77] vna celada para resistir a los españoles la entrada y no pudieron vieronlos: y ansi los españoles començaron a pelear casi vn dia duro la pelea a la noche retruxeronse a sus estancias

The next day the Spaniards set fire to that house, in which there were many statues of idols. The Spaniards were now battling against the Mexica inside their stronghold. They did no harm to the women and children, but only to the men who were fighting. That day night put an end to the battle.

The next day the Spaniards and all their friends began [198] to move toward where the Mexica were in their stronghold. The Mexica tried to make an ambush to resist the Spaniards' entry, but they were unable to; they were seen, so the Spaniards began the battle. The fighting lasted almost all day; at night they withdrew to their quarters.

Auh in otlatvic, in ie ic macuil[fol. 77v]ilhuitl: ie no ceppa vel quicētlaz in toiaouh in Españoles: yoan in ixquich in techiaoalotoc, vel cemolin, vel techiavaloque, techololhuique, aocac campa vel huia vel nexoxocolo, vel nepapatzolo, vel miequintin patzmicque, nequequeçaloc. Auh in cenca ie intech onaci, ce civatl quivallatequia, quimixatequia, quimixapapatza in toiaovan.

Auh in tlatoani in Quauhtemoctzin yoan in tiiacavan in Coiovevetzi in Temilotzin, Topantemoctzin. Auelitoctzin. Mixcoatlailotlactzin. Tlacutzin, Petlauhtzin. Nimā ic conanq̄ ce vei tiacauh, itoca Tlapaltecatl opuchtzin coatlan ichā niman ie ic quichichioa, conaquique, in quetzalteculotl: itlaviz catca in Auitzotzin: quito in Quauhtemoctzin. Inin tlaviztli, itlaviz catca [fol. 78] in noteichiuhcauh [200] in notatzi Auitzotzin, ma iehoatl conitqui ma ipan ommiqui ma cōtemaviçolti ma ipan tetlattiti ma quittacan in toiaovan ma quimaviçocan. Auh in oconaquique vel temamauhti, vel maviztic in neci: auh navinti in quinnavatique in quivalpalevitiazque, in quivallamatilitiazque, quivalmacaque in imiuh catca tlacateculotl, tlacumitl, iacatecpaio. Auh inic iuh quichiuhque in, iuhquin ma intlapoal muchiuh in tlatoque in Mexica:

farther ⟨than Amaxac⟩. The battle lasted a full day.

And when it dawned on the fifth day, our enemies the Spaniards and all who surrounded us again attacked all together; they surrounded us entirely, herded us together. There was no place to go; people shoved, pressed, and trampled one another; many died in the press. But one woman came to very close quarters with our enemies, throwing water at them, throwing water in their faces, making it stream down their faces.

And then the ruler Quauhtemoctzin and the warriors Coyohuehuetzin, Temilotzin, Topantemoctzin, the Mixcoatlailotlac Ahuelitoctzin, Tlacotzin, and Petlauhtzin took a great warrior named Tlapaltecatl opochtzin, whose home was in Coatlan, and outfitted him, dressing him in a quetzal-owl costume. That had been the device of Ahuitzotl. Quauhtemoctzin said, "This was the device of my progenitor,[200] my father Ahuitzotl. Let him wear it, let him die in it. Let him dazzle people with it, let him show them something; let our enemies see and admire it." When they put it on him he looked very frightening and splendid. And they ordered four [others] to come helping him, to accompany him. They gave him the darts of the devil, darts of wooden rods with flint tips. And the reason they did this was that it was as though the fate of the rulers of the Mexica were being determined.

y a la mañana determinaron de romper y cercaronlos de todas partes de manera que por ninguna parte podian salir y estãdo en esta estrechura murieron muchos ningunos [199] y mugeres pisados y acozeados y estando en esta pelea las mugeres tambien peleauan cegando a los contrarios con el agua de las acequias arrojandosela con los remos.

Estando ya los mexicanos acosados de todas partes de los enemigos acordaron de tomar pronostico o aguero si era ya acabada su ventura o si los quedaua lugar de escapar de aquel grã peligro en que estauã: y hablo el señor de mexico que se llamaua Quauhtemoctzin, y dixo a los p̃ncipales que con el estauã el vno de los quales se llamaua Coioueuetzin, y otro Temilotzin, y otro Topã[fol. 77v]temoctzin, y otro Auelitoctzin, y otro Miscoatlaylotlactzin, y otro Tlacotzin, y otro Petlauhtzin hagamus esperiencia a uer si podemos escapar deste peligro ẽ que estamus venga vno de los mas valientes que ay entre nosotros y vistase las armas y diuisas que eran de mi padre Auitzotzin: luego llamaron a vn mancebo valiente hombre que se llamaua Tlapaltecatl opuchtzin que era del barrio de coatlan donde es agora la perrocha [201] de sᵃ catalina en el tlatilulco: aquel le hablo el señor Quauhtemoctzin y le dixo. Veys aqui estas armas que se llaman Quetzalteculotl que eran armas de mi padre Avitzotzin vistetelas y pelea con ellas mataras algunos: vean estas armas n̄ros enemigos podra ser que se espanten en verlas: y como se las vistieron parecio vna cosa espantable y mãdaron a quatro capitanes que fuesẽ delante del de cada parte dos aq̃l que yua armado con las armas de Auitzotzin en las quales tenian gran aguero que saliendo luego [fol. 78] los enemigos auian de huyr: dierõle Tambien el arco y la saeta de vitzilobuchtli que tenian tanbien guardado por

In the morning they decided to let loose full force, and they surrounded them on all sides so that they could not get out anywhere. Being so hemmed in, many children [198] and women died, trampled and kicked. Finding themselves in this battle, the women fought too, blinding their enemies with water from the canals, splashing it on them with paddles.

With the Mexica now pressed on all sides by the foe, they agreed to test through prognostication or omens whether their fate were sealed or they still had room to escape from the great danger confronting them. The lord of Mexico, called Quauhtemoctzin, spoke and said to the leaders with him, one of whom was called Coyohuchuetzin, another Temilotzin, another Topantemoctzin, another Ahuelitoctzin, another Mixcoatlailotlactzin, another Tlacotzin, and another Petlauhtzin, "Let us make an experiment to see if we can escape this danger in which we find ourselves. Let one of the most valiant among us come and don the arms and insignia that belonged to my father Ahuitzotzin." Then they called a youth, a man of courage, called Tlapaltecatl Opochtzin, who was from the district of Coatlan in Tlatelolco, where the parish [201] of Santa Catalina is now. The lord Quauhtemoctzin spoke to him, telling him, "You see here this warrior's costume, called a *quetzaltecolotl,* which was the costume of my father Ahuitzotzin. Put it on; fight in it, and you will kill some people. Let our enemies see this costume; it could be that they will be frightened by seeing it." When they dressed him in it, he appeared a frightening spectacle. They ordered four captains to go ahead of him, two on each side of the one in the costume of Ahuitzotzin, being very confident that with the power of the omen, when he appeared the enemy would flee. They also gave him the

quito in Civacoatl Tlacutzin. Mexicae tlatilulcae, atlei inic mexico ocatca, inic ommanca mexicaiutl: in mitoa in vncan inavatil in vitzilobuchtli in tepā quitlaça ca çan iee in xiuhcoatl, in mamalhoaztli in o tepā quitlaztinenca in toiaupan in ie anconcui Mexicae in inaoatil in mitl: çan nimā vm[fol. 78v]pa anquitlachieltizque in īvicpa toiaovan, amo çan tlalpan anquimaiavizque cenca intech in anquitlaçazque: auh intla ce, anoço vme mominaz: auh in ano ce, anoço vme in maçiz toiaouh ca nel totlapoal, oc achitzin tinacazitztiazque, oc quenin quimonequiltiz in totecuio: [203] niman ie ic iauh in quetzalteculotl, in quetzalli iuhquin xexeliuhtiuh.

The Cihuacoatl Tlacotzin said, "O Mexica, o Tlatelolca, is there nothing left of the way it was in Mexico, of the way the Mexican state was, which was said to be the envoy of Huitzilopochtli that he sends against people, as he used to send the fire serpent, the fire drill at our enemies? O Mexica, you are taking his envoy the dart; you are to aim it only at our enemies. You are not just to cast it on the ground, but hurl it very close to them. And if one or two of them are hit, or if one or two of our enemies are captured, then it is truly our fate that for a little while longer we will ⟨find favor⟩, while our lord so wishes." [203] Then the quetzal-owl went, with the quetzal feathers waving.

Auh in oquittaque in toiaovan, iuhquin tepetl vitomi vel muchintin momauhtique in Españoles, cenca quinmauhti, iuhquin ma itla ipan quittaque: niman ic tlapanco tlecoc in quetzalteculotl. Auh in cequintin toiaovan in o vel quittaque moquetzque: niman ic quivalcuepque, quivaltocaque: ie no ceppa no quincuep quintocac in quetzalteculotl, [fol. 79] niman ie ic quinamoia in quetzalli, yoan in teucuitlatl: auh niman ic vmpa valhuetz in tlapanco, amo mic, amo quivicaque in toiaovan: ie no ieintin in axivaque in toiauvā ça ic cen ontzotzon in iauiotl [206] ic cactimoman, aoctle muchiuh: niman ic iaque in toiaovan, cactimoman, aoctle muchiuh inic oniovan.

When our enemies saw him, it was as though a mountain had fallen. Every one of the Spaniards was frightened; he intimidated them, they seemed to respect him a great deal. Then the quetzal-owl climbed up on the roof. But when some of our enemies had taken a good look at him they rose and turned him back, pursuing him. Then the quetzal-owl turned them again and pursued them. Then he snatched up the precious feathers and gold and dropped down off the roof. He did not die, and our enemies did not carry him off. Also three of our enemies were captured. At that the war stopped for good. [206] There was silence, nothing more happened. Then our enemies went away. It was silent and nothing more happened until it got dark.

Auh in imuztlaioc, çan nimā aoctle muchiuh, aocac navati, ça pachiuhtoc in macevalli. Auh in iehoantin Españoles aoc no tle ay, ça onoque, quimonitztoque in

And the next day nothing more happened at all, no one made a sound. The common people just lay collapsed. The Spaniards did nothing more either, but lay

reliquias y tenian fe en aquel arco y saeta
que quādo saliesen no podian ser vencidos
aq̄lla saeta tenia vn casquillo de pedernal

estando estos cinco puestos a punto: vn
principal mexicano que se llamaua Cioacoatl Tlacotzin, dio vozes diziendo a los
cinco que estauan a punto O mexicanos o
tlatilulcanos el fundamento y fortaleza de
los mexicanos en Vitzilobuchtli ess esta [202]
el qual arrojaua sobre los enemigos su saeta
que se llamaua Xiuhcoatl y mamaloaztli la
misma saeta lleuays agora vosotros que es
aguero de todos nosotros mirad que la en-
dereçays contra v̄ros enemigos para que
haga tiro y no se pierda en valde y si por
uentura con ella matardes o captiuardes alguno tenemos cendidumbre [204] y pronostico que no nos perderemos desta uez sino
que [fol. 78v] quiere n̄ro dios ayudarnos y
dh̄as estas palabras aquel que estaua armado
con los otros quatro començaron a yr contra los enemigos:

y los enemigos como los vieron asi los
españoles como los indios cayolos grāde espanto no los parecio cosa humana y aquel
que yua armado cō quetzalteculotl subiose
a vna açotea: y los enemigos pararonse a
mirarle; que cosa era aquella y como
conozieron que era hombre y no demonio
acometieronle peleando y hizieronle huyr:
El Quetzalteculotl [205] torno tras ellos con
los que con el yuan, y hizolos huyr: y subio
otra uez en el tlapanco donde los tlaxcaltecas tenian quetzales y cosa de oro roba-
das, y tomoselas y boluio a saltar del tlapanco abaxo y no se hizo mal ninguno ni
le podieron captiuar los enemigos mas ātes
los que yuā con el capituaron tres de los
enemigos: y por entonce ceso la pelea
boluieronse todos a sus rrāchos,

y el dia siguiente Tanpoco pelearon.

bow and arrow of Huitzilopochtli, which
they had also kept as relics, and they had
faith that when that bow and arrow were
brought out, they could not be defeated.
That arrow had a head of flint.

When these five were all ready, a Mexica leader called Cihuacoatl Tlacotzin
called out, saying to the five who were
ready, "O Mexica, O Tlatelolca, the foundation and strength of the Mexica through
Huitzilopochtli is [202] that he cast at the
enemy his arrow, called *xiuhcoatl* and
*mamalhuaztli*. Now you bear the same
arrow, which is the omen for all of us. See
that you aim it against your enemies so that
it hits and does not miss. If perhaps you kill
or capture someone with it, we will have a
certain [204] sign that we will not be lost this
time, but that our god wants to help us."
After these words were said, the one who
wore the insignia, together with the other
four, began to go against the foe.

When the enemies, Spaniards as well as
Indians, saw them, great fright possessed
them; it did not seem human to them. The
one wearing the *quetzaltecolotl* device
climbed up on a roof terrace. The enemies
stopped to look at him and see what manner of thing it was; when they recognized
that it was a man and not a demon, they attacked him, giving battle, and made him
flee. The one with the *quetzaltecolotl* [205]
turned against them, with those who accompanied him, and made them flee. He
climbed on the *tlapanco* again, where the
Tlaxcalans had *quetzales* and items of gold
that they had stolen, and he took them and
leaped down from the *tlapanco* again. He
received no harm whatever, nor could the
enemies capture him; rather, those who
accompanied him captured three of the
enemy. For the time being the battle
ceased, and they all returned to their huts.

The following day they did not fight
either.

macevaltin aoctle mantoc, cencā ça onoq̄.

Auh nican moteneoa in izq̄ntin tiiaca-van, in vevei oquichtin, in vel imixco catca iauiotl, in iauteceaia in ipan icaca iauiotl. Tlacuchcalcatl, Coiovevetzin, Tzilaca-tecutli Temilotzin: in iehoantin in [fol. 79v] ca tlatilulca. Auh in tenuchca, iehoan-tin in. Cioacoatl tlacutzin, vitznaoatl Motelchiuhtzin: o ca iehoātin in, in ve-veintin tiiacavan catca in tlatilulco, yoan inic tenuchtitlan.

39

Inic cempoalli oncaxtolli onnavi capi-tulo: vncā mitoa in quenin iehoantin Me-xica in iquac o vel quincaltechpachoto in nez in mottac Eztetl: [208] iuhq̄nma ilhui-cacpa valla. Auh inic valneztia iuhquin vei tlexuchtli.

Auh in ovalioac: niman ie ic quiquiiavi, avachquiquiiavi, ie tlaquauhiova in nez tletl: in iuh mottac, in iuh nez, iuhquin il-huicacpa valla, iuhquin ecamalacutl, mo-mamalacachotiuh, motevilacachotiuh, iuhquin cuecuepocatiuh tlexuchtli, cequi vevei, ce[fol. 80]qui çan tepitoton, cequi ça iuhquin tlemoiutl, iuhquin ecatepuz-tli, [210] moquetza, cenca icoioca, tetecuica, titicuica, çan quiiavalo in atenamitl; co-ionacazco in valitztia: nimā ic ia in ane-pantla, vmpa popolivito, aiac motenvitec, aiac navat:

auh in imuztlaioc, aoc no tle muchiuh, ça onoac, çano onoque in toiaovan. Auh in capitan tlapāco vallachixtica in amaxac, Aztavatzin itlapanco, cevalcalco, tlatlapalli in cevalcalli, quimonitztica in macevaltin, cololhuitoque in Españoles, mononotz-toque.

still, looking at the people. Nothing was going on, they just lay still.

Here are mentioned all the warriors, the men of great valor, in whose countenances was war, who directed the battle and pre-sided over it: the Tlacochcalcatl Coyo-huehuetzin and the lord of Tzilacan, Temilotzin—these are Tlatilolca. And these are Tenochca: the Cihuacoatl Tla-cotzin and the Huitznahuatl Motelchiuh-tzin. These were the great warriors of Tlatelolco and Tenochtitlan.

Thirty-ninth chapter, where it is said how when [the Spaniards] had forced the Mexica to the very wall, there appeared and was seen a blood-colored fire [208] that seemed to come from the sky. It appeared like a great blazing coal as it came.

When night came, it rained and sprin-kled off and on. It was very dark when a fire appeared. It looked and appeared as if it was coming from the sky, like a whirl-wind. It went spinning around and around, turning on itself; as it went it seemed to explode into coals, some large, some small, some just like sparks. It seemed to take on the aspect of a "wind-axe." [210] It sputtered, crackled, and snapped. It cir-cled the walls at the water, heading toward Coyonacazco, then it went into the midst of the water and disappeared there. No one struck his hand against his mouth, no one uttered a sound.

And the next day, again nothing hap-pened. Everyone just lay still, and so did our enemies. And the Captain was looking down from a rooftop in Amaxac, the roof of Aztahuatzin. From a varicolored canopy he was looking out at the people. The Spaniards crowded about him, consulting with one another.

Aqui se ponen los²⁰⁷ [fol. 79] nombres de los capitanes y valientes hombres mexicanos y tlatilulcanos que se hallaron en esta guerra vno dellos era Tlacochcalcatl que quiere dezir Capitan general que se llamaua Coioueuetzin, otro Tzilacatecutli, otro Temilotzin, [fol. 79v] estos eran tlatilulcanos de los mexicanos, vno se llamaua Cioacoatl Tlacotzin, otro Vitznaoacatl, otro Motelchiuhtzin: estos eran valientes hombres de mexico, y del Tlatilulco.

Here are given the²⁰⁷ names of the captains and brave men, Mexica and Tlatelolca, who took part in this war. One of them was the Tlacochcalcatl, which means captain-general, called Coyohuehuetzin; another Tzilacateuctli, another Temilotzin; these were Tlatelolca. Of the Mexica, one was called Cihuacoatl Tlacotzin, another Huitznahuacatl, another Motelchiuhtzin. They were brave men of Mexico and of Tlatelolco.

39

Capitulo .39. de como los del Tlatilulco quando estauan cercados vieron venir huego del cielo sobre si de color de sangre.

Chapter Thirty-nine, of how the Tlatelolca, when they were encircled, saw a blood-colored fire come upon them from the sky.

El dia siguiente cerca de medianoche lluuia menudo y a desora vierõ los mexicanos vn hoego asi como torbellino que echaua de si brasas grãdes y menores y centellas muchas remolineando y respendando²⁰⁹ estallando y anduuo alrededor del cercado o corral de los mexicanos donde estauã todos cercados que se llama coyonacazco: y como vuo cer[fol. 80]cado el corral tiro derecho hazia el medio de la laguna alli desaparecio: y los mexicanos no dieron grita como soelen hazer en tales visiones todos callaron por miedo de los enemigos:

The next day, about midnight, it was drizzling, and suddenly out of nowhere the Mexica saw a fire, like a whirlwind, throwing off large and small coals, and many sparks whirling, flashing,²⁰⁹ and exploding. It went around the fence or enclosure of the Mexica, where they were all surrounded at a place called Coyonacazco; when it had circled the enclosure it shot straight toward the middle of the lake and disappeared there. The Mexica did not shout out as they usually do with such visions; they all kept quiet for fear of the enemy.

otro dia despues desto no pelearon, todos estuuieron en sus rranchos, y don hernando cortes subiose encima de vna açotea de vna casa del barrio de Amaxac; esta casa era de vn principal Tlatilulcano que se llamaua Aztaoatzin, desde aquel Tlapanco estaua mirando hazia el cercado de los enemigos: alli encima de aquel Tlapanco le tenian hecho vn pauellon colorado desde donde estaua mirãdo, y muchos españoles estauã alrededor del hablãdo los vnos cõ los otros.

The day after this they did not fight; they all stayed in their huts. Don Hernando Cortés climbed up on the roof terrace of a house in the district of Amaxac. This house belonged to a Tlatelolca leader called Aztahuatzin. From that *tlapanco* he looked toward the enclosure of the enemy; there on top of that *tlapanco* they had set up for him a red canopy from which he looked out, and many Spaniards were around him, speaking with one another.

Auh in Quauhtemoctzin; yoan in oc cequintin tlatoque. Civacoatl Tlacutzin. Tlillancalqui. vitznaoatl. Petlauhtzin. Motelchiuhtzi mexicatl. Achcauhtli, Tecutlamacazcatzin. Niman ie iehoantin in Tla[fol. 8ov]tilulco tlatoque. Tlacuchcalcatl. Coiovevetzin. Tlacateccatl. Temilotzin. Ticociavacatl. Topantemoctzin. Mixcoatlailotlactzin. Auelitoctzin, vitznaoatl. Vitzilivitzin. Tepanecatl vitzitzin: in muchintin in tlatoque, mocentlaliticatca tolmaiecan mononotztoca in quenin muchioaz in tlein tictequitizque: auh in quenin intlan toncalaquizque.

Niman ie ic quivica in Quauhtemoctzin, acaltica, çan ommote: vmētin in convicaque, itlan ietiaque. Teputzitoloc tequioa, yoan Iaztachimal ixolouh in Quauhtemoctzin. Auh ce quitlanelhuitia itoca Ceniautl: auh in iquac ie quivica in Quauhtemoctzin: nimā ie ic mochoquilia in ixquich macevalli [fol. 81] quitoque. Ie iauh in tlacatl xocoiotl in Quauhtemoctzin ie iauh quinmomacaz in teteu in Españoles.

And Quauhtemoctzin and the other rulers—the Cihuacoatl Tlacotzin, the Tlillancalqui Petlauhtzin, the Huitznahuatl Motelchiuhtzin mexicatl, the Achcauhtli Teuctlamacazqui [chief lordly priest], and then the rulers of Tlatelolco, the Tlacochcalcatl Coyohuehuetzin, the Tlacateccatl Temilotzin, the Ticocyahuacatl Topantemoctzin, the Mixcoatlailotlac Ahuelitoctzin, the Huitznahuatl Huitzilihuitzin, and the Tepanecatl Huitzitzin—all of the rulers were gathered at Tolmayeccan consulting about what was to be done, what our tribute duty should be, and how we should submit to them.

Then they took Quauhtemoctzin in a boat. In it were only two people accompanying him, going with him: Tepotzitoloc, a seasoned warrior, and Iaztachimal, Quauhtemoctzin's page, with one person who poled them along, named Cenyaotl. When they were about to take Quauhtemoctzin, all the people wept, saying, "There goes the lord Quauhtemoctzin, going to give himself to the gods, the Spaniards."

Es muy verisimile que el capitan Don hernādo cortes auia embiado muchos mensajeros al señor de mexico Quauhtemoctzin para que se rendiesen ante que los matasen a todos, pues ya no tenian ningun remedio y en este punto en que estaua agora el [fol. 8ov] negocio de la guerra es cosa muy cierta que ya el señor de mexico Quauhtemoctzin auia dado la palabra a los mensajeros de [211] capitan Don hernando cortes que se queria rendir y a este proposito se puso en el pauellon en el tlapanco: el capitan don hernādo cortes esperando a que viniese a su presencia el señor de mexico Quauhtemoctzin con los demas principales a ponerse en sus manos

y ansi estādo sobre el tlapāco Don hernādo cortes en su pauellon: El señor de mexico Quauhtemoctzin con todos los principales q̄ con el estauā vinieronse adonde estaua el marques en canoas: Quauhtemoctzin yva en vna canoa y yvan dos pajes con el que lleuauan sus armas y vno solo yva remādo en la canoa q̄ se llamaua Cenyautl: y quando le lleuauan a la presencia del capitan Don hernādo cortes començaron toda la gente mexicana que estaua en el corral diziendo. Ya ua n̄ro señor rey a ponerse en las manos de los dioses españoles.

It is very plausible that Captain don Hernando Cortés had sent many messengers to the lord of Mexico, Quauhtemoctzin, that they should surrender before they were all killed, because they no longer had any remedy. At this point in the progress of the war, it is very certain that the lord of Mexico, Quauhtemoctzin, had given his word to the messengers of[211] Captain don Hernando Cortés that he wanted to surrender, and it is for that purpose that Captain don Hernando Cortés took up position under the canopy on the *tlapanco,* waiting for Quauhtemoctzin the lord of Mexico to come into his presence with the other leaders to place himself in his hands.

With don Hernando Cortés thus on the *tlapanco* under his canopy, the lord of Mexico, Quauhtemoctzin, and all the leaders who were with him came in canoes to where the Marqués was. Quauhtemoctzin went in a canoe; two pages went with him, bearing their arms, and a single one went along paddling the canoe, called Cenyaotl. When they were taking him to see Captain don Hernando Cortés, all the Mexica who were in the enclosure began ⟨to lament⟩, saying, "Our lord king is going to place himself in the hands of the Spanish gods."

## Autor

De las cosas arriba dͪħas, parece claramente, quanto temporizo, y diximulo el capitan Don hernādo cortes: con estos mexicanos, por no los destruyr del todo, ni acabarlos de matar, porque segun lo arriba [fol. 81] dicho muchas vezes podieron acabarlos de destruyr; y no lo hizo esperando siempre a que se rendiesen para que no fuesen destruydos del todo:

## Author:

From the things said above it appears clearly how much Captain don Hernando Cortés temporized and overlooked things with these Mexica in order not to destroy them completely nor kill them all, because according to what was said above they could have finished destroying them many times, but he did not do it, always waiting for them to surrender so that they would not be completely destroyed.

Inic ompoalli capitulo vnca mitoa in
quenin iehoantin tlatilulca yoã tenuchca
yoan in intlatocauh in intlan oncalacque
Espanoles: auh in tlein muchiuh in iquac ie
intlã cate./.

Auh in oconaxitito in ocontlalhoa-
caquixtito: niman ie ic much vallachia in
Españoles, quivalanque, imatitech quivalanque in Españoles niman ie ic quitlecavia
in tlapanco ixpan conquetzato in Capitan
in iautachcauh. Auh in o ixpan conquetzato, nimã ie ic quitta, quimoottitia,
quipepepetla in Quauhtemoctzin: niman
ic itlan quitlalique yoan contlazque in
tlequiquiztli, aiac ic quimotlaque, çan
impan qui[fol. 81v]quixtique çan imicpac
quiz in macevalti: niman ic cẽtetl convicaque, concalaquique in acalli: vmpa
cõvicaque in ichan Coiovevetzin. Auh in
oacique: nimã ic tlecoque in tlapanco:
niman ie ic no ceppa temictia miec in
vncan mic: auh çã choloque, çan ic
vmpolivito in iauiotl:

nec valtzatzioa: quitoa. Ie ixquich ma
quixoa, xicmoqualtitin in quiltzintli: in o
iuh quicacque in niman ie ic oneoa in
macevalli: niman ie ic vi, çan atlan. Auh in
oquiçato vei vtli ipan, ie no ceppa cequin
vmpa quinmictia, ic qualãque in Españoles
in oc no çan cequintin quitqui in imma-
quauh yoan inchimal; in calla onoca qui-
valmelauhque in amaxac vallamelaoa, in
vncan vel [fol. 82] vmaxac: vncan xexeliuh
in macevalli, ixquich tepeiacac itztia, ixquich xoxoviltitlã itztia, ixquich nonoalco
itztia. Auh in xollocopa, yoan in maçatzin-
tamalcopa, aiac vmpa itztia.

Auh in ixquich acaltica onoca yoan in
tlapechco catca, yoan in tolmaiecan çan
atlan in iaque: in aca ixillan acitiuh in atl, in
aca ielchiquipan, in aca iquechtlan acitiuh:
auh in aca vel polaqui, in vncan vecatlan:
in pipiltzitzinti temamamalo, tlachoquiz-

Fortieth chapter, where it is said how
the Tlatelolca and Tenochca and their
ruler submitted to the Spaniards, and what
happened when they were among them.

And when they had gotten him there
and put him on land, all the Spaniards were
waiting. They came to take him; the Spaniards grasped him by the hand, took him
up to the roof, and stood him before the
Captain, the war leader. When they stood
him before him, he looked at Quauhtemoctzin, took a good look at him,
stroked his hair; then they seated him next
to him. And they fired off the guns; they
hit no one, but they aimed over the people, the [shots] just went over their heads.
Then they took a [cannon], put it in a
boat, and took it to the home of Coyohuehuetzin. When they got there, they
took it up on the roof. Then again they
killed people; many died there. But [the
Mexica] just fled, and the war came to
an end.

Then everyone shouted, saying, "It's
over! Let everyone leave! Go eat greens!"
When they heard this, the people departed; they just went into the water. But
when they went out on the highway, again
they killed some people, which angered
the Spaniards; a few of them were carrying
their shields and war clubs. Those who
lived in houses went straight to Amaxac,
where the road forks. There the people divided, some going toward Tepeyacac,
some toward Xoxohuiltitlan, some toward
Nonoalco. But no one went toward
Xoloco and Maçatzintamalco.

And all who lived in boats and on plat-
forms [in the water] and those at Tolmayeccan just went into the water. The water
came to the stomachs of some, to the
chests of others, to the necks of others, and
some sank entirely into the deep water.

Capitulo .40. de como los del Tlatilulco
se dieron a los españoles con los mexicanos
y su señor que con ellos estaua.

Desque llegaron a tierra el señor de
mexico Quauhtemoctzin, con los que con
el yuan, saltaron en tierra cerca de la casa,
donde estaua el capitan: y los españoles que
estauan cerca del agua, tomaron por las
manos a Quauhtemoctzin, amigablemente,
y lleuaronle adonde estaua el capitan Don
hernãdo cortes encima de la açotea: y
como llego adonde estaua el capitan, luego
el le abraço, y mostro muchas señales de
amor al dicho Quauhtemoctzin, y todos
los españoles le estauã mirãdo con grã
alegria: y luego soltaron todos los tiros por
alegria de la [fol. 81v] conclusion de la
guerra, quando esto acontescio salieron dos
canoas de mexicanos y entraron en la casa
de vn principal que se llamaua Coioueuetzin donde estauan indios Tlaxcaltecas y
reboluieronse los vnos con los otros y
murieron alli algunos: y los mexicanos
huyeron y ascondieronse.

Despues de aver hecho esto luego
mando el capitan Don hernando cortes
apregonar que todos los que estauan en el
corral saliesen libremente y se fuesen a sus
casas y como començaron a salir los mexicanos se lleuauã sus armas y yvan agaui-
llados y dondequiera q̃ topauã a algunos
indios de los amigos de los españoles
matauãlos y desto se enojaron mucho los
españoles y a bueltas de los que se yvan algunos de los mismos vezinos del Tlatilulco
dexaron sus casas y se fueron pensando que
avn los matarian ansi²¹² esperasen en sus
casas vno se fueron hazia Tlacuba y otros
hazia Sanct X̅poual:

y los que tenian casas en el agua vnos
dellos se fueron en canoas, otros salieron
apeando por el agua, otros nadando, y lle-
uan sus haziedas y sus hijos a cuestas salian
muchos de noche y otros de dia

Chapter Forty, of how the Tlatelolca
surrendered to the Spaniards along with
the Mexica and their lord who was with
them.

When the lord of Mexico, Quauhtemoctzin, and those who accompanied
him touched land, they disembarked close
to the house where the Captain was. The
Spaniards who were close to the water
took Quauhtemoctzin by the hand in a
friendly fashion and conducted him to
where Captain don Hernando Cortés was,
on the roof terrace. When he got to where
the Captain was, he embraced the said
Quauhtemoctzin and showed many signs
of affection, and all of the Spaniards were
gazing at him with great joy. Then they
discharged all the cannon for joy over the
conclusion of the war. When this happened, two canoes full of Mexica appeared
and entered the house of a leader called
Coyohuehuetzin, where the Tlaxcalan Indians were. They got into an altercation
and some people were killed there, and the
Mexica ran away and hid.

After this was done, Captain don Hernando Cortés ordered it proclaimed that all
who were in the enclosure should come
out freely and go to their homes. When
the Mexica began to come out, they were
carrying their weapons and went in gangs.
Wherever they encountered any Indians
who were friends of the Spaniards, they
would kill them. At this the Spaniards became very angry. Following those who
were leaving, some of the very citizens of
Tlatelolco abandoned their houses and
went away, thinking that they would kill
them if²¹² they stayed in their houses.
Some went toward Tacuba, others toward
San Cristóbal.

Some of those who had their houses in
the water left in canoes, others wading
through the water, others swimming.
They carried their belongings and their
children on their backs. Many left by
night, others by day.

tleoa: cequinti mopapaquiltitivi, maaviel-
titivi: in oconnepanoto vtli Auh in acaleque, in ixquich acale ça ioaltica in quiz,
yoā tel cemilhuitl in quizque iuhquin
moquequeztivi inic vi.


Auh in izquican antica tetlatlaçaltiaia in
Españoles [fol. 82v] in teucuitlatl quitemoa
amo tle ipan quitta, in chalchivitl, in quetzalli yoan in xivitl: novian nemia in inxilla[213] in incuetitlan, in cioatzitzinti. Auh in
toquichtin novian nemi in imaxtlatitlan,
yoan in incamac. yoan quimanaia, quin-
pepenaia in Cioa in chipavaque, in Cuztic
innacaio in cuztique. Auh in cequintin
cioa inic motetlaçaltiaia, miçoquivique,
yoan tatapatli in quimocuetiq̄ tzotzomatli
in quimovipiltique, çan moch tzotzomatli
in intech quitlalique. Auh no cequintin
pepenaloque in toquichtin iehoantin in
chicaoaque in iniolloco oquichtin yoā in
quin telpupuchtotonti [fol. 83] in quinti-
tlanizque, in intitlanvan iezque, in moteneoa intlamacazcaoan: cequintin nimā quin-
camatlatiq̄ cequintin quincamaicuiloque:
cequintin quintenicuiloque.


Auh in omomā chimalli; inic tixitinque,
in xiuhtonalli ei calli. Auh in cemilhuitlapoalli ce coatl:[215]


Auh in iquac in ōmotemacato in
Quauhtemoctzin: nimā quivicaque in acachinanco in ie ioa. Auh in imuztlaioc in ie
achiton tonatiuh, ie no ceppa vallaque in
Españoles: vel miequintin, no çaniuh tlantivitze,[217] in moiauchichiuhtivitze, tepuzvipilli, in tepuzquacalalatli: auh aoctle in
intepuzmaquauh, yoan aoctle in inchimal,
ça mu[fol. 83v]chintin valmoiacapacho-
tiaque iztac canaoac ica quintlaieltiaia in
mimicque in ie iyaia, in ie potoni: muchintin vallacxipanvitiaque, quivalquitz-
quitiaque itilmatitech in Quauhtemoctzin,

The little children were carried on people's backs. There was a general wail; but
some went rejoicing and amusing themselves as they went along the road. Most of
the owners of boats left at night, though
some left by day. They seemed to knock
against one another as they went.

And along every stretch [of road] the
Spaniards took things from people by
force. They were looking for gold; they
cared nothing for green-stone, precious
feathers, or turquoise. They looked everywhere with the women, on their abdomens,[213] under their skirts. And they
looked everywhere with the men, under
their loincloths and in their mouths. And
[the Spaniards] took, picked out the beautiful women, with yellow bodies. And
how some women got loose was that they
covered their faces with mud and put on
ragged blouses and skirts, clothing themselves all in rags. And some men were
picked out, those who were strong and in
the prime of life, and those who were
barely youths, to run errands for them and
be their errand boys, called their *tlamacazque* [priests, acolytes]. Then they
burned some of them on the mouth
[branded them]; some they branded on the
cheeks, some on the mouth.

And when the weapons were laid down
and we collapsed, the year count was
Three House, and the day count was One
Serpent.[215]

And when Quauhtemoctzin went to
give himself up, they took him to Acachinanco; it was already dark. And the
next day, when there was a little sun, the
Spaniards came again, a great many of
them; they too had reached the end.[217]
They came equipped for battle, with iron
cuirasses and iron helmets, but not with
their iron swords and their shields. They all
came pressing narrow white cloths to their
noses because the dead made them sick, for
they were smelling bad and stinking. They
all came on foot, holding Quauhtemoc-

[fol. 82] Los españoles y sus amigos pusieronse en todos los caminos y robauā [fol. 82v] a los que pasauā tomandolos el oro q̄ lleuauan y escudrināndolos todos sus hatos y todas sus vestiduras y ninguna cosa otra tomauan sino el oro y las mugeres moças hermosas y algunas de las mugeres por escaparse desfracauāse²¹⁴ poniendo lodo en la cara, y vestiendose de handrajos: Tambien tomauan mancebos y hombres recios para esclauos pusieronlos nombres tlamacazque y a muchos dellos herraron en la cara.

[fol. 83] Rendieronse los mexicanos, y despartiose la guerra en la cuenta de los años, que se dize tres casas, y ē la cuenta de los dias: en el signo que se llama Ce coatl.

The Spaniards and their friends stationed themselves on all the roads and robbed those who went by, taking the gold they carried and scrutinizing all their gear and clothing; they took nothing but the gold and women who were young and beautiful. In order to escape, some of the women disguised²¹⁴ themselves, putting mud on their faces and dressing in rags. They also took youths and strong men for slaves, calling them *tlamacazque;* they branded the faces of many of them.

The Mexica surrendered and the war ended in the year count [during the year] called Three Houses, and in the day count on the sign called Ce Coatl.

Al señor de mexico Quauhtemoctzin el mismo dia que se rendio le lleuarō al lugar de acachinanco con todos los principales adonde era la²¹⁶ aposento de Don hernādo cortes: y luego otro dia vinieron muchos españoles al tlatilulco todos ordenados a punto de guerra y todos atapauā las narizes por el hedor de los muertos que estauā por enterrar y trayan consigo al señor de mexico Quauhtemoctzin, y a otro principal que se llama Coanacotzin, y a otro que se llamaua Tetlepāquetzatzin, [fol. 83v] y los demas principales que guardauan el tesoro,

The same day that the lord of Mexico, Quauhtemoctzin, surrendered, they took him with all the leaders to the place Acachinanco, where the²¹⁶ lodging of don Hernando Cortés was. Then the next day many Spaniards came to Tlatelolco, all in order and ready for battle. They all covered their noses because of the stench of the dead who were unburied. They brought with them the lord of Mexico, Quauhtemoctzin, and another leader called Coanacochtzin, and another called Tetlepanquetzatzin, and the other leaders who guarded the treasure.

Coanacotzin, Tetlepanquetzatzin, çan ieixtin valmantiaque. Auh in Cioacoatl tlacutzin: Tlillancalqui. Petlauhtzin, vitznaoatl, motelchiuhtzin mexicatl. Achcauhtli. Tecutlamacazqui, Coatzin, tlatlati, tlaçuliautl,[218] in iehoantin in quipiaia in ixquich teucuitlatl:

niman vmpa tlamelauhque in atactzinco, in vncan ichan in tiiacauh in tlacuchcalcatl, in Coiovevetzin: pipilivi in [fol. 84] Espanoles, ie vmmecatl[219] motilinia, veca tlantivi, veca acitivi: auh in oacito in ichā coiovevetzin, nimā ic tlecoque in tlapanco, in tlapechco: niman ic motlalique, tlatlapalquachtli in quicevalcaltique capitan, nimā ic oncā ommotlali in Marques, itlan ommotlali in Malintzin:

auh in Quauhtemoctzin itlan ca in Capitan: in quimolpilia Quetzalichpetztli, tlatlacuhuitectli, vitzitzilin hivio inic ocuiltecaio, omach catzaoac, çan quixcavitica: nimā contoquilitica in Coanacutzin, tetzcucu tlatoani: in quimolpilitica, çan vel ichtilmatli, xoxochiteio, xochimoiaoac, omach no catzaoac: nimā cōtoquilitica. Tetlepanquetza[fol. 84v]tzi, tlacuban tlatoani, çāno iuhqui in quimolpilitica in ichtilmatli, o no vel catzactix, o uel catzaoac: nimā contoquilitica. Mixcoatlailotlac, avelitoctzin: tlatzacutica Iopicatl, pupucatzin, pilli: cectlapal onoque in tenochca. Tlacutzin. Petlauhtzin. Motelchiuhtzin mexicatl, achcauhtli, tecutlamacazqui, coatzin tlatlati, Tlaculiautl.[220]

41

Inic ompoalli oce capitulo vncā mitoa in tlatolli inic quinnonotz do hernando Cortes in ixquichtin altepetl ipā tlatoque, in nican Mexico: auh tetzcucu, tlacuba, in iquac ie omoman chimalli, in quintemoliaia in cuztic teucuitlatl, in vncan qui-

tzin, Coanacochtzin, and Tetlepanquetzatzin by their capes; only the three of them came ⟨in line⟩. And the Cihuacoatl Tlacotzin, the Tlillancalqui Petlauhtzin, the Huitznahuatl Motelchiuhtzin mexicatl, the Achcauhtli Teuctlamacazqui [senior lordly priest] Coatzin, and the treasurer Tlaçolyaotl[218] guarded all of the gold.

Then they went straight to Atactzinco, where the home of the warrior the Tlacochcalcatl Coyohuehuetzin was. The Spaniards were in a line stretching for two mecatl,[219] reaching far off to its end. And when they reached the home of Coyohuehuetzin, they went up on the roof to a platform. Then they sat down. They placed a canopy of varicolored cloth over the Marqués; then he sat down, and Marina sat beside him.

And Quauhtemoctzin was next to the Captain. He had tied on a shining maguey-fiber cloak, each half different, covered with hummingbird feathers, Ocuillan style. It was very dirty; it was all he had. Then Coanacochtzin, the ruler of Tetzcoco, was next. He had tied on only a plain maguey-fiber cloak with a flowered border, with a spreading design of flowers; it too was very dirty. Next was Tetlepanquetzatzin, the ruler of Tlacopan, who likewise had tied on a maguey cloak; it too was dirtied, very dirty. Next was the Mixcoatlailotlac Ahuelitoctzin. Last was Yopicatl Popocatzin, a nobleman. To the side were the Tenochca Tlacotzin, Petlauhtzin, Motelchiuhtzin mexicatl, the Achcauhtli Teuctlamacazqui Coatzin, and the treasurer Tlaçolyaotl.[220]

Forty-first chapter, where is told the speech that don Hernando Cortés gave to all the rulers in the altepetl of Mexico here, Tetzcoco, and Tlacopan, when the weapons were laid down, questioning them about the gold they had left scattered at the

y fueron derechos al lugar donde estaua el corral, donde se auian hecho, fuertes los mexicanos que se llamaua Atactzinco y ētraron en la casa del Tlacuchcalcatl que se llamaua Coioueuetzin: y luego subieron al açotea, y sentaronse y pusieron alli vn pauellon al capitā Don hernando cortes: y sentose en su silla.

[fol. 84] La yndia que era interprete que se llamaua Marina pusose cerca del capitan y de la otra parte el señor de mexico Quauhtemoctzin tenia cubierta vna manta que se llama Quetzalychpetztli y estaua cabe el señor de Tetzcuco que se llamaua Coanacotzin y tenia cubierta vna manta de nequē que se llama Xoxochiteio estaua tābien alli otro principal que se llamaua Tetlepanquetzatzin señor de Tlacuba tenia cubierta otra manta pobre y suzia, tambiē estaua alli otro principal que se llamaua Miscoatlaylotlactzin, y otro se llamaua Auelitoctzin a la postre de todos estaua otro principal que se llamaua yupicatl pupucatzin, de la otra parte estauan vnos principales mexicanos vno de los quales se llamaua Tlacutzin, otro Petlauhtzin, otro Motelchiuhtzin, otro Mexicatl, otro achcauhtli, otro Teutlamacazqui, otro Coatzintlatlati, otro tlaçulyautl

41

[fol. 84v] Capitulo .41. de la platica que hizo el capitan Don hernando cortes, a los señores de mexico, tetzcucu, y tlacuba: despues de la victoria, procurando por el oro, que se auia perdido, quando salierō huyendo de mexico.

They went straight to where the enclosure was in which the Mexica had fortified themselves, called Atactzinco, and went into the house of the Tlacochcalcatl, who was called Coyohuehuetzin. Then they went up on the roof terrace and sat down; they put up a canopy there for Captain don Hernando Cortés, and he sat down in his chair.

The Indian woman who was interpreter, called Marina, placed herself close to the Captain, and on the other side was the lord of Mexico, Quauhtemoctzin; he was covered with a cloak called *quetzalichpetztli*. Next to him was the lord of Tetzcoco, called Coanacochtzin; he was covered with a cloak of maguey called *xoxochitenyo*. Another leader was also there, named Tetlepanquetzatzin, lord of Tacuba; he was covered with another poor and dirty cloak. Another leader was also there, called Mixcoatlailotlactzin, and another called Ahuelitoctzin. Last of all was another leader named Yopicatl Popocatzin. On the other side were some Mexica leaders, one of whom was called Tlacotzin, another Petlauhtzin, another Motelchiuhtzin, another Mexicatl, another Achcauhtli, another Teutlamacazqui, another Coatzintlatlati, and another Tlaçolyaotl.

Chapter Forty-one, of the speech that Captain don Hernando Cortés made to the lords of Mexico, Tetzcoco, and Tacuba after the victory, seeking the gold that had been lost when they left Mexico fleeing.

cenmantiquizque tultecaacaluco, in iquac quizque, choloque mexico.

[fol. 85] Niman ie ic quinnonotza in Marques in Capitan in tlatoque: quimilhuia. Catli in teucuitlatl? in omopiaia Mexico: niman ie ic vallaquixtilo in acalco in ixquich in teucuitlatl, in teucuitlapanitl, in teucuitlacopilli, in teucuitlamatemecatl, in teucuitlacotzevatl, in teucuitlaquacalalatli, in teucuitlacomalli: muchi ixpan contecaque in capitan, çã much iehoan in Españoles in vallaquixtique:

niman ie ic quitoa in Capitan. çan ie ixquich in in teucuitlatl? in omopiaia Mexico, muchi anquinextizque? ca vel quitemoa in totecuiovan:

Nimã ie ic ontlatoa in Tlacutzin. [fol. 85v] Tla quimocaquiti in totecuio in teutl, ca o ipan maxitico in totecpan, ca much ticxaxantzacque, amo nel much quimotquilique in totecuiovan?

niman quivalito in Malintzin. quimitalhuia in Capitan, Quemaca ca much ticcuique, muchi omocentlali, yoan muchi omumachioti: auh ca much techtlaçaltique in vncã tulteca acaloco, much oncã techtepevaltique, much quinextizque:

nimã ie ic tlananquilia in Cioacoatl tlacutzin. tla quimocaquiti in teutl in Capitã. Cavel acalco moquetza in tenuchcatl, ca amo ichivil, ca çan ineixcavil quichiuh in tlatilulcatl, in acal[fol. 86]tica tlaiecoque, in quiniacatzacuilito in totecuiovã amo nel iehoantin muchi quicuique in tlatilulca:

nimã ie ic vallatoa in Quauhtemoctzin: quivalilhui in Cioacoatl, tlein tiquitoa Cioacoatle: maço quicuiq̃ in tlatilulca, amo ic çaçacoque in tlamaceuhque? amo muchi quinextique? amo texopan in monechico? auh tlein oconmocuilique in totecuiovan amo iehoatl in? commapilhui in teucuitlatl in Quauhtemoctzin:

Tolteca canal when they came out and fled from Mexico.

Then the Marqués, the Captain, spoke to the rulers, saying to them, "Where is the gold that was kept in Mexico?" Then they took out of the boats all the gold: the golden banners, the golden miters, the golden arm bands, the golden leg bands, the golden helmets, the golden disks. They laid it all before the Captain, but the Spaniards came to remove it all.

Then the Captain said, "Is this all the gold that was kept in Mexico? You are to produce it all, for our lords are seeking it urgently."

Then Tlacotzin spoke up: "If our lord the god will pay heed, did our lords not take with them all that was brought to our palace when he was there, all of which was turned into bars?"

Then Marina replied, "The Captain says, 'Yes, we took everything that was assembled, and it was stamped. But they made us let it go at the Tolteca canal, they made us drop it there. They are to produce all of it.'"

Then the Cihuacoatl Tlacotzin replied, "Let the god, the Captain, pay heed. The Tenochca ⟨do not appear⟩ in boats, it is not their affair; rather the Tlatelolca took it upon themselves alone to fight in boats and to intercept our lords. Was it not perhaps the Tlatelolca who took it all?"

Then Quauhtemoctzin spoke in turn, replying to the Cihuacoatl, "What are you saying, Cihuacoatl? Although the Tlatelolca took it, were not those who took things apprehended? Did they not produce everything? Was it not collected at Texopan? And is this not what our lords took?" Quauhtemoctzin pointed to the gold with his finger.

[fol. 85] Como estuuieron juntos los tres señores de mexico, y tetzcuco, y tlacuba, con sus principales delāte de Don hernādo cortes, mando a Marina que les dixese donde esta el oro que auia dexado en mexico? Y luego los mexicanos le sacaron todas las joyas que tenian ascondidas en vna canoa llena, y todo lo pusieron delante del capitan, y de los españoles que con el estauā:

y como lo vio dixo no ay mas oro que este en mexico? Sacaldo todo, que es menester todo:

y luego vn principal que llamauan Tlacutzin hablo a Marina respōdiendo: Di a n̄ro señor y dios, que quando llego a las casas reales, la primera vez vio todo lo que avia, y todas las salas cerramos con adoues, no sabemus que se hizo el oro que auia tenemos que todo lo lleuaron ellos, y no tenemos mas desto agora;

y el capitan respondio diziendo que es [fol. 85v] verdad que todo lo tomamos? pero todo nos lo tomaron en aquel paso del acequia que se llama Toltecaacaloco, es menester que luego parezca.

Y luego respondio vn principal mexicano que se llamaua Cioacoatl Tlacutzin, y dixo a Marina dile al dios capitan q̄ nosotros los mexicanos no peleamos por el agua con canoas ni sabemos esta manera de pelea que solos los del tlatilulco que peleauan por el agua atajaron a n̄ros señores los españoles y creemos que solos ellos lo tomaron:

y luego respondio Quauhtemoctzin y dixo al principal Cioacoatl que es lo que dizes aunque es asi, que los del Tlatilulco lo tomaron por ello fueron presos, y todo lo tornaron en el lugar de Texopan se junto todo, y esto es lo que esta aqui y no ay mas;

When the three lords of Mexico, Tetzcoco, and Tacuba were assembled with their subordinate leaders before don Hernando Cortés, he ordered Marina to ask them where the gold was that he had left in Mexico. Then the Mexica got out for him all the precious items they had hidden in a full canoe and put it all before the Captain and the Spaniards who were with him.

When he saw it, he said, "Is there no more gold than this in Mexico? Get it all out, for it is all needed."

Then a leader named Tlacotzin spoke in answer to Marina, "Tell our lord and god that when he came to the palace the first time he saw everything that there was. We closed all the rooms with adobe bricks; we don't know what happened to the gold that was there. We believe that they took it all with them, and we have no more than this now."

The Captain answered, saying, "It is true that we took it all, but they took it all from us in crossing the canal called Toltecaacaloco. It is necessary that it be produced immediately."

Then a Mexica leader called Cihuacoatl Tlacotzin answered, saying to Marina, "Tell the god and captain that we Mexica do not fight on the water with canoes, nor do we understand this kind of fighting. Only the Tlatelolca who were fighting on the water intercepted our lords the Spaniards, and we believe that they alone took it."

Then Quauhtemoctzin answered, saying to the leader Cihuacoatl, "What are you saying? Although it is true that the Tlatelolca took it, they were apprehended for it and returned it all. It was all assembled in the place Texopan, and it is what is here. There is no more."

nimā quivalilhui in Malintzin. quimitalhuia in capitan Çan ie ixquich in?

niman ic conito in cioacoatl, aço aca
quiquixti in Macevalli, atel motlatemoliz,
aquimottiliz in totecuio in capi[fol.
86v]tan:

nimā ie no ceppa quivalito in Malintzin,
quimitalhuia in Capitan Matlacpoalli anquinextizque in teucuitlatl ixquich in: qui-
valtamachiuh imatica, quivaliavallali in
ima:

ie no ceppa ontlananquili in civacoatl:
quito. Aço ça aca ipan mocueti in civa-
tzintli, amotemoliz, aquimottiliz: [221]

niman ie ic ontlatoa in Mixcoatlailotlac,
avelitoctzin: quito. tla quimocaquiti in tlacatl in totecuio in Capitan, in oc vnca
Motecuçoma, in iquac ontepevaloia cana,
ca cemolini in Mexicatl, in tlatilulcatl, in
tepanecatl in aculhoa: in ixquich tepanecatl, in ixquich acul[fol. 87]hoa yoan in ixquich chinampanecatl, ca ticemolini, in
tontepeva: auh in onia altepetl, ca nimā ie
ic valnecuepalo, ceceniaca cōmati in imaltepeuh. Auh çatepan valhui in altepevaque
in ie pevallaca, quivalitqui in intlacalaquil,
intlatqui valmuchiuhtiuh in chalchivitl in
teucuitlatl, in quetzalli yoan in oc cequi
tlaçotetl, in teuxivitl, in xiuhtototl, in
tlauhquechol: quioalmacaia in Motecuçoma, çan cē vmpa valaci, çā vmpa val-
mocemaci in tenuchtitlan in ixquich
tlacalaquili in teucuitlatl.

Then Marina replied to him, "The
Captain says, 'Is this all?'"

Then the Cihuacoatl said, "Perhaps
some of the common folk removed it, but
it will be investigated, our lord the Captain
will see it."

Then again Marina replied, "The Captain says that you are to produce two hundred pieces of gold of this size." She measured it with her hands, making a circle
with her hands.

Again the Cihuacoatl replied, saying,
"Perhaps some woman put it in her skirt.
It will be sought; he will see it." [221]

Then the Mixcoatlailotlac Ahuelitoctzin
spoke up, saying, "May the lord our lord,
the Captain, pay heed. When Moteucçoma was still alive, when there was a conquest somewhere, the Mexica, the Tlatelolca, the Tepaneca, and the Acolhuaque
all went together. All of us, some Tepaneca, some Acolhuaque, and some
people of the chinampas, moved together
when we went to conquer, but when the
altepetl fell, then everyone came back,
each one heading for his own altepetl. And
afterward came the people of that altepetl,
the ones conquered, bringing their tribute;
what they carried was green-stone, gold,
precious feathers, and other precious
stones, turquoise, cotinga and spoonbill
feathers, and they came and gave it to Moteucçoma. It arrived all together, all the
tribute and gold arrived together in Tenochtitlan."

dixo luego Marina: el ñīo capitan dize que no esta aqui todo:

y respondio el principal Cioacoatl por uentura algun maceoal a tomado algo. Buscarse a: y traerse a a la presencia del capitan

[fol. 86v] Otra uez dixo Marina el señor capitan, dize que busqueys docientos tesoelos de oro tan grandes, como asi: y señaloles con las manos, el grandor de vna patena de caliz:

otra uez hablo el principal Cioacoatl, y dixo por uentura algunas de las mugeres lo lleuaron ascondido debaxo, de las nauas, buscarse a, y traerse a a la presencia del señor capitan:

luego alli hablo otro p̃ncipal, que se llamaua Miscoatlaylotlac auelitoctzin, dile al señor capitan que quando viuia Motecuçoma el estilo que se tenia en conquistar era este que yuan los mexicanos, y los tetzcucanos, y los de Tlacuba, y los de las chinampas, todos juntos yvan sobre el pueblo o prouincia que queriã conquistar: [fol. 87] y despues que la auian conquistados, luego se boluian a sus casas, y a sus pueblos: y despues venian los señores de los pueblos que auian sido conquistados, y trayan su tributo de oro, y de piedras preciosas, y de plumajes ricos: y todo lo dauan a Motecuçoma, todo el oro venia a su poder.

Then Marina said, "Our Captain says that it is not all here."

The leader Cihuacoatl answered, "Perhaps some *macehual* has taken something. It will be sought and brought into the presence of the Captain."

Again Marina said, "The lord Captain says you should look for two hundred disks of gold this big," and she signaled with her hands the size of a chalice plate.

Again the leader Cihuacoatl spoke, saying, "Perhaps some of the women took it hidden underneath their skirts. It will be looked for and brought into the presence of the lord Captain."

Then another leader, named Mixcoatlailotlac Ahuelitoctzin, spoke up, saying, "Tell the lord Captain that when Moteucçoma was alive, the custom that was maintained in conquering was this: the Mexica, the Tetzcoca, the people of Tacuba, and the people of the *chinampas* went all together against the settlement or province that they wanted to conquer, and after they had conquered it, they all went back to their homes and their settlements. Afterward came the lords of the settlements that had been conquered, bringing their tribute of gold, precious stones, and rich plumage, and they gave it all to Moteucçoma. All the gold came into his custody."

# EXTRACT FROM THE
# ANNALS OF TLATELOLCO

*Nahuatl*

[p. 27] Matlactlomey tochtli xiuitl yquitoqz spañoles atla no yquac miquito mexica tloapa¹ . Ce acatl xiuitl ypā quiçatō spañoles ȳ tecpātlayacac . nima ye yc vitz yn capita .

yn iquac oquiçaco tecpātlayacac nima ye quinamiqui cuetlaxtecatl yc ūcā quimamaca ȳ teucuitlatonatiuh centetl coztic centetl yztac² yoā tezcacuitlapilli . yoā teucuitlaquaapaztli . teucuitlaquatecuçiztli yoā quetzallapanecayotl . epchimalli yn capitan yxpan tlamictiloc yee yquallan yn eztli quauhxicaltica quimacaya capita yee yc quimicti yn eztli quimacaya quiuitec espadatica yee yc xitinque ȳ tenamique

ynhin yxquich quimamacato Capitan ynoma motecuzoma ça ye ⟨in⟩ ilotiz ȳ capitan yehuatl ytequiuh mochiuh ȳ cuetlaxtecatl .

ça nimā yquac acitiuetzico tenochtitla yn acico quecholli cemilhuitonalli chicuey ecatl . yn ovnacico tenochtitlan : nima [y]e tiquimamaca ȳ totolli . ȳ totoltetl yn iztac tlaolli . yn iztac tlaxcalli nima ye tateca . nima ye maçatlaqualli ticallaqz yoā quauitl . Cecni quiteca yn itetlamamac tenochcatl cecni quiteca yn itetlamamac tlatilulcatl .

Auh ȳ capitan nimā ye yc vnpeva atenco : quicauhtia ȳ don pedro alvarado tonatiuh . nima ye quitemolia motecuçoma yn quenin quilhuiquistilia ynteuh . nima ye quimilhuia quenami ma xictlalica . yn quesquich ytlatlatquio ma xicchiuaca

yn iquac tenauati tonatiuh ye yl[p]itoc motecuçoma yoā ȳ tlatilulco ytzquauhtzi tlacuchcalcatl . yquac quipiloque acolhuaca pilli neçaualquentzi atenantitech . yc ome mic nauhtla tlatoani ytoca coualpopocatzi quimiminqz yn ocomiminque y⟨e⟩ nemitican tlatlac .

ynic tlapia tenochca quauhquiauac Centlapal yncal ma tenochca centlapal yncal ma tlatilulca :

yehoāti quimonilhuico ynic mochichiuaz vitzilopochtli [p. 28] Nima ye quitlalia y uitzilopochtli moch yc chichiuhtica yn iamatlatqui auh yn ixquich ytlatlatquio muchi y quicencauhque nima ye ycuicoanoua y mesica yn iuh quichiuaya y cemilhuitl . can oc vel mochiuh

ynic omilhuitl cuicoanoque ye yquac mique ȳ tenochca yn tlatilulca . ȳ cuicoanoua çā pepetlauhtinenca çan isquich yncuechi³ yxixiuh . ȳtempilol[***h] ȳcozqui . ymaz-

# EXTRACT FROM THE
# ANNALS OF TLATELOLCO

*English Translation*

In the year of Thirteen Rabbit the Spaniards were seen on the water. It was also when [some] Mexica went to the ocean[1] and died. In the year of One Reed the Spaniards appeared at Tecpantlayacac. Thereupon the Captain came.

When he appeared at Tecpantlayacac, Cuetlaxtecatl met him; there he gave him suns of precious metal, one yellow [gold] and one white [silver],[2] and a mirror for the back, and a golden helmet, and a golden shell headcover, and a head fan of plumes, and a shell shield. Sacrifices were made before the Captain, at which he was angered. They gave the Captain blood in an eagle vessel, and because of it he killed the person who was giving him blood, striking him with a sword. At that, the meeting party dispersed.

Moteucçoma himself gave all this to the Captain [so that] the Captain would go back. [Presenting the gift] was the task of the Cuetlaxtecatl.

He [Cortés] reached Tenochtitlan very quickly; he arrived [in the month of] Quecholli, on a day Eight Wind. When he reached Tenochtitlan, we gave him turkey hens, turkey eggs, shelled white maize, and white tortillas, as well as providing water, as well as delivering deer fodder and wood. The Tenochca made their contribution separately, and the Tlatelolca made their contribution separately.

Then the Captain left for the seashore; he left behind don Pedro de Alvarado, Tonatiuh [the Sun]. Then he asked Moteucçoma how they celebrated the festivity of their god. He said to him, "How is it? Set up all the equipment for it and do it."

When Tonatiuh gave the order, Moteucçoma was already being detained, along with Itzquauhtzin, the Tlacochcalcatl in Tlatelolco. At this time they hanged the nobleman of Acolhuacan, Neçahualquentzin, at the wall near the water. The second who died was the ruler of Nauhtla, named Cohualpopocatzin. They shot him with arrows; when they had shot him, he was burned while alive.

As to how the Tenochca ⟨stood guard, or were in charge⟩ at Quauhquiahuac, on one side were the houses of the Tenochca, on the other side the houses of the Tlatelolca.

They told them that Huitzilopochtli should be adorned. Then they set up Huitzilopochtli, outfitted with all his paper garments and all his accoutrements; they prepared it all. Then the Mexica danced and sang, doing it all day, which they were able to do.

The second day that they danced and sang was when the Tenochca and Tlatelolca died. While dancing they went bare [of weapons], with only their net cloaks,[3] their

taxcl ȳchochol . Y ueuetzonaya⁴ ueuentzitzi ymihiyeteco ymayacach yehoā achto
quīpeualtiqz vnca quimatlatlazqz quītentlatlazque nima ye yc micoa yn isquchti
Cuicoanoaya muchinti tlatlataque vnca mique

ȳ techpeualti ye techmictia yey hora . yn ovntemictiqz teutualco nima ye callaqui ȳ
callitic ynic moch quimictiqz yn atecaya . y maçatlaqualli quitocaya . ȳ tezia yn tlach-
panque . yn tlapiaya .

Auh yn tlatoani motecuzomazi tenochtitla quivicatinemi . yn itzquauhzi tlacuchcalcatl tlatilulco ȳ quintlacaualtiaya Spañoles quimilhuiaya totecuiouane ma ysquich tle
amailia motolinia maceualli cuix ychimal cuix ymaquauh yetinemi . Ça mopetlauil-
titinemi .
Yn açico Capitan . ye otechmicti tonatiuh ye cēpoualilhuitl techpoyomicti ȳ
tonatiuh . yñic via atēco c[a]pitan y inic onacico amo yaotica namicoc çan iuian yn
oncallaquico . Quin imoztlaoc yn tiquintocaque tlacavacac ye yc vntzinti yaoyotl .

Nima ye yc quiça yoaltica tecuhylhuiticā quizque ye yquac y vmique toltecaacaloco
. vncan tiquintlatepeualtique .
ye yuh yoaltica quiçazque oc achtopa motlachielito maçatzintamalco yn otlachieto
ye yquac y youaltica quizqz
ome tecpa⁵ . xiuitl yca ye yquac mic y motecuhçomatzi no yquac mic yn itzquauhzi . tlatilulco tlacuchcalcatl .
yn oonehuaque motlalito acueco . qu[i] mopeuito omotlalito⁶ teucalhuiaca . one-
hoaq[z] çoltepec . onehuaqz vnca motlalito tepotzotla . onehvaqz omotlalito citlaltepec . onehoaqz motlalito temazcalapa . vnca namicoqz macoqz totolli totoltet[l] .
tlaolli . vncā yyocuitiloque . ye yc calaqz motlalito . tlaxcallan

Nima ye yc momanā cocolliztli : tlatlaciztli tlachinol[p. 29]totonqui çauatl .
Y ye quentel quiça cocoliztli nima ye yc ualleua vnpa quiçato tepeyacac achto
vncan . tlalpolo Nima ye yc valleva pillauan onquiçaco tlapechuaca yzcalli . matlac-
poualticā quiçaco vmotlalico tetzcoco . vncā vnpoualti . niman ye yc vallevac ye no
cepa quiualtocac çitlaltepec . tlacopan vmotecaco tecpa :

auh y ye yxquich chicuhnauhtecatl xaltocamecatl . quauhtitlancalcatl . tenayocatl .
azcapotzalcatl . tlacopanecatl coyoacatl muchinti nica valcallaque : Chicomilhuitl yn
techicallico çan oncā onoca tlacopa .
ye no cepa y cuitlauic ya ça ye no yehoatl ȳ quitocaqz yn uncan quizqz ye no
vmotecato yn tetzco[co] . Napoaltica ye no cepa quiçaco vaxtepec quauhnavac vnca
valtemoc xochmilco vnca miqz tlatilulca ye no cepa çan vnpa quiz yn ūpa valla tetzcoco ye no vmotecato . tlalliztacapa ye no miqz y tlatilulca .

ynic ye no vmotecato tetzcoco yquac peuh y ye momimictia⁷ tenochca . yey calli
xiuitl ypa quimictiqz yn inpillo Ciuacoatl tziuacpopocatzi yoa Cipactzi . tencuecue-
notzi . ypilhua motecuhçomatzi axayaca . xoxopeualloc⁸ quimictique

turquoise [ornaments], their lip plugs, their necklaces, their forked heron-feather ornaments, their deer's hooves. The old men who beat the cylindrical drums[4] had their tobacco pots and their rattles. It was them they first attacked; they struck off their hands and lips. Then all who were dancing, and all who were looking on, died there.

When they attacked us, they were killing us for three hours. When they had finished killing people in the courtyard of the temple precinct, they went into the buildings and killed those who carried water, provided deer fodder, ground maize, swept, and kept watch.

And the ruler Moteucçoma of Tenochtitlan, accompanied by Itzquauhtzin, the Tlacochcalcatl of Tlatelolco, was trying to hold the Spaniards back. They said to them, "O our lords, let it be enough. What are you doing? The people are suffering. Do they have shields and war clubs? They go unarmed."

When the Captain arrived, Tonatiuh had already killed us; it had been twenty days since Tonatiuh had treacherously killed us while the Captain was gone to the seashore. When he arrived, he was not met with battle; he entered uncontested. Only the next day did we pursue them, and there was a clamor, with which the war began.

Then they came out at night; during [the month of] Teucilhuitl they came out. At that time they died at the Tolteca canal; there we made them drop things.

When they were about to come out at night, they first went to Maçatzintamalco to have a look around; when they had had a look they left by night.

In Two Flint Knife[5] year, Moteucçoma died; it was also when Itzquauhtzin, the Tlacochcalcatl of Tlatelolco, died.

When they left, they established themselves[6] at Acueco. Then they departed and established themselves at Teocalhueyacan. They departed [and made a stop at] Çoltepec. They departed and established themselves at Tepotzotlan. They departed and established themselves at Citlaltepec. They departed and established themselves at Temazcalapan. There they were met and were given turkey hens, eggs, and shelled maize, and they rested. Then they entered Tlaxcala to establish themselves.

Then a plague broke out of coughing, fever, and pox.

When the plague lessened somewhat, [the Spaniards] came back; they appeared at Tepeyacac. First they laid waste there. Then they came in this direction at the [feast of the] drunkenness of children; they appeared at Tlapechhuacan during [the month of] Izcalli. They had been gone two hundred days. They established themselves at Tetzcoco, where they spent forty days. Then they came and again went through Citlaltepec. They established themselves at the palace in Tlacopan.

And the people of Xaltocan, Quauhtitlan, Tenanyocan, Azcapotzalco, Tlacopan, and Coyoacan all entered in here. For seven days they fought us, just staying at Tlacopan.

Again they went back, going the way they came, and went to establish themselves in Tetzcoco again. After eighty days they appeared again at Oaxtepec and Cuernavaca; from there they went to Xochimilco; Tlatelolca died there. They left there again and came to Tetzcoco to establish themselves again. At Tlaliztacapan, again Tlatelolca died.

When they established themselves at Tetzcoco again was when the Tenochca began to fight among themselves.[7] In the year Three House they killed their lord the Cihuacoatl Tzihuacpopocatzin, along with Cipactzin and Tencuecuenotzin, children of Moteucçoma and Axayacatl. They were kicked to death.[8]

ynī y mopoloqz tenochca ça monetechuiqz y momimictique . ypanpa y yehoantin i pipilti mictiloque quitlaoculiaya ypā tlatoaya y maceualli ynic monechicoz yztac tlaolli totolli totoltetl ynic tetlā quincallaquizqz [9] maceualli .

tlamacazqz achcacauhti tiachcaua ȳ temictique tecuhtlatoqz yn cuallanqz . ynic mictiloqz pipilti

quitoqz ȳ temictique . Cuix tiualpillotiaque ye ycempoalloc y yequene totech m[o]pilloque totech moquetzaco [10] toxcatl .

ye yc c[e] motecato y ye techicali . ye yuh matlaquilhuitl techicalli [11] . yn quiçaco yacal . y cempoalilhuitl ynic quixcaui y mical nonovalco yc oca maçatzintamalco .

yn iquac quiçaco yacal yztacalco quiçaco ye yquac tetlan vncallac [12] yztacalcatl no vnpa vallicatia nimā vnca motecaco acalli acachinanco : niman ye no vnca moxacaltia vexotzincatl tlaxcaltecatl necoc vmac .

Nima ye yc moyaua yn imacal yn tlatilulcatl ypa mical yn otli nonoalcatl yc oca maçatzintamalco mical . Auh y xoxouiltitla yn tepeyacac ayac mical

çā ticpixqz ȳ titlatilulca yn otli yn iquac onacico ymacal çan ymoztlaoc quicauhqz xoloco omilhuitl yecalliuac [13] vitzilla :
ye yquac y ye momimictiqz [14] tenochca : y quimolhuiqz Catliqz topilhua aço ye cepa contlaçazqz ⟨aç⟩oquichtizqz

Ca naui y quimōcuicuitiuezqz y ye quimictia yacatia Comictiqz quauhnochtli tlacateco tiachcauh cuapa viznauac tiachcauh tlenamacaqz amātla tlenamacac . tlallo-can [p. 30] tlenamacac . ynin y mopoloque ynic opa momimictiqz tenochca .

Contecaco vnepantla tlequiquiztli tecama quiuatitiqz [15] yn otli yn oquitlazqz tlequi-quiztli quauhquiauac yn [uetzi]co .

nima ye yc cemollini tenochcatl nima ye y quinapaloa yn uitzilopoch [16] quiualcal-laquiqz tlatilulco Contecaco amaxac telpochcalli . Auh yn intlatocauh contlalico y yacacolco quauhtemoctzi Auh y ye yxquich maceualli ye yquac quicauh yn iauh yn itepeuh tenochtitlan catca ynic callaquico tlatilulco tocalla acitimoquetzaco . nima ye yc motlalico nouian tocaltitla totlapanco .

Auh ye tzatzi yn impiloa yn intecuhtlatocaua . quitoqz . totecuioane Mexicae tlati-lulcae atoqueztelçi [17] . ça tocacalpixca amo m⟨a⟩axitizque ȳ calpixcātli ȳ tlalli . yz cat-qui amocococauh ȳ tlauiztli yn oamechpieliaya yn amotlatocauh yn chimalli tlauiztli ī tecuecuextli ȳ quetzallalpilloni ȳ teucuitlanacochtli . yn chalchiuhtli . Ca yxquich amaxca amotlatqui . Ma amoiollicatzi ma amihiyocauilliti canpa tiuallaque ca timexica ca titlatilulca muchocatiuiz yn tlatoua ye yquac quimacaque yn tlauiztli yn teucuitlaio yn quetzallo .

Auh y yehvanti tzatzitinenqz yn otlica ȳ caltzalla yn tianquizco xipanoc tetlyaco

These Tenochca who brought themselves down simply had internecine conflicts. The reason these nobles were killed is that they were favoring the common people and trying to see to it that shelled white maize, turkey hens, and eggs should be collected so that they could ⟨have them submit (to the Spaniards)⟩.[9]

It was ordinary priests, high priests, and ⟨war?⟩ leaders who did the killing; the lords in official positions were angry that the nobles were killed.

The killers said, "Have we ⟨come as lords? become lords⟩? It has been twenty days now. They depended on us and ⟨turned to us⟩ at [the festivity and massacre of] Toxcatl."[10]

[The Spaniards] established themselves permanently and began fighting us. After they had fought us[11] for ten days, their boats appeared. For twenty days the fighting was exclusively at Nonoalco, and second, at Maçatzintamalco.

When their boats appeared, they appeared at Iztaccalco; at that time the people of Iztaccalco ⟨submitted⟩;[12] from there they came ahead this way, then they stationed the boats at Acachinanco. Then also the Huexotzinca and Tlaxcalans set up temporary huts for themselves there on both sides of the road.

Then the Tlatelolca's boats dispersed. The Nonoalca fought on the road, and there was also fighting at Maçatzintamalco, but at Xoxohuiltitlan and Tepeyacac no one fought.

Only we Tlatelolca held the road when their boats arrived. The next day, they abandoned Xoloco. There was fighting[13] for two days at Huitzillan.

At this time the Tenochca fought among themselves.[14] They said to one another, "Where are our children? Are they ⟨going to use them in the war⟩? Will they ever ⟨grow up⟩?"

They quickly seized four people and began killing them. The first they killed was Quauhnochtli, leader at the Tlacatecco [temple of Huitzilopochtli]; [then] Quapan, leader at Huitznahuac [temple of Tezcatlipoca], and incense-offering priests; the priest at Amantlan; and the priest at Tlalocan. These are the ones who lost their lives the second time the Tenochca fought among themselves.

[The Spaniards] came and set up a gun in the middle of the road at Tecaman. They aimed it[15] along the road in this direction; when they fired the gun, [the shot] landed at Quauhquiahuac [Eagle Gate].

Then all the Tenochca decamped. They took Huitzilopochtli[16] in their arms and brought him into Tlatelolco, establishing him at the *telpochcalli* [youths' house] in Amaxac. And they set up their ruler Quauhtemoctzin at Yacacolco, and at that time all the common people left their former altepetl of Tenochtitlan; on coming into Tlatelolco they stopped among our houses; then they settled down everywhere against the walls of our houses and on our roofs.

And their lords and lordly officials began to proclaim, saying, "O our lords, Mexica Tlatelolca, the stewards' warehouses are no longer ⟨by any means⟩[17] ours alone. ⟨[The Spaniards?] are not to have access to the warehouses and the land.⟩ Here is your property, the devices that your ruler was keeping for you, the shields, the wrist bands, the plumes to be girded on, the golden earplugs, the green-stones; it is all your property and possession. Be calm, do not lose heart. Whence have we come? We are Mexica, we are Tlatelolca." All came crying as they talked. At that time they gave them devices covered with gold and plumes.

And those who went about proclaiming in the roads and passageways and at the

tlaco ciuacoatl motelchiuh yn iquac viznauatl xochitl acolnauacati . anavacatl tlacochcalcatl ytzpotonqui covaçaca covayvitl oyximachoc . tezcacoacatl . vanitl oq̄z mix-
coatlaillotlac yn asca teuhcalcatl tentlil[18] . yehvantin i yn ⟨t⟩zazitinenqz yn isquich
quiteneuhtinenque yn omito yn iquac valcallaque tlatilulco .


Auh yz cate yn tlacaqz . Coyoaqz . tlacopaneca . azcapotzalca . tenayoca . quauhti-
tlancalqz . toltitlancalque . chicuhnauhteca . tetzcoco Coanacotzi . Cuitlauac [p. 31] .
tepechpan yzyocan yni ça moch evanti yn tlatoque yn quicanque yn iuh q̄toq̄ intlatol
yn tenochcan .
av in ixq̄ch cavitl yn ticalivaque aocan monexiti yn tenochcatl yn izq̄ otli y nica y
yacacolco yn atizcapa[19] y covatlā y nonovalco[20] y xoxoviltitla ȳ tepeyacac ça novia toneiscavil mochiuh ȳ titlatilolca çano yvi yn acalotli moch toneiscavil mochiuh

av i tenochcatl y teq̄va catcan onca quaçontec av in achcauhtli o moch moqua-
çonteq̄ av i quachic yn otomitl ça moquaquimilotinemi aoca [i]x[q]uezq̄ yn ixq̄ch cavitl ticalivaq̄ yn itlatocauh ça moch evantin i tlatilolca ȳ cololviticate

av in icivava moch no q̄pinaviq̄ q̄mavaq̄ q̄ilviq̄ tenochca . ca ⟨çamonoq̄⟩ amo
apinava ayc civatl amotla no moxauhtoca av in içivava mochoq̄litinemi yn q̄tlatlauhtia
ȳ tlatilolca av ie tlachia yn avaq̄ ȳ tepevaq̄ e valayva yn aoca netzi tenochca

av in tlatilolcatl ye y⟨x⟩polivi y quachic yn otomitl y yaoteq̄va ye yc miq̄ ȳ tleq̄q̄ztli
yn tepozmitl
e valayva yn acolvacan yn tlatovani ȳ tecōcōltzin evanti nonoçaloco ȳ tlatilulco
ticocyavacatl topātemoctzi tezcacovacatl poyecatzin tlacatecatl temilotzi tlacochcalcatl
coyovevetzi tzivatecpanecatl matlalacatzi

q̄milvico yn ititlava yn acolvaca tecocoltzi conilvia ca techvaliva ȳ tlacatl y couacatl
ȳ tecocoltzi ca comitalvia tla q̄caq̄ca y mexica y tlatilolca a e y toneva a e chichinaca yn
iyolo yn inacayo motolinia . auh çano yvi nevatl a otonevac a ochichinacac y noyolo
yn tleyntzi noconocovia yn noq̄milco y nocuexaco y novia nemi y nechtlacvic⟨o⟩lia
a mochiuh opoliuh yn ava y tepeva Ca noconitova manoço yyocan contlali tenochcatl
ma yoca opolivi ayatle noconchivaz oc noconchia yn itlatol q̄n q̄tozq̄ q̄zq̄lvitl con-
tla⟨tz⟩qz ca isq̄ch q̄mocaq̄ti[c]a y notlatol

ye concuepa yn tlatolli yn tlatilolco tlatoq̄ q̄monilvia otechmocnelili yn ticauhtzin
atel evatl ynic tona ynic tota yn acolva yn chichimecatl ca yz ca q̄mocaq̄tia a e cepovali
q̄neq̄a y mochivazq̄a yn iuh q̄valmitalvia[21] av in axca can oc niquitac ca o vel mixtlati
caocac motenochcaçaçilia ca e ceq̄ moquauhtitlacalcatlapiq̄a ceq̄ tenayoca azcapozalco
coyovaca e motlamiya can oc niq̄ta auh evatl ye motlatilolcaçaçilia q̄n oc nicchivaz
otlacauhq̄n iyollotzi oq̄mocnelili y moq̄q̄ça y movillana a e toconchia yn iyyo yn
itla[p. 32]tol[22] yn totecoyovan


ye yuh epoualli ticalliua y ye quinomauico spañoles yn tzatzico ytoca Castaneda
ytocayoca yyauhtenco tzatzico quiualhuicac tlaxcalteca y ye quiualtzatzilia yaotlapia y

market⟨s⟩ at Xipanoc and Tetliyaco were Tlacotzin the Cihuacoatl; Motelchiuh, who was then Huitznahuatl; Xochitl, who was Acolnahuacatl; the Tlacochcalcatl Itz-potonqui; Coaçaca Coaihuitl, who was recognized as Tezcacoacatl; Huanitl Oquiz-tzin the Mixcoatlailotlac; and Tentlil, currently Teocalcatl. [18] These are the ones who went about proclaiming, who went about saying what has been mentioned when they entered Tlatelolco.

And here are those who listened: [the rulers] of Coyoacan, Tlacopan, Azcapotzalco, Tenanyocan, Quauhtitlan, Toltitlan, Chiucnauhtlan, Coanacochtzin of Tetzcoco, Cuitlahuac, Tepechpan, and Itzyocan. These are all the rulers who heard what the Tenochca said.

And during all this time, while we were being attacked, the Tenochca appeared no-where on all the roads here in Yacacolco, Atizaapan, [19] Coatlan, Nonoalco, [20] Xoxo-huiltitlan, and Tepeyacac. They became the responsibility of the Tlatelolca alone, and likewise the canals all became our exclusive responsibility.

And the Tenochca who were war captains cut off their hair [to avoid recognition], and all the subordinate leaders cut their hair, and the scraped-heads and the Otomis wrapped up their heads. Nowhere did they show their faces during the time when we were being attacked; only all the Tlatelolca surrounded their leader.

And all their women also shamed and scolded the Tenochca, saying to them, "You are just lying inactive, you have no shame. A woman will never decorate herself to be next to you." Their women went about weeping and imploring the Tlatelolca; and seeing this, the citizens sent word, but nowhere did the Tenochca appear.

But the Tlatelolca scraped-heads and Otomis, the war leaders, were dying from the guns and iron bolts.

The ruler of Acolhuacan, Tencocoltzin, sent word. Those with whom they came to talk were the Ticocyahuacatl of Tlatelolco, Topantemoctzin; the Tezcacoacatl Poyecatzin; the Tlacateccatl Temilotzin; the Tlacochcalcatl Coyohuehuetzin; and the Cihuatecpanecatl Matlalacatzin.

The messengers of Tencocoltzin of Acolhuacan came to say to them, "The lord ⟨Coacatl⟩ Tencocoltzin sends us here and says, 'May the Mexica Tlateloca hear; their hearts burn and smart, their bodies are afflicted. And my heart too has burned and smarted. Whatever little thing I buy for myself [and put] in my bundle or in the folds of my cloak, they look everywhere and take it from me. The citizens are already lost. I say, let the Tenochca be left alone, let them perish by themselves. I will do nothing yet; I will await word of what [the Tlatelolca] say and how many days ⟨they are defer-ring it⟩. This is all of my statement that they are to hear.' "

Then the Tlatelolca rulers responded to the speech, telling them, "Thank you, our younger brothers; the Chichimecatl of Acolhuacan is our protector. Here is what he is to hear. Twenty days ago ⟨they⟩ wanted what he says to be done, [21] but now, where have we seen [the Tenochca]? They have entirely hidden their faces. No one pro-claims himself a Tenochca any more, for some pretend to be from Quauhtitlan, and some claim to be from Tenanyocan, Azcapotzalco, or Coyoacan. Where do we still see any of them? And those ⟨whom we do⟩ proclaim themselves Tlatelolca. What are we to do? [Tencocoltzin] has been kind. Those who toddle and crawl owe him thanks. We await word [22] from our lords."

After we had been being attacked for sixty days, and the Spaniards were coming [fighting] in person, one named Castañeda came shouting at the place called Iyauh-

tenantitla tlaxoxiuhco ytoca ytzpancalqui achcauhtli chapoltzi omesti tlapaltecatl [23]
cuesacaltzi .

quiualhuia xiualhuia acame yn ūcā [ancate]
auh ye comolhuia tleȳ quitozqz ma ça tocōcaquiti
nima ye yc acalco motlaliqz çan oc veca motecaqz q̇monilhuia tleȳ anquito[z]nequi

ye quiualhuia [24] ȳ tlaxcalteca Can amocha [25]
quimonilhuia Ca ye qualli amehvā yn amotemoua xiualhuia amechnotza teutl capitan
yc nima vel onquizqz nima ye yc quiuica y nonoalco ayauhcalco vncā capitan yoa
malintzi yoā tonatiuh y Sandoual vnca cenquiztimani yn altepetl ypan tlatoque .

tlatolo . Conilhuia ȳ capitā Ca ouallaqz tlatilulca otiq̇manato .

quiualilhuiā malintzi tla xiualhuia . ca cōmitalhuia ȳ capitan . quē momati y mesica
cuix cenca oc piltontli quauhtemoc Amo quitlavculia ȳ piltzintli yn ciuatzintli y ye
iuhqui ye [26] poliui ueuentzi Ca nica mani ȳ tlatoqz tlaxcalla vexotzīco . cholola .
chalco . acolhvaca quauhnauac xochmilco mizquic cuitlauac Colhuaca

Conitoa . a uey ynic teca omocacaiauh ȳ tenochcatl n⟨o⟩ tonehvac yn iyollo yn atl
ipā tepetl ipa tlatoca . auh ynhi ma yyoca quiuallalica tenochcatl ma yyoca vnpopoliui
Cuix atle yc tonehoa yn iyollo tlatilulca yn iuh opoliuhqz ynic ȳca omocacaiauhqz .

nima ye quiualilhuia tlatoqz Cuix a⁰ yuhqui anquitoa yn ātlatoqz .
Conitoa . ca q̄maca . ma yuh q̄mocaq̇ti y to⁰ teutl ma yyoca q̇ualalica tenochcatl ma
yyoca vnpopoliui . O ca yuhqui hi ȳ tlatolli anquinotquilia [27] motechiuhcava :

ca conitoa teutl : ma quilhuiti ȳ quauhtemoc ma mononotzaca ma yyoca Cōtlaliqz
tenochcatl oc ye nechca noniquania teucalhuiaca yn quenin amononotzazque vnpa
notech acitiuh yn motlatol [28] . auh yn acalli oc ye coyoaca miquania .

yn ocōcaque ça quiuatoque [29] Can oc tiquimanazque yn quimotemolia . Ca otoui-
tique ma cuelle toconihyouica
Ca yuin yn impa mihito ȳ tenochca vnpa ynca necētlalliloc . ça acalticā vntzatzito y
ça aucmo uelli yyoca quintlalia tenochca . y ye iuhqui [p. 33] yeque⟨n⟩e yc ⟨to⟩tech
moquetzque y necalliztli

niman açitimoquetzaco Cuepopa auh ȳ yacacolco Cozcaquauhco vnca moye⟨c⟩o
tlatepozmiuiaia coyoueueçi nauinti .
Auh yn acalli motecaco texopa yeylhuiti y necalliztli vnca : techualleuitique nimā
vncā açico teuthualco nauilhuiti necalliztli

Auh y nica niman açico yacacolco ye yquac vncā axiuaque Spañoles tlilhuacan vtli
ypa niman ye yxquich aua tepeua macuiltzontli yn unca mic y ça ineyxcauil tlatilulcatl .

yquac tontotzonpantique yn titlatilulca yexca y māca tzonpantli y manca teuthualco

tenco. He brought the Tlaxcalans. He shouted in this direction to those who stood watch at the rampart at Tlaxoxiuhco, who were one named Chapoltzin, leader of the Itzpan people, along with the Tlapaltecatl[23] Cuexacaltzin.

He said to them, "Come here, whoever is there."

They said to each other, "What will they say? Let's just go listen to him."

Then they got in a boat and, stationing themselves at a distance, said to them, "What do you want to say?"

The Tlaxcalans responded,[24] "Where is your home?"[25]

They said to them, "Very well, you are being sought. Come; the god, the Captain is summoning you."

Then they left; then they took them to Nonoalco, at Ayauhcalco, where the Captain, Marina, Tonatiuh [Alvarado], Sandoval, and all the rulers of the various altepetl were gathered.

When they spoke, they said to the Captain, "The Tlatelolca have come; we went to get them."

Marina told them in reply, "Do come here; the Captain says, 'What do the Mexica think? Is Quauhtemoc still such a small child? He has no pity on the children and women; the old men have already[26] perished. Here are the rulers of Tlaxcala, Huejotzinco, Cholula, Chalco, Acolhuacan, Cuernavaca, Xochimilco, Mizquic, Cuitlahuac, and Culhuacan.'"

[The Tlatelolca] said, "The Tenochca have taken great advantage of people; the hearts of the rulers in the [various] altepetl have been pained. Well then, let them leave the Tenochca by themselves, let them perish alone. Perhaps the Tlatelolca will not be pained by it, the way they perished because they took advantage of them."

Then [Cortés] replied to the rulers, "Perhaps it is not as you rulers say."

They said, "Yes, indeed it is; may our lord the god so hear it. Let them leave the Tenochca by themselves, let them perish alone. That is the word that you are to carry[27] to your subordinates."

The god said, "Let them go tell Quauhtemoc. Let them consult, let them leave the Tenochca by themselves. Meanwhile, I am moving to Teocalhueyacan; word from you[28] about what you have decided will reach me there. And the boats are moving to Coyoacan for a while."

When they heard this, they just replied,[29] "Where are we to get hold of the people they are looking for? We have had a difficult time of it; let us make an effort."

Thus were the Tenochca discussed and agreement reached about them. But [when the Tlatelolca were] in the boat, they shouted, "It is no longer possible to leave the Tenochca by themselves! At this point, after all, they have ⟨relied on us⟩ in the fighting!"

Then [the Spaniards] reached Cuepopan, and at Yacacolco, in Cozcaquauhco, Coyohuehuetzin fought, shooting crossbow bolts, and ⟨hit⟩ four.

And the boats stationed themselves at Texopan. The fighting lasted three days, and they drove us from there. Then they reached the temple courtyard; the fighting lasted four days.

And when they reached Yacacolco here, Spaniards were captured on the Tlilhuacan road, as well as all the people from the various altepetl. Two thousand died there, and the Tlatelolca were exclusively responsible for it.

At this time we Tlatelolca set up skull racks; skull racks were in three places. One

tlilla yn vnca çoçotoca yn intzonteco totecuioua ³⁰ yc vca yacacolco no vnca çoçotoca
yn intzōteco ȳ totecuioua yoā vntetl cauallo ytzonteco yquesca çacatla ciuateucalli
yxpa Ça yneyxcauil yn tlatilulca

Auh y ye yuhqui techualleuitique açitimoquezaco tianquizco ye yquac yxpoliuh yn
tlatilulcatl vey ocelotl vey tiacauh . yc omoçema y necalliztli

ye yquac y mocentlazque micalque tlatilulca çiua teuiuiteque tlamamaque tlauiztli
onactinenque yn īcue moch cacoquistique ynic vel tetocaya

ye yuhqui vncā conquachcaltico capitan tianquizco momozco ye yquac no qui-
quetzque quauhtematlac yn ūca momozco yn uncā tianquizco matlaquilhuiti necalliztli .

Auh yxquich hi yn topa [mo]chiuh yn tiquitaque ȳ ticmauizoqz ȳ techocti ȳ tetla-
[ocolti] ynic titlaihiouique ³¹ . yn atl tiquiqz tequixquiatl xantetl ypa tlatetzotzontli yn
atlacomolli ça teneneyxcauil chimaltitlā ȳ pieloya yn oc nen aca moteyc[cequi]liz-
nequi ça chimaltitla tiquaque ȳ tzonpanquauitl yn tequixquiçacatl ȳ xa⟨n⟩tetl ȳ cuez-
palli quimichi teutlaquilli ³² . Ocuilli titonetechquaqz yn iquac tlepan quimontlaliaya y
ye ycuci ynacayo vncan con⟨cuic⟩ tleco quiquaya .

Auh ȳ topatiuh mochiuh ³³ yn ipatiuh mochiuh ȳ telpochtli ȳ tlamacazqui yn ich-
pochtli ȳ piltzintli y ye yxquich maçeualli yn ipatiuh mochiuh ça omatecochtli tlaolli
ça matlactli axaxayacatlaxcalli tequixquiçacatlaxcalli ça çenpoualli topatiuh mochiuh
yn teucuitlatl yn chalchiuitl yn quachtli ȳ quetzalli y ye yxquich tlaçotli auctle ypa
motac ça tetepeui

[p. 34] yn o yuh cōquetzque quauhtematlatl tiāquizco ³⁴ ye yquac concauaco y
yaomic acolnauacatl xochitl tenochtitlan ycha ye yuh cenpoualilhuitl quicatinemi ȳ
quicauaco tianquizco tlatilulco motlami amo motenochcaito ynic quiualhuicaqz
nenecoc quiualaantiaque yoa ce tepozmitl ce tlequiquiztli y quiualpixtia

yn ocōquezaco copalnamacoa nima ye yc valtzatzi vallaz p⟨i⟩lli nima ye yc oui
tlatilulca canato vnteaca vitznauac tiachcauh toueyo .

yn oconaque xochitl quiualnauatia y viznauac tiachcauh quilhuia ca quitquitiuh ȳ
tlatolli xochitl yn oquinonotz quauhtemoc topantemoc ³⁵ tehvatl ticnonotzaquiuh ȳ
capitan .

yn iquac concauaco nimā yc moman yn chimalli aucmo necalliva aocac ano . Auh
nima ye quiuica contlalito axocotzinco Ciuateucalco .

yn ocōtlalito nima ye yc ui quilhuizqz topātemoczi coyoueuetzi temiloçi e niman
yc no ye yn ītlatocauh tenochca . Conilhuia nopiltzitzine Ca oconcauaco yn amote-
chiuhcauh acolnauacatl xochitl quil tleȳ ynahuatil amechmomaquiliz .

Nimā ye yc mononoza Comolhuia quen anquitoa
nimā yc mochīti tzatziteuaqz macaçocmo nicā quiualhuicaca : Ca yuhquī tonex-

was in the temple courtyard at Tlillan, where the heads of our lords [the Spaniards] were strung; [30] the second place was in Yacacolco, where the heads of our lords were strung, along with the heads of two horses; the third place was in Çacatla, facing the Cihuateocalli [Woman-Temple]. It was the exclusive accomplishment of the Tlatelolca.

After this they drove us from there and reached the marketplace. That was when the great Tlatelolca warriors were entirely vanquished. With that the fighting stopped once and for all.

That was when the Tlatelolca women all let loose, fighting, striking people, taking captives. They put on warriors' devices, all raising their skirts so that they could give pursuit.

At this point they made a canopy for the Captain on a sacrificial platform in the marketplace. This was also when they set up the catapult there on the platform. The fighting in the marketplace lasted ten days.

And all this is what happened to us and what we saw and beheld. What we suffered is cause for tears and sorrow. [31] The water we drank was salt. Adobe bricks ⟨dipped in⟩ a well were an exclusive possession, guarded under a shield. If someone tried to toast something, [it had to be guarded] with a shield. We ate colorín wood, grass from the salt flats, adobe, lizards, mice, things full of dust. [32] We fought over eating worms; when they put them on the fire and their flesh began to cook, they picked them out of the fire and ate them.

And we had a price. [33] There was a price for a youth, a priest, a maiden, or a little child. The price for any ordinary person was just two handfuls of shelled maize. Ten cakes of water flies or twenty of grass from the salt flats was our price. Gold, greenstones, tribute cloth, plumes, and all precious things were considered as nothing and just spilled on the ground.

When they had set up the catapult in the marketplace, [34] then they came to deliver Xochitl, the Acolnahuacatl. He died in the war [but was still alive at this time]; Tenochtitlan was his home. For twenty days they had ⟨had him with them⟩; they came to the marketplace to deliver him. He attributed himself to Tlatelolco; he did not call himself a Tenochca. When they brought him, they came taking him on both sides, and a crossbowman and a harquebusier came guarding him.

When they left him at Copalnamacoyan, they shouted out, "Here will come a nobleman." Then the Tlatelolca went to get him; the leader was Tohueyo, a leader from Huitznahuac.

When they had taken Xochitl, the Huitznahuac leader came to report [to Quauhtemoc] and told him, "Xochitl is carrying a message." Quauhtemoc told Topantemoc, [35] "You will come to talk to the Captain."

When they came to deliver [Xochitl], the war stopped. There was no more fighting, no one was taken prisoner. Then they took [Xochitl] and put him in the Cihuateocalli at Axocotzinco.

When they had put him there, they went to tell Topantemoctzin, Coyohuehuetzin, and Temilotzin, and thereupon also the ruler of the Tenochca. They said to them, "O my lords, they have come and delivered your agent the Acolnahuacatl Xochitl. It is said he has some message to give you."

Then they consulted and said to one another, "What do you say?"

Then they all cried out, "Let him not be brought here, for our sacrifices when we

tlaual omochiuh . Ca oticamapouhqz ca oticopalpouhqz ma çano ye quiualqui yn
itlatol yn ocanato .

ynic ça ye no ye yauh viznauac tiachcauh toueyo ȳ quicuiz ȳ tlatolli . Nima ye yc
quitlatoltia quitilmacaltique[36] quitemolia yn tlatolli ȳ quiualitquitia

quitoa acolnauacatl xochitl . Ca quimitalhuia teutl Capitan yoā y malinzi . tla quicaqui quauhtemoc ȳ coyoueue topātemoc amo quitlaoculia y maceualli ȳ piltzintli yn
ueuēzi yn illamatzi ca ça yxquich y nica Cuix oc vel ce netlalolli : auh y nima yxquich
: ma ualla chipauac ciuatl chipauac tlaolli totoli totoltetl chipauac tlaxcalli . Auh
Canoço mocia[37] quē quitoz ma yyoca quiuallalica tenochcatl ma yioca vnpopoliu[i]

[p. 35] yn oconcuic tlatolli viznahuac tiachcauh toueyo nima ye yc yauh quimacaz ȳ
tlatolli tlatilulco tlatoqz ⟨tetlan⟩ vnca meuititica ȳ tenochca yntlatocauh quauhtemoc
ȳ ocōcaque yn isquich ȳ tlatolli quiuatquic[38] acolnauacatl xochitl nima ye yc mononoza tlatilulco tlatoque Comolhuia quē anquitoa quē amononoza .

Nima ye quiualitoa Coyoueuetzi tlacuchcalcatl tla quiualnozaca ⟨teua⟩ conilhuia
tla xiuallauh quen antlachia quē anquita yn amotlapiello .

Conitoa teua a⟨ma⟩tlamatqui amatequi Nopilçīçīne ma xicmocaquitica tleynel
tiquitozqz Ca ça nauilhuitl yn titlanapualtizqz Auh y mach yehvatl yn inavatil y vitzilopochtli cayatle vetzi Cuix ychtaca a anquimotilizque ma oc tonaçica ca ça nauilhuitl yn titlanapoualtilizque .

Auh y ye yuhqui amo mouelcaqui . ye no yc peuh y yaoyotl ça ye no ⟨no ic⟩
conistito cōpeualtito yaoyotl viznauac tiachcauh toueyo yc yequene tecemolinique
amaxac açitimoquezaco necalilliztli

nima ye yc nequequeçalo ça tlacapa netlaloloc yn atl tlacatica tzop tlacatica ⟨te⟩ ça
ye y ⟨maquiz/miquiz⟩ .

yuin yn opoliuh y mexicatl tlatilulcatl yn oquicauh yn iauh yn itepeuh y ye uncā
Amaxac yn ixquich y[e]ticatca auctle tochimal tomaquauh auctle tochimal auctle
ti⟨c⟩quani yuh ce youal yn topā quiauh

y ye yuhqui yn ovnalquiz nimā ye yc ui y coyoueuezi topantemoczi temilozi auh
yn quauhtemoczi Concauaco ȳ quauhtemoczi yn ūcā catca Capitan dō p⁰ aluarado
malinzi

[p. 36] Yn ovnanoqz yquac peuh y ye quiça maçeualli yn campa motztilitia yni
quixoa yn oc aca tzotzomatzintli yc motzinilacatzotiuh

ciuatzintli nouiā ȳ quitlatemolia x̄p̄ianoti quitlaxilia yn iquetzi nouia nemi yn [in-
nacazco] yn icamac yn ixilla[39] yn itzontitla

Ca ye yui ȳ quiz maceualli ynic nouia moyauac yn atl ipan tepetl ypa ȳ texomolco
tecaltech maaquito :

ynic tixitinque ca yey calli xiuitl yca poliuh altepetl ynic tixitinqz ypā nexochimaco
Cemilhuitonalli Ce Couatl

yn o iuh tixitinque ȳ tlatilulco tlatoque motlalito quauhtitla ȳ topantemoczi tla-
cuchcalcatzintli Coyoueuetzi . temilotzi . ye vey tiacauh y vei oquichtli ça cani moqui-
quistia ça ytzotzomatzi yetinemi . No yuhqui Ciuatzintli ça tzotzontecomayo ȳ qui-
mocuetia tlacuiloltzintli quimouipiltia

read in the paper and the incense were such that the one who went to get him should receive the message."

So the same Huitznahuac leader, Tohueyo, went to receive the message. He caused [Xochitl] to speak and interrogated him about the message he brought.[36]

The Acolnahuacatl Xochitl said, "The god, the Captain, and Marina say, 'Let Quauhtemoc, Coyohuehue, and Topantemoc hear. They have no pity on the people, the little children, the old men and women. ⟨It is over here. Is there to be another rout?⟩ And then let everything be brought: beautiful women, shelled white maize, turkey hens, eggs, white bread. But perhaps one should wait[37] to see what the reply is. Let the Tenochca be left by themselves, let them perish alone.' "

When the Huitznahuac leader Tohueyo had received the message, he went to give it to the Tlatelolca rulers; sitting among them was the ruler of the Tenochca, Quauhtemoc. When they had heard the whole message that the Acolnahuacatl Xochitl brought,[38] the Tlatelolca rulers said to one another, "What do you say? What is your advice?"

Then the Tlacochcalcatl Coyohuehuetzin said, "Let them summon the Teohua [custodian of the god]." [When he arrived,] he said to him, "Come; what is your [pl.] view? How do you see what is in your custody [the ritual calendar]?"

The Teohua, learned with papers, cutter of papers, said, "My lords, listen to what we will say. In only four days, eighty will have passed [since the fighting began]. Perhaps it is the order of Huitzilopochtli that [nothing should be done when that term] is not yet fulfilled. Perhaps you will see [what should be done] secretly ⟨have it revealed to you⟩. Let us wait out the eighty days, for there are only four more."

But when the time came, it was not approved ⟨by the god⟩. The war began again. It was the same Tohueyo, Huitznahuac leader, who faced ⟨the enemy⟩ and began the war, with which finally they moved everyone to Amaxac, and the fighting reached there.

Then people were trampled; one ran just on top of people. The water filled up with people. It was through people that ⟨one saved oneself? one died?⟩.

Thus were defeated the Mexica Tlatelolca, who relinquished their altepetl. There at Amaxac, as to all we had with us, we no longer had shields or war clubs, we no longer had anything to eat. It rained on us all night.

When it was done, when it was over, Coyohuehuetzin, Topantemoctzin, and Temilotzin went and delivered Quauhtemoctzin to the place where the Captain, don Pedro de Alvarado, and Marina were.

When they had been taken into custody, the people began to leave, heading for where there was a way out. Some still had some rags to wrap around their bottoms.

The Christians searched all over the women; they pulled down their skirts and went all over their bodies, in their mouths, on their abdomens,[39] in their hair.

Thus the people left, scattering among the altepetl all around, going into the corners or against the sides of other people's houses.

When we dispersed and the altepetl was lost, it was Three House year. We dispersed in [the month of] Nexochimaco, on a day One Serpent.

When we had dispersed, the Tlatelolca rulers Topantemoctzin, the Tlacochcalcatl Coyohuehuetzin, and Temilotzin went to settle in Quauhtitlan. Great warriors had to find a way to live somewhere or other, wearing nothing but rags. Likewise the women put on just skirts with a skull pattern and painted blouses.

ynic ye nentlamati tlatoqz ye ypa mononotza y ye no cepa tixpoliui y cetzin oc
oquizqz macehualli y ye tichtacamictilo acolhuaca otontla

ye yc mononotza ȳ quitlaoculia macehualli ye quitoa y ma tiuia ma tictlatlauhtito
yn to° tlatoani Capitan
  Nima ye yc motemoua teucuitlatl tetlatemolilo ye tetlatlanilo yn açoc aca achi teucuitlatl y chimaltitech tlauiztitech oquicuic oquimopielti yn anoço ytenteuh ytenpilol
: yn anoçoc aca oquitla oquiquistili yn iteua yn azo teucuitlatl yn anoço yyacametz
anoço ȳpilol y ye yxquich nima ye yc monechicoa .

  y ye yuhqui yn omonechico yn oc quesquich onez : nima ye yc quiualisquetza yn
intechiuhcauh tlapaltecatl Cuexacaltzi tecpanecazintli vitzitzi viznauac tiachcauh
toueyo . Cuytlachcoacal poçonçi yehuantin i yn quicauato teucuitlatl Coyouaca .

  yn oonacique conilhuia Capitan totecuioe tlatoanie mizualmotlatlauhtilia y mote-
chiuhcaua [p. 37] ȳ tlatilulca tlatoque Conitoa Ma qui[mo]caquiti yn tlacatl ȳ to°
M[otolinia] yn imaceualtzi ca ye conihiohuia yn auacā tepeva[cā] ȳ texomolco tecaltech . Ca ye yca mocacaiava yn acolhva yn otomitl ye quichtacamictia Auh [yni ca] yz
catqui yni quiualmotlatlauhtilia Ca yehvatl yn īteteuh yn inacoch y motechiuhcauh
auh yn toteuua yn intech ocatca : auh ȳ chimaltitech vca catca ye yxpan contequilia ye
tanatitia .
  Auh yn oquitac ȳ Capitan ȳ malinçi ça niman y ce yquallani q̇toa : Cuix ye ȳ yn
temolo ye ȳ quimotemolia y nicā toltecaacalloco anqui⟨∗∗∗⟩tlaçaltique Campa ca ma
neci .
  Nima ye y conitoa motitlāqz . Ca oquimanili ȳ quauhtemoczi . y ciuacoatl auh y
viznauatl a yehuāti Comati yn campa ca ma quīmotlatlanili .
  Yn oquicac yequene yc vel quimonilpi tepoztli quimōtlatlalili .
  Quiualilhuia malinçi Ca conitoa . Capitan . Ma uia ma quinonotzati yn ītlatocava
onechmocneliliqz azo nelli ye motolinia maceualli ye yca necacayauallo ma ualhuia
ma motecaqui yn īchā tlatilulco yn ixquich yntlal ma ypa motecaca tlatilulca yoa
xiquim[o]lhuilic[a yn] tlatilulca tlatoqz ȳ tenochtitlan aucac motecaz Canel ȳtepeualpā
ȳ teteuh ca ye yncha ma mouicaca
  y ye yuhqui yn oyaque tlatilulca tlatoqz yntitlaua nimā ye yc intech moquetza te-
nochtitlā tlatoqz ȳ quintlatoltia . ye yquac quic[x]itlatique yn quauhtemoctzi .

  Auh ça vallathui ȳ quiualhuicaqz vallilpitiaqz quauhti[tech] quimoniylpico quauh-
titech ychan auitzotzi yn acatl yacapa vncā quiz ȳ espada tlequiquiztli yn imasca
totecuioua ȳ quintlaçaltiqz .
  Auh yn teucuitlatl quiquistito Cuitlauactonco ycha ytzpotonqui . Yn ocōquistico
totecuioua ye no cepa quiuica Coyoaca ylpitiui
  [p. 38] Ye unca mic ȳ teua ȳ quipiaya vitzilopoch [40] yn quitemoliaya yn campa onoc
ytlatqui tlacatecolotl ynehvā totec tlamacazqui tlenamacac .

  ye yquac qui[momachi]tocaque ynic teyacāqz Xaltoca quachilco ȳ pieloya ytlatqui
yn ūpa quiçacato . yn onez ymomesti quinpilloque maçatla onepantla .

For this reason the rulers were discontent and consulted about it, [saying], "We are perishing for a second time. Some of the people who left are being murdered among the Otomis of Acolhuacan."

Then they consulted, favoring the people, and said, "Let us go implore our lord ruler the Captain."

Then there was a search for gold. People were searched and interrogated to see whether someone perhaps had taken and kept a little gold on his shield or device, or his lip plug or lip pendant, or if someone perhaps had taken something of gold from his gods, perhaps their half-moon nose ornament or their pendant. It was all then collected.

When whatever was found had been collected, they selected as their representatives the Tlapaltecatl Cuexacaltzin, the Tecpanecatl Huitziltzin, the Huitznahuac leader Tohueyo, and the Cuitlachcoacatl Poçontzin; these are the ones who went to deliver the gold to Coyoacan.

When they arrived, they said to the Captain, "O our lord, o ruler, your subordinates the Tlatelolca rulers come to implore you; may the lord take heed. His vassals are afflicted, they are suffering in the various altepetl in the corners and against the sides of other people's houses. The Acolhuaque and Otomis are taking advantage of them, murdering them. Well then, that is what they come to ask about. Here are the lip- and earplugs of your servants, and what was on our gods and on our shields." They laid it before him in baskets.

But when the Captain and Marina saw it they became angry and said, "Is that what is being looked for? What is being sought is what you caused to be lost at the Tolteca canal. Where is it? Let it be produced."

Then the messengers said, "Quauhtemoc took it, and the Cihuacoatl and the Huitznahuatl. They know where it is. Let them be interrogated."

When [Cortés] heard this, he had them tied up tightly, putting them in irons.

Marina replied to them, "The Captain says, 'Let them go and consult their rulers. I thank them. Perhaps the people are truly afflicted and advantage is being taken of them. Let them come back to settle in their home, Tlatelolco; let the Tlatelolca settle on all their land. And tell the Tlatelolca rulers that no one is to settle in Tenochtitlan yet, for it is the conquered area of the gods and is already their home. May they go.'"

When this had happened and the messengers of the Tlatelolca rulers had left, they turned to the Tenochtitlan rulers and interrogated them. At this time they burned Quauhtemoctzin on the feet.

And at dawn they brought them, tied to poles, and they came and tied them to poles at the home [palace] of Ahuitzotzin in Acatliyacapan. The swords and guns belonging to our lords, that they made them drop, came to light there.

And they went to Cuitlahuactonco, to the home of Itzpotonqui, to extricate the gold. When our lords had retrieved it, they took them again, bound, to Coyoacan.

At that point died the Teohua, who was in charge of Huitzilopochtli,[40] and they were interrogating him about where the appurtenances of the demon were located, along with the incense-offering priest of Totec.

At that time they confessed, so that they led people to Xaltocan, to Quachichilco, where his appurtenances, which they had transported there, were being guarded. When the things had been found, they hanged them both in the middle of the road at Maçatlan.

Y ye yuhqui yquac peuh y ye ualcallaqui maceualli ynic motecaco tlatilulco naui tochtli Xiuitl yca . Nimā ye yc uitz ȳ temillotzi vmotlalico capoltitla . auh ȳ dō Juᵒ veuenzi omotlalico aticpac . Auh ȳ coyoueueçi ȳ topātemoczi quauhtitla mique

yn otontotecaco nican tlatilulco çan oc tyyoque ayamo motecaco ȳ toᵒ x̄p̄ıanoti çan oc yc techyollalique ȳ coyoaca yxquichcauitique

vnca quipilloqz vizilopochco tlatoani macuilxochitzi nima ye colhoaca tlatoani pizozi ⟨no⟩ vncā quipilloqz yoan quauhtitla tlacatecatl yoā tlillancalqui quīpelloqual-tique . niman ye xochmilca [no] quinperroqualtique : yoā tetzcoca ecamastlaçi quipel-loqualtiqz ça mocauaco ayac quiualhuicac çan ymamatlacuilollo quiuatquiqz⁴¹ nauīti ce choloqz ça yey in acico Coyoaqz⁴² .

Auh y ye onoqz Coyoaca ye vnca xexeliuh y nouian altepetl niman ye yc momace-valmaca yn ixquich nouian altepetl ye yquac ⟨tenemactic⟩ ye yquac nemaceualmacoc .

Nima ye y quiualtoma tenochtitlan tlatoqz : yn oquiualtonqz ye ui yn azcapotzalco ye vnpa mononotzato ynic yaocallaquizquia meztitla vnpa valmocuepato tolla .

Nima ye yc yaotlatoan Capitan vaxyacac yehuāti via Acolhuaca . Nima ye meztitla nimā Michuaca Niman⁴³

After this, the people began to come back to settle here in Tlatelolco, in the year of Four Rabbit. Then Temilotzin came and settled in Capoltitlan, and don Juan Huehuentzin came to settle in Aticpac, but Coyohuehuetzin and Topantemoctzin died in Quauhtitlan.

When we came to settle here in Tlatelolco, we were still all alone. Our lords the Christians had not yet come to settle; they gave us consolation by staying for the time being in Coyoacan.

There they hanged the ruler of Huitzilopochco, Macuilxochitzin, as well as the ruler of Culhuacan, Pitzotzin. They also hanged the Tlacateccatl of Quauhtitlan, and they had the Tlillancalqui eaten by dogs. They also had some people of Xochimilco eaten by dogs. And they had some Tetzcoca, one of whom was Ecamaxtlatzin, eaten by dogs. They just came to stay. No one accompanied them, they just brought[41] their codices. There were four of them. One fled, and only three got to Coyoacan.[42]

And while [the Spaniards] were dwelling at Coyoacan, the altepetl all around were distributed. Then all the altepetl everywhere were given [to the Spaniards] as vassals; [the Spaniards] were given their portion of vassals.

Then they released the Tenochtitlan rulers; when they released them, they went to Azcapotzalco. They went there to consult about a military expedition to Metztitlan; they came back from Tula [presumably without having gone to Metztitlan].

Then the Captain proclaimed war in Oaxaca; they had gone to Acolhuacan. Then Metztitlan, then Michoacan, then . . .[43]

# EXTRACT FROM THE CODEX AUBIN

*Nahuatl*

[ce acatl] ¹ Nica miq̄co ȳ moteuhcçomatzin yvā yquac açico ȳ marques

ⱤIn iq̄c q̄npeuhq̄ y mexica in x̄p̄ianome camo çānen huallāq̄ ca ytencopatzinco in tote° ca q̄monavatilli in sancto pᵉ q̄molhuili xiq̄navatican in cavallelosme oc centetl tlalli ipā yazque ynic açico ȳ nican xii frayles

[p. 82] ⱤIn ipā micq̄ yn aviyanime ychpochvan yezquia ȳ moteuhcçomatzin quitoque in x̄p̄ianome Vallazque civa yehuantin ȳ mochpochvā Quito ȳ moteuhcçomatzin Tla quicaquican ȳ mexica

ⱤIn ipan açico castillan tlaca ye cēpovalli ōmacuilli de nouiembre ypan quecholli oquiuh matlaquilhuitl tacizque in quecholli niman ic valmoma in deziembre .v. 20 ² atemoztli. tititl. yzcalli .v. quavitleva xillopevaliztli tonçoztontli. veytoçoztli. toxcatl.

In ipan in toxcatl yn acoquiçaya in diablo quimmictique in cuicoyanovaya ynic peuh in cuicoyanoliztli çan quitla ȳ moteuhcçoma quilhui yn malintzin Tla quimocaquiti in teotl ca otonaçico yn ilhuiuh in toteouh ca axcā matlaquilhuitl Auh ynin aça oc toconquixtia catle ma tayzque ca çan tititotizque yn iquac in ye quitlecavia in tzovalli tell icavacazque ca çan ye ixquich

Auh niman quito in capidan Ca ye qualli ma quichivazque ca onicac

Niman ic ompeuhque quimillochtito yn oc cequintin vallaca castillan tlaca ça yehuatl in tonatiuh mocauhtia Auh yn iq̄c yn oaçito ȳ itlapovalpan niman ye quitova ȳ moteuhcçoma . Tla quicaquican yn inantzitzinhuan ca yz catqui [p. 83] niquilhui in teotl Ca otaçico yn ilhuiuh ypan in toteouh ca toconilhuiq̄xtilizque Niman quito Xicchivacan In axcan quen tonyez ³

Nimā q̇toque ȳ pipiltin Tla q̇nvalnotzacā in tiachcavā Auh yn oonyaque nimā ye q̇nnavatia q̇milhuia Cenca oc ye toconana yn iuh mochivani

Auh quitoque in tiachcavā Ma çan chicavac mana

Niman quito yn ecatzin tlacateccatl Tla xicmocaquiltican intlacatle tixpan ca yn iuh mochiuh in cholollan yn çan q̇ncaltzacque yn axcan ma no yuh techiuhti ma cecentecpantli chimalli totlapiel mochiva

Niman q̇to ȳ moteucçoma Cuix toyaopan in ticate ma motelchiva

Niman quito in tlacateccatl Ca ye qualli

# EXTRACT FROM THE CODEX AUBIN

*English Translation*

[One Reed.] [1] Here Moteucçoma died, and this is when the Marqués arrived.

⊄ This is when the Christians conquered the Mexica; they came not by accident, but at the order of our Lord, for he gave orders to the Holy Father. He said to him, "Order the cavaliers to go to another land," so that the twelve friars arrived here.

⊄ In this year the prostitutes who were supposed to be daughters of Moteucçoma died. The Christians said, "Let women be brought, your daughters." Moteucçoma said, "Let the Mexica hear, . . ."

⊄ In this year the Castilians arrived, on the twenty-fifth of November, in Quecholli, just before the tenth day of Quecholli. Then came December [. . .] [2] Atemoztli, Tititl, Izcalli, five [days of Nemontemi], Quahuitl ehua, Xipehualiztli, Toçoztontli, Hueitoçoztli, Toxcatl.

In Toxcatl, when the devil was raised up, they killed those who were snake-dancing. Moteucçoma just requested [permission] for the dancing to begin. He said to Marina, "Let the god hear. The day of the festivity of our god has come; today is the tenth day. Well then, shouldn't we still celebrate it? We won't do anything. We will just dance; when they are about to take up the dough [image], they will make a clamor, that's all."

Then the Captain said, "Very well, let them do it; I have understood."

Then they departed to make the other Castilians who had come go back; only The Sun stayed behind. And when the day of [the festivity] came, Moteucçoma said, "Let his mothers ⟨the devotees of Huitzilopochtli⟩ hear; here is what I said to the god: 'The day has come when we are to celebrate the festivity of our god.' Then he said, 'Do it.' Now what shall we do?" [3]

Then the nobles said, "Let the leaders ⟨war captains⟩ be called." And when they got there they notified them and said to them, "We are still ⟨gathering recommendations⟩ about what should be done."

And the leaders said, "Let it be taken ⟨with strength, spirit⟩"

Then the Tlacateccatl Ecatzin said, "Listen, if we don't keep in mind what happened in Cholula, where they closed them inside the building, look out that they don't do the same thing to us. Let us have groups of twenty with shields stand guard for us."

Then Moteucçoma said, "Are we among enemies? Disregard it."

Then the Tlacateccatl said, "Very well."

Niman ye ic peva in cuicatl in teyacana telpochtequitiva teçacatl conacquia ytoca tolnavacatl quatlaçol yn opeuh cuicatl niman ye ic cecenyaca valↄça in x̄p̄ianome tetlan ↄↄça niman ic nanavintin momamanato in q̄xovayan

niman ye contlacoviteↄto in teyacana ce tlacatl quiyacavitecque yn ixiptla diablo niman quimōmavivitequito in tlatzotzonaya ca ontetl yn inveueuh centetl atēpa [p. 84] quitzotzunaya niman ye quequeçallo⁴ yc ixpoliova

niman ce tlacatl tlenamacac acatlyyacapā valitztia tzatzitivitz quitotivitz Mexicaye tle amay aocac yyollo quimati aquique yn immac mani malchimalli In iquauh çan axoyaquavitl⁵ yn oquittaque niman ye motepotztia yuhↄn ça mototupeuhtiaque

niman yc ōmocaltzacque In ipan caltzauhcticatca Etzalqualiztli cempovaltica ypā Etzalqualiztli yn ichtaca valↄz yn itlatol ȳ moteuhcçoma quimilhui in tiachcavan Tla ↄcaquicā ȳ mexica ca ye omilhuitl yn atle quiqua yn īmaçavan yn teteo otlatlan in tolcuextli yn ↄqualtia Auh yn axcā ye ontetl yn comontivetzi Auh inin ma oc moxonexcaltican in tiachcavā ma amo tipoliuhti ca ȳnezca yn tachcavā

Niman quitoque Ca ye qualli . Niman ye monavatia çan yovaltica in callaquia ȳ maçatlaqualli
Auh niman valla in capidān yquac in ye no chicomilhuitl ypan necallivac ypan in yaque tlaxcallan in tecuilhuitontli yquac mic y moteuhcçoma
Yn oōmic niman quivalmamaltiq̄ yn itoca apanecatl niman ompa [p. 85] quivicac in vitzillan çan ye ompan quivaltocaque ye no ye ompa quivicac ȳn ecatitlā çan ye ompa quivalmiminquc ye no ye ompa quivicac in tecpantzinco çāno quivaltocaque ye no ceppa quivicac yn acatlyyacapa q̄n ye ompa canque quito yn apanecatl . Totecuiyouane motollinia ȳ moteuhcçoma cuix nicmamatinemiz

Nimā quitoque in pipiltin Xoconanacan Niman quimonteq̄uhtique in calpixque niman quitlatique
Niman veitecuilhuitl tlaxochimaco Xocotl vetzi ochpaniztli yn ōmotlatocatlali yn cuitlavatzin niman ye hecoztli niman ye tepeilhuitl niman ye quecholli ypā mic in cuitlavatzin panquetzaliztli niman ye atemoztli tititl yzcalli atlcavallo yn ipan ommotlatocatlalli in quauhtemoctzin tlacaxipevaliztli in quimonpeuh chalca yuan xocotitlan tlaca niman q̄ttaque tehuan movahuanque toçoztontli ypan ȳ micque pipiltin tzivacpopoca xoxupevalloc tzivactzin tencuecuenotl [p. 86] axcayaca⁶ totlevicol


℄ Inic micque tzivacpopoca quinnavali yn quauhtemoc amantlan tlenamacac quimilhui In tiachcavā ye omilhuitl ȳ notlan valcecemilhuitia in tzivacpopoca ma ytla nechayti

Niman quitoque in tiachcavan Maca quimoyollitlacalhui yn tlacatl tlacoculizcuitiz ma ticcavacā ma yauh
Niman ye monavatia in tlamacazque no yehuantin in tiachcavā in temictizque niman ye quitetemova yn oquittaque moveuetzquillitivi in q̄uhtemoctzī nimā yquechtlan canato ↄlhuia oc xivalla on niccauhtze Nimā ye quivivitequi

Then began the singing. A warrior youth leader named Tolnahuacatl Quatlaçol went ahead, wearing an ornament in his lip. When the singing began, each of the Christians came out and passed among people, then groups of four stationed themselves at the exits.

Then they cut the one who was leading in half. One of them struck the nose off the image of the devil. Then they cut off the hands of the drummers, who had two cylindrical drums; they were beating one at the edge of the water. Then people were trampled,[4] and great numbers perished.

Then an incense-offering priest coming from Acatliyacapan came shouting, saying, "O Mexica, what are you doing? No one is aware. Who has weapons in his hands?" Their staves were only fir boughs.[5] When they saw [what was happening], they turned around and ran, shoving one another as they went.

Then [the Spaniards] closed themselves up in a building; they were enclosed during Etzalqualiztli for twenty days. During Etzalqualiztli secret word came out from Moteucçoma; he said to the leaders, "Let the Mexica hear; for two days the deer of the gods have eaten nothing. The reed matting they had been eating has run out. Now for two days they have been agitated. Now let the leaders first give their advice, lest we perish. [What is] the opinion of the leaders?"

Then they said, "Very well [i.e., the horses should be fed]." Then orders were given that the deer fodder should be delivered just at night.

And then the Captain came. At this time there was fighting for another seven days. In Teucilhuitontli they went to Tlaxcala. This was when Moteucçoma died.

When he had died, they made one called Apanecatl come carrying him. Then he took him to Huitzillan, but they chased him back away from there. Then he also took him to Ecatitlan, but there they shot arrows at him. Again he took him to Tecpantzinco, where they likewise chased him back out. Again he took him to Acatliyacapan; there they finally received him. Apanecatl said, "My lords, something must be done about Moteucçoma. Am I to go about carrying him [forever]?"

Then the noblemen said, "Take him." Then they put the stewards in charge of him and burned him.

Then [came] Hueiteucilhuitl, Tlaxochimaco, Xocotl huetzi. In Ochpaniztli Cuitlahuatzin was installed as ruler. Then came Ecoztli, then Tepeilhuitl, then Quecholli. Cuitlahuatzin died in Panquetzaliztli. Then came Atemoztli, Tititl, Izcalli, Atl cahualo, during which Quauhtemoc was installed as ruler. In Tlacaxipehualiztli he conquered the Chalca and Xocotitlan people; then they saw him ⟨i.e., were brought to Tenochtitlan⟩ and were painted with stripes [for sacrifice] along with others. In Toçoztontli the noblemen Tzihuacpopoca, Xoxopehualoc, Tzihuactzin, Tencuecuenotl, Axayaca,[6] and ⟨Totlehuicol⟩ died.

ℭ As to how Tzihuacpopoca [and the others] died, Quauhtemoc gave orders to an incense-offering priest of Amantlan. He said to the leaders, "For two days Tzihuacpopoca has been coming and spending the whole day at my side; let him not do me harm."

Then the leaders said, "Let him not offend the lord; he [Quauhtemoc] will be aggrieved. Let us take leave of him [Tzihuacpopoca], let him depart."

Then the priests along with the leaders were ordered to kill them. Then they went looking for him. When they saw him, Quauhtemoc went along laughing, then he took him by the neck and said, "Come here a moment, my younger brother." Then he struck him.

Huey toçoztli nimā ye toxcatl Etzalq̄liztli ypan in techcēpevaltiq̄ in x̄p̄īanome tecuilhuitontli huey tecuilhuitl. niman ye miccaylhuitontli. Ic napovaltonatiuh ynic axiuac
mexicayotl tenochcayotl

[ome tecpatl] 7 x Yc x tla°ni ochpaniztli yn ōmotlatocatlalli cuitlavatzin çā napo-
valilhuitl yn tlatocat quecholli tlami yn ipā mic totumonaliztli ynic omic yq̄c yaque in
tlaxcalla castillan tlaca

[p. 87] 1521 [yei calli] 8 x Yc xi ȳ tla°ni ypā nemontemi quauitleva ȳ motlatocatlalli
quauhtemoctzin yvā oncā moyavac ȳ mexicayotl tenochcayotl yq̄c valcencalacq̄ in Españoles

1522 [nahui tochtli] 9 x 4 . tochtli yn onuca coyovacan marq̄s yq̄c ompa q̄ncētlalli ȳ
tlatoque q̄uhtemoctzin tlacotzin oq̄ztzin vanitzin yq̄c ompeuh ȳ marques pantlan
cuextlan yq̄c nez in xicocuitlacandella

Then came Hueitoçoztlil, then Toxcatl, Etzalqualiztli, during which the Christians entirely conquered us. [Then] Teucilhuitontli, Hueiteucilhuitl, then Miccailhuitontli. In eighty days the corporate entity of Mexico Tenochtitlan was taken.

[Two Flint Knife.][7] ⚅ The tenth ruler was installed in Ochpaniztli, Cuitlahuatzin. He ruled for only eighty days; he died at the end of Quecholli of the pustules [small-pox], when the Castilians had gone to Tlaxcala.

1521. [Three House.][8] ⚅ The eleventh ruler, Quauhtemoc, was installed during Nemontemi and Quahuitl ehua. And at this point the corporate entity of Mexico Tenochtitlan collapsed; this was when the Spaniards came in once and for all.

1522. [Four Rabbit.][9] ⚅ Four Rabbit. The Marqués was staying in Coyoacan. This was when he assembled the rulers Quauhtemoc, Tlacotzin, Oquiztzin, and Huanitzin; this was when the Marqués left for Pantlan and Cuextlan. This is when beeswax candles were first seen. . . .

# 4.

# FRAGMENTS FROM THE
# ANNALS OF QUAUHTITLAN

*Nahuatl*

[p. 16] Auh yn yehuatl quinatzin yn tepotzotlan tlatohuani catca yn omoteneuh ytatzin Aztatzontzin ca quin yehuatl contzinti yn tepotzotlan tlatocayotl . auh ynin quinatzin quin iquac momiquilli yn iquac onaçico españoles yn castilteca quin yuh ye nauhpohualli momiquilli yn iquac tecuilhuitica quizque españoles ompa quizque yn tepotzotlan yn caxtilteca yquac nauhpohualtiloc yn tlatohuani catca quinatzin = auh yn o yuh momiquilli quinatzin yn tepotzotlan tlatohuani catca yn itatzin Aztatzontzin niman yn tepotzotlan conmotlatocatlalli yn omoteneuh Don Pedro macuilxochitzin yn itelpoch aztatzontzin yehuatl ontlatocatito yn tepotzotlan

[p. 68] Auh yn iquac tlatocattiticatca yn moteucçomatzin ypan yn yancuican huallaque nican yn españoles . yancuican oncan quiçaco yn oncan açico yn ytocayocan chalchiuhcueyecan . auh yn yquac ȳ oquimatque yn huell oquittaque yn itlamocuitlahuicahuan yn moteucçomatzin yn cuetlaxtlan tlaca yn inteyacancauh catca ytoca cuetlaxtecatl Pinotl . niman onpeuhque yn quimittato yn x̄p̄īanotin yn yquac quimittaque ypan quinmatia teteo . auh çatepan quintocayotique x̄p̄ītianotin [1] . ynic quitohuaya teteo . ca tlatlacatecollo yc quintocayotiaya . nauhecatl tonatiuh . quetzalcohuatl et^a . Auh yn iquac oquimatque yn oquicacque ȳ x̄p̄īanotin ca yehuatl huey tlatohuani yn moteucçoma . yn oncan Mexico . auh nimā quihuallihuallique yntetlapaloaya yn x̄p̄īanotin yc quihuallapalloque yn moteucçomatzin yehuantin quihualytquique yn ompa tlamocuitlahuiyaya yn quimocuitlahuiyaya tlacallaquilli . ynic çe yehuatl yn oticteneuhque yn itoca cuetlaxtecatl Pinotl . ynic ome tentlil . ynic ey cuitlalpitoc . auh yz catqui yn intetlapallohuaya x̄p̄īanotin yehuatl yn yn quimacaco moteucçomatzin = centetl xayo xoxoctic . auh ontetl capatli = centetl tliltic = centetl chichiltic = auh ontlamantli cactli çapatos = çe cuchillo = centetl sombrero . yhuā çentetl gorra = yhuan çentetl paño = yhuan çentetl taça = yhuan çequi cozcatl

# 4.
# FRAGMENTS FROM THE
# ANNALS OF QUAUHTITLAN

*English Translation*

And it was that Quinatzin, former ruler of Tepotzotlan, father of the aforementioned Aztatzontzin, who first founded the Tepotzotlan rulership. And this Quinatzin had just died when the Spaniards, the Castilians, arrived. He had just died eighty days before when the Spaniards came by; they came by Tepotzotlan during Teucilhuitl, at which time it had been eighty days since the late ruler Quinatzin [died]. And when Quinatzin, the former ruler of Tepotzotlan, father of Aztatzontzin, had died, the aforementioned don Pedro Macuilxochitzin installed his son Aztatzontzin as ruler, and he went to Tepotzotlan to rule.

When Moteucçoma was ruling, during his time the Spaniards first came here. They first appeared and arrived at the place called Chalchiuhcueyecan. And when those who were in charge of things for Moteucçoma, the Cuetlaxtlan people, whose leader was named the Cuetlaxtecatl Pinotl, found out about it and considered it well, they set off to see the Christians. When they saw them, they regarded them as gods; later they called them Christians. [1] The reason they said they were gods is that they called devils [gods]: Nauhecatl Tonatiuh, Quetzalcoatl, etc. And when the Christians had found out and understood that that great ruler Moteucçoma was in Mexico, the Christians sent him gifts of greeting, with which they saluted Moteucçoma. Those who took care of things there, who took care of the tribute, brought them to him. First was the one we have mentioned, named Cuetlaxtecatl Pinotl; second, Tentlil; third, Cuitlalpitoc. And here are the things the Christians gave Moteucçomatzin as a greeting: a green frock; two capes, one black and one red; two pairs of footwear, shoes; a knife; a hat; a cap; a woolen cloth; a cup; and some beads.

# 5.
# EXTRACT FROM
# HISTORIA TOLTECA-CHICHIMECA

*Nahuatl*

---

[fol. 49v] ⊄ xiii. tochtl. xiuitl. ⊄ Inic machiyaco yn atenco ȳ castillan tlaca yn iq̃c vallāq̃

[fol. 50v] ⊄ .i. Acatl. xiuitl. [1] ⊄ Inic açico ȳ castillā tlaca auh yn valla ȳtoca marques. auh yn açico ompa ȳ tlaxcallā yevantin quinamiq̃ yn tlaxcalteca yn tlatoque quitla-pallo̅q̃ quitlatlauhtique

⊄ yvan yc tlalpollo̅q̃ ȳ chollolla çano ypā ȳ ce acatl xiuitl.

⊄ yvan. oncā quicavaco yniquipiaya ȳ tlatocayotl yn tepeyacac tlacatl. auh ȳ quipixqui onpovalxiuhtica omatlactica omeyca.

⊄ Ivā oncā momiquilli ȳ tlatovani ȳ tequanitzin oncā motlatocatlallia ȳ don alonso de castaneda

.ii. tecpatl. xiuitl. ⊄ Inic tipoliuhque q̃vhtinchā yvan tepeyacac yvan tecallco yvan tecamachallco yvan quechollac. ompa timochintin titomaquixtito yn atoyac tiquauh-tichā tlaca titecallca titepeyacac tlaca.

.iii. calli siuitl. ⊄ Oncā ticpevalltiq̃ ynic ya titetlayecolltia ytencopa ȳ marques. auh ȳ tictlayecolltiq̃ ytoca françisgo de ordona ȳ ticmacaq̃. matlactli ayatl. no matlactli. maxtlatl. [2] no matlactli. vipilli. no matlactli. cueytl. yvan matlactlatemātli. coztic teo-cuitlatl yvan matlactetl totolin yvan centzontli tlaolli çan tanatica motomachi [3]

---

[fol. 51] iiii. tochtl xiuitl. ⊄ ōcā valaq̃ teopixq̃ .xii.

v. acatl xiuitl.

vi. tecpatl xiuitl.

vii. calli xiuitl. ⊄ oncā ticpevaltique yn tlacotli ȳ tictemaca y nepa yvh ya ⟨e⟩xiuitl otimacoq̃ omētin spanoles ȳ ya tiquintlayecoltia.

viii. tochtl. xiuitl. ⊄ oncan ticcauhq̃ yn tocuē yn xicotenco teteltitlan yn ipan catqui xicotencatl.

.ix. acatl xiuitl.

.x. tecpatl xiuitl. ⊄ patolq̃chtli.

xi. calli xiuitli.

xii tochtli. xiuitl. ⊄ Oncā motlalli totatzin tepeyacac ȳtoca fray juᵒ de livas oncā tzin-tic ȳ tlaneltoquiliztli yn christianoyotl yvan oncā nequahateq̃loc nenamictilloc.

⊄ xiii. Acatl. xiuitl.

⊄ Ivā çano yevatl ȳ xiuitl yn ipā timacoq̃ tasançio ynic ya ticchiva tequixaxalli

# EXTRACT FROM
# HISTORIA TOLTECA-CHICHIMECA

*English Translation*

℀ Thirteen Rabbit year. ℀ At this time the Spaniards were sighted at the seashore, when they came.

℀ One Reed year. [1] ℀ At this time the Spaniards arrived, and the one called the Marqués came. And when they arrived, the Tlaxcalans met them in Tlaxcala; the rulers greeted them and addressed them politely ⟨or gave them gifts⟩.

℀ And at this time they wrought destruction at Cholula, also in One Reed year.

℀ And at that point the Tepeyacac people relinquished the rulership they had held; they had held it for fifty-three years.

℀ And at that point the ruler Tequanitzin died, and don Alonso de Castañeda assumed the rulership.

Two Flint Knife year. ℀ At this time we of Quauhtinchan, Tepeyacac, Tecalco, Tecamachalco, and Quecholac were defeated. We all, we people of Quauhtinchan, Tecalco, and Tepeyacac, took refuge at the river [or the river Atoyac].

Three Horse year. ℀ At that point we began to serve people at the orders of the Marqués, and the person we served was named Francisco de Orduña. What we gave him was ten light cloaks, also ten loincloths, [2] also ten woman's blouses, also ten skirts, and ten pieces of gold, ten hen turkeys, and four hundred measures of shelled maize, just measured with a small woven palm basket. [3]

Four Rabbit year. ℀ At that point twelve friars came.

Five Reed year.

Six Flint Knife year.

Seven House year. ℀ At that point we began to give labor service to people; it had been three years that we had been given to two Spaniards and were serving them.

Eight Rabbit year. ℀ At that point we relinquished our fields in Xicotenco Teteltitlan; the people of Xicotenco are on them.

Nine Reed year.

Ten Flint Knife year. ℀ [We gave the type of tribute cloak called] *patolquachtli.*

Eleven House year.

Twelve Rabbit year. ℀ At that point our father, named fray Juan de Rivas, established himself in Tepeyacac. At that point was founded the faith, Christianity, and at that point people were baptized and married.

℀ Thirteen Reed year.

℀ Also in this year we were given a tribute quota, so that we ⟨gave various things⟩,

yvan matlactzontli tlaolli yvā caxtolquavacalli oce ȳ trigo tictocazque yvan. nauh-
tecpantli yn etl quavacalli yvan nauhtecpantl ȳ chilli yvan caxtolli oce yn chiā quavacalli yvā caxtolli oce yn iztatl yvan centecpantli totollin yvā centecpantli omatlactli
macevalli oncā poliuhq̄ yn patolquachtli ȳ tiq̄macaya yn imomextin Alōso valençia
yvan juᵒ perez de artiaga. auh ȳ tictemacaq̄ yn patolquachtli yexiquipilli yn nauhxiuh-
tica Ⅱ yvan ocā piloloc don thomas tecpanecatl. Ⅱ yvan oncā motlali totatzin tepeyacac ytoca fray juᵒ de livas

Ⅱ .i. Tecpatl. xiuitl.
Ⅱ In ipā motlalique ȳ cuetlaxcovapā ȳ castillan tlaca yn achto oncā motlalli ytoca saia-
villez⁴ ȳ tepachovaya / yvan oncā ticpevalltiq̄ yn itzcallotl y ya mochiva oncā ticcauhq̄
ȳ tequixaxali.

Ⅱ .ii. Calli xiuitl. Ⅱ Inic vitza juez ytoca Sanctoval quivaliva. presitente mexico
ypampa tepantli yn itechcopa totomivaque ynic motepantiaya yxpan mochiuh yn
totatzin fray x̄p̄oval de çamola testicos mochiuh

.iii. tochtl. xiuitl. Ⅱ Inic momamal yn iteocaltzin ȳ sanct juᵒ bapᵗᵃ / yvā ōcā tiçacamoq̄
otlamaxallco.
.iiii. Acatl. xiuitl. Ⅱ Inic momamal yn iteocaltzin sanct franᶜᵒ ȳ tepeyacac yvan val-
miq̄ni yn intianquiz oncā tlaytec.
[fol. 51v] .v. tecpatl. xiuitl.
.vi. calli xiuitl.
.vii. tochtl xiuitl. Ⅱ Dō augustin.
.viii. acatl xiuitl.
.ix. tecpatl xiuitl.
.x. Calli. xiuitl. Ⅱ Inic opa valla ȳ don agustin osorrio juez ypampa tlalli y nicā quauh-
tinchā quivalliva yn don antonio de mētoça visorrey. auh texticos mochiuhq̄ totatzi-
tzivā fray juᵒ de livas fray diᵒ de oralde
.xi. tochtl. xiuitl.
Ⅱ In ipā mocuic yn itlatocayotzin ȳ Emperador magestad oncā yācuicā motlalliq̄ aⱠ-
desme thoribio martinez baltasar. vetznavatzintli yvan. Regidores. alguaziles mayordomo escribano motlaliq̄

.xii. Acatl. xiuitl. Ⅱ Oncā ticpevaltiq̄ yn ça tomines mochiva ȳ totlatocavh ticmaca.
ce peso. auh ȳ juᵒ perez. ce peso yvā navi tomin. oncā ticauhque yn veyac quachtli
yxiptla mochiuh ȳ tomines / yvā oncā macoq̄ ȳ çacatl. ȳ chichimeca. Atzomiyatla.


.xiii. tecpatl. xiuitl. Ⅱ Oncā yancuican ōcā motlalli governador don felipe de mendoça
yvan aⱠdesme juᵒ batista don diᵒ de galiçia

Ⅱ Ocā omollnamiqui ȳ tepantli yn ya yepovallxiuitl ypan castolxiuitl ypan exiuitl yn
oquiquetzico yn mexica. ȳ xilloxochcatl. yn quavitencatl ȳ tocuiltecatl ȳ tlauhpanecatl
ȳ atepanecatl yn itencopa y tlatovani yn axayacatzī yn iquac quimacuilcāquixtico yn
altepetl yn quauhtenchā y mexica. / auh oncā oquillnamicque ȳ tlatoq̄ ȳ quavhtichan-
tlaca y don alonso de castaneda ȳ don diᵒ de Rojas yn don peᵒ de luna ȳ don felipe de

and four thousand [measures] of maize, and sixteen measures of wheat that we were to plant, and eighty measures of beans, and eighty [measures] of chiles, and sixteen measures of chia, and sixteen [pieces of] salt, and twenty turkey hens, and thirty commoners [to work]. At that time the *patolquachtlis* that we had been giving to both Alonso de Valencia and Juan Pérez de Artiaga were stopped. We gave twenty-four thousand of them during four years. ⊄ And don Tomás, the Tecpanecatl [lord], was hanged at that point. ⊄ And at that point our father named fray Juan de Rivas established himself at Tepeyacac.

⊄ One Flint Knife year.

⊄ In this year the Spaniards settled at Cuetlaxcohuapan [Puebla]. The person who first established himself there and governed was named [Saiavillez]. [4] And at that point we began in fact [to pay the tribute in the kind of cloak called an] *itzcallotl;* at that point we relinquished ⟨paying various kinds of tribute⟩.

⊄ Two House year. ⊄ At this time came the judge named Sandoval; the president [of the Audiencia of New Spain] sent him here about the boundaries, concerning how the Totomihuaque formed their boundary. It took place in the presence of our father fray Cristóbal de Zamora, who acted as witness.

Three Rabbit year. ⊄ At this time the church of San Juan Bautista was inaugurated. And we cleared ground for cultivation at Otlamaxalco.

Four Reed year. ⊄ At this time the church of San Francisco in Tepeyacac was inaugurated, and their market was moved ⟨from Tlaitec⟩.

Five Flint Knife year.

Six House year.

Seven Rabbit year. ⊄ Don Agustín ⟨came as judge⟩.

Eight Reed year.

Nine Flint Knife year.

Ten House year. ⊄ For the second time don Agustín de Osorio came as judge concerning the lands here in Quauhtinchan. Don Antonio de Mendoza, the viceroy, sent him, and our fathers fray Juan de Rivas and fray Diego de Olarte served as witnesses.

Eleven Rabbit year.

⊄ In this year the emperor his majesty's rulership was assumed [i.e., Spanish-style municipal government was introduced]. For the first time alcaldes were placed in office, Toribio Martínez and Baltasar Huitznahuatzintli, and also regidores, constables, a majordomo, and a notary.

Twelve Reed year. ⊄ At that point we began just raising money to give to our ruler, one peso, and to Juan Pérez one peso and four tomines. At that point we gave up [paying in] long tribute cloaks; the money was substituted instead. And at that point the [duty of delivering] dried grass [for hay] was given to the Chichimeca at Atzomiatla.

Thirteen Flint Knife year. ⊄ At that time don Felipe de Mendoza assumed office as governor for the first time, along with the alcaldes Juan Bautista and don Diego de Galicia.

⊄ At that point attention was given to the boundaries that the Mexica—the Xiloxochcatl, the Quahuitencatl, the Tocuiltecatl, the Tlauhpanecatl, the Atepanecatl— had set up seventy-eight years before by order of the ruler Axayacatzin when the Mexica came to divide the altepetl of Quauhtinchan into five parts.

And at that point the Quauhtinchan rulers, don Alonso de Castañeda, don Diego

mēdoça don baltasar de tores don di⁰ galiçia yn don baltasar de lup[***] yn quinque-
chillico yn mexicatl yn intepā yn axaxalpā ȳ chichicalotla ȳ chimaçolco yn ocotochatlauhtli ȳ tlatzcayo yn acatlā yn atlecuillo yn tzotollo ȳ tecopilli yn atzontli ȳ ya yxquich cavitl ȳ quiqua ȳ tepeyacac tlaca yn intlal ȳ quauhtichātlaca oquixpantillito yn
tlatovani ȳ don Antonio de mēdoça visorey yniquintlalpā tlaq̃ yn quauhtichan tlaca ȳ
tepeyacac tlaca auh oquimovelquiti⁵ ȳ tlatovani y.⁶

de Rojas, don Pedro de Luna, don Felipe de Mendoza, don Baltasar de Torres, don Diego de Galicia, and don Baltasar de Lup[…], pointed out the boundaries that the Mexica had set up at Axaxalpan, Chichicalotla, Chimalçolco, Ocotochatlauhtli, Tlatzcayo, Acatlan, Atlecuillo, Tzotollo, Tecopilli, and Atzontli, where meanwhile the Tepeyacac people had been sustaining themselves from the lands of the Quauhtinchan people. They put it before the lord viceroy, don Antonio de Mendoza, how the people of Tepeyacac had been sustaining themselves from the lands of the Quauhtinchan people, and the lord heard[5] it favorably.[6]

# LETTER OF THE CABILDO OF
# HUEJOTZINGO TO THE KING, 1560

*Nahuatl*

---

C R Mᵗ

Totecuioe totlatocatzine yn tiRey Don felipe n̄r̄o señor cenca timitzvecapāmaviz-
nepechtequilia tocnoteca tocnomati mixpantzinco y vel timavizvecapatlatouani yn
ipaltzinco in ixquichivelli in ipalnemovani yn dios Amo tomaçehual inic tic-
tenamiquizque mocxitzin ça vecapa timitztonepechtequililia in cenca tivecapa
tix̄p̄īano in vel titevellamachticatzī . yn dios toteᵒ ca teuatzin vel tixiptlatzī i nican
tlalticpac yn titechmopachilhuia in titechmoyacanilia yn itechcopa in x̄p̄īanoyotl in
tehuanti in tixquichti in titlachivalhua yn timaçehualhuan in ipalnemovani yn dios
ihuan in tehuatzin in timomaçevaltzitziva in timotetlaecolticatzitziva i nicā titlaca i
nicā tichaneque ȳ nueva España movicpatzinco toçemitztoque movicpatzinco tocon-
çentlazticate yn tix in toyollo timitzotocentemachilia in ixpantzinco in toteᵒ dios ca
momactzinco otechmotlalili inic titechmopializ ihua motetzinco otechmopouilli ynic
timotlacavā tiazque inic timotetlaecolticahuan tiazq̄ ma icatzinco yn toᵒ dios ihuan ma
ica in çenca maviztic in çenca vecapa motlatocayotzin Xitechmelnamiquili xitechval-
motlaocolithuili ca çenca vei tonetoliniliz tonetequipachol in topā mochiva yn nicā
nueva Espana tichaneque ⁊

Totecuioe totlatocatzine ȳ tirrey don felipe n̄r̄o señor mixpantzinco totlatoltica
tontonextia tontoquetza yn tivexutzinca in timitztlapilia yn moçiudad . tichaneque
Neuatl nigouerᵒʳ ihuan in tiałłdesme tirregidoresme ihuā titeteucti tipipilti in timotlacavā timotetlaecolticahuā yn çenca timitztocnotlatlauhtilia / omochiuh ototlaueliltic
çenca vei cenca etic in topan catqui in tlaocoyaliztli y netequipacholiztli ancā topā aci
ancā totech açi in motetlaocolilitzī . in moteicnoitalitzī amo ticmaçeva amo tiq̇cnopil-
huia ȳ motlatocayotzī Auh ca in ixquich cavitl ynic topā açico yn momaçevalhua españoles ixquich cavitl movicpatzinco tonitztinemi tontlatemachitinemi yn quemania
topan açíq̇uh yn motetlaocolilitzī no iuhqui otictemachitinenca oticchixtinenca yn
itetlaocolilitzī ȳ çenca momahuiztlaçotatzī in tlatohuani cemanahuac yn don carlos
empador catca Auh ipampa yn axcan toteᶜ totlatocatzine / tontocnopechteca yn mixpantzinco ma ticmacevaca ȳ motetlaocolilitzī ma mitzmoyollotili in cenca huei tetla-
ocolini teicnoitani in dios inic topā mochivaz motetlaocolilitzin ca in ticcaqui yn iuh
tilhuillo ca çenca ticnovacatzintli titlatlacatzintli in ivicpa yn ixquichti momaçevalhuā
yn iquac ce ticmoc̄noitilia yn mixpantzinco neçih momaçeval in motolinia yuh mitoa
ca nima ticmocnoittilia yca in cenca mahuiztic motlatocayotzin yhuā in icatzinco yn

# LETTER OF THE CABILDO OF
# HUEJOTZINGO TO THE KING, 1560

*English Translation*

Catholic Royal Majesty:

Our lord sovereign, you the king don Felipe our lord, we bow low in great reverence to your high dignity, we prostrate and humble ourselves before you, very high and feared king through omnipotent God, giver of life. We have not deserved to kiss your feet, only from afar we bow down to you, you who are most high and Christian and very pleasing to God our lord, for you are his true representative here on earth, you who govern us and lead us in things of Christianity. All of us creatures and subjects of the life-giving God, we poor vassals and servants of your majesty, we people here, we who dwell here in New Spain, all together we look to you, our spirits go out toward you; we have complete confidence in you in the eyes of our lord God, for he put us in your hands to guard us, and he assigned us to you for us to be your servants and your helpers. By our lord God and by your very honored and very high majesty, remember us, have compassion with us, for very great is the poverty and concern visited on us who dwell here in New Spain.

Our lord sovereign, King don Felipe our lord, through our words we appear and rise before you, we of Huejotzingo who guard for you your city—we citizens, I the governor and we the alcaldes and regidores and we the lords and nobles, your men and your servants. Very humbly we address ourselves to you: Oh unfortunate are we, very great and heavy sadness and concern lie upon us, nowhere do your pity and compassion come to us and reach us, we do not deserve, we do not attain your rulership. And ever since your subjects the Spaniards arrived among us, we have been looking toward you, we have been confidently expecting that sometime your pity would reach us, as we also had confidence in and were awaiting the mercy of your very revered dear father the ruler of the world, don Carlos the late emperor. Therefore now, our lord sovereign, we bow humbly before you; may we deserve your pity, may the very greatly compassionate and merciful God inspire you so that your pity is exercised on us, for we hear, and so it is said to us, that you are very merciful and humane toward all your vassals; and when a vassal of yours appears before you in affliction, so it is said, then you have pity on him with your very revered majesty, and by the grace of omnipotent God you help him. May we now also deserve and attain the same, for

ixquichivelli in dios ticmochivilia Ma no iuhqui axcā ticmaçevaca tiquicnopilhuica ca
in momoztlae topā aci topan mochivā y netoliniliztli yn netequipacholliztli ynic tito-
choquilia titotlaocoltia omochiuh ototlaveliltic canpa tiazque yn timocnomaçevaltzi-
tzivā yn tivexutzinca yn moçiudad . tinemi intlacamo veca timetztica ca miyacp[o]a
mixpantzinco tineçizquia tel cenca ticnequi tiquellevia in ma mixpantzinco taçica ti-
neçicā ammo tiveliti yeica ca cenca titotolinia ca antle neçi in totech monequiz yn
otlica yn acalco ȳ tiquazque yvā inic titetlaxtlavizque ynic huel motetzinco taçizque
yeica ȳ axcā çan totlatoltica mixpantzinco toneçi ihuā mixpantzinco tocontlalia yn
tocnomacevallatol ma çan ica in çenca vei in moxp̄ianoyo ihuā cenca mavizvecapa
motlatocayotzī ma xicmohuelcaquiti inin tocnotlatol ꓽ

Totecuioe totlatocatzine yn ayamo aca techilhui techiximachti yn moteyo yn mo-
tlatollo in ticenvecapamahuiztlatoani y noviā tiRey in titlaçenpachoa ihuā yn ayamo
ticaquitiloque in timachtiloque yn iteyotzin yn itocatzī in toteᵒ dios yn ayamo topā
açic yn tlaneltoquiliztli ȳ ayamo tixp̄ianome yn iquac topā onaçico ȳ motetlaecolticavā
españoles inic valla in mocapitā general Don herᵈᵒ cortes yn maçonelivi yn ayamo
tictiximachilique in ixquichivelli in cenca tetlaocoliani in sanctissimā trinidad yn il-
huicava ȳ tlalticpaque yn toᵒ dios techmomaçehualtili in ica ytetlaocolilitzin techyol-
loti ynic timitztotlatocatizque ynic motetzinco tipouizꝗ inic timotlacahuā timomacevalhuā titochiuhque ayac çe altepetl techpanavia ynic nica neuva españa ynic yacuica
yacachto movictzinco titotlazque timitztomacaque no ihuā ayac yc techmamauhti
ayac techcuitlahuilti ca ça uel yehuatzī ȳ dios techmomacevaltili toyollocacopa motetzinco titopouhque ynic tiquintopacaçelilique in yācuica huallaꝗ Españoles in topā
açico nica nueva España ca hueca ticauhque yn tocal inic tiquizque ynic veca
tiquinamiquito cenpouali leguas inic tiyaque inic tiquintlapaloto in yehuatl capitā general don herᵈᵒ cortes ihuan oc çequinti quihualyacā vel tiquintopaccaceliliꝗ tiquin-
tonahuatequilique vel tiquinchoquiztlapalloque yn maçoçonelivi ȳ amo tiquimixi-
matia Auh in tothahuā yn tocolhuā yn amo no quimatia ca çan itetlaocolilitzintica yn
toᵒ dios ynic huell o . tiquimixmatque ca tohuanpoua ynic tiquintotlaçotilique oncan ¹ tiꝗnpevaltiqz ye tiquintlaqualtia in ye tiquintlaecoltia cequinti hualmococotaque
inic tiquinapaloque tiquimemeque yn oc çenca miyac ic otiquintlaecoltique yn amo
vel nicā tiquitozque maçihui in yeuatl moteneva mitoa tlaxcaltecatl ca otlapallevi ca ça
vel tevā ticuitlaviltique inic tlapalleviz ihuan tevan tictlacavaltique inic amo quiyao-
chivaz . yn maçonelivi tictlacahualtique ca ya iuh ya castolilhuitl quiyaochivaya
quimicatia ² Auh yn teuā in maçanel ce motolinia español ynman quen ticchiuhꝗ inma
itech taçique nimā ayac ³ ynin amo tiztlacati ca huel quimati in ixꝗchti conguistadores
yn omomiquiliꝗ ihuā axca çequinti monemitia

Auh in iquac yn oconpehualtique yn intepeualiz in inteyaochivaliz ca nimā vel no
titocencauhque ynic tiquintopallevilique ca ça vel ixquich totech quiz ȳ toyaopātlat-
qui in totlaviz in titac ca huel mochi taxca auh amo çan titlaixquetzque ca vel tonoma
tiyaque in titlatocati ihuā in ixquich yn topilloa ihuā in ixꝗchti tomaçevalhua tiquivi-
caque ynic tiquipallevique yn Españoles amo çaniyo yaoyotica in tiquipalevique çano
ihuā yn ixquich ȳtech monec otiquimacaꝗ tiquintlaqualtiꝗ tiquintlaquetique . Auh in
yaopā quincocovaya yn anoço ça vel mococovaya tiquinapallotinēca tiquimemeti-
nenca auh in ixquich ȳ yaopan tequitl inic tlachichivalloya mochi tehuanti ticchiuh-
que Auh inic vel quinpeuhque yn mexicatl in acaltica vel tevāti tictequipanoque ti-
quinmacaque yn quahuitl yvan in ocotzotl ynic quichiuhque acalli yn Españoles . Auh
in iquac oquinpeuhque yn mexicatl ihuan in ixquich ytech pouia ayc otiquintlal-

every day such poverty and affliction reaches us and is visited on us that we weep and mourn. Oh unfortunate are we, what is to become of us, we your poor vassals, we of Huejotzingo, we who live in your city? If you were not so far away, many times we would appear before you. Though we greatly wish and desire to reach you and appear before you, we are unable, because we are very poor and do not have what is needed for the journey, things to eat on the boat nor the means to pay people for things in order to be able to reach you. Therefore now we appear before you only through our words; we set before you our poor commoners' words. May you only in your very great Christianity and very revered high majesty attend well to this our prayer.

Our lord sovereign, before anyone told us of or made us acquainted with your fame and your story, most high and feared universal king who rules all, and before we were told or taught the glory and name of our lord God, before the faith reached us, and before we were Christians, when your servants the Spaniards reached us and your captain-general don Hernando Cortés arrived, although we were not yet acquainted with the omnipotent, very compassionate holy Trinity, our lord God the master of heaven and earth caused us to deserve that in his mercy he inspired us so that we took you as our king to belong to you and become your people and your subjects; not a single altepetl surpassed us here in New Spain in that first and earliest we threw ourselves toward you, we gave ourselves to you, and furthermore no one intimidated us, no one forced us into it, but truly God caused us to deserve that voluntarily we adhered to you so that we gladly received the newly arrived Spaniards who reached us here in New Spain, for we left our homes behind to go a great distance to meet them; we went twenty leagues to greet captain-general don Hernando Cortés and the others whom he led. We received them very gladly, we embraced them, we saluted them with many tears, though we were not acquainted with them, nor did our fathers and grandfathers know them; but by the mercy of our lord God we truly recognized them as our neighbors, so that we loved them; nowhere [1] did we attack them. We began to feed them and serve them; some arrived sick, so that we carried them in our arms and on our backs, and we served them in many other ways, which we are not able to say here. Although the people who are called and named Tlaxcalans indeed helped, yet we strongly pressed them to give aid, and we admonished them not to make war; but although we so admonished them, they made war and fought [2] for fifteen days. But we, when even one Spaniard was afflicted, then we managed to reach him; [there was no one else]. [3] We do not lie in this, for all the conquerors know it well, those who have died and some now living.

And when they began their conquest and war making, then also we prepared ourselves well to aid them, for out came all of our arms and insignia, our provisions and all our equipment, and we not merely named someone, we went in person, we who rule, and we took all our nobles and all of our vassals to aid the Spaniards. We helped them not only in warfare, but also we gave them everything they needed; we fed and clothed them, we would go carrying in our arms and on our backs those whom they wounded in war or who were simply very ill, and we did all the tasks in preparing for war. And it was we who worked so that they could conquer the Mexica with boats; we gave them the wood and pitch with which the Spaniards made the boats. And when they conquered the Mexica and all belonging to them, we never abandoned them or left them behind in it. And when they went to conquer Michoacan, Jalisco,

cauique ammo no yc tiquimicapacauhque Auh in iquac tepevato yn michvaca in xalixco in colhuacā[4] yhuā in ompa ī panco auh in ompa ȳ vaxcac yn tequante[op]ec[5] in quauhtemalla . ça ce ȳ ya ic nica nueva España in tepeuhque in teyaochiuhque inic quitzonquixtique yn intepevaliz ayc tiquintlalcavique amo no itla tiquimitlacalhuique in inyaotiliz yn manel tiçeme yc tipololoque yn manoçē tomaçeval niman ayac ca vel ticyecchiuhque yn totequiuh Auh in yehuanti tlaxcalteca ca quezquinti pipiltin yn piloloque ynic amo qualli quichiuhque yn yaoyotl miyacca hualcholloque in miyacpa quitlacoque ȳ yaoyotl ynin amo tiquiztlacati ca huel yevan quimomachitia yn cōguita-dores

Totecuioe totlatocatzine no ihuā mixpantzinco tiquitohua ticnextia inic topa açi-coh in motatzitziuā p̄resme in matlactli omome yn sanct fran^{c.o} ipilhuā in quihual-mivali in cenca vecapa tepixcatlatoani s^{o} p̄re iuā in tehuatzin tiquivalmivalli ynic an-techmotlaocolilique inic techmachtico ȳ Evangelio inic techmachtico in sancta fe catolica in tlaneltoquiliztli ynic techiximachitico in içel teotl ȳ dios tote^{o} Auh in teuanti Tivexu^{ca} ȳ moçiudad tichaneque çanoihuī techmocnelili in dios te[c]hyolloti inic tiquintopaccaçelilique yn iquac ipan valcallacque yn altepetl vexutzinco Vel toyollocacopā tiquintomaviztilique tiquintotlaçotilique in iquac techmona-huatequilique inic tictlalcavizque yn nepapā tlateotoquiliztli yn tlavelilocayotl ça nimā toyollocacopan ticcauhque no ihuā techmocnelilique in tiquintelchiuhque tiquin-popoloque tiquintlatique in tetl in quavitl ticteteotiaya ca oticchiuhque huel toyol-locacopa tiquinpopoloque tiquixixinique tiquintlatique yn teocalti no yquac ȳ ya techmomaquilia ȳ s^{o} Evangelio in sancta fe catolica vel ica toçeyaliz totlanequiliz oti-cuique oticanque ayac ic techmamauhti ayac techcuitlahuilti ça vel toçializtica otic-tzitzquique ihuā in izquitlamantli s̄cr̄os otechmomaďlique yhuiā yocoxcā totech otic-tlalique totech oticpachoque ça nima aic ce yn ma pilli anoço maçevaltzintli yc tololinoc yn anoço yc tlatiloc in ixquich noviā omochiuh inic nicā nohuia[6] España in miequi altepeme cuitlaviltiloq̄ yc toliniloque yn aço piloloque yn anoço tlatiloque inic amo quicavaznequia in tlateotoquiliztli . ihuan yn amo iyollocacopa quiçeliaya in Evang^{o} ihua in tlaneltoquiliztli oc cenca yeuanti in tlaxcalteca can[7] quintopevaya quintlaçaya ȳ p̄reme yn amo quiçeliaya in tlaneltoquiliztli ca miyaquinti tlaçopipilti yc tlatiloque ihuan çequinti piloloque Inic ocompehualtique In inotzaloca in itlaecol-tiloca in to^{o} dios Auh in tevantin in tihuexotzinca in timocnomaçevaltzitziuā ayc ytla otimitztitlacalhuique mochipa otimitztotlaecoltilique in izquitlamantli otiquival-mivalli motecopatzinco tinavatilo[8] Vel ixquich yvian yocoxca ticana ticui ca tel çan itetlaocolilitzintica yn dios ticchivā ca amo tonoma catle tohuelli yeica axcan ma çan icatzinco ma çan ipaltzinco ȳ dios xitechmocaquilili Inin totlatol in izquitlamantli mixpantzinco ticnextia tiquitoa inic titechmotlaocoliliz inic topa ticmochiviliz yn motlatocayotzin inic titechmoyollaliliz titechmopalleviliz inic çeçemilhuitl tichoca ti-tlaocoya çenca tinentlamati tipatzmiqui ihuan iuhqui ya xiniznequi ya poliviznequi in maltepetzī yn moçiudad vexu^{co} Iz catqui in topa ya mochiva yn axcā in topā quitlalia in motlapixcatzitzivā yn officiales yoan ī fiscal doctor maldonado çenca vey in tlacal-laquili in motetzinco poui çenxiquipilli pesos tom̄es ihuan caxtoltzontli pesos yhuan ontzontli pesos tomī no ixquich in tlaolli hanegas in totlacallaquil yn ticchivazque ꞏ

Totecuiyoe totlatocatzine ca aic yuhqui topā omochiuh yn ixquich cavitl topan açico in motetlaecolticatzitziua in momaçevalhuā Españoles ca ȳ yeuatl yn motetla-ecolticatzī yn don her^{do} cortes capitā general catca in margues del valle yn ixquich cavitl o nica monemiti tonavac vel mochipa otechmotlaçotili otechpaccanemiti ayc

and Colhuacan,[4] and at Pánuco and Oaxaca, Tehuantepec,[5] and Guatemala, and all over New Spain here where they conquered and made war until they finished their conquests, we never abandoned them, nor did we do anything detracting from their war making, though some of us were destroyed in it, ⟨though not a single one of our subjects was left⟩, for we truly performed our duty properly. But as to those Tlaxcalans, several of their nobles were hanged for making war poorly; in many places they ran away, and often they did badly in the war. In this we do not lie, for the conquerors themselves know it.

Our lord sovereign, we also declare and manifest before you that your fathers the twelve children of Saint Francis came to us, whom the very high priestly ruler the Holy Father sent and whom you sent, both granting us the favor that they came to teach us the gospel, to teach us the holy Catholic faith, the belief, to make us acquainted with the single deity God our Lord, and likewise God favored and inspired us, us of Huejotzingo, who dwell in your city, so that we gladly received them. When they entered the altepetl of Huejotzingo, of our own free will we honored them and showed them esteem. When they embraced us so that we would abandon the wicked belief in many gods, we forthwith voluntarily relinquished it; likewise they did us the good deed [of telling us] to despise, destroy, and burn the stones and wood that we worshiped as gods, and we did it; very willingly we destroyed, demolished, and burned the temples. Also when they gave us the holy gospel, the holy Catholic faith, with very good will and desire we received and grasped it; no one intimidated us into it, no one forced us, but very willingly we seized it, and we quietly and peacefully arranged and ordered among ourselves all the sacraments they gave us. Not once was anyone, whether nobleman or commoner, ever tortured or burned over this, as was done on every hand here in New[6] Spain. People of many altepetl were forced and tortured, were hanged or burned because they did not want to relinquish idolatry, and unwillingly they received the gospel and faith. Especially those Tlaxcalans[7] pushed out and rejected the fathers, and would not receive the faith, for many of the high nobles were burned, and some hanged, for combating the advocacy and service of our lord God. But we of Huejotzingo, we your poor vassals, we never did anything in your harm, always we served you in every command you sent and what at your command we were ordered.[8] Quietly and peacefully we accept and take absolutely all of it, though only through the mercy of God do we do so, for it is not within our personal power. Hence now, by and through God, may you hear these our words, all that we declare and manifest before you, so that you will do us the favor of exercising on us your rulership to console us and aid us in [this trouble] with which we daily weep and sorrow. We are afflicted and sore pressed, and your altepetl and city of Huejotzingo is as if it is about to crumble and disappear. Here is what is happening to us: now your stewards the royal officials and the prosecuting attorney Dr. Maldonado are assessing us a very great tribute to belong to you. The tribute we are to give is 14,800 pesos in money, and an equal number of fanegas of maize.

Our lord sovereign, never has such happened to us in the whole time since your servants and vassals the Spaniards came to us, for your servant don Hernando Cortés, former captain-general, the Marqués del Valle, as long as he lived here among us always greatly cherished us and kept us happy; he never disturbed or agitated us. Al-

otechacoma ayc otechcomoni macihuī in ticmacaya tlacallaquili ca çan techixyeyecal-
huiaya maçonelli in coztic teocuitlatl ȳ ticmacaya ca ça vel tepito çaço quexquich çaço
quenami in maca nel huel coztic ca çan quipaccaceliaya ayc techavac ayc techtequipa-
cho yeica ca vel ixpā catca ca vel quimomachitiaya inic çenca vei o yc tictlaecoltique
ticpallevique no miyacpa techilhuiaya inic mixpantzinco topan tlatoz . techpalleviz
mitzmomachitiliz in ixc̣ch yc otimitztopallevilique inic otimitztotlaecoltiliq̄ Auh in
iquac mixpantzinco vya in iquac oticmoneltilili yn oticmotlaocolili yn oticmaviztili
ticmotlaxtlavilli inic omitzmotlaecoltilico i nica nueva España auh aço çan techelcauh
in mixpantzinco quenoçonel tiquitozq̄ camo taçia camo t⟨o⟩tlacaḍa in mixpātzinco
ac nel in topā tlatoz omochiuh ototlaveliltic ypampa axcā tontocēcava mixpantzinco
totlatocatzine toteꞔ Auh in iquac tiquivalmivalli in mixiptlatzitzivan yn presidente
oꞮꞯpo . don sebastian Ramirez yvā in oydores ȳ llicen^{d.o} salmeron yn llicendo cahinos[9]
. quiluca maldonado ca vel yeuantī quineltilico quichicavaco yn mihiyotzī yn mo-
tlatoltzī inic topampa tiquimonavatili i nicā titlaca ȳ nueva España tichaneque cenca
miyac tlamantli yc otechpallevique yc otechcaxanique ȳ cenca vevey totlacallaquil
ocatca yvā in miyac tlamātli in totlatequipanoliz catca vel ixquich ipa . techmaqui-
xtique vel ixquich techpopolhuilique Auh in tevanti timocnomaçevaltzitzinva in
tivexutzinca yn moçiudad tichaneque ca topa ovalmovicac ypan callaquico yn altepetl Vexutzinco yn llicen^{d.o} salmerō ca nimā quimothuili in altepetl inic çenca
motolinitica in ica totlacallaquil in coztic teocuitlatl Epouallatemātotontī in çexiuhtica
ticcallaquia Auh inic techtolinia yehica amo nicā neçi in coztic teocuitlatl amo nicā
catqui yn ipan taltepeuh ca ça novia tictemovaya yc nimā quipopollo motecopatzinco
yn llicen^{d.o} salmero yc conixiptlacayoti quipatcayoti yn tomīes in techtlalili totlacallaquil macuiltzontli pesos ihuan ompovalli ōmatlactli pesos tomīes Auh ca ixquich
cauitl in techtlalili isquich cavitl otiqualchiuhtaque in timitztomaquilitivitze inic
timomacevalhuā ynic motetzīco tipoui aic otiḍcxicauhque ayc otiquitlacoq̄ Vel mochi
oticaxiltique Auh yn axca cenca titiçahuia cenca titomauhtia tiquitova cuix itla otiquitlacoque cuix itla anq[u]alli ayectlic oticchiuhque in mohuicpatzinco in titotecuiyo
in titotlatocauh anoço yeuatzī in ixc̣chivelli dios itla otiquitlacoque yn ivictzinco . aço
itla oticmocaquiti in totlavelilocayo inic cenca vei axcā topan vetzī yn tlacallaquili
chicopa oquipanavi in ixquich otiqualtequitaque in macuiltzotli pesos Auh in tiquitoa
in mixpantzinco ca amo vecahuaz inic cenpoliuiz inic xixiniz in moçiudad Vexu^{co}
yehica ca amo quiximatia Tlacallaquili yn totavā in tocolhuā yn tachtouā ayac qui-
tlacallaquiliaya ca çā mixcavica catca Auh in tevanti in tipipilti yn tiquipia momaçe-
valhuan ca çenca ya titotolinia aocmo totech neçi in pillotl ya tiquinenevilia in maçe-
valti yn iuhqui ḍqua in iuhqui quimoquentia ya no iuhqui totech ca / oc cenca
telellaçiꞔ vel otopan tzonquiçaco in netoliniliztli in iuhqui catca totavā tocolhuā tachtouā in iuh motlacamatia yn iuh maviztique catca nimā aocmo achi totech ca⸗
   O Totecuiyoe totlatocatzine in tiRey ca ipan timitzontomachitiā yn ilhuicac mo-
etztica yn icel teotl dios ca vel ipan timitztomachita in titotatzī ma xitechmo-
tlaocolitivili ma xitechvalmocnoitivili ma oc cenca yevanti xiquimelnamiquilli in
çacatla in quauhtla yn moquixtia yn monemitia ca yevanti in techoctia in tech-
tlaocoltia vel tixpa vel tiquitzticate in inetoliniliz . vel yeuanti ypampa in tontlatoā in
mixpantzinco inic amo çatepā totech yc tim[o]quallanitiz In iquac opopoliuhque
anoço oxixinque yn momaçevaltzitzivā onca tlami y in tocnotlatol ⸗
   Auh ca cenca miyac inic motolinitica inic motequipachotica in moçiudad . vexu^{co}
yn amo nicā vel timitzticuilhuilizque Auh ca itech ticcaua in totlaçotatzī p̄re fray

though we gave him tribute, he assigned it to us only with moderation; even though we gave him gold, it was only very little; no matter how much, no matter in what way, or if not very pure, he just received it gladly. He never reprimanded us or gave us concern, because it was evident to him and he understood well how very greatly we served and aided him. Also he told us many times that he would speak in our favor before you, that he would help us and inform you of all the ways in which we have aided and served you. And when he went before you, then you confirmed him and were merciful to him, you honored and rewarded him for the way he had served you here in New Spain. But perhaps before you he forgot us. What are we to say? We did not reach you, we were not given audience before you. Who then will speak for us? Unfortunate are we. Therefore now we place ourselves entirely before you, our sovereign lord. And when you sent your representatives, the Presidente and Bishop don Sebastián Ramírez, and the Audiencia judges, Licentiate Salmerón, Licentiates Ceinos,[9] Quiroga, and Maldonado, they themselves realized and confirmed the orders you gave for us people here, us who live in New Spain. In many things they aided us and lightened the very great tributes we had, and with many things that were our tasks they delivered us from and pardoned us all of it. And we your poor vassals, we of Huejotzingo who dwell in your city, when Licentiate Salmerón came to us and entered the altepetl of Huejotzingo, he saw how troubled the altepetl was with our tribute in gold, sixty pieces that we gave each year. The reason it troubled us is that gold is not gathered here and is not to be found here in our altepetl, though we searched for it everywhere. Then at once Licentiate Salmerón abolished it on your behalf and substituted and exchanged money for it; he set our tribute in money at 2,050 pesos. And ever since he assigned it to us, we have kept doing it; we hasten to give it to you, for we are your subjects and belong to you. We have never neglected it, we have never done it badly, we have given the full amount. But now we are greatly taken aback and very afraid and we ask, have we done something wrong, have we behaved badly and ill toward you, our lord sovereign, or have we committed some sin against almighty God? Perhaps you have heard something of our wickedness and for that reason now this very great tribute has fallen upon us, seven times exceeding all we had gone along paying before, the 2,000 pesos. And we declare to you that it will not be long before your city of Huejotzingo completely disappears and crumbles, because our fathers, grandfathers, and great-grandfathers knew no tribute and gave tribute to no one, but were independent. We nobles who have charge of your subjects are now truly very poor. Nobility is seen among us no longer. Now we resemble the commoners; as they eat and dress, so do we. We have been very greatly afflicted, and our poverty has reached its culmination. Of the way in which our fathers and grandfathers and great-grandfathers were rich and honored, there is no longer the slightest trace among us.

O our lord sovereign king, we rely on you as on God the one deity who dwells in heaven, we consider you our very father. Take pity on us, have compassion with us. May you especially remember those who subsist and live in the wilds, those who move us to tears and pity. Their poverty is before our eyes, we are gazing directly at it, wherefore we speak out before you so that afterward you will not become angry with us when your subjects have disappeared or dispersed. There ends this our humble supplication.

We cannot write here for you the very many ways in which your city of Huejotzingo is poor and stricken; we are leaving that to our dear father fray Alonso de

alonso de buendia sanct fran<sup>co</sup> ipiltzin intla yevatzī quimonequiltiz ycel teutl dios inic
vell ompa açiz ȳ mixpantzinco Ca uel yehuatl mitzmocaquitiliz yn oc miyac tlamantli
In tonētlamachiliz in tonetoliniliz ca huel quimomachitia vell oquitac yn çiudad vexu-
tzīco onxihuitl nicā guardian ocatca Ma yehuatl mixpantzinco quitoz quipouaz ca
huel itech titotlacanequi Vel itech otitoçencauhque ya isquich ynic mixpātzinco
tonaçi toneçi ynin Amatl omochiuh ypa çiudad Vexu<sup>co</sup> ya ic cenpohualilhuitl oma-
tlaquilhuitl mani metztli De Julio ynic oquichtli in totecuio . Jesu . x<sup>o</sup> ya etzontli
xihuitl ypan caxtolpoualli xivitl yvan Epoualli xivitl

Yn cenca hueca timitztocnonepechtequilia timocnomacevaltzitzihua

don leonardo Ramirez governador   don matheo de la corona aⱥde   diego alameda
aⱥde   don felipe de mendoça aⱥde   hernando de meneses   miguel de aluarado
alonso pimentel   agustin osorio   dō fran<sup>co</sup> vazquez   don di<sup>o</sup> de chavez   juan de
almo[***]   di<sup>o</sup> de niça   agustin d. s<sup>o</sup> thomas   di<sup>o</sup> xuarez tori<sup>o</sup> d. s ⟨x<sup>o</sup>⟩val mot<sup>a</sup>

Buendía, child of Saint Francis, if God the one deity should will that he arrive safely before you. He himself will be able to tell you many more things about our anguish and poverty, because he learned and saw it well while he was father guardian [of the Franciscan monastery] here in the city of Huejotzingo for two years. We hope that he will tell and relate it to you, for we have much confidence in him and have placed ourselves completely in his hands. This is all with which we come and appear before you. This letter was done in the city of Huejotzingo on the thirtieth day of the month of July, in the year of the birth of our lord Jesus Christ 1560.

Your poor vassals who bow down humbly to you from very far,

Don Leonardo Ramírez, governor. Don Mateo de la Corona, alcalde. Diego Alameda, alcalde. Don Felipe de Mendoza, alcalde. Hernando de Meneses. Miguel de Alvarado. Alonso Pimentel. Agustín Osorio. Don Francisco Vásquez. Don Diego de Chaves. Juan de Almo[. . .]. Diego de Niza. Agustín de Santo Tomás. Diego Juárez. Toribio de San [Cristó]bal Motolinia.

COMMENTARY

# COMMENTARY

## 1. BOOK TWELVE OF THE FLORENTINE CODEX

1. FUERO (in the Spanish)    For "fueron." Syllable-final *n* is frequently omitted in the writer's practice, probably corresponding to his speech; instances of this kind will not be noted henceforth. I say "for" in such cases relating to the Spanish section of the manuscript simply to indicate a more readily intelligible form. In some instances the more standard form may have been the one intended by the writer, but in others it was not; for the most part it seems impossible to attain certainty on which interpretation applies in a particular passage. Partly for this reason, I put the more standard forms, which I spell as I imagine Sahagún might have, in quotes as finite constructions possibly intended either by the writer or by a previous copyist instead of putting them in italics as purely abstract standard forms. I have followed the same practice in the Nahuatl texts.

2. ESTORIA (in the Spanish)    For "(h)istoria." The merging of unstressed *e* and *i*, as here, is a common phenomenon in the writing of Spanish loans in Nahuatl texts, though *i* for Spanish *e* is seen more often than the opposite, as here. The preceding words beginning *e* may have affected the form chosen.

3. NICĀ CHANEQUE (in the Nahuatl)    Possibly the intention here, as in the Spanish version, is that the Spaniards were not known by the local people. My translation is guided by the fact that nonactive verbs in Nahuatl do not specify an agent. Perhaps, however, the phrase "in nicā chaneque" is an implicit dative: "[the Spaniards] were not known [to] the people who live here."

4. DESTA (in the Spanish)    For "a esta."

5. TLATEMMA (in the Nahuatl)    Read "tlatemmachoia." See Sahagún 1950–1982: 13.2. Although the verb often means "to be lazy, inactive," and so appears later in the text, here its second meaning, "to tell one's troubles," seems more apt. When I say "read" in relation to Nahuatl passages, I am fairly confident that the subsequent form was the intention of the writer. Such is not the case with the readings offered for dubious, deficient, or deviant forms in the Spanish text; see n. 1 above.

6. SENAL (in the Spanish)    For "señal." The omission of the tilde, probably a phenomenon of speech as well as of orthography, is quite common in the text and will not be noted henceforth.

7. CHAPITEL (in the Spanish)   The word is defined as the head of a pillar, but the intention here seems to be the pillar itself, as in the Nahuatl.

8. ITEIOC (in the Nahuatl)   This form, which would be "his rock (inalienable, locative)," is a mistake for "itepeioc," 'his mountain'; Sahagún 1950–1982: 13.2, points out that the Real Palacio manuscript in fact has "itepeyoc."

9. ÇAN (in the Nahuatl)   The word is inadvertently repeated in the manuscript.

10. TANMAÑO (in the Spanish)   For "tamaño." The insertion of a syllable-final *n* is rarer in this text than the omission of one, but in Nahuatl writing in general it is a very common phenomenon. Some cases in this text have to do with the confusion between verbal singulars and plurals. Henceforth, inserted *n* will not be noted.

11. OMMOTZCALO (in the Nahuatl)   Forms related to *itzcalli* have the meaning "high" as well as "sideways, inclined."

12. MASTELEJOS (in the Spanish)   For "astillejos."

13. TEUCINIACATL (in the Nahuatl)   Read "Teuciniocatl."

14. PARA VENDERLOS SO COLOR DE VER QUE COSA ERA AQUELLA (in the Spanish)   The phrase is reversed; properly it should say "para ver que cosa era aquella, so color de venderlos [in standard grammar, venderlas]."

15. EN LA HISTORIA DESTE DIOS (in the Spanish)   That is, elsewhere in the Florentine Codex.

16. DONDE (in the Spanish)   For "de donde."

17. COACOZCAIO (in the Nahuatl)   The Spanish version's "Ecacozcaio" seems preferable.

18. TOLECIO (in the Nahuatl)   I provisionally follow Sahagún 1950–1982: 13.6 in the rendering of this form. "Covered with turkey blood," however, ought to have been written "Totolezio." More tempting, if improbable, would be "Toltecaio" 'in Toltec style.'

19. IN IVELIACA (in the Nahuatl)   I have neither seen nor hit upon any adequate explanation of this word. The Spanish version suggests "what they had seen," which also has logic on its side.

20. Q̄N (in the Spanish)   For "quando."

21. NAUHTLAN TOZTLAN (in the Nahuatl)   Despite the punctuation and capitalization, Nauhtlan and Toztlan might be one place, as in the Spanish version.

22. MICTLANQUACTLA (in the Spanish)   For "mictlanquauhtla."

23. AUSAN (in the Spanish)   For "auian."

24. QUARDENSE (in the Spanish)   For "guardense."

25. LO (in the Spanish)   For standard "los." Final *s*, especially as a plural ending, but also in other cases, is frequently omitted in the text, and such instances will not be noted henceforth.

26. TLAONAOATI (in the Nahuatl)   Read "tlanaoati."

27. COATZONTECOMETICA (in the Nahuatl)   Read "coatzontecomatica."

28. TOSQUESAS (in the Spanish)   For "turquesas." The *o* for *u* is normal in Nahuatl writing in general and in this text in particular. The *s* for *r* may be a visual error; it

may also be a simple mechanical error, because the word receives a standard spelling just above.

29. COLCAGAUA (in the Spanish)    For "colgaua."

30. RODELLA (in the Spanish)    For "rodela."

31. FORTA (in the Spanish)    Possibly for "suerte."

32. MOTECUCOMA (in the Nahuatl)    Read "Motecuçoma."

33. XICMOTLATLAUHTILICAN (in the Nahuatl)    The verb *tlatlauhtia* can mean either "to pray to" or "to address politely." In chap. 5 it clearly has the latter meaning.

34. LLA (in the Spanish)    For "llama."

35. AC NEL ICAC, HA IEPPA NEHOATL (in the Nahuatl)    These two idioms are not well understood and seem not to be recorded anywhere else. I have built on the Spanish version, but the result is more than normally speculative.

36. LEUAUAN (in the Spanish)    For "lauaua," though perhaps the writer intended the final *n* as a plural.

37. DESPORTADE (in the Spanish)    For "despertalde."

38. CERIMONIA (in the Spanish)    This word is more standardly written "ceremonia," but the form in the text is also seen in sixteenth-century Spanish writing.

39. INNAOATIL (in the Nahuatl)    Or "when they heard about the report of the guns," or "when they heard how the projectiles of the guns hit"?

40. TEPUZTLI (in the Nahuatl)    *Tepoztli,* having referred to copper and perhaps to any usable nonprecious metal in preconquest times, quickly came to mean the iron (and steel) the Spaniards brought with them. If we are to imagine the messengers actually saying the things reported here, the meaning was probably simply "metal."

41. TLACATLAQUALLI (in the Nahuatl)    The dictionaries justify the translation "fasting food," but by its elements the construction could also mean "people's food."

42. MONECTICAQUA (in the Nahuatl)    It appears that the manuscript originally had "monectiquaqua." The first *qu* was then written over in a fashion transforming it approximately into *tic,* leaving something that could be read as "monecticticaqua" or "monectiticaqua," but the intention was clearly what is given in the text here.

43. IN TLACIUHQUE, IN NANAOALTI (in the Nahuatl)    The translations for different kinds of shamans and prognosticators are necessarily arbitrary and inexact, because the set of English terms does not offer precise equivalents. In any case, our understanding of the roles among the Nahuas is not very exact, and even when we have a fair notion, it is not clear that different aspects corresponded to different specialists.

44. ATZTZAPUTL (in the Nahuatl)    For the names of the foods I rely chiefly on Sahagún 1950–1982: 13.22, which has references and some specific botanical names. The terms left in Nahuatl are not understood. The intention of "atztzaputl" is probably "atzatzaputl." See Sahagún 1950–1982: 13.22, n. 7.

45. A (in the Spanish)    Incorrect and superfluous by the normal rules of Spanish grammar.

46. SU (in the Spanish)    For "so." Henceforth no note will be taken of the frequent cases of *u* for standard *o* and vice versa.

47. FUESEN (in the Spanish)    Normal Spanish grammar would demand "fuese."

48. SOBRE EL (in the Spanish)    Through inadvertence "y sobre el" was written between this and "y sobre su reyno."

49. CANAS (in the Spanish)    Fol. 13v ends with the excess letters "respon."

50. CINCALCO (in the Nahuatl)    Possibly Mictlan is literally the land of the dead, Tonatiuh ichan the home of the sun, and Tlalocan the verdant seat of the rain and earth god, much as in the Spanish version, but it is also possible that all four places named were caves with reputations as places of access to supernatural realms.

51. QUAUHTLAXCALLA (in the Nahuatl)    The form contains a prefatory *quauh-*, sometimes seen optionally combined with altepetl names on formal occasions. I am not sure whether the element derives from *quahuitl* 'tree, wood, forest', in which case it might have a connotation of mock humility, or from *quauhtli* 'eagle', in which case it would connote pride and martial vigor.

52. QUAUHTEXCALLAN (in the Spanish)    The Spanish version takes *quauh-* as part of the name, which it is not, and has "-texcalla" rather than "-tlaxcalla" as in the Nahuatl; see n. 51 just above.

53. LES (in the Spanish)    "Les" has been changed from an earlier "los."

54. XOXOQUIVI (in the Nahuatl)    I have not found a satisfactory analysis for this word and rely on the analogous preceding phrase.

55. COMO VIEREN (in the Spanish)    The second *o* in "como" serves twice, a second time in what must be read as "ovieren."

56. ESTRAUO (in the Spanish)    For "estrago."

57. MU (in the Spanish)    For "muy."

58. DEL (in the Spanish)    For "y el."

59. ES (in the Spanish)    For "en."

60. TLALCALTECAS (in the Spanish)    For "Tlaxcaltecas."

61. CUINOÇO (in the Nahuatl)    Read "cuix noço."

62. ESPANOLES (in the Nahuatl)    As here, the manuscript frequently has the word without a tilde. Henceforth no notice is taken of this variant, which likely represented speech (Nahuatl lacked a palatalized *n* and often geminated the *n* instead).

63. LOS CHALCO (in the Spanish)    The word "los" seems superfluous, though the intention may have been "los chalca," "los chalcas," "los chalcos," or some such.

64. OCONCAVILI (in the Nahuatl)    This form appears to be from the verb *cahua* 'to leave, abandon', but the function of the applicative here is a mystery.

65. TECA OMOQUAVITEC, CA TECA OMOQUIMILO (in the Nahuatl)    These are presumably little-attested idiomatic expressions. Perhaps the sense is "he has done stupid things to people and hidden himself from them." The Spanish version may rest on a better comprehension of the idioms.

66. ÇAN IE IUHQUIN ICAMAC OMMAQUIQUE (in the Nahuatl)    Another unsolved idiom, perhaps referring to the apparition's blistering the enchanters with words.

67. MOCECHTLE (in the Nahuatl)    Read "moceloquichtle."

68. CHIPAN (in the Spanish)    For "chinanpan" or the like.

69. CHALCATLATOQUE (in the Nahuatl)   It seems that a section on the Spanish entry into Chalco is missing. The Spanish version apparently tries to make up for it after the fact.

70. YTZTAPALAPAN (in the Spanish)   The manuscript has a period in addition to a comma after this word.

71. TLACOMACHOZQUE (in the Nahuatl)   Read "tlacamachozque."

72. DE (in the Spanish)   In the manuscript, the word is inadvertently repeated.

73. ARTILLE (in the Spanish)   For "artilleria."

74. IN TEIACANA (in the Nahuatl)   In the manuscript, the letters "in te" are inadvertently repeated at the page break.

75. IN CACALTZALAN (in the Nahuatl)   Or "into the alleyways."

76. DESDE (in the Spanish)   For "deste."

77. IMANANQUILLOĀ (in the Nahuatl)   The intention is apparently "inananquilloā."

78. IAQUETIVITZ (in the Nahuatl)   I can offer no explanation of the main verb in this construction.

79. A LUGAR (in the Spanish)   An earlier version no doubt had "al lugar" or "a un lugar" instead.

80. CONNEPECHTEQUILIA (in the Nahuatl)   It appears that, as in the Spanish, the bowing should precede the standing straight.

81. A (in the Spanish)   In normal usage this word should be "en."

82. MALITZIN (in the Nahuatl)   Syllable-final nasals were often omitted in Nahuatl speech and writing. Thus this form instead of the usual "Malintzin" is probably more than a simple mistake.

83. A (in the Spanish)   The word is repeated through inadvertence.

84. HUELQUE (in the Spanish)   For "huelgue."

85. ITZQUAUHTZIN: (in the Spanish)   The colon is inadvertently repeated at the beginning of fol. 26.

86. QUITZIZQUIQUE (in the Nahuatl)   Read "quitzitzquique." The present case is possibly a simple slip, but final tz was sometimes lenited in this fashion, and the same substitution is found below at n. 93.

87. DE (in the Spanish)   For "le."

88. UEVETZIN (in the Nahuatl)   Read "uevetzi." The writer probably intended this word to be a contraction of "uevetzi" and "in" and then added "in" after all.

89. TOTOLLALEOATZALLI (in the Nahuatl)   Read "totollatleoatzalli." This form is possibly more than a simple error; see the same word below at n. 133.

90. AOCMO IUIC QUIÇA (in the Nahuatl)   In the manuscript, the phrase is inadvertently repeated (as "aocmo ivic quiça,").

91. A (in the Spanish)   Superfluous and incorrect by normal Spanish grammar.

92. NE (in the Spanish)   For "ni."

93. QUITZITZIZQUITIUI (in the Nahuatl)   Read "quitzitzitzquitiui." See also n. 86 above.

94. TLATLATILCALI (in the Nahuatl)    Read "tlatlatilcalli." Nevertheless, the form "cali" for *calli* is found as a variant in texts of many kinds.

95. TEOCUITLACOTZECOATL (in the Nahuatl)    Read "teocuitlacotzeoatl."

96. TLATLATILCALI (in the Nahuatl)    See n. 94 above.

97. IUHQUIN MOCECENQUETZA, . . . IUHQUIN IIZTAIA INIOLLO (in the Nahuatl) Three of these four idioms are extremely obscure in the context. It is mainly the Spanish version that gives one some sense of the thrust.

98. XINVITZOLLI (in the Nahuatl)    Read "xivitzolli." The *n*, however, probably represents the first, unvoiced portion of a geminate [w].

99. XIQUALCUICĀ (in the Nahuatl)    Read "xicualcuicā." It is not uncommon, however, to find *qua* representing standard *chua*.

100. MAUHCAC (in the Nahuatl)    Apparently one is to read "mauhca."

101. IE (in the Nahuatl)    The word is inadvertently repeated in the manuscript.

102. IVEI[MAXTLI] (in the Nahuatl)    The element "-maxtli," the possessed form of *maxtlatl* 'loincloth', was omitted in the manuscript, though an empty space has been left where it should have been.

103. TEXOACAXILQUI (in the Nahuatl)    Here I rely on Sahagún 1950–1982: 13.53.

104. IUHQUIN NECECEQUETZALO, IUHQUIN INIOIOLIPĀ (in the Nahuatl)    The same uncertainties with these idioms obtain as at n. 97, where they are also used in tandem.

105. ICUECHI (in the Nahuatl)    Here I have followed Sahagún 1950–1982: 13.53.

106. IN YIAQUE: . . . IN TELPUCHIAQUE (in the Nahuatl)    Here I have followed Sahagún 1950–1982: 13.54; I have been unable to identify the form "yiaque" or "iaque." Conceivably it could be the plural of *yaqui,* a preterit agentive from *yauh* 'to go', with the meaning "one who has gone," but no such usage has come to my attention. The *y* added to the first example makes one think of the word *iyac* 'something or someone with a stench'.

107. MOPOÇAOA (in the Nahuatl)    I rely here on Sahagún 1950–1982: 13.56.

108. MINACACHALLI (in the Nahuatl)    The translation of this word is based on Sahagún 1950–1982: 13.56.

109. INDIOS (in the Spanish)    In the manuscript at this point, originally "niños" 'children' was written, and then only partly changed to "indios."

110. EN (in the Spanish)    For "con."

111. TETELPUCHCALI (in the Nahuatl)    Read "tetelpuchcalli." See n. 94 above.

112. DIUERSAS PARTES (in the Spanish)    By the normal standards of Spanish grammar, "en" is missing before "diuersas."

113. DE CASA (in the Spanish)    By normal Spanish grammar, "la" is missing between these two words.

114. SE CESEYS (in the Spanish)    This combination is not grammatical by normal standards.

115. MA MOTLACAVALTICAN (in the Nahuatl)    It is not clear where Itzquauhtzin leaves off reporting what Moteucçoma said and begins talking on his own.

116. AMO CE YIOQUICHOAN? (in the Nahuatl)    Strictly speaking, the translation given would require that the second sentence of the quote be in the second person,

which it is not. An alternate translation would be "You rogue, what does Moteucçoma say, and not just one of his men?" In view of the Spanish version, possibly "one of his men" has homosexual connotations.

117. TEPANCALLI (in the Nahuatl)    From the Spanish version and common sense it is easy to presume an error for *tecpancalli* 'palace', but it may be correct, as the word means "enclosure."

118. ENTRARSE (in the Spanish)    For "entrase" or "entrasse."

119. ENTRADOS (in the Spanish)    Normal grammar would demand "entrado."

120. SPECIAL (in the Spanish)    Spanish writing of the sixteenth century sometimes elided *e* before *sp,* as in the frequently seen "Spaña."

121. LAS (in the Spanish)    For "los."

122. MOCA TLALLOAQUE (in the Nahuatl)    The word "moca" seems superfluous in this expression, and indeed one would have expected "tlalloque" rather than "tlalloaque."

123. TIERRAS (in the Spanish)    For "tiros."

124. LOS (in the Spanish)    For "las."

125. DESPERAUĀ (in the Spanish)    For "despeñauā."

126. TETELPUCHCALI (in the Nahuatl)    See nn. 94 and 111 above.

127. IQUIIAOAIOC (in the Nahuatl)    The word is inadvertently repeated in the manuscript.

128. DE (in the Spanish)    The word is inadvertently repeated in the manuscript.

129. MIXCOATECHIALTITLĀ (in the Nahuatl)    The first part of the word, "mixcoa-," is inadvertently repeated in the manuscript.

130. Q̄N (in the Spanish)    For "quando."

131. AQUE (in the Spanish)    For "aqui."

132. ALLI (in the Spanish)    The word is inadvertently repeated in the manuscript.

133. TOTOLLALEVATZALLI (in the Nahuatl)    See n. 89 above.

134. DONDE (in the Spanish)    Normal grammar would demand "de donde."

135. COZTALANPOPUL, COZTEMILOLTIQUE (in the Nahuatl)    Sahagún 1950–1982: 13.71 has "anointed yellow, painted yellow." The words are obscure to me.

136. LAS (in the Spanish)    For "los."

137. DARGAS (in the Spanish)    For "adargas."

138. ANTE (in the Spanish)    Normal usage would demand "antes de."

139. OTOMIES DE TLAXCALTECAS (in the Spanish)    The word "de" seems superfluous, as though there were a mixture of the two phrases "otomies de Tlaxcala" and "otomies tlaxcaltecas."

140. DESDE (in the Spanish)    For "deste."

141. A (in the Spanish)    By normal grammar this word should not be present.

142. VEL TOIACACPA OQUIQUIXTI IN NETOLINILIZTLI (in the Nahuatl)    Such I take to be the thrust of this expression, of which I have seen no other example. It seems to say, more literally, "they have taken affliction [to? from?] our very noses."

143. Tlacalaquili (in the Nahuatl)    Read "tlacalaquilli"; most of the other cases of "-li" for -*lli* involve some form of the word *calli*.

144. Iz (in the Nahuatl)    Perhaps for "ie."

145. Argullo (in the Spanish)    For "orgullo."

146. Mocacaq̄ (in the Nahuatl)    I follow Sahagún 1950–1982: 13.76, in translating this construction, which I have not been able to analyze.

147. Luego (in the Spanish)    A "los" is missing after this word.

148. Matlacpoalli oçe, oncaxtolli (in the Nahuatl)    The number given is larger than the total of the days and months listed, which even counting Teucilhuitl as a whole month comes to 215 or 216, depending on what is counted. The discrepancy arises from the omission of the month of Atemoztli between Panquetzaliztli and Tititl toward the beginning.

149. Vmpoalilhuitl (in the Nahuatl); ochenta y cinco (in the Spanish)    Note the discrepancy between the Spanish and the Nahuatl versions on the number of days of peace.

150. Ic caxtolpoalli omume (in the Nahuatl)    "Seventeenth" is correct; two months are omitted on the list.

151. Comiençaua (in the Spanish)    For standard "començaua."

152. Vatztia (in the Nahuatl)    As remarked in Sahagún 1950–1982: 13.83, the intention is probably "valitztia" or the like. Although *hual-* would seem misplaced, the thrust of the passage and the Spanish version reinforce the notion that the basic verb form is *itztiuh* 'to head toward'.

153. Se (in the Spanish)    The word "llama" is missing after this.

154. Por su parte (in the Spanish)    Or "Captain don Hernando Cortés for his part also attacked the Mexica. . . ."

155. Lengua (in the Spanish)    Presumably "laguna" is intended, but conceivably the meaning could be a strip of land running out into the water.

156. En aquel derecho de Sancto antonio yglesia (in the Spanish)    The syntax of the Spanish is heavily influenced by Nahuatl here.

157. Xauan (in the Spanish)    For "dexauan."

158. Mec (in the Nahuatl)    Read "nec."

159. Este (in the Spanish)    Normal usage would demand "en" before this word.

160. Quintotona (in the Nahuatl)    Read "quintotoca."

161. Ningunos (in the Spanish)    The number of the verb demands "ninguno."

162. Iztac tetl (in the Nahuatl)    Literally "white stone," this phrase would appear to have had some still undiscovered technical meaning.

163. In tlatoque (in the Nahuatl)    Several parts of the preceding passage can be interpreted in different ways. I have let myself be guided to an extent by the Spanish version.

164. Ma tlaieiecavi (in the Nahuatl)    Or "let the fighting begin," and the same just below.

165. MA XIMOTLACOTILI (in the Nahuatl)    The verb *tlacoti* 'to do work like that of a slave, to perform (humble) service', and the like, seems sometimes to have had the specific sense of performing rites and sacrifices.

166. DE LOS (in the Spanish)    In the manuscript, the words "y de" are marked out following "de los." The end result seems to be not quite what was intended.

167. SACARONLOS (in the Spanish)    The text has "los" both before and after the verb; standard grammar would demand "les" in any case.

168. CASTAÑEDA XICOTENCATL: IQUETZALTEMAL IETINEMI (in the Nahuatl)    The prominent Spaniard Rodrigo de Castañeda (see the Spanish version) entered into the spirit of Mesoamerican combat to the extent of wearing indigenous devices and taunting his enemies in the prescribed fashion; as we see here, he even acquired an indigenous name or epithet, Xicotencatl, which was a dynastic name among the Tlaxcalans.

169. TODOL (in the Spanish)    For "todo el."

170. DERECHOS (in the Spanish)    For standard "derecho."

171. TLALHOACAN (in the Nahuatl)    Although the sense could be "dry land," a place-name is called for; Tlilhuacan suggests itself, and it is confirmed by the Spanish version.

172. ESFORCANDO (in the Spanish)    For "esforçando."

173. TODO LODOSO QUE NO PODIAN ANDAR POR EL (in the Spanish)    The Nahuatl version is noncommittal on what made the road slippery. One is inclined to think of blood, but Sahagún thought it was mud.

174. LOS (in the Spanish)    This "los" is excess; probably the writer first omitted "a" as in Nahuatl syntax, then remembered it, and ended up with "los" duplicated.

175. TLAQUILI (in the Nahuatl)    Sahagún 1950–1982: 13.104, prefers "frilled flower," a medicinal herb. In either case, the word would end in "-lli" in the writer's normal practice.

176. CELADA (in the Spanish)    In normal usage, something on the order of "en" should precede this word.

177. ABRIANLAS (in the Spanish)    The element "las" is superfluous and incorrect in normal grammar.

178. CERRAUANLOS (in the Spanish)    The text has "los" both before and after the verb, much as in the case at n. 167 above.

179. ONOIAQUE (in the Nahuatl)    Read "oniaque."

180. LAC (in the Spanish)    For "la."

181. FOL. 71    Erroneously numbered 80 in the manuscript.

182. SIGUIAN (in the Spanish)    For "seguian."

183. ACAACALCO (in the Nahuatl)    Read "acalco."

184. QUITLAQUALANILIA (in the Nahuatl)    Although the form appears to be based on *qualani* 'to become angry', and probably on *qualania* 'to make someone angry', I have not attained a secure analysis.

185. BUS (in the Spanish)    For "busca."

186. COMENCARON (in the Spanish)    For "començaron."

187. INEZCOAIAN (in the Nahuatl)    The translation demands that the intention is "inezçoaian," not at all unlikely in view of the fact that omission of the cedilla is a fairly common phenomenon.

188. MUMUZTLI (in the Spanish)    *Momoztli* was a generic term for a sacrificial platform or altar. It is not entirely clear, however, that Sahagún does not (mistakenly) intend the word as the temple's proper name, as he apparently did with the locative form of the name on fol. 66v.

189. MIXPEPETZA (in the Nahuatl)    Possibly the intention is "mixpepetzoa."

190. TLATILUCATL (in the Nahuatl)    Read "tlatilulcatl."

191. HIZIERON (in the Spanish)    For "hirieron."

192. MANERA (in the Spanish)    For "madera."

193. RROCAUĀ (in the Spanish)    For "derrocauā."

194. TELPUCHCALI (in the Nahuatl)    See nn. 94, 111, and 126 above.

195. TECHPUCHCALLI (in the Spanish)    For "Telpuchcalli."

196. RESTIR (in the Spanish)    For "resistir."

197. OQUICHICATIVITZE (in the Nahuatl)    I remain unsure whether this means men or women fighting like men.

198. DE (in the Spanish)    Normal usage demands "a."

199. NINGUNOS (in the Spanish)    For "niños."

200. NOTEICHIUHCAUH (in the Nahuatl)    This form, in which the first *i* is erroneous, is partially corrected from an earlier error.

201. PERROCHA (in the Spanish)    For "parrochia" (or other spellings, but all have a penultimate *i*).

202. ESS ESTA (in the Spanish)    Apparently for "es esto."

203. TOTECUIO (in the Nahuatl)    Several elements in the translation of the preceding speech are more than normally speculative.

204. CENDIDUMBRE (in the Spanish)    For "certidumbre."

205. QUETZALTECULOTL (in the Spanish)    In the manuscript, through inadvertence the *que* of this word was written twice.

206. IAUIOTL (in the Nahuatl)    This term could be interpreted as meaning the individual battle, but the fact that there was no more serious fighting, and the use of the phrase *ic cen* 'for good, once and for all, entirely' lead one to think that the whole war is meant.

207. AQUI SE PONEN LOS (in the Spanish)    In the manuscript, these words are inadvertently repeated at the beginning of fol. 79.

208. EZTETL (in the Nahuatl)    I take the intention to be "Eztletl." Compare the Spanish version and the Nahuatl text below.

209. RESPENDANDO (in the Spanish)    Apparently for something on the order of "resplandeciendo."

210. ECATEPUZTLI (in the Nahuatl)    Scattered attestations of this term in Nahuatl annals, though they give us no exact translation, imply that an *ecatepoztli* was some sort of meteorological phenomenon.

211. DE (in the Spanish)   For standard "del."

212. ANSI (in the Spanish)   For "si"; confusion seems to have arisen from inadvertent repetition of "-an" from the preceding word.

213. INXILLA (in the Nahuatl)   A word of broad application, *xillan* encompassed (in addition to metaphorical meanings) abdomen, belly, and womb, and the reference here might be to inspection of the vagina.

214. DESFRACAUĀSE (in the Spanish)   For "disfraçauāse."

215. CE COATL (in the Nahuatl)   The month is not given, but this date is not compatible with the elaborate calendrical account given in chaps. 27 and 28. Here the war ends in Three House (coinciding with 1521); there it was already well into Four Rabbit (1522) when the Spaniards returned from Tlaxcala to begin the siege. Factual accuracy is not the main point of interest here, but chaps. 27 and 28 extend the Spaniards' absence far too long.

216. LA (in the Spanish)   For "el."

217. NO ÇANIUH TLANTIVITZE (in the Nahuatl)   The meaning of this phrase is especially obscure.

218. CIOACOATL . . . TLAÇULIAUTL (in the Nahuatl)   Which titles go with which names remains somewhat speculative, but I believe the correspondence in the translation of the Nahuatl is better than in the Spanish version.

219. VMMECATL (in the Nahuatl)   The *mecatl* (literally, "rope") was a varying and in any case little understood measure used primarily in laying out fields.

220. TLACULIAUTL (in the Nahuatl)   Read "Tlaçuliautl."

221. AQUIMOTTILIZ (in the Nahuatl)   The *a* prefixed to some verbs here and above appears not to be a negative.

## 2. EXTRACT FROM THE ANNALS OF TLATELOLCO

1. TLOAPAN   Read "teoapan."

2. YZTAC   Presumably the moon.

3. YNCUECHI   See Book Twelve of the Florentine Codex at n. 105.

4. UEUETZONAYA   Read "ueuetzotzonaya."

5. TECPA   Read "tecpatl" (unless it be imagined that the word is compounded with the following "xiuitl," which seems unlikely in view of the intervening punctuation).

6. OMOTLALITO   Overnight stops are meant here, but the same word is used as for going to Tlaxcala to make a much longer stay.

7. MOMIMICTIA   *Momictia* can also mean "kill each other," and it may well have that meaning here.

8. CIPACTZI . . . XOXOPEUALLOC   Previous translators have taken it that Cipactzin and Tencuecuenotzin were the same person; further that "xoxopehualloc" is the name of a person; and further that this Xoxopehualoc and Axayacatl were sons of Moteucçoma. I cannot be sure that they were not right. Indeed, compare the Codex Aubin selection at n. 6.

9. TETLĀ QUINCALLAQUIZQZ   The idiom *tetlan calaqui* means "to submit to an enemy" or "to make peace"; it can also have its literal meaning, "to enter among other people." I have at times thought that what the nobles were trying to do was to collect food so that the people from outside could be quartered in Tenochtitlan during the siege.

10. TOTECH M[O]PILLOQUE TOTECH MOQUETZACO   This passage is extremely obscure. But previous translations emphasizing hanging people are not lexically or grammatically viable. In Molina's dictionary (1970), *itech ninopiloa* is "to grasp onto" something; I have not found *itech ninoquetza,* but the related *itech ninotlaquechia* means "to stand or rest on" something.

11. TECHICALLI   In the manuscript, the last five letters of the word ("calli") are inadvertently repeated.

12. TETLAN VNCALLAC   Another possibility would be that they took refuge in Tenochtitlan; see above, n. 9.

13. YECALLIUAC   Read "ycalliuac."

14. MOMIMICTIQZ   In the manuscript, "mo" is inadvertently repeated at the beginning of the word.

15. QUIUATITIQZ   Apparently one is to read "quiualititiqz."

16. UITZILOPOCH   Read "uitzilopochtli."

17. ATOQUEZTELÇI   The last part of this construction apparently corresponds to standard *quenteltzin* 'so-so, a bit'. The intention of the rest is not clear to me.

18. VIZNAUATL . . . TENTLIL   I have made some improvements over previous translations in interpreting the list, but many of the pairings of names and titles, and even the identifications as name or title, are still highly dubious. Several appellations were written in above the line, creating uncertainties about the intended order.

19. ATIZCAPA   In the Nahuatl, read "atizaapa."

20. NONOVALCO   Through inadvertent repetition, the manuscript has "nononovalco."

21. E CEPOVALI . . . QVALMITALVIA   Or "twenty days ago what he suggests needed to be done"?

22. YN IYYO YN ITLATOL   In the manuscript, through inadvertent repetition the letters "yn iyo n itla" appear at the beginning of p. 32.

23. TLAPALTECATL   Or from Tlapallan?

24. QUIUALHUIA   Read "quiualilhuia."

25. CAN AMOCHA   The reply of the Tlatelolca is apparently missing, that is, it was never written into the manuscript, for there is no space between the two statements of the Tlaxcalans.

26. YE   As *c* and *e* are often virtually impossible to distinguish from each other, this word might be interpreted as "yc"; yet the parallel with the preceding "ye" makes it extremely probable that "ye" is the intention.

27. ANQUINOTQUILIA   Read "anquimotquilia."

28. MOTLATOL   Crossed out in the manuscript is "amo-," which would have been better.

29. QUIUATOQUE    Read "quiualitoque."

30. TOTECUIOUA    MS 22$^{bis}$, p. 47, adds at this point "yhua oncan quitlalique yn vatella yn caçiz Ecatzin tlacatecatl tlapanecatl Popocatzin" ("and there they placed the banner⟨s⟩ that the Tlacateccatl Ecatzin and Tlapanecatl Popocatzin captured").

31. TITLAIHIOUIQUE    MS 22$^{bis}$, pp. 47–48, adds at this point "auh yn otlica omitl xaxamãtoc tzontli momoyauhtoc calli tzontlapouhtoc calli chichiliuhtoc / Ocuilti moyacatlamina otlica Auh yn caltech hahalacatoc yn quatextli Auh yn atl ça yuhqui chichiltic ça yuhqui tlapallatl ca yuh tiquique tiquia tequixquiatl Auh oc ypa tictetzotozonaya xamitl" ("And on the roads lay shattered bones and scattered hair; the houses were unroofed, red [with blood]; worms crawled on the roads; and the walls of the houses were slippery with brains. And the water seemed red, as though it were dyed, and thus we drank it. We drank salt water, and we hammered on the adobe"). The end of the interpolation impinges on the text of the other manuscript, which is repeated in MS 22$^{bis}$ along with the variation on it. The exact thrust of the form "moyacatlamina" is not clear; simply "motlamina" would give the sense in the translation (and in previous renderings); because *yacatl* is "nose," it is possible that what is meant is that worms were crawling in and out the noses of dead bodies.

Through Angel María Garibay, whose translation in several ways improves on the two preceding ones, this passage has become the most famous one associated with the annals of Tlatelolco. Garibay recast the section as a verse lament, and he translated "omitl" as "darts" (*mitl* is arrow, dart, or spear), which then gave rise to the English "Broken Spears." Garibay did so even though both previous translators had correctly rendered the word as "bones," and there is no room for doubt that 22$^{bis}$ says "omitl;" it is one of the clearest things in the manuscript, and it is entirely consonant with the rest of the passage, which has none of the earmarks of Nahuatl song and verse.

32. TEUTLAQUILLI    Or the reference may be to the plant mentioned by Anderson and Dibble in Book Twelve; see n. 175 to text 1, above.

33. TOPATIUH MOCHIUH    I.e., apparently people were selling themselves or dependents as slaves for food.

34. TIĀQUIZCO    At this point MS 22$^{bis}$ (p. 48) interpolates, infelicitously, "auh yehuatzin Quauhtemoctzin quimohuiquilia ȳ malti amo yuh quicahua yn tecahuato achcauhti tlatlacateca necoc quitititza quimititlapanaya yoma Quauhtemoctzin" ("And Quauhtemoctzin took the prisoners with him. He did not leave them alone; leading priests from the Tlacatecco went to deliver people; they seized them on both sides, and Quauhtemoctzin himself broke open their abdomens").

35. QUAUHTEMOC TOPANTEMOC    Or vice versa?

36. QUITILMACALTIQUE    This word, meaning "they provided him with a cloth cover or canopy," seems out of place here, as if taken through a copying error from the earlier section mentioning the canopy for Cortés.

37. MOCIA    Read "mochia."

38. QUIUATQUIC    Read "quiualitquic."

39. IXILLA    Or in their vaginas; see n. 213 to text 1, above.

40. VITZILOPOCH    It is not clear from the facsimile whether in the original the readily legible "vitzilopoch" is followed by "-tli".

41. Quiuatquiqz    Read "quiualitquiqz."

42. Coyoaqz    No one so far has succeeded in making much sense of the immediately preceding sentences, and I am far from claiming to have found the solution.

43. Niman    MS 22^bis, p. 53, adds "then Honduras, Guatemala, and Tehuantepec." It also notes that this is the end of the document being copied: "Ca zan oncan tlami ynic omopouh ynin amatl yn iuhqui omochiuh" ("there ends the reading of this document as it was done").


### 3. EXTRACT FROM THE CODEX AUBIN

1. Ce acatl, One Reed    The year is represented pictographically.

2. .v. 20    The meaning is not clear to me. Possibly the two numerals are to be added to give 25, the same date as given for November, but even then the intention would not be clear. The meaning might be "five twenties," i.e., five Nahua months, but again this reading does not seem to fit the context.

3. Tonyez    Read "tonyezque."

4. Quequeçallo    The reading is not certain.

5. Axoyaquavitl    As at n. 4, the reading is not certain.

6. Axcayaca    The reading is not certain; in any case, the intention seems to be "axayaca."

7. Ome tecpatl, Two Flint Knife    The year is represented pictographically.

8. Yei calli, Three House    The year is represented pictographically.

9. Nahui tochtli, Four Rabbit    The year is represented pictographically as well as alphabetically.


### 4. FRAGMENTS FROM THE ANNALS OF QUAUHTITLAN

1. X̄pitianotin    Presumably the intention was "x̄p̄ianotin" as elsewhere in this document.


### 5. EXTRACT FROM HISTORIA TOLTECA-CHICHIMECA

1. .I. Acatl. xiuitl    Roughly equivalent to the year 1519.

2. Maxtlatl    A c was later inserted above the line, making "maxtlactl" and confusing the word with "matlactli," 'ten', which is found on both sides.

3. Motomachi    Apparently the intention is "motamachiuh." The basket referred to is of the type called in modern Mexican Spanish a *tenate*.

4. Saiavillez    This form seems too far from any Spanish name to be sure of the intention (the intention, that is, of some earlier copy, which probably had a more recognizable spelling). One thinks of Sayavedra, but there are several discrepancies. The person in charge of the founding of Puebla was Licenciado Juan Salmerón; Salmerón

likewise seems too distant. Kirchhoff, Güemes, and Reyes García (1976: 231) give in their translation "fray Avillez" (presumably for Avilés), but the original clearly has *s*, not *f*, not to speak of the *r* that must be presumed to be missing, or of the fact that the Spanish title *fray* was used exclusively with first names.

5. OQUIMOVELQUITI    Read "oquimovelcaquiti."

6. Y    The manuscript breaks off abruptly here; apparently a folio or more is missing.

## 6. LETTER OF THE CABILDO OF
## HUEJOTZINGO TO THE KING, 1560

1. ONCAN    Read "ancan."

2. QUIMICATIA    Read "quimicalia."

3. NIMĀ AYAC    The phrase appears to have a still unidentified idiomatic meaning.

4. COLHUACĀ    This name apparently refers to the present Culiacán on the west coast of Mexico.

5. TEQUANTE[OP]EC    The expected form would be "tequantepec."

6. NOHUIA    This word, meaning "everywhere," is used where Spanish "nueva" or "nueua," 'new' is intended (the slip seems to have been caused by the appearance of the same word just above in the text).

7. CAN    Read "çan."

8. TINAVATILO    In the manuscript, the letters "tinava" are repeated at the beginning of the word.

9. CAHINOS    Read "çahinos."

# APPENDIX

*Captions for the Illustrations of*
*Book Twelve of the Florentine Codex*

1. The Spaniards disembark.

2. Spaniards advancing in formation.

3 (fol. 1). The Spaniards assault the main temple in Mexico.

4 (fol. 1). The first omen: the tongue of flame in the sky.

5 (fol. 2). The third omen: the burning of the temple of Xiuhteuctli.

6 (fol. 2). The second omen: the burning of a temple of Huitzilopochtli.

7 (fol. 2). The fourth omen: the tripartite comet.

8 (fol. 2v). The sixth omen: the woman who wept in the night.

9 (fol. 3). The eighth omen: the appearance of two-headed people.

10 (fol. 3). The seventh omen: the bird with a mirror on its head.

11 (fol. 5). Moteucçoma's stewards bring the Spaniards' gifts to him.

12 (fol. 8v). Moteucçoma's emissaries present gifts to Cortés.

13 (fol. 8v). The Spaniards put the emissaries in irons.

14 (fol. 9). The Spaniards discharge their firearms to impress the emissaries.

15 (fol. 9v). The Spaniards revive the emissaries with food and drink.

16 (fol. 9v). The emissaries hasten back to land.

17 (fol. 10v). Moteucçoma has a captive sacrificed before the emissaries.

18 (fol. 11v). Spaniards and their war equipment.

19 (fol. 11v). The emissaries describe the Spaniards to Moteucçoma.

20 (fol. 12v). Moteucçoma's emissaries offer food to the Spaniards.

21 (fol. 13). Moteucçoma and the Mexica lament on being told of the Spaniards' power.

22 (fol. 14). Cortés and the Mexica converse through Marina.

23 (fol. 14v). Moteucçoma contemplates flight.

24 (fol. 17). The Spaniards are received in Tlaxcala.

25 (fol. 18). Moteucçoma's emissaries meet the Spaniards at the pass between Iztactepetl and Popocatepetl.

26 (fol. 18). The emissaries return to tell Moteucçoma of the meeting.

27 (fol. 18v). Moteucçoma's sorcerers encounter Tezcatlipoca in disguise.

28 (fol. 20). The vision of Mexico's temples burning.

29 (fol. 21). The road to Mexico is blocked with maguey.

30 (fol. 21v). The Spaniards and the Four Lords speak peace.

31–43 (fols. 22–24). The Spaniards enter Mexico.

44 (fol. 26v). Supplies for the Spaniards.

45 (fol. 26). Moteucçoma and the Spaniards converse through Marina.

46 (fol. 26v). The Spaniards seize Moteucçoma.

47 (fol. 26v). The Spaniards take Moteucçoma with them into the palace.

48 (fol. 27v). Moteucçoma shows the Spaniards the treasure house.

49 (fol. 28). The Spaniards and their allies seize the treasure.

50 (fol. 28). The treasure is melted down.

51 (fol. 29). Marina makes an announcement to the Mexica.

52 (fol. 29). The Mexica deliver supplies for the Spaniards.

53 (fol. 29). Items delivered to the Spaniards.

54 (fol. 29v). Alvarado wishes to see the festivity of Toxcatl.

55–56 (fol. 30). The Spaniards observe the preparations for the festivity.

57–60 (fols. 29v–31). The image of Huitzilopochtli is prepared.

61 (fol. 31v). Huitzilopochtli's face is uncovered, and offerings are laid down.

62 (fol. 31v). Dancing and singing during the festivity of Toxcatl.

63 (fol. 32). The fully prepared Huitzilopochtli on the temple steps during the ceremonies.

64 (fol. 32). An unruly celebrant in the festivity is punished.

65 (fol. 32v). A celebrant prepares to leave the ceremony to relieve himself.

66–70 (fols. 33–33v). Spaniards kill the celebrants in the temple courtyard.

71 (fol. 34). The Mexica are told of the massacre.

72 (fol. 34). Fighting between Mexica and Spaniards begins.

73 (fol. 36). The Spaniards are besieged in the palace.

74 (fol. 36). Moteucçoma is put in irons.

75 (fol. 36). The dead are collected.

76 (fol. 36v). Itzquauhtzin addresses the Mexica.

77 (fol. 36v). The Mexica detect supplies being carried into the palace.

78–79 (fol. 38v). Reinforcements arrive for the Spaniards.

80 (fol. 39). This image appears to feature primarily an indigenous person using a digging stick, plus some arms and devices associated with the Mexica.

81 (fol. 39). The Spaniards use their firearms with great effect.

82 (fol. 39v). The Spaniards expel the Mexica from the great temple.

83 (fol. 40v). The Spaniards cast the bodies of Moteucçoma and Itzquauhtzin into the water.

84 (fol. 40v). Moteucçoma's body is retrieved.

85 (fol. 40v). Moteucçoma's body is burned.

86 (fol. 41). Itzquauhtzin's body is removed.

87 (fol. 41). Itzquauhtzin's body is burned, to the tears of the Tlatelolca.

88 (fol. 42v). The Spaniards and their allies emerge from the palace.

89 (fol. 42v). The Mexica detect the Spaniards leaving.

90 (fol. 43). Combat on the causeway.

91 (fol. 43). The Spaniards fall in the water.

92 (fol. 43). The Mexica pursue the fleeing Spaniards.

93 (fol. 44). The people of Teocalhueyacan come to the Spaniards with food and greetings.

94 (fol. 45). The Mexica recover and dispose of bodies in the Tolteca canal.

95 (fol. 45). The Mexica carry off spoils.

96 (fol. 45). The Mexica search in the water for spoils.

97 (fol. 45v). Combat at Calacoayan.

98 (fol. 45v). The Spaniards go up to Teocalhueyacan.

99 (fol. 47v). The people of Teocalhueyacan receive the Spaniards.

100 (fol. 47v). The people of Teocalhueyacan complain of Moteucçoma to Cortés.

101 (fol. 47v). The Spaniards play martial music as they prepare to leave Teocalhueyacan.

102 (fol. 48). The Spaniards approach Tepotzotlan.

103 (fol. 48). The Mexica pursue the Spaniards.

104 (fol. 48). The Spaniards approach Citlaltepec; the people hide.

105 (fol. 48v). The Spaniards reach Xoloc, the people taking refuge on the mountain, while a temple burns.

106 (fol. 49). The Spaniards reach Aztaquemecan.

107 (fol. 50v). The Mexica observe the Spaniards leaving.

108 (fol. 51). The Mexica pursue the Spaniards near Tonan Mountain.

109 (fol. 51). The Spaniards turn on the Mexica.

110 (fol. 51). The Mexica collect and dispose of their dead.

111 (fol. 51v). The Mexica put a temple in order.

112 (fol. 52v). The Mexica decorate and display their gods.

113 (fol. 53v). Epidemic of smallpox in Mexico.

114–16 (fol. 54). Return of the Spaniards to Mexico.

117 (fol. 55). The Spaniards' brigantines in the lake.

118 (fol. 55v). The Spaniards attack Çoquipan.

119 (fol. 56). Spanish artillery knocks down a wall at Xolloco.

120 (fol. 56). Fighting around Çoquipan or Xolloco.

121 (fol. 56v). Spanish artillery knocks down a wall at Huitzillan.

122 (fol. 56v). Indigenous allies of the Spaniards fill in a canal with stones.

123 (fol. 58). Spanish horsemen at Huitzillan.

124 (fol. 58). A Spanish horseman lances a Tlatelolca warrior.

125 (fol. 58). The warrior's companions unhorse the Spaniard.

126 (fol. 58v). Warriors come to land and enter among the houses.

127 (fol. 58v). The Spaniards are attacked on both sides.

128 (fol. 58v). The Mexica take a cannon abandoned by the Spaniards to Tetama-çolco to drop it in the water.

129 (fol. 59). The Spaniards chase the Tenochca from Tenochtitlan.

130 (fol. 59v). Tzilacatzin hurling stones at the Spaniards.

131 (fol. 60). The Tlatelolca fight the Spaniards near Nonoalco as refugees leave Tenochtitlan in flames.

132 (fol. 60). More fighting near Nonoalco.

133 (fol. 60). The Spaniards come in great force.

134 (fol. 60v). Three guises of Tzilacatzin.

135–136 (fol. 61). The Tlatelolca force the Spaniards and their allies to withdraw.

137 (fol. 63). People of Xochimilco and other settlements arrive in boats.

138 (fol. 63). Quauhtemoc and another lord (probably Mayehuatzin).

139–142 (fol. 63v). The Mexica attack the Xochimilca and the others, saving those whom they had seized and taking some of them captive.

143 (fol. 64). Quauhtemoc and Mayehuatzin kill some of the perpetrators.

144–145 (fols. 64–64v). The Spaniards come to Iyauhtenco.

146–148 (fol. 66). The Mexica force the Spaniards back to the boats, capturing and disrobing some of them.

149–151 (fol. 67). The Mexica capture Spaniards, horses, and allies.

152–153 (fol. 67v). The Mexica sacrifice Spaniards and allies.

154 (fol. 68). The heads of sacrificed Spaniards and horses displayed.

155 (fol. 68v). The Spaniards enter the marketplace of Tlatelolco.

156 (fol. 69v). The Spaniards set fire to the main temple of Tlatelolco.

157 (fol. 69v). Fighting in the marketplace of Tlatelolco.

158 (fol. 69v). The Mexica hurl stones from the rooftops into the Tlatelolco square.

# BIBLIOGRAPHY

Anderson, Arthur J. O., Frances Berdan, and James Lockhart
1976
*Beyond the Codices*. Berkeley and Los Angeles: University of California Press.

Andrews, J. Richard
1975
*Introduction to Classical Nahuatl*. Austin: University of Texas Press.

Assadourian, Carlos Sempat, and Andrea Martínez Baracs, eds.
1991
*Tlaxcala: textos de su historia, siglo XVI*. México: Gobierno del Estado de Tlaxcala.

Bierhorst, John, trans.
1985
*Cantares Mexicanos: Songs of the Aztecs*. Stanford, Calif.: Stanford University Press.

Campbell, R. Joe, and Mary L. Clayton
1988
Bernardino de Sahagún's Contributions to the Lexicon of Classical Nahuatl. In Klor de Alva, Nicholson, and Quiñones Keber 1988, pp. 295–314.

Carochi, Horacio
1983
*Arte de la lengua mexicana con la declaración de los adverbios della*. Facsimile of the 1645 edition, with intro. by Miguel León-Portilla. México: Instituto de Investigaciones Filológicas, Instituto de Investigaciones Históricas, Universidad Nacional Autónoma de México.

Carrasco, Pedro
1972
La casa y hacienda de un señor tlalhuica. *Estudios de Cultura Náhuatl* 10: 22–54.

*Cartas de Indias*
1877
Madrid: Imprenta de Manuel G. Hernández.

Chimalpahin Quauhtlehuanitzin, don Domingo de San Antón Muñón
1963–1965
*Die Relationen Chimalpahin's zur Geschichte Mexico's*, ed. Günter Zimmermann. 2 vols. Hamburg: Cram, De Gruyter.

Cline, S. L., ed.  
n.d.

*The Book of Tributes: Early Sixteenth-Century Nahuatl Censuses from Morelos.* Forthcoming as Nahuatl Studies Series no. 4, UCLA Latin American Center.

———— and Miguel  
León-Portilla, eds.  
1984

*The Testaments of Culhuacan.* Nahuatl Studies Series no. 1, UCLA Latin American Center. Los Angeles: UCLA Latin American Center Publications.

Dibble, Charles E.  
1982

Sahagún's Historia. In Sahagún 1950–1982: 1.9–23.

————, ed.  
1963

*Historia de la nación mexicana.* México: Porrúa.

Edmonson, Munro S.,  
ed.  
1974

*Sixteenth-Century Mexico: The Work of Sahagún.* Albuquerque: University of New Mexico Press.

Farriss, Nancy M.  
1984

*Maya Society Under Colonial Rule.* Princeton, N.J.: Princeton University Press.

Garibay K., Angel María  
1943

Huehuetlatolli, Documento A. *Tlalocan* 1.1: 31–53, 1.2: 81–107.

Gibson, Charles  
1952

*Tlaxcala in the Sixteenth Century.* New Haven, Conn.: Yale University Press.

————  
1964

*The Aztecs Under Spanish Rule: A History of the Indians of the Valley of Mexico, 1519–1810.* Stanford, Calif.: Stanford University Press.

Gillespie, Susan D.  
1989

*The Aztec Kings: The Construction of Rulership in Mexica History.* Tucson: University of Arizona Press.

Hinz, Eike, Claudine  
Hartau, and Marie-Luise  
Heimann-Koenen, eds.  
1983

*Aztekischer Zensus. Zur indianischen Wirtschaft und Gesellschaft im Marquesado um 1540: Aus dem ''Libro de Tributos'' (Col. Ant. Ms. 551) im Archivo Histórico, México.* 2 vols. Hannover: Verlag für Ethnologie.

Karttunen, Frances, and  
James Lockhart  
1976

*Nahuatl in the Middle Years: Language Contact Phenomena in Texts of the Colonial Period.* University of California Publications in Linguistics no. 85. Berkeley and Los Angeles: University of California Press.

————, eds.  
1987

*The Art of Nahuatl Speech: The Bancroft Dialogues.* Nahuatl Studies Series no. 2, UCLA Latin American Center. Los Angeles: UCLA Latin American Center Publications.

Kirchhoff, Paul, Lina  
Odena Güemes, and Luis  
Reyes García  
1976

*Historia tolteca-chichimeca.* México: Instituto Nacional de Antropología e Historia.

Klor de Alva, J. Jorge, H.
B. Nicholson, and Eloise
Quiñones Keber, eds.
1988

*The Work of Bernardino de Sahagún: Pioneer Ethnographer of Sixteenth-Century Aztec Mexico*. Albany, N.Y. and Austin: Institute for Mesoamerican Studies, State University of New York at Albany, University of Texas Press.

Launey, Michel
1979

*Introduction à la langue et à la littérature aztèques*, vol. 1: *Grammaire*. Paris: L'Harmattan.

León-Portilla, Miguel
1976

*Visión de los vencidos: Relaciones indígenas de la conquista*. With texts translated by Angel María Garibay K. 7th ed. México: Biblioteca del Estudiante Universitario, Universidad Nacional Autónoma de México.

———
1992

*The Broken Spears: The Aztec Account of the Conquest of Mexico* (expanded translation of *Visión de los vencidos*, with foreword by J. Jorge Klor de Alva). Boston: Beacon Press.

Lockhart, James
1968

*Spanish Peru, 1532–1560*. Madison: University of Wisconsin Press.

———
1972

*The Men of Cajamarca: A Social and Biographical Study of the First Conquerors of Peru*. Austin: University of Texas Press.

———
1985

Some Nahua Concepts in Postconquest Guise. *History of European Ideas* 6:465–482.

———
1991

*Nahuas and Spaniards: Postconquest Central Mexican History and Philology*. Stanford, Calif.: Stanford University Press and UCLA Latin American Center Publications.

———
1992

*The Nahuas After the Conquest: A Social and Cultural History of the Indians of Central Mexico, Sixteenth Through Eighteenth Centuries*. Stanford, Calif.: Stanford University Press.

———, Frances Berdan,
and Arthur J. O.
Anderson
1986

*The Tlaxcalan Actas: A Compendium of the Records of the Cabildo of Tlaxcala (1545–1627)*. Salt Lake City: University of Utah Press.

——— and Enrique
Otte, eds.
1976

*Letters and People of the Spanish Indies, Sixteenth Century*. New York: Cambridge University Press.

——— and Stuart B.
Schwartz
1983

*Early Latin America: A History of Colonial Spanish America and Brazil*. New York: Cambridge University Press.

Martínez, José Luis
1982

*El códice florentino y la Historia general de Sahagún*. México: Archivo General de la Nación.

Mengin, Ernst, trans. and ed.
1939

Unos Annales Históricos de la Nacion Mexicana. Die Manuscrits Mexicains nr. 22 und 22 $^{bis}$ der Bibliothèque Nationale de Paris. *Baessler-Archiv: Beiträge zur Völkerkunde* 22.69–168.

————, ed.
1945

Unos Annales Históricos de la Nacion Mexicàna." *Corpus Codicum Americanorum Medii Aevi*, vol. 2. Copenhagen: E. Munksgaard.

Molina, fray Alonso de
1970

*Vocabulario en lengua castellana y mexicana y mexicana y castellana* (1571). México: Porrúa.

Muñoz Camargo, Diego
1984

*Descripción de la ciudad y provincia de Tlaxcala,* ed. René Acuña. México: Instituto de Investigaciones Antropológicas, Universidad Nacional Autónoma de México.

Olwer, Luis Nicolau d', and Howard F. Cline
1973

Sahagún and His Works. In Robert Wauchope, ed., *Handbook of Middle American Indians* 13 (*Guide to Ethnohistorical Sources,* pt. 2, ed. Howard F. Cline and John B. Glass), pp. 186–206. Austin: University of Texas Press.

Prescott, William H.
1931

*History of the Conquest of Mexico.* New York: Modern Library.

Ruiz de Alarcón, Hernando
1984

*Treatise on the Heathen Superstitions that today live among the Indians native to this New Spain, 1629,* trans. and ed. J. Richard Andrews and Ross Hassig. Norman: University of Oklahoma Press.

Sahagún, fray Bernardino de
1905–1907

*Historia de las cosas de la Nueva España: Edición parcial en fascimile de los Códices Matritenses. . . .* 4 vols. Madrid: Hauser y Menet.

————
1950–1982

*Florentine Codex: General History of the Things of New Spain,* trans. Arthur J. O. Anderson and Charles E. Dibble. 13 pts. Salt Lake City, Utah, and Santa Fe, New Mexico: University of Utah Press and School of American Research, Santa Fe.

————
1975

*Historia general de las cosas de Nueva España,* ed. Angel María Garibay K. 3d ed. México: Porrúa.

————
1978

*The War of Conquest: How It Was Waged Here in Mexico,* trans. Arthur J. O. Anderson and Charles E. Dibble. Salt Lake City: University of Utah Press.

————
1979

*Códice florentino.* MS 218–220 de la colección Palatina de la Biblioteca Medicea Laurenziana. Facsimile edition. 3 vols. Florence: Giunti Barbera and the Archivo General de la Nación.

————
1989

*Conquest of New Spain, 1585 Revision,* trans. Howard F. Cline and ed. S. L. Cline. Salt Lake City: University of Utah Press.

Taylor, William B.
1972

*Landlord and Peasant in Colonial Oaxaca*. Stanford, Calif.: Stanford University Press.

———
1979

*Drinking, Homicide, and Rebellion in Colonial Mexican Villages*. Stanford, Calif.: Stanford University Press.

Tezozomoc, don Hernando [Fernando] de Alvarado
1949

*Crónica mexicayotl,* trans. and ed. Adrián León. Publicaciones del Instituto de Historia ser. 1 no. 10. México: Imprenta Universitaria.

Todorov, Tzvetan
1984

*The Conquest of America*. New York: Harper & Row.

Toscano, Salvador, ed.
1948

*Anales de Tlatelolco . . . y Códice de Tlatelolco*. México: Porrúa.

Velázquez, Primo Feliciano, trans. and ed.
1975

*Códice Chimalpopoca: Anales de Cuauhtitlan y Leyenda de los soles*. 2d. ed. México: Instituto de Investigaciones Históricas, Universidad Nacional Autónoma de México.

# INDEX